BEST PRACTICES SERIES

Designing a Total Data Solution

Technology, Implementation, and Deployment

THE AUERBACH BEST PRACTICES SERIES

Broadband Networking
James Trulove, Editor
ISBN: 0-8493-9821-5

Business Continuity Planning
Ken Doughty, Editor
ISBN: 0-8493-0907-7

Designing a Total Data Solution: Technology, Implementation, and Deployment
Roxanne E. Burkey and Charles V. Breakfield, Editors
ISBN: 0-8493-0893-3

High Performance Web Databases: Design, Development, and Deployment
Sanjiv Purba, Editor
ISBN: 0-8493-0882-8

Electronic Messaging
Nancy Cox, Editor
ISBN: 0-8493-9825-8

Enterprise Systems Integration
John Wyzalek, Editor
ISBN: 0-8493-9837-1

Financial Services Information Systems
Jessica Keyes, Editor
ISBN: 0-8493-9834-7

Healthcare Information Systems
Phillip L. Davidson, Editor
ISBN: 0-8493-9963-7

Internet Management
Jessica Keyes, Editor
ISBN: 0-8493-9987-4

Multi-Operating System Networking: Living with UNIX, NetWare, and NT
Raj Rajagopal, Editor
ISBN: 0-8493-9831-2

Network Design
Gilbert Held, Editor,
ISBN: 0-8493-0859-3

Network Manager's Handbook
John Lusa, Editor
ISBN: 0-8493-9841-X

Project Management
Paul C. Tinnirello, Editor
ISBN: 0-8493-9998-X

Server Management
Gilbert Held, Editor
ISBN: 0-8493-9823-1

Web-to-Host Connectivity
Lisa Lindgren and Anura Gurugé, Editors
ISBN: 0-8493-0835-6

Winning the Outsourcing Game: Making the Best Deals and Making Them Work
Janet Butler, Editor
ISBN: 0-8493-0875-5

BEST PRACTICES SERIES

Designing a Total Data Solution

Technology, Implementation, and Deployment

Editors

ROXANNE E. BURKEY
CHARLES V. BREAKFIELD

AUERBACH

Boca Raton London New York Washington, D.C.

Chapter 4 ©1996, International Technology Group. Reproduced with permission.

Library of Congress Cataloging-in-Publication Data

Designing a total data storage solution : technology, implementation, and deployment
edited by Roxanne E. Burkey, Charles V. Breakfield.
p. cm. -- (Best practices)
Includes bibliographical references and index.
ISBN 0-8493-0893-3 (alk. paper)
1. Database design. 2. Database management. 3. Data warehousing. I. Burkey, Roxanne E. II. Breakfield, Charles V. III. Best practices series (Boca Raton, Fla.)

QA76.9.D26 D48 2000
005.74--dc21 00-044216

Direct all inquiries to CRC Press LLC, 2000 N.W. Corporate Blvd., Boca Raton, Florida 33431.

Auerbach is an imprint of CRC Press LLC

No claim to original U.S. Government works
International Standard Book Number 0-8493-0893-3
Library of Congress Card Number 00-044216
Printed in the United States of America 1 2 3 4 5 6 7 8 9 0
Printed on acid-free paper

Contributors

CHRIS AIVAZIAN, CISSP, *Vice President, Data Security and Disaster Recovery, Fleet Bank NA, Melville, New York*
GERALD L. BAHR, *Networking Consultant, Roswell, Georgia*
NIJAZ BAJGORIC, *Faculty, Bogazici University, Istanbul, Turkey*
CHARLES BANYAY, *Manager, Deloitte & Touche Consulting Group, Toronto, Ontario, Canada*
RICHARD A. BELLAVER, *Associate Professor, Center for Information and Communication Sciences, Ball State University, Muncie, Indiana*
EILEEN M. BIRGE, *Director, BSG Alliance/IT, Houston, Texas*
CHARLES V. BREAKFIELD, MBA, MCSE, *Manager, Architecture and Design, Complex Call Centers, Nortel Networks, Richardson, Texas*
ROXANNE E. BURKEY, *Manager, Architecture and Design, eSolutions Team, Nortel Networks, Richardson, Texas*
JENNIFER L. COSTLEY, *Vice President of Technology, Banker's Trust Company, New York, New York*
PAUL DAVIS, *Director of Strategic Marketing, WRQ, Seattle, Washington*
EDWARD F. DROHAN, *President, Business Development Services of NY, Inc., New York, New York*
DORIC EARLE, MBA, *Senior Manager for Advanced Customer Care Engineering and Support, eBusiness Initiative, Nortel Networks, Richardson, Texas*
ELIZABETH N. FONG, *Computer Systems Laboratory, National Institute of Standards and Technology, Gaithersburg, Maryland*
DR. RICHARD FORD, *Technical Director, Command Software Systems, Inc., Jupiter, Florida*
IDO GILEADI, *Senior Manager, ICS, Deloitte & Touche Consulting, Toronto, Ontario, Canada*
AMITAVA HALDAR, *Senior Systems Analyst, AIC Consulting, Chapel Hill, North Carolina*
KATHRYN A. HARVILL, *Computer Systems Laboratory, National Institute of Standards and Technology, Gaithersburg, Maryland*
GILBERT HELD, *Director, 4-Degree Consulting, Macon, Georgia*
BRIAN JEFFERY, *Managing Director, International Technology Group, Mountain View, California*
LISA M. LINDGREN, *Independent Consultant, Gilford, New Hampshire*

Jennifer Little, *Program Manager, AmerInd, Inc., Alexandria, Virginia*
Gary Lord, *Partner, KPMG Peat Marwick, Palo Alto, California*
Jeffrey J. Lowder, *Chief, Network Security, United States Air Force Academy, Colorado Springs, Colorado*
David Mattox, *Lead Technical Staff, The MITRE Corporation, Reston, Virginia*
Stewart S. Miller, *President and Owner, Executive Information Services, Carlsbad, California*
Nathan J. Muller, *Independent Consultant, Huntsville, Alabama*
David Nelson, *Director of Marketing, Wingra Technologies, Madison, Wisconsin*
Network Associates, Inc., *Santa Clara, California*
William E. Perry, CPA, CISA, CQA, *Executive Director, Quality Assurance Institute, Orlando, Florida*
T.M. Rajkumar, *Associate Professor of MIS, Miami University, Oxford, Ohio*
Len Seligman, *Principal Technical Staff, The MITRE Corporation, Reston, Virginia*
Charles L. Sheppard, *Computer Systems Laboratory, National Institute of Standards and Technology, Gaithersburg, Maryland*
Kenneth Smith, *Senior Technical Staff, The MITRE Corporation, Reston, Virginia*
Martin D. Solomon, *Database Technology Architect, C.W. Costello, Middletown, Connecticut*
Michael J.D. Sutton, Adm.A., CMC, ISP, MIT, *Director, Business Process and Document Management Services Group, Ottawa, Ontario, Canada*
Richard J. Tobacco, *Brand Manager, Communications Server, OS/390, Network Computing Software, IBM*
John R. Vacca, *Information Technology Consultant, Pomeroy, Ohio*
James Woods, *Independent Consultant, Lewisville, Texas*
Marie A. Wright, *Associate Professor of Management Information Systems, Western Connecticut State University, Danbury, Connecticut*
Leo A. Wrobel, *President, Premier Network Services, Inc., Dallas, Texas*

Contents

Introduction

Designing a Total Data Storage Solution: Technology, Implementation, and Deployment

BUSINESS MODELS HAVE ALTERED. Old formulas on just saving the company money no longer apply to a data management solution. Stressful but successful careers in data management are based on how well money is invested in technology for use by the enterprise, with realistic expectations set for returns on those investments. It is all too easy to say, "No, we are not going to spend anything, everything is running well"; but this thinking only mortgages an enterprise's future for short-term profits for a scant few quarters. Shortsightedness does not push an enterprise to the forefront of its industry, nor into a leadership role. Enterprise survivability is now based on how well the data management design provides the information needed, on demand. Realization of effective data management begins with a centered Chief Information Officer (CIO) capable of capitalizing on wise technical investments to protect long-term enterprise earnings growth.

As a professional, one tries not to make any career-limiting decisions (CLD); however, there is always the apprehension that exists when one takes on an enterprise's data management positioning. If one has taken on the challenge as a new Chief Information Officer (CIO) because the exiting predecessor made a CLD, one is faced with many questions. How will one make a difference to prevent becoming the next corporate casualty? To a certain extent, as with all ambitious rising professionals, one has become a corporate mercenary for hire at the next earnings plateau. By aspiring to the elite status of CIO, one is now into a career category that has a high mortality rate tightly coupled with the high potential returns on career investment. As a practical adaptation of the Japanese *bushido* code (way of the warrior), business is war and in today's enterprise landscape there are no prisoners.

A CIO, of even a moderately sized enterprise, is required to rapidly understand the nature of the current data management systems environment that often has global reach, deal with available and emerging technologies, and demonstrate good judgment of how changes to technology within the environment will impact the enterprise. Any new or existing CIO is presented a series of unique challenges to understanding the operations, technology, business requirements, as well as the enterprise growth and positioning within the world marketplace. A crucial piece of this puzzle is to know the data handling of the enterprise as well as the methods to ensure data integrity while maintaining a fully functioning data operation. The feint of heart did not apply, nor do they belong in these positions. All rising professionals take advantage of the available tools and realize that application of the tools is most of the battle.

This book is such a tool. It helps walk the novice and seasoned professional through the data management system areas that require critical insight within a short time of joining an enterprise—at both the 30,000-foot level as well as with a magnifying glass to view the necessary granularity. Exploration of the best methods of detailed planning for technology expansion to maintain a competitive edge is provided for enterprise adaptation. Frank, detailed discussions of the components that make up the total cost of ownership, financial impact of technology integration is covered to provide a foundation for expenditure justification or returns on investment. This business perspective for technology integration covers a broad spectrum of step-by-step planning of the essential technology components for even the very complex data management environments. The goal is to minimize false steps or poor choices that often result in a CIO making a CLD.

The book is broken into five sections that each deal with a specific segment of the data management systems environment. Some overlap in areas occurs because the perspective of each reader is from a different frame of reference and the differences in the internal enterprise hierarchy. It moves the CIO through the path of understanding the environment to planning for the future growth and positioning.

The CIO must first take the time to understand the environment. With all the potential positioning of staff, the CIO must have the tools to gain a realistic perspective. This is much like Modest Moussorgsky's "Pictures At An Exhibition"; that is, different views of reality as defined by the artist. Imagine that the CIO has wandered into the exhibition and now must participate in a digital environment. Each view plays uniquely and has a different approach. It is up to the CIO to adapt to these different views of the data environment and then play to the appropriate business tune. As is the case in most professional fields, the CIO must understand the available operating charter of the enterprise and then harmonize to the music being played. The music for CIOs is to determine whether they are facing a distributed or centralized environment, the cost containment versus the technically advantaged, merged or downsizing companies, and, of course, the hardware infrastructure.

Once the foundational infrastructure is clarified, the CIO rapidly parachutes into the heart of the new data jungle. CIO survivability in this data jungle depends on adapting quickly and consuming details and organizing the jungle into a well-planned garden. Although one describes the job to friends and family as a manager of 1s and 0s, one must leverage incredibly complex data structures for storing information into rows of data that can be readily harvested. The job here is to logically sow the 1s and 0s into a data architecture positioned for the demand of the user community. This overall architecture and the execution of the data structure, including potential migration for a better layout, are under the guidance of the CIO. Data architecture delves deep into various structures as well as the mixed data types prevalent in today's enterprise, including video and audio. It leads one through basic structures and the tools availability to ensure data integrity. It covers the standards necessary for solid data management systems that are expandable to meet enterprise data growth.

With the data architecture firmly in place, the CIO provides the buffet for users to select how and what data to access. The struggle of who owns the data and how it should be used is offered in detail. The critical nature of correct data to the correct user at the correct time is essential for competition by enterprises. Data is only valuable in-so-far as it can be accessed and manipulated. If the end users or the data management staff are unable to reach the data, the value is lost. Building bridges between dissimilar systems and fortifying the hardware platform that supplies the data is like moving through the buffet line. Each user has the real choice of selection, including how, where, and how much. Data access answers the difficult questions of:

- Who needs the data and how are they reaching it?
- What are the best methods for maintaining critical data access?
- Where should different media types be placed for user access?
- When can software be managed?
- How does the user get to the right information?

Market leadership is often based on the ability of enterprise staff to have rapid, correct data access and it is the CIO who is responsible for keeping the data buffet filled.

The single largest ongoing function of any CIO is ensuring the proper procedures for data management. Safeguarding an integral portion of enterprise resources is clearly a difficult task, much like settling in for a long siege. This section looks at preparing for all the potential disruptions to the data environment. Planning for security against internal and external attacks is reviewed to make certain processes are in place to maintain the data operations. Enterprises tend to spend enormous amounts of money on structuring and accessing data, but attention to the requirements of data management is often left with too little and it is realized too late. Data management covers topics from encryption methods to full-blown disaster recovery planning. Securing corporate data adds a layer of complexity to data managing and includes not just restricted access to prying eyes, but also from malicious attacks and computer viruses. There is no one methodology or product that can be invoked to manage one's enterprise data at every layer from all threats, but deploying several different products with the right processes combined will fortify the enterprise's data stockpile. A hero is often the person in the right place, at the right time, with the right tools.

With all of the above in place, the CIO can now plan to venture where the enterprise has never been before. The choices and plans shape the way the enterprise can embrace the future now. The technology choices presented allow for many different paths that must work now, as well as position to meet the next onslaught of enterprise churn. Deploying technology is, in fact, the relentless crushing of time into shorter intervals. The telegraph line replaced the Pony Express (letter carriers); airplanes and trucks replaced trains and wagons for rapid transport of people and goods; telephones replaced telegraphs for communications; computers replaced adding machines and human ciphers; and faster computers replaced slower computers. Telephones and computers are rapidly pushing together as information travels the same wires.

The Internet is the newest iteration of crushing time into even smaller increments. The term Web-year is now used to describe six-month time frames. Thus, corporate data must be available quicker to support corporate customers and end users. Web pages offering product information must be delivered quicker and transactions must be completed sooner if a company is to survive global competition. Product lead times are shortened, deliveries are just in time, transactions are now not next week, and all of it needs to be done without losing the personalized relationship customers expect. The future now provides insight into how to evaluate and use technology to the advantage of the enterprise. If the foundations in place are solid, the solutions are doable. As the CIO, one must deliver that data management infrastructure to the enterprise corporate community. One has one Web-year to succeed.

Section I
Understanding the Environment

AN ENTERPRISE'S DATA MANAGEMENT SYSTEMS CAN RANGE FROM THE SIMPLISTIC TO THE COMPLEX, depending on:

- when operations began
- type of business
- evolution of the enterprise
- ability to understand and implement new technology

It is critical when entering a new enterprise as CIO of the data management systems department to understand how the environment reached its current state. For days, many questions and doubts will surface. Therefore, it is important that the CIO be armed with some principles and facts as a baseline.

Is the new company built on a centralized or decentralized model for using data handling technology, or is it a hybrid combination of the two? If it is assumed that the new CIO was brought in not to maintain the status quo, but to evolve the systems infrastructure, then understanding the current architecture is the beginning point.

Of course if the new CIO was brought in as part of the new management team, then first efforts might require one to orchestrate integrating data handling infrastructures between two merging companies. If that is the case, then one's concerns are not only with regard to the merger of different data structures, but also the dissimilar security requirements of each organization.

First and foremost on the mind of a successful CIO is that data management systems are almost always treated as overhead cost to doing business. If one intends to have any longevity in the data world, it is critical to constantly look for ways to save expenditures. Locating all possible economies of scale to be found and evolving one's data management group and the enterprise's competitive position (not to mention one's career) while pinching pennies is possible, if one knows what one is getting into each step of the way.

The toughest question always is, "Will this new technology actually help save money or just consume more resources that just are not available nor budgeted?" Should one outsource data processing ability to save money or does that put loyalties at the mercy of an outsider? How does one weigh the risk of outsourcing verses the hard dollar costs of data management infrastructure ownership? Will the Internet and outsourcing solve all problems?

This section delves into these issues with tools to develop and gain an understanding of the heart of the data management environment from the most common aspects. Understanding the environment is the first step toward successfully positioning the enterprise to meet the technology changes under consideration. It will lead the CIO through the steps to understanding the environment with the following chapters providing a well-rounded foundation for the professional new to the position or those who are refocusing the data management systems.

- Best Practices for Managing the Decentralized IT Organization
- Controlling Information During Mergers, Acquisitions, and Downsizing
- Cost-effective Management Practices for the Data Center
- Assessing the Real Costs of a Major System Change
- Application Servers: The Next Wave in Corporate Intranets and Internet Access

Chapter 1
Best Practices for Managing the Decentralized IT Organization

Eileen M. Birge

OVER THE YEARS, COMPANIES HAVE PROVIDED IT SERVICES TO THEIR BUSINESS UNITS THROUGH A VARIETY OF ORGANIZATIONAL MODELS — centralized, decentralized, outsourced, and insourced. Recent technical developments and trends, however, have made adoption of the decentralized model more likely than in the past.

The heavy emphasis on client/server systems has reduced dependency on the corporate mainframe. For many companies, the drivers to decentralized organization and a migration to client/server computing are the same: the belief that systems development in the past has been too slow and will not support the rapid pace of business change.

Because the capital expenditure portions of a project are less visible in client/server environments, client/server computing has also made business units better prepared to fund their own applications development activities. Experimentation with personal computers and local area networks (LANs) has increased self-reliance. Many of the disciplines provided by a corporate IT department such as extensive security, disaster recovery, data backup, and source code control may not be present in the business unit applications — and not missed until a problem arises.

The trend toward decentralization is clear. In 1995 almost one in two surveyed businesses planned cuts in IT staff. More than 85 percent of the surveyed companies had reorganized within the last 18 months — and half of these organizations had moved some aspect of IT to the line of business units. At a late 1990s CIO Forum meeting in Houston, 100 percent of the attendees

0-8493-0893-3/00/$0.00+$.50

indicated that they had experienced a major reorganization within the last 12 months or would within the next 12.

Will these reorganizations be successful? Or will another round of CIO ousters be followed by more reorganizations and more stress? There are several factors that seem to increase the success rate of the new decentralized IT organization. This article discusses success factors that help IT managers and their organizations achieve the benefits of decentralization without experiencing many of the costs. Briefly, these steps are as follows:

- Initiate organizational change.
- Align IT with corporate strategy.
- Prepare a qualitative vision of success.
- Ensure realignment based on facts not emotions.
- Keep IT expenditures visible.
- Develop applications in the field but develop developers centrally.
- Maintain control of infrastructure development.
- Outsource selectively and carefully.
- Operate as a consulting organization.
- Move project initiation, approval, and financing to the business units.
- Communicate effectively and continuously.

INITIATING ORGANIZATIONAL CHANGE

In more than half of the companies undergoing an IT reorganization, the CEO or the CFO initiates the change, often in response to business unit complaints about service levels, systems delays, or lack of IT responsiveness to a changing business environment. When CEOs or CFOs initiate a move, they may view IT as a cost center rather than as a contributor to the business strategy. CEO/CFO reorganizations therefore often involve significant outsourcing, downsizing, and other activities aimed at controlling expenses.

The first thing IT managers should do to ensure a successful decentralization effort is to take control of the change process by initiating change rather than reacting to it. Taking the initiative allows an IT manager to implement change based on the other success factors and with a better understanding of the real advantages and pitfalls of decentralization. For example, if the CEO/CFO mandates that all IT functions move to the business units with virtually nothing remaining at the corporate level, then the IT organization often has no budget or sponsorship for infrastructure, research and development, knowledge sharing, or staff training.

ALIGNING IT WITH CORPORATE STRATEGY

The need for IT to align itself with corporate strategy should be self-evident — but in too many companies, IT operates in a strategic vacuum. How can IT managers align their organizations with corporate strategy when management fails to effectively communicate the strategy? It makes a great deal of difference to an IT group, for example, if a company sees itself as a low-cost producer of newspapers versus a high value-added dispenser of information. The systems, technologies, skill sets, cost structure, and objectives associated with the latter strategy are far more complex than for the former. The high value-added dispenser of information may be involved with World Wide Web publishing (and paid electronic subscription), customer-driven information digests and alerts, electronically submitted (and billed) advertising, and electronic clipping and digest services for customers. Complex new systems require a different organizational strategy than a simpler focus on maintaining the status quo and making only incremental improvements.

But what happens if an IT manager does not know what the corporate strategy is? First, the manager should try to infer the implicit strategy from corporate behavior. If this behavior seems random (which is a scary thought), then the IT manager should, at a minimum, outline the likely impact of various strategies on the aligned IT organization. Two simplified strategy scenarios from the package delivery sector provide some examples.

Focus on High-Quality Aggressive Service. In this first scenario, the corporation sees itself as a high-quality, reliable provider of express mail and package delivery services with plans to expand into the high-cost but same-day critical delivery arenas. Meeting customer information and service-level expectations are critical success factors for the business.

Resulting IT Alignment. The IT organization must be prepared to develop new systems and technologies based on a variety of media forms (e.g., the Internet, telephone, proprietary dialup) that let customers access immediate information on package status and arrange package pickup. To proactively identify and resolve problem areas, the IT organization should improve quality control and exception reporting. Effective systems that integrate commercial flight information need to be developed to support the same-day-delivery business. The IT budget will increase as a result of this strategy.

Focus on Low-Cost Services. In this scenario, the company sees itself as the low-cost provider of package delivery services. Most of its capital expenditures are directed toward the purchase of aircraft and delivery vehicles with lower operating costs. Current reporting on cost of service is sufficient to manage this business.

Resulting IT Alignment. The IT organization should focus on maintaining current systems and moving systems to other platforms only as a result of rigorous cost justification. IT should concentrate on outsourcing areas that are more cost effectively handled by others.

Once the sample scenarios are developed, the IT manager should review them with executive management and convey the importance of receiving feedback on which scenario most closely matches management's vision. IT managers should emphasize that management feedback will be used to guide the direction of the IT organization for the next few years.

PREPARING A QUALITATIVE VISION OF SUCCESS

With a clear corporate strategy in hand, IT managers should prepare a qualitative vision that helps focus their departments and can be tested against the strategy for fit. The vision should be a page or less in length and avoid mention of specific technologies. Questions to consider when composing the vision include:

- Where do you want the IT organization to be three years from now?
- How do you want management to describe the IT organization at the end of this time period?

IT managers are looking of course to ensure that executives describe the IT organization as making a positive contribution to corporate strategy. Statements such as "The high performance of our IT department allowed us to reduce the time period from contact to sales close by 50%" or "IT input into our strategy planning sessions is essential — IT personnel help us see the possibilities of using information to improve our business" are the goal.

ENSURING A REALIGNMENT BASED ON FACTS NOT EMOTIONS

IT managers should assess each IT function to determine its logical physical and organizational home and communicate that logic to business units. User departments, for example, often express a desire to have their own LAN administrator based on their belief that the presence of such an individual would improve service. However, it is easy for an IT manager to demonstrate that centralized LAN administration is far cheaper, safer, and provides better service that departmentalized LAN services. A recent study by the Gartner Group indicated that a user population of 1,250 would cost almost $3 million more over a three-year period to support through a departmental model versus a centralized model. Recent software developments make it even easier and more effective to run a centralized LAN administration activity than in the past.

Determining the logical home of an IT function also entails dissecting the functions to their lowest level. Asset management, for example, is a prime candidate for both centralization and outsourcing, yet the function may not be explicitly recognized within the department. In today's IT shops, asset control gets done (more or less) but may not be actively managed.

KEEPING IT EXPENDITURES VISIBLE

Today's US corporations spend, on average, about 5% of revenues on information technology. Gartner studies project that this will rise to 9% over time — but that the share spent by central IT will decrease.

IT managers should not abandon stewardship of this expenditure — even if it is outside their control. Accounting and reporting systems should aid in aggregating and analyzing all IT expenditures regardless of budgetary authority — or expenditure type.

In addition, because IT expenditures are a mix of capital and expense items and separate analysis of each can be misleading, expenditure analysis should focus on both kinds of items. This ongoing analysis helps IT managers make outsourcing decisions, benchmark against comparable companies, and determine what percentage of time and money should go to ongoing operations versus improvements and development.

DEVELOPING APPLICATIONS IN THE FIELD...DEVELOPING DEVELOPERS CENTRALLY

Bringing IT to the Users

Because applications development and maintenance are best done at the customer site — not just in the same building but also on the same floor and in the same work areas — IT managers should ensure that the development team moves to the project's departmental home at project outset. Seating should be mixed to ensure that IT people and customers are indistinguishable, a goal that is reinforced by having IT staff adopt the customers' dress code.

IT managers who implement these steps help increase user ownership of the finished product, reduce the "us against them" mentality that too often pervades development projects, and make knowledgeable users far more accessible. Bringing IT to users is also more practical than trying to relocate user experts to IT for a project's duration. Most important, developing applications in the field defuses one of the major reasons business units demand their own IT staffs in the first place — it makes them feel as if they already have one.

Retaining Centralized Staff Development

The need for effective staff nurturing increases with the IT staff's increased worries about maintaining their technical skills in an era of rapid change. The most productive IT personnel present a constant retention challenge — the best and the brightest want to move on to the next skill just as they are becoming truly productive with a current skill.

The challenges posed by skill mastery and employee development warrant keeping the career management of IT professionals under a central umbrella. A central group offers more in the way of advancement opportunities, cross-training, and diverse assignments — the very items that motivate the high-performing IT professional.

MAINTAINING CONTROL OF INFRASTRUCTURE DEVELOPMENT

Because business units are willing and eager to pay for applications but not necessarily for a new, easier-to-manage Network Operating System, IT managers must ensure that funding and visibility for infrastructure items like network operating system (NOS), source code control, and standards remain centralized. This results in lower maintenance and administrative costs, because, for example, the network operating system (NOS) configurations and wiring closet in Topeka will look just the same as those in San Diego. IT managers will find that making the business case for infrastructure improvements is much easier when they are talking about the organization as a whole.

IT managers should interpret the term infrastructure rather broadly to include, in many cases, common business applications. Companies are adopting complete integrated products such as SAP and Baan to replace their core legacy applications. Because these products provide maximum benefits to the corporation when adopted by all units, it is logical, for example, to develop a SAP implementation team that can consistently roll out the application to the business units — with the benefit of prior units' experience.

Infrastructure also includes the tools and methods application used by developers and implementation of knowledge sharing. A tool-building organization should be responsible for tools selection, development, harvesting (in conjunction with project personnel), and methodologies. Because this group can quickly lose contact with the real world, staff that has recent experience in business unit applications development or maintenance should be rotated through the function. The experience of BSG Alliance/IT indicates that one harvester/tool builder for every 50 developers can mean a 10% to 15% productivity improvement in the developer group.

OUTSOURCING SELECTIVELY AND CAREFULLY

Industry publications indicate that between 85% and 95% of major companies will outsource one or more IT functions before the end of the decade. Outsourcing is going to happen — so IT managers who ignore outsourcing will have it done to them rather than through them.

A one-year honeymoon and a nine-year divorce is an oft-repeated description of past mega-outsourcing deals. IT managers not yet involved in an extensive outsourcing arrangement have the benefit of learning from the experience of early adopters. Some of the lessons learned include:

- Avoid unnecessary 10-year outsourcing deals. Three years is a good maximum length for the arrangement.
- Use multiple vendors to take advantage of the best of breed and avoid excessive dependency on one vendor.
- Determine in advance the objectives for the outsourcing deal. Early outsourcing arrangements were often focused on costs savings. Today the most commonly cited objective is access to people with the right skill sets.
- Experiment with functions that have easier-to-measure success factors, such as network operations, asset management, and phone administration. Each of these areas has specific service-level agreements and performance measures.
- Use attorneys and consultants with an established track record in this area.

OPERATING AS A CONSULTING ORGANIZATION

The IT organization is a business that should sell to its customers — the business units — just as a consulting organization would. IT managers can achieve a consulting relationship by establishing a single point of contact between the IT department and the line of business. The individual who fills this role acts as a consultant and sits in on the strategy planning sessions of the business unit. He or she should be both a skilled IT and a business professional familiar with the unit's goals, financial resources, products, and tactics.

The single point of contact should also serve as the general contractor for the business unit, meaning that the IT organization is the prime contractor responsible for the performance and quality of outside subcontractors. This avoids the problems that arise when business units contract directly with a vendor to deliver an application and then pass it on to the IT organization to maintain.

IT managers should also ensure that the IT organization bills for its services and prepares status reports and change orders highlighting variances, completion dates, and other activities. Status reports should also be tested for effectiveness regarding both development and maintenance activities. Too often, maintenance becomes a major cost (as much as 70% of total IT expenditures), but its results are difficult to quantify at year's end. An analysis of maintenance also helps an IT manager decide if IT staff is doing true maintenance (i.e., updating code to accommodate a new business practice) or providing production support (i.e., fixing bugs that prevent the successful completion of work).

Users who are billed for IT services will expect fixed-fee contracts rather than an open-ended purchase order. As a result, IT managers should plan on doing some projects on a fixed-fee basis — but only after advising users about the cost of change orders. Overruns on fixed-fee projects are charged to the IT department and affect the profit and loss statement.

Operating as a consulting unit supports other success factors — working at the customer site, providing assignment rotation, and maintaining the partner/customer relationship. Furthermore, it imposes a market discipline on the IT organization. If the business units are unwilling to pay for all the services IT offers or do not want to pay for the services of selected individuals, IT managers may need to cut back on staff — presumably always pruning the least productive providers. Under this scenario, the applications development/maintenance portion of the IT budget is set by what users are willing to pay rather than by what was spent last year plus 3%.

MOVING PROJECT INITIATION, APPROVAL, AND FINANCING TO THE BUSINESS UNITS

Because user satisfaction is directly related to control, applications development and maintenance should be funded and approved by the business units. In this way, the capital expenditure or expense affects their capital program or profit and loss statement. The ability to authorize projects, cancel projects, and change projects increases both real and perceived satisfaction and removes IT from the position of having to deny or postpone project requests. Instead, if a business unit can pay for a project, IT makes an explicit commitment to getting approved projects done (even if this requires the use of outside contractors or consultants).

Decentralized project approval lets users make a clearer assessment of how IT expenditures compare to competing capital projects so that they can decide, for example, whether scrubbers should be installed at the factory or a new inventory control system should be acquired. It also seems to increase the job satisfaction of IT personnel: several studies indicate that IT staff working in customer-controlled sites feel closer to their customers and believe their systems are more usable.

Decentralized project approval does run the risk of sub-optimizing the overall corporate investment in IT expenditures. IT managers can mitigate this risk to some degree by training the individual acting as single point of contact to analyze proposed projects in terms of their strategic relevance to the company. If too high a percentage of expenditures are going to non-strategic projects, IT managers may need to try some guided selling to business units.

COMMUNICATING EFFECTIVELY AND CONTINUOUSLY

Why do most business executives like the idea of a decentralized IT organization? Do they want more control? More responsiveness? Surprisingly, the most common factor behind the move toward decentralization is the need for better understanding of what the IT shop does.

An IT manager's competitors (i.e., well-known consulting houses) are well aware that most business executives feel left in the dark by the IT organization. So they sponsor seminars, hold executive briefings, and send out mailings to help enlighten their target audience. Similarly once a company becomes a customer of a consulting firm, a senior-level person from the consultancy makes a point to establish relationships with business unit leadership and provide them with ongoing information about how the work is going. The single point of contact should adopt this role as well.

IT managers should also solicit feedback by holding formal meetings with business leaders at least twice a year. They should ask the following questions: If the IT group were a vendor to this company, would you provide a positive reference to another customer? Why or why not? What could the IT organization do differently to improve? Although some companies have extensive quality assurance processes — the true measure of quality is a customer recommendation.

RECOMMENDED COURSE OF ACTION

IT managers can achieve the benefits of decentralized organization without experiencing many of the costs. By presenting the IT group to corporate customers as a vendor of IT development services, IT managers give customers the control to purchase IT services. Customers drive what applications work is done based on their needs and not on the ability or availability of IT services. At the same time, IT managers provide a logical permanent structure for IT a professional that enhances career development for retention of high performers. Work that is vital to the ongoing operations of the company but less visible to the user (i.e., communications and LAN administration) is supported centrally to increase service levels, reduce costs, and achieve the benefits of selective outsourcing.

Chapter 2
Controlling Information During Mergers, Acquisitions, and Downsizing

Chris Aivazian

THE FOLLOWING ACTION PLANS AND ACTIVITIES ARE TAKEN FROM ACTUAL ACQUISITION EXPERIENCES. In one case, a medium-sized financial institution acquired a similar corporation about half its size. As with all mergers and acquisitions, the acquired organization began to experience the anxieties associated with change. Morale and productivity were on the decline, and damaging rumors began to circulate. Management had to react immediately. The acquired organization's Information Technology Division undertook a review of its systems, processes, operations, and resources to ensure that they were in a position to maintain business-as-usual internally for the Division and externally for their business partners and customers, that they identified key people and resources in their organization who were critical to the Division's ability to ensure business continuity, and that they identified areas of risk to the organization and initiated the necessary action plans to either eliminate or minimize these risks.

The actual experiences are reported by a middle manager responsible for information security in the acquired organization.

The middle-level managers of the IT Division got together and decided to create an action plan for managing risks during the transition. The document created contained an overview of general risk areas, and actions that planned to address those risks. The managers identified all critical functions, applications, and personnel and kept the document confidential.

0-8493-0893-3/00/$0.00+$.50

They rated the risks and discussed the tactics to mitigate each risk as follows.

Each issue relative to keeping the organization and its systems up and running was listed. Each issue — along with its criticality, the probability of its occurrence, the impact, the contingency plan to be taken if necessary, and the team leader (including a suitable alternate) responsible for its implementation and follow-up — was itemized. An example of one item on this list would be the loss of key programming staff; the criticality was rated high, the probability was rated high, the impact was that production problems may not be resolved in a timely fashion, and the contingency plan was to offer monetary incentives and to re-deploy other programmers to critical areas.

Then, the minimum staffing requirement for each department and section was identified. This list was subsequently used to calculate the monetary incentives necessary to ensure that key staff remain to support the organization throughout the conversion process. A document containing a skills/experience inventory for each staff member was also created. This document helped to identify areas where cross-training was needed, and areas where additional staffing might be required in order to get through the transition period. The managers met regularly and reviewed changes in status and staff turnover. This enabled monitoring of all aspects of the transition as it was progressing, and allowed quick reaction as the environment kept changing.

In another plan of action, to keep the organization stable and operating efficiently, it was necessary to convince senior management to consider generous stay-on bonuses, over and above the standard severance packages. It was quickly discovered that talented staff resigned anyway, leaving a good number of their severance dollars behind. This happened because all people have different tolerance levels for risk, and some people cannot bear the uncertainty of not knowing the state of their future employment. When these talented individuals resigned, and left their severance dollars behind, the managers convinced senior management to keep this money in the pool for the remaining employees, and not to reclaim it. As key personnel left the organization, other non-key staff had to assume new key responsibilities, and had to be compensated accordingly. Periodically, the stay-on bonus issue was revisited, and detailed letters of assurance to each eligible employee were issued. This made it possible to retain some talented individuals when they may have otherwise opted for employment opportunities elsewhere.

In another action plan, information security awareness was kept at high levels, and a contest was used to keep morale high. A simple reward was offered, like lunch for two, for each new idea submitted as an awareness poster. The winners were recognized by receiving a free lunch for themselves and a friend, by having their names appear prominently on their contribution, and by having their poster displayed in public areas like the cafeteria and elevator lobbies. It is surprising to see how many new entries can be generated by offering a simple, low-cost reward. This plan had the added benefit of infusing fresh ideas and material into the existing awareness program. Special activities were also planned to improve morale, and some of these were in the form of fishing trips, baseball games, picnics, and movie theater outings.

Other action plans undertaken included changing the predictability of certain information security controls. Random changes were made to password expiration dates and workstation time-out values for staff working in sensitive technology areas.

Also created was a new document that managers can complete and send to our Corporate Security and Information Security departments as their staff resign. This form contains a checklist of items the former employee had in his/her possession, like a company credit card, a company cell phone, a beeper, or an identification badge. This form was forwarded to all areas responsible for reclaiming such items. This process helps us reconcile the list of terminations the Human Resources department submits, and helps several support departments keep current with the steady flow of resignations.

By implementing safeguards like these, it was possible to avoid disruptions to processing, which kept the organization running effectively, keep morale relatively high, which contributed to a fairly stable workforce, and reward key staff at a stressful time when they needed it most.

It is also necessary to avoid certain courses of action.

It is necessary to avoid imposing new policies that imply that employees can no longer be trusted. You must weigh the pros and cons of issuing heavy-handed warnings or directives that could backfire and have the opposite effect. In an example within another organization experiencing a similar transition, a directive was being prepared, which would have required the previously unenforced, 2-week mandatory vacation policy to be immediately reinstated. After some objections by middle managers, senior management re-evaluated this option and decided not to make a change that could have had the effect of lowering morale, by implying that management no longer trusts its employees. In this case, the potential gain was not worth the added risk.

Within that same organization, another example of avoiding a course of action was to convince the acquiring organization not to impose new limits on the use of confidential employee assistance programs and job counseling, even though the programs began to experience significant increases in usage, and therefore, cost. During these stressful periods, it was discovered that it is not a good idea to be overly restrictive with funds when it can be damaging to people-oriented programs like these. Companies must remember that people are their number one resource during tension-filled periods.

It should also be remembered that, during certain transition periods like mergers and acquisitions, middle managers and supervisors are not immune to the effects of the majority of these changes. They are exposed to the same stresses as the rest of the staff, and their needs must be supported just as well.

The remainder of this document summarizes suggestions that each information security manager is probably putting into practice today. They can serve as a checklist to follow, especially during unstable times.

OPERATIONS AND PHYSICAL SECURITY

- Change management procedures and new system implementations must be closely monitored. Enforce authorized signature requirements, and consider adding more senior staff to the authorization process.
- Speak with all shift managers, network control center managers, and help desk managers. Explain the need for closer scrutiny of all non-company personnel in their areas, and ask them to politely challenge all visitors for proper identification. Ask them to pay close attention to, and report any unusual activities or occurrences, especially during the off-hours.
- Review evacuation plans and perform unannounced tests periodically.
- Question all requests for exception access to production data even if it is read-only, and especially ones stemming from high-risk areas.
- If your organization has a systems development life-cycle process, ensure that it is adhered to.
- Implement a policy of either allowing only two persons or no persons in sensitive areas. Use security guards and/or closed-circuit TV systems for monitoring.
- Review existing employee safety procedures, as the organization's first priority is the safety of personnel.
- Instruct security guard force to check all badges, and check for removal passes for all company equipment, as it tends to disappear more frequently during transition periods. Inform them of terminated employees who may pose problems later on. Ask them to be diligent, especially during the off-hours.
- Perform surprise visits to Data Centers. Question any unusual activity.
- Review the adequacy of backup and recovery procedures. Test disaster recovery and contingency plans more frequently. Re-check your door locks, controlled access doors, man-traps, etc. Perform unscheduled,

surprise tests. Review emergency contact lists and ensure that they are up-to-date.
- Review all off-site documentation for accuracy and currency.

COMMUNICATIONS AND NETWORK SECURITY

- Have a good Internet/intranet policy in place. Decide whether to allow downloads or not. If allowed, is there a process to scan and test the software? Check firewall access logs often. Perform penetration testing to see if any exposures were forgotten.
- Check all physical controls, environmental controls, change management controls, backup controls, and disaster recovery controls.
- Speak with LAN system administrators and review the roles and responsibilities of managers, administrators, and users.
- Replace traditional password systems with one-time token-based password systems. If that is not practical, change passwords frequently and make them hard to guess.
- Control the use of LAN traffic analyzers (sniffers).
- Contact organizations like the Carnegie Mellon University's Computer Emergency Response Team (CERT) to obtain the latest computer security alerts related to external and internal threats to computer systems.

MAINFRAME, MID-RANGE AND PC SECURITY

- Review activity logs daily, paying close attention to security violations and unusual patterns. Investigate all potential breaches promptly.
- Check for regular software and data backups, and for the adequacy of backup media storage and retrieval.
- Ensure PCs are included as part of the regular audit process.
- All mobile computers (laptops, notebooks, notepads, etc.) should be carried in hard cases, and not in the soft cases that most often tell the world that there's a laptop contained therein. All mobile PCs should have a security product installed and activated, with the three minimum controls enabled: ID and password to sign-on, inactivity timeout, and boot protection.
- Remember to review dial-up systems and their logs. Keep the list of authorized users complete and up-to-date.

EMPLOYEE SECURITY CONCERNS

- Communicate, communicate, and communicate. People need to know what is going on. Even if there is nothing to say, periodically assemble staff and tell them that there is nothing to say. Communicate both good news and bad news. Most employees act like adults and can accept the bad along with the good.

- Ensure that there is a good monetary rewards program for staff retention. Consider periodic bonus payments tied to specific project completion within specified time frames.
- Have Information Security staff work with Human Resources to implement a program to promote good ethics and trust. Experts agree that ethical behavior is best taught in the classroom rather than on the job. Instruction materials are widely available, most likely from the Human Resources department.
- Most experts agree that damage by employees is estimated at least 80% of the total. Outsiders and natural events account for the remaining 20%.
- Increase all levels of training. This may be more costly, but will help improve morale, retain certain talented individuals, and prepare people for their next career.

INFORMATION SECURITY STAFF

- Information Security professionals are not immune to organizational changes. Be prepared to take swift and immediate actions if it becomes necessary to release an information security staff member. Severe actions like physically escorting the employee out of the building, and immediate revocation of all their system access rights may be warranted.

VIRUSES

- Be sure to have an up-to-date virus detection software package installed and activated on all workstations. Most vendors today supply integrated, multi-platform, detection and eradication software that is very effective.
- Ensure the existence of a local Computer Emergency Response Team to deal with potential problems like virus infestations and hacker attacks. Team representation should include working members from all technology areas, and not managers alone. Have CERT policies up-to-date. Be sure that all members are aware of their roles and responsibilities, and that they are able to train a suitable replacement in case they leave the team.
- Remember backup procedures. The most common — and least expensive — method of recovery from a virus is a noninfected backup copy.

MISCELLANEOUS CONTROLS

- Voice Mail system passwords should follow the same guidelines for password changes. The same should apply to E-mail. Awareness materials should point out the need to secure facsimile transmissions and general paper output.

- Automated intrusion detection systems should be put into place. Although these systems are in the infancy stage of their development life cycle, they do provide a good level of automation, and can free up the human intervention during the detection phases.
- Speak with financial controls organization and ask them to review their accounting controls. Double-entry bookkeeping processes are strong control systems. Minimize outstanding balances on dormant and suspense accounts. Closely monitor all activity on these types of accounts.
- Put into place an incident reporting process coupled with a loss monitoring system. This can take the form of a problem management committee.
- Implement a good system of hiring controls, including drug testing, fingerprinting, new employee orientation, and consider including information security controls as positive contributors to job performance in the job description and in the performance review process for all employees.
- Ensure that all policies, procedures, guidelines, and standards are clear, concise, endorsed by the uppermost levels of management, and most importantly, enforceable.
- Revisit procedures for sensitive controls like encryption keys, key escrow processes, and fire-proof vault access procedures. Be sure the principles of rotation of duties, dual control, separation of duties, need-to-know, rule of least privilege, and cross-training are strictly enforced. This can be a challenge since during periods of transition, staff is generally being reduced. Perform a careful risk analysis, and do not skimp on sensitive controls.
- Increase the frequency and scope of systems audits. Perform self-audits regularly, and monitor logs daily.
- Arrange periodic (weekly?) meetings with a committee made up of members from Information Security, Audit, Physical Security, Human Resources, Compliance, Disaster Recovery/Contingency Planning, and Risk Management. Exchange information regularly. This type of crisis intervention team should discuss risks, threats, prevention, detection, and resolution. Be specific with documentation, but keep proceedings confidential.
- Work closely with the Human Resources department and make sure that advance notification of all terminations and transfers is done. Have a central depository of all system access so that rapid, complete, and instant revocation can occur. Do not forget contractors, consultants, part-time, and per-diem staff. Remember that the use of consultants usually increases during times when the regular work force is on the decline. These controls, although always important, require additional consideration during transition periods.

- Be sure to have a system of senior management oversight and reporting. The Information Security function needs endorsement from the upper-most levels of management.
- Establish a network of Security Liaisons. These extensions of the information security function need to be constantly trained as they are the eyes and ears of the information security organization. Develop special training programs to prepare the organization for increased threats.
- Make personnel accountable for their actions. Institute a system for periodic review of the organization policies by staff, and if possible, obtain a signature indicating receipt of such policies.
- Change violation thresholds periodically and covertly. It is possible to begin to uncover new patterns that may have gone undetected under the old values. Studies have revealed that computer crime succeeds in stable and predictable environments and conditions.
- Before installing new controls and security practices, make a special effort to obtain the acceptance of those affected by them. As mentioned earlier, avoid heavy-handed direct warnings about doing harmful acts that may backfire.
- Be prepared to collect evidence of wrongdoing, and to litigate if necessary. Use the resources in the Legal department prior to instituting any actions.
- Institute training and educate staff about social engineering. Increase information security visibility through posters, special alert memos, videos, newsletters, bulletins, and other awareness materials.
- Consider using the organization's E-mail when there is a need to communicate awareness information quickly.
- Encourage staff to report unusual activities in their work areas. Set up a telephone hot-line to receive confidential intelligence information. Set up a procedure to confidentially process and react to the information collected.
- Offer special job and career counseling and alternative employment opportunities. Emphasize the importance of preserving one's career as more important than current job changes.

CONCLUSION

These are simply suggestions that may or may not apply to all organizations. Obviously, a university's security needs differ from those of a bank. Look at each situation individually, and apply some of these principles wherever possible. If this is done, there will not only be a system of prudent security controls and practices in place, but one that will have gone a long way toward protecting the organization in difficult transition periods.

Chapter 3
Cost-Effective Management Practices for the Data Center

Gilbert Held

IS MANAGERS HAVE THE RESPONSIBILITY TO MAINTAIN THE HIGHEST POSSIBLE LEVEL OF ECONOMIC EFFICIENCY IN THE DATA CENTER. Toward this end, they must have knowledge of the expeODNnditures in the data center and its operations, and they must be aware of all methods for reducing these costs. This chapter outlines the core set of data center activities and functions that together represent the major expenses in operating a data center. For each activity and function, methods to control costs are presented. In addition, several examples illustrate the use of software productivity tools that can have a substantial effect on the ability to support internal and external customers, economize on the use of disk space, set up appointments and meetings in an efficient manner, and perform other efficiency-enhancing tasks.

MAJOR LINE-ITEM EXPENSES

The major line-item expenses associated with a typical data center are as follows:

- Staff:
  - Employees
  - Contractor personnel
- Hardware:
  - Capital expenses
  - Noncapital and lease expenses
- Software:
  - Purchases

0-8493-0893-3/00/$0.00+$.50

- Leases
- Maintenance
- Utilities
- Communications facilities
- Supplies

Although the expenditure for any particular line item and its percentage of total expenses varies among data centers, in aggregate these items represent between 90 and 95% of all data center expenditures. IS managers should use the list of line items in contemplating methods to control the major expenses associated with data center operations; these methods provide the potential for large paybacks.

REDUCING STAFF COSTS

For most organizations, direct and indirect payroll expenses over a period of time will significantly exceed all other costs associated with data center operations. Thus, methods for controlling staff costs can provide the manager with a significant level of success in controlling the cost of a data center. Three of the more cost-effective methods managers should consider are a lights-out operation, downsizing, and the use of productivity tools.

Lights-Out Operation

The term *lights-out* is used as a synonym for an unattended data center. A lights-out operation implies an obvious reduction in staffing costs because the data center operates without personnel.

Most organizations that implement a lights-out data center restrict unattended operations to second and third shifts when the need for manual intervention can be minimized through the use of such automation programs as job schedulers, task managers, and automated tape libraries. Even the few organizations that have implemented a third-shift lights-out data center must periodically run the data center with employees — drive heads must be cleaned, printed output has to be moved to the distribution center, and backup tapes must be transported to an off-site storage location. Nevertheless, utility programs can considerably reduce staffing needs, permitting a near lights-out operation to rapidly pay for itself through the avoidance of second- and third-shift premiums as well as a reduction in the number of primary shift employees.

A wide selection of traditional mainframe automation software is available for purchase or leasing. Such products include applications for job scheduling, disk management, and multiple-console support utility programs.

Job Schedulers. A job scheduler is a utility program that allows data center personnel to define criteria, which the program then uses to queue jobs for execution. Some queues may be assigned a high priority to perform an immediate or near-immediate execution; placement in other queues may result in a deferred execution (e.g., in the evening). Job-scheduling software can perform a task previously performed by one or more data center employees.

Tape Management Software. This option provides a data center with a volume-tracking capability, enabling tape librarians to more effectively manage hundreds, thousands, or tens of thousands of tapes and to locate and mount requested tapes much more rapidly.

Disk Management Software. This software enhances the data center's ability to allocate online storage to users and to back up data onto tapes or cartridges. In addition, some disk management storage utilities include a data compression feature, which compresses data during a tape backup operation. For organizations with more than a few hundred tapes, disk management software is used to compress onto one tape data that would usually require the storage capacity of three or more tapes. This saving can offset the cost of the program and probably provide even more payback.

Multiple-Console Support. A multiple-console support program provides large data centers with the ability to have personnel control computer operations outside the data center. Managers at an appropriate security level may be permitted to use their terminals or access the computer through a microcomputer, enabling them to assign priority to jobs and perform other functions.

LAN/WAN Administration. In addition to its applicability to data center operations, a lights-out operating philosophy is applicable to the corporate local area network (LAN) and the wide area network (WAN). Third-party programs are available to automate many key LAN functions, such as initiating file backup operations of each server on the network at predefined times or after software downloads.

Downsizing

The four major expenses associated with staffing a data center are:

- The number of employees and pay rates
- Contractor support
- Overtime
- Shift operations and differential pay

For most organizations, the number of employees directly supporting data center operations and their pay rates and benefits represent the largest staff expense. Some organizations have outsourced all or a portion of data center operations, either to reduce costs or to obtain an experienced pool of employees at locations where the hiring of data processing personnel is difficult. As an alternative to outsourcing, downsizing data center operations is a practical method of controlling or reducing staffing expenses.

With a downsizing strategy, a company encourages employees reaching retirement age to leave the company. A fraction of these employees is replaced by younger, lower-paid personnel. This method considerably reduces direct personnel expenses. However, the IS manager must consider that many of those employees urged to retire early represent a pillar of knowledge and experience: the manager may not find it practical to lose this resource. Thus, most managers may wish to take a close look at productivity tools, contractor support, overtime, and shift operations in the quest to control staffing expenses.

Productivity Tools. In addition to those automation tools previously mentioned to achieve a near lights-out operation, there are hundreds of programs for automating operations on platforms, ranging from mainframes to LAN servers.

An automation tool replaces a repetitive process by automating its operation. As a result of the tool's use, employee productivity increases or fewer employees are needed to perform an activity. By comparison, a productivity tool allows an employee to perform a job more efficiently but is not designed to replace a repetitive process.

The use of one or more productivity tools permits scarce resources in the form of organizational employees to work more efficiently and effectively. Although there are literally thousands of programs that can be classified as productivity tools, many, if not most, can be classified into a core set of categories. Those categories include illustration or drawing programs, remote control programs, electronic mail and calendar scheduling programs, text retrieval programs, monitoring programs, and archiving and compression performing programs. The use of programs in one or more of the previously mentioned program categories can have a substantial effect on the ability of employees to perform their job assignments. In this section, the benefits that can be obtained through the use of programs in each of the preceding categories will be discussed.

For example, a remote control software program allows a LAN administrator to access and control networks at other corporate locations. One administrator can administrate multiple networks at different geographical locations as if the administrator's personal computer were locally attached to each network. The productivity tool is used to extend the span of control of employees and provide a mechanism to more cost-effectively control distributed networks. Similarly, remote control software products, such as Hewlett-Packard's series of distributed systems (DS) control programs, allow a central site operator to control the operation of minicomputers at distributed data centers, thereby reducing the need to hire additional operational staff. In both these examples, the operations are random processes and the productivity tool extends the operational capability of an employee, but it does not replace the process.

Illustration/Drawing Program. One common activity performed in a data center involves the periodic creation of hardware, communications, and personnel schematic diagrams. Through the use of an appropriate illustration or drawing program, the schematic diagram process can be significantly enhanced.

For example, Visio, a Windows-based program from Shapeware Corp., includes over 20 built-in templates that facilitate the drawing of different objects and symbols. By selecting the network template, the symbols for a server and bus-based local area network can be moved into the program's drawing window. Using a drawing program with built-in templates can considerably reduce the time and effort involved in creating different types of diagrams. Thus, the use of Visio or a similar drawing program can substantially boost employee productivity when a requirement exists for preparing different types of schematic diagrams.

Remote Control Programs. A variety of functions can be supported through the use of remote control software products, ranging in scope from LAN administration to enabling technical experts in a corporation at one location to test and troubleshoot different types of problems that might occur at another corporate location either around the block or thousands of miles away.

Electronic Mail and Calendar/Scheduling Programs. The use of a calendar/scheduling capability within an electronic mail program, such as Novell GroupWise, greatly facilitates the establishment of meetings and conferences, as well as the dissemination of information. For example, by granting other users access to your calendar, they can determine if you are available for a meeting before attempting to schedule the meeting.

Text Location and Retrieval Programs. One common data center problem involves the location of information necessary to use different hardware and software products. In an IBM mainframe environment, it is often common for several offices to be used to stack various programming and hardware-related manuals. Not only is this a waste of office space, but, in addition, it is difficult for more than one person at a time to effectively use the same manual. Recognizing these problems, IBM and other hardware and software vendors now commonly make their manuals available on CD-ROM. Although a single CD-ROM can store the equivalent of a stack of manuals 50 feet high, its utility is restricted unless it is placed on a LAN and users are provided with text retrieval software that facilitates its use.

Placing the CD-ROM on a LAN permits multiple users to simultaneously view different manuals contained on the disk while appropriate text retrieval software functions as a mechanism that facilitates searching the contents of the disk or a selected portion of the disk. In this way, the contents of a 600M byte CD-ROM can be searched in seconds, permitting access to keyboard references that would be time-consuming or even impossible to perform when using paper manuals that require use of the index of 50 or more manuals as a search mechanism. Because many vendor programming and hardware-related manuals are conspicuous by their lack of an index, the use of text location and retrieval programs can considerably enhance user productivity by facilitating the location of desired information.

Monitoring Programs. Data center managers can select from a wide range of monitoring programs to view the performance of computer hardware and network operations. Some programs, such as CPU monitors, provide information about the use of mainframe resources that can provide a considerable amount of assistance in tuning an organization's hardware to the work flow executed on it. For example, use of a monitoring program might help determine that delays in program execution are primarily the result of disk constraints. An upgrade of older 3380s to 3390 disk technology could therefore improve the flow of jobs through the mainframe.

A second area where monitoring programs can be of considerable assistance concerns the state of the corporate network. Through the use of the Simple Network Management Protocol (SNMP) and Remote Monitoring (RMON) probes, the activity occurring on remote network segments can be viewed from a central location.

Consider the use of SimpleView, an SNMP RMON manager developed by Triticom Corp. for managing SNMP-compliant hardware and software devices. The addresses of an Ethernet and Token-Ring probe can be entered into the Network Map Window, with the Ethernet probe then being selected. Unlike some SNMP programs that require users to identify variables to be retrieved from a probe's management information base (MIB) by their numeric address in the global naming tree, SimpleView supports an MIB Walk feature in which the variable names associated with global naming tree entries are identified by their text description (e.g., sysObjectID). By simply selecting a variable by its name, information about the network management variable can be retrieved from the selected probe without having to know the numeric sequence identifier associated with the MIB entry.

Another valuable feature associated with SimpleView is its support of the SNMP GetNext command. This command permits a user to retrieve the value of the next management variable after an initial location in the global naming tree is specified. Once the sysObject ID is selected from the MIB Walk window, use of subsequent GetNext commands displays the MIB Variable to be retrieved in terms of its position in the global naming tree.

Use of an SNMP management console thus provides the ability to retrieve information from different types of network probes. This in turn can enable trained personnel at one company location to view the operation of remote networks to include examining the state of their health and initiating corrective action if they should note a network-related problem.

Archiving and Compression Performing Programs. Owing to the growth in client/server computing, a new function has been added to many corporate data centers. That function is the development, testing, and distribution of programs and data files.

The distribution of programs and data files is considerably facilitated through the use of an archiving and compression performing program, such as the popular PKZIP, ARJ, ARC, and similar programs. Using any of these programs reduces the data storage required to distribute program and data files if the distribution occurs via diskette, magnetic tape or cartridge, removable disk, or on another type of physical media. If distribution occurs by telecommunications, the reduced storage achieved from archiving and compressing one or more programs and data files results in a reduction in communications time. Thus, using an archiving and compression performing program can reduce both data storage and communications time associated with the distribution of programs and data files. It is important to consider the user interface when selecting an appropriate archiving and compression performing program, because the interface greatly affects the productivity of employees using the program. Unfortunately, almost all archiving and compression performing programs are command-based, requiring users to enter strings of codes to perform such operations as viewing the contents of an archive. One exception to the command base use of archiving and compression performing programs is WinZip, a Windows-based program developed by Nico Mak Computing.

Contractors. For most organizations, contractor support is used to provide a level of expertise not available from in-house employees. Because most contractor employees are billed at an annual salary level that is 30 to 50% higher than employee salary levels, eliminating or minimizing the use of this resource can result in considerable savings. One way to eliminate or reduce the use of contractor personnel is to identify the skills they perform that are not available from current employees. The IS manager can review the records of employees to determine whether they are capable of learning the skills performed by contractor personnel. If so, the manager could then contemplate having employees take the appropriate vendor courses and attend public seminars to acquire the previously contractor-supplied skills. Once employees obtain adequate skill levels, they can work with contractor employees for a period of time to obtain on-the-job training, eventually phasing out contractor support.

Overtime. By controlling overtime and shift operations, the IS manager may also be able to maintain data center operations within budget. Overtime, in many instances, gradually becomes an unnecessary expense. For example, overtime usually begins as a mechanism to perform a necessary operation, such as extending shift coverage to support the testing of new software or a similar function. Without appropriate controls, it becomes easy for employees to request and receive permission to use overtime to substitute for sick, vacationing, or otherwise absent workers. All too often, overtime use expands significantly and can become the proverbial budget buster. Alternatives to overtime, such as compensatory time, should be considered.

Shift Operations. Shift operations not only require the use of additional employees but cause premium pay rates through shift differentials. Controlling shift operations has the potential for significantly controlling personnel costs. Possible methods of reducing shift operations include:

- Obtaining additional processing and peripheral device capacity to finish jobs earlier
- Altering the job flow mixture to execute jobs that do not require operator intervention after the prime shift
- Requiring non-prime shift jobs to be executed on specific days and at specific times

HARDWARE COSTS

Over the life cycle of a computer system, its hardware cost typically represents the second or third largest expenditure of funds. Controlling the cost of hardware is a means for the IS manager to maintain expenditures within budget.

Capital and Non-Capital Expenses

Most organizations subdivide hardware expenditures into capital and non-capital expenses. Capital expenses must be depreciated over a period of years even though paid for upon acquisition. Non-capital hardware expenses can be written off during the year the equipment is required. However, the current limit for this category of hardware is $17,500. Because most hardware expenditures exceed this limit, this chapter discusses hardware that is capitalized.

The several practical methods for controlling the cost of capitalized equipment include:

- Obtaining plug-compatible peripherals to satisfy peripheral expansion requirements
- Using a lease to minimize one-time expenditures of new equipment additions
- Buying used equipment to satisfy some or all of the data center's processing and peripheral expansion requirements
- Platform reduction

The major risk in acquiring used equipment is the availability and cost of maintenance. If availability of maintenance is not a problem and the cost is reasonable, employing used equipment can considerably reduce equipment costs.

Platform Reduction. Platform reduction refers to downsizing client/server technology as a replacement for conventional mainframe and minicomputer-based applications. The rationale for considering a platform reduction is economics. A Pentium-based server is capable of operating at 50 millions of instructions per second (MIPS) for a fraction of the cost of an equivalent MIPS mainframe. Of course, previously developed applications must also be moved off the mainframe, which is not a trivial task. Organizations with extensive mainframe applications can require anywhere from 18 months to 2 or more years to move a series of mainframe applications to client/server technology. The additional expense of moving applications to a new platform includes a period in which many programmers are no longer available to enhance existing applications because their primary effort is focused on program conversion. The most successful platform reduction efforts are those that can identify an orderly migration of applications or the successful replacement of mainframe applications with client/server applications.

Example. An organization has an IBM 3090E supporting employees using Lotus 1-2-3/M, WordPerfect, a CICS application, and PROFS for electronic mail. The mainframe versions of 1-2-3 and WordPerfect can be replaced by equivalent and more functional client/server products. PROFS can be replaced by 10 or more LAN E-mail programs. Thus, only the customized CICS application would require a conversion effect. An orderly migration to client/server technology may entail installing the network, training employees to use the LAN, loading the ready-made client/server programs, and providing any additional user training. The conversion of the customized CICS applications to run on the client/server platform would be planned to coincide with the end of this transition effort. Such planning minimizes the time required to move to a new computing platform. In addition, such a plan would enable the organization to expediently cancel mainframe software licenses and maintenance service, which can range between $10,000 and $25,000 a month for a 3090E. An expeditious and orderly migration to a computing platform can have a considerable financial impact on the organization's bottom line.

SOFTWARE COSTS

Line-item expenses associated with software are generally subdivided into purchase and lease products. For example, the computer operating system and utilities may be available only on a lease basis, whereas application programs may be available for purchase only.

Leasing and Purchasing. In examining lease versus purchasing software, the IS manager should be aware that many mainframe products are priced on a monthly lease basis. The expense of leasing for 30 months usually equals the cost of purchasing the product. Excluding the potential interest earned on the difference between the expense associated with an immediate purchase and the lease of software, the organization should generally purchase any software product that it anticipates using for more than 30 months. If it purchases such a product, the organization will begin to accrue savings on software after using it for 30 months. The savings cumulatively increase each month the product is used after this break-even point.

Multiple Processors. Another area in which IS managers can control software costs involves multiple-processor data centers. Because most computer manufacturers charge a monthly fee for each processor use site, based on the number of and types of computers the processor operates on, reducing production installation to one or a few computers can provide savings.

Example. A data center with multiple IBM 3090 processors uses CICS and PROFS as well as other IBM software products. If multiple copies of each software product were licensed to run on each processor, the software licensing fee would significantly exceed the licensing fee charged for running CICS on one processor and PROFS on the second processor. In this case, it might be beneficial to establish a cross-domain network to enable users to access either processor from a common front-end processor channel attached to each 3090 computer system.

For client/server applications, the financial savings possible from obtaining LAN-compliant software rather than individual copies of a product can be considerable. For example, a database program that is sold for $499 on an individual basis may be obtained as a network-compliant program capable of supporting 50 concurrent users for $1995. The IS manager should examine the different types of PC software licenses and the cost of individual versus LAN licenses.

MAINTENANCE

Although hardware is usually thought of as the main source of maintenance expenses, many software products have a maintenance cost to be considered in correctly budgeting data center expenditures. Concerning hardware maintenance, the IS manager can control his expense through:

- Third-party maintenance
- Conversion of on-site to on-call support
- Replacing old equipment with newer, more sophisticated products

Although savings from the use of third-party maintenance and the conversion of on-site to on-call maintenance support are relatively self-explanatory, the topic of reducing expenditures by replacing old equipment with more sophisticated products requires some elaboration.

Most computer manufacturers guarantee the availability of spare parts for a specified time, such as 5 years from product introduction. After that time, spare parts may or may not be available from the original equipment manufacturer. If not, the organization may be forced to pay inflated prices for spare parts from third-party equipment vendors to prolong the life of aging hardware. In addition, monthly maintenance fees are usually based on the age of the hardware, with maintenance costs rising as equipment life increases. At a certain point, it becomes more economical to purchase or lease newer equipment than to pay rising maintenance costs that can exceed the monthly lease and maintenance costs of the newer equipment.

As for software maintenance costs, most vendors price maintenance according to the numbers and types of computers on which their software product operates. The IS manager can control software maintenance costs by following the suggestion previously discussed for software — reducing the number of products used by dedicating specific processors to specific functions, instead of running copies of the same product on each processor.

UTILITIES AND CONSERVATION PRACTICES

Conservation can serve as a practical method for controlling the cost of data center operations. Two of the most practical utility costs over which an IS manager may have significant control are water and electricity.

If the data center processors use chilled water for cooling, the manager should stipulate that the water be recirculated. Not only does it reduce the organization's water bill, it will also reduce the electric bill and possibly even the sewage bill. After chilled water is used for processor cooling, the water temperature is usually below that of natural water. Therefore, a smaller amount of energy is required to recool the used water than to chill new water. Because many cities and counties bill sewage charges on the basis of the amount of water consumed, recirculating chilled water also reduces water consumption. This in turn reduces the organization's sewage bill.

Equipment Replacement

The cost of operating old equipment usually exceeds that of more sophisticated products designed to use very large-scale integrated (VLSI) circuitry. For some data center configurations, including front-end processors, disk drives, and mainframes that may run 24 hours a day, 7 days a week throughout the year, the cost of electricity can be significant. By examining equipment for components that can consume an inordinate amount of energy, performing an operational analysis, and replacing equipment when justified, the IS manager can realize considerable operational cost savings.

Examples. A data center is located in a large metropolitan area such as New York City or Los Angeles, where the cost of electricity can easily exceed 10¢ per kiloWatt-hour (KWH).

Some front-end processors manufactured in the mid-1980s consume 15,000 Watts per hour, whereas more modern equipment using VLSI circuitry may require 3500 Watts per hour. Because most front-end processors are run continuously except during upgrading or periodic maintenance, they can be estimated to consume power 24 hours a day, 350 days a year — or 8400 hours a year. If the front-end processor consumes 15,000 Watts of electricity per hour, it will use 126,000 kiloWatts of power (15,000 Watts * 8400 hours/year). At a cost of 10¢ per KHW, the cost of providing power to the processor becomes $12,600 during the year.

For the newer front-end processor that consumes 3500 Watts of electricity per hour, the yearly cost of power would be reduced to $2940, or a decrease of $9660. Over the typical 5-year life of most front-end processors, the extra cost of electrical consumption of the older processor would exceed $48,000. This cost by itself would probably not justify acquiring new equipment. However, considered in tandem with older equipment, this alternative could provide a sufficient level of savings to justify the acquisition of new equipment.

COMMUNICATIONS

If the data center provides computational support for remote locations, the IS manager should consider analyzing its expenditures for voice and data communications. Depending on the number of remote locations and traffic volumes between those sites and the data center, the manager may find several methods to control the organization's communications cost. Two of the more practical methods are the development of a T1 backbone network and negotiation of a Tariff 12 agreement.

T1 Backbone Network. A T1 backbone network permits voice and data to share transmission on high-speed digital circuits. A T1 circuit provides the capacity of 24 voice-grade channels at a monthly cost of approximately 8 voice channels. If the organization's voice and data traffic requirements between two locations exceed 8 individual voice lines, T1 circuits can significantly reduce the cost of communications.

Tariff 12 Negotiations. This tariff enables organizations with large communications requirements to negotiate special rates with AT&T and other communications carriers. According to vendor information, discounts in excess of 50% have been obtained for multiyear contracts with a value of $5 million to $10 million per year. For organizations with communications requirements that do not justify Tariff 12 negotiations, savings may still be achieved with regard to each carrier providing service between the organizations' remote locations and its data center. In addition to investigating AT&T, MCI Communications Corp., and U.S. Sprint, the manager may wish to examine the cost of transmission facilities of alternative local access carriers, such as Metropolitan Fiber Systems of Chicago, which provides local access to long-distance carriers in more than 50 cities throughout the U.S. The choice of this alternative may permit the manager to reduce the cost of the organization's local and long-distance communications.

SUPPLIES

One of the most overlooked areas for controlling the cost of data center operations is consumable supplies. Most consumable supplies are purchased repeatedly throughout the year. The IS manager can reduce the cost of consumable supplies by grouping the requirements of several departments, consolidating expenditures on a monthly or quarterly basis to purchase larger quantities of needed supplies. This action typically results in a decrease in the unit cost per 100 disks, per cartons of 1000 sheets of multipart paper and similar supplies.

Another technique is forecasting supply requirements for longer time periods. For example, purchasing multipart paper on a quarterly basis instead of each month may reduce both the per-carton cost of paper and the shipping charges. Further savings are also possible where reports can be stored on the network for access by many without the costs associated with printing and storage of printed materials. A total review of printed reports should be considered semiannually to eliminate unnecessary report generation at either the data center or remote print service location.

CONCLUSION

This chapter describes several practical actions IS managers can consider to control data center costs. Although only a subset of these actions may be applicable to a particular data center, by considering each action as a separate entity, the IS manager is able to effectively consider the cost of many line items that cumulatively represent the major cost of operating a data center. This process is a helpful way to review current expenditures and serves as a guide to the various options for containing or reducing data center operations costs. In an era of budgetary constraints, such cost-control actions will only increase in importance to all managers.

Chapter 4

Assessing the Real Costs of a Major System Change

Brian Jeffery

THE WIDESPREAD ASSUMPTION OF THE LATE 1980S THAT DOWNSIZING FROM MAINFRAMES WOULD REDUCE IT COSTS FOR JUST ABOUT ANY BUSINESS sparked what has come to be an increasingly confusing debate about the costs of computing. Today, evidence from a wide range of sources challenges this assumption. Users have become increasingly disturbed about the high costs of decentralizing IT resources. There is also a growing realization that the cost structures of mission-critical systems have remarkably little to do with underlying technologies.

As user experiences with major platform changes have shown, no one system is inherently more or less expensive than another. Real costs depend greatly on the applications and workload profiles of individual organizations. Cost profiles vary by industry, by type and size of business, as well as by geographical location.

Underlying hardware and software technologies are also less important than the way the IT department is organized, the quality of IT management and staff, and the efficiency with which IT resources are used, including the effectiveness of cost accounting and control procedures. IT managers who are considering a major system change involving new computing platforms need to better understand IT cost structures and how these structures change over time. Lack of understanding of these areas can result in a business applying the wrong solutions to the wrong problems — and wasting a great deal of money.

This chapter discusses the key factors affecting IT costs in any business. It offers IT managers suggestions on how to avoid common mistakes in forecasting the costs of computing and guidelines for using comparisons with other companies to more effectively determine real computing costs.

0-8493-0893-3/00/$0.00+$.50

COMPOSITION OF IT BUDGETS

The cost of providing IT services to a business involves a wide range of items. These include not only hardware and software acquisitions, but also personnel and their associated costs, along with the costs of maintenance, telecommunications, facilities, supplies, and various other related items and outside services.

A 1993 survey of corporate IT budgets in the US conducted by Computer Economics, Inc., of Carlsbad CA found that the largest single IT cost item was personnel (42.1%), followed by hardware (28.9%), software (11.9%), and "other" (17.1%). The category of "other" included telecommunications, outside services, supplies, facilities, and miscellaneous items. IT managers should pay particular attention to this category because although the individual items in it may each represent only a fraction of total IT costs, their percentage is far from insignificant. Most of these costs remain the same or increase during major system changes.

Businesses often make the mistake of focusing solely on one-time investment outlays, primarily hardware acquisitions, rather than on longer-term operating costs. This approach inevitably misses the main components of the company's total IT costs. Organizations that make this mistake are likely to experience a U-curve effect, as illustrated in Exhibit 4-1. Costs may follow original projections while a new system is in the start-up and test stage, but as soon as the system enters production and handles real workloads, IT spending escalates rapidly as new costs are incurred.

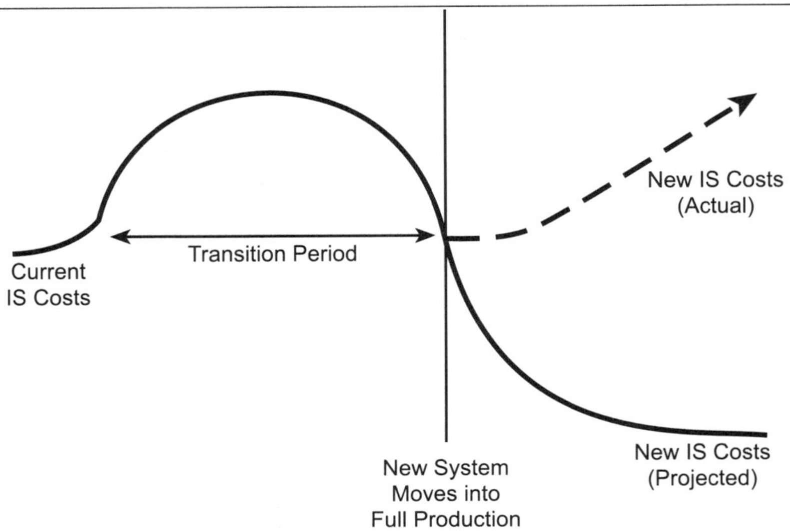

Exhibit 4-1. U-curve effect of a new system on total it costs.

QUANTIFYING PRODUCTION WORKLOADS

In any production environment, a minimum six sets of workload parameters affect a system's capacity requirements and hence its costs. They are:

- Numbers of active users.
- Volumes of data generated and used by applications.
- Type, size, and volume of transactions.
- Type, size, and volume of database queries.
- Type, size, and number of documents generated and printed.
- Batch workloads, including data consolidations, backup operations, and production printing.

These parameters can vary widely within a company, as well as between different types and sizes of businesses in different industries. As a result, use of standardized, generic measurements for quantifying system performance is one of the most common causes of cost underestimates.

Because there is no such thing as a generic business, any valid computing cost comparisons must be specific to the needs of an individual business organization. Most standardized measurement techniques have little relevance to the performance that will actually be experienced by users in any given production environment.

For example, much of the industry debate about Millions of Instructions Per Second is based on a fundamental error. Instruction sets, as well as the complexity and size of instructions, and the system processes that are instructed vary widely between systems.

Millions of Instructions Per Second has no validity in a cross-architecture comparison. In addition, millions of instructions per second (MIPS) represent only a measure of CPU performance. In any real production environment, the performance actually experienced by users is influenced by hundreds of different parameters.

Measurements of transaction performance, such as TPC/A, TPC/B, or TPC/C, are based on stylized suites of software and workloads. These rarely correspond to the applications portfolios, transaction volumes, or workload characteristics of a specific business. Variations between different types of transactions have a major effect on capacity requirements, and hence on costs.

The use of any single benchmark is inherently misleading because few production systems handle a single type of workload. Transactions and queries may vary widely from application to application, and the overall processing mix is likely to include batch as well as other types of system operations.

Thus, any cost comparison between different systems should be based on quantified workloads that correspond to the business's current and future requirements.

Database Query Volumes

Particular attention should be paid to query volumes. Although the effects of transaction and batch workloads are typically well documented for IT environments, large volumes of user-initiated database queries are a more recent phenomenon. Their effects are still poorly understood and rarely documented in most organizations.

Businesses that move to client/server computing commonly experience annual increases in query volumes of from 30% to 40%. Moreover, these types of increases may continue for at least five years. Although most transactions can be measured in kilobytes, queries easily run to megabytes of data. Long, sequential queries generate particularly heavy loading. Thus, once client/server computing comes into large-scale use within an organization, heavier demands are placed on processor, database, and storage capacity.

In many organizations, queries can rapidly dominate computing workloads, with costs exceeding those for supporting Online Transaction Processing applications. IT costs in this type of situation normally go up, not down. It is better to plan for this growth ahead of time.

SERVICE LEVELS

Service levels include response time, availability, hours of operation, and disaster recovery coverage. They are not addressed by generic performance indicators such as Millions of Instructions Per Second or TPC metrics and are not always visible in workload calculations. However, service levels have a major impact on costs.

Many businesses do not factor in service-level requirements when evaluating different types of systems. The requirements need to be explicitly quantified. All platforms under evaluation should include costs for configurations that will meet the required levels.

Response Time

Response time is the time it takes a system to respond to a user-initiated request for an application or data resource. Decreasing response time generally requires additional investments in processors, storage, I/O or communications capacity, or (more likely) all of these.

In traditional mainframe-based Online Transaction Processing applications, response time equates to the time required to perform a transaction or display data on a terminal. For more complex IT environments, response time is more likely to be the time required to process a database query, locate and retrieve a file, and deliver a document in electronic or hard copy form. Delivering fast response time according to these criteria is both more difficult and more expensive than it is for traditional mainframe applications.

Availability

Availability is the absence of outages. Standard performance benchmarks, and even detailed measurements of system performance based on specific workloads, provide no direct insight into availability levels. Such benchmarks do not indicate how prone a system will be to outages, nor what it will cost to prevent outages.

Even in a relatively protected data center environment, outages have a wide range of common causes. These include bugs in system and applications software, hardware and network failures, as well as operator errors. When computing resources are moved closer to end users, user error also becomes a major source of disruptions.

Production environments contain large numbers of interdependent hardware and software components, any of which represent a potential point of failure. Even the most reliable system experiences some failures.

Thus, maintaining high availability levels may require specialized equipment and software, along with procedures to mask the effects of outages from users and enable service to be resumed as rapidly as possible with minimum disruption to applications and loss of data. The less reliable the core system, the more such measures will be necessary.

Availability can be realized at several levels. Subsystem duplexing and resilient system designs have cost premiums. For example, to move from the ability to restart a system within 30 minutes to the ability to restart within a few minutes can increase costs by orders of magnitude.

Hours of Operation

Running multiple shifts or otherwise extending the hours of operation increases staffing requirements. Even if automated operations tools are used, it will usually be necessary to maintain personnel onsite to deal with emergencies.

Disaster Recovery

Disaster recovery coverage requires specialized facilities and procedures to allow service to be resumed for critical applications and data in the event of a catastrophic outage. Depending on the level of coverage, standby processor and storage capacity may be necessary or an external service may be used. Costs can be substantial, even for a relatively small IT installation.

SOFTWARE LOADING

The cost of any system depends greatly on the type of software it runs. In this respect, again, there is no such thing as a generic configuration or cost for any platform. Apart from licenses and software maintenance or support fees, software selections have major implications for system capacity. It is possible for two systems running similar workloads, but equipped with different sets of applications and systems software, to have radically different costs.

For example, large, highly integrated applications can consume substantially more computing resources than a comparable set of individual applications. Complex linkages between and within applications can generate a great deal of overhead. Similarly, certain types of development tools, databases, file systems, and operating systems also generate higher levels of processor, storage, and I/O consumption.

Exhibit 4-2 contains a representative list of the resource management tools required to cover most or all the functions necessary to ensure the integrity of the computing installation. If these tools are not in place, organizations are likely to run considerable business risks and incur excessive costs. Use of effective management tools is important with any type of workload. It is obligatory when high levels of availability and data integrity are required. In a mainframe-class installation, tools can consume up to 30% of total system capacity and license fees can easily run into hundreds of thousands of dollars.

EFFICIENCY OF IT RESOURCES

Capacity Utilization

Most computing systems operate at less than maximum capacity most of the time. However, allowance must be made for loading during peak periods. Margins are usually built into capacity planning to prevent performance degradation or data loss when hardware and software facilities begin to be pushed to their limits. If the system is properly managed, unused capacity can be minimized.

When planning costs, IT managers must distinguish between a system's theoretical and used capacity. Failure to account for this is one of the more frequent causes of cost overruns among users moving to new systems. It may be necessary to add additional capacity to handle peak workloads. For example, properly managed disk storage subsystems may have high levels of occupancy (85% and over is the norm in efficient installations). There is a close relationship between data volumes used in applications and actual disk capacity. Inactive data is more frequently dumped to tape, thus reducing disk capacity requirements and corresponding hardware

Exhibit 4-2. A representative list of resource management tools.

SYSTEM LEVEL
System Management/Administration

PERFORMANCE MANAGEMENT
Performance Monitoring/Diagnostics
Performance Tuning/Management
Capacity Planning
Applications Optimization

STORAGE MANAGEMENT
Host Backup/Restore
Hierarchical Storage Management
Disk Management
Disk Defragmentation
Tape Management
Tape Automation
Volume/ File Management

CONFIGURATION/EVENT MANAGEMENT
Configuration Management
Change/Installation Management
Fault Reporting/Management
Problem Tracking/Resolution

DATA MANAGEMENT
Database Administration
Security

HIGH AVAILABILITY
Power/Environmental Monitoring
Disk Mirroring/RAID
Fallover/Restart
Disaster Recovery Planning

NETWORK MANAGEMENT
Operations Management/Control
Change Management
Configuration Management
Problem Management
Resource Monitoring/Accounting
Software Distribution/License Control

Exhibit 4-2. A representative list of resource management tools. (continued)

OPERATIONS
Print/Output Management
Job Rescheduling/Queuing/Restart
Resource Allocation
Workload Management
Load Balancing
Console Management
Automated Operations

ADMINISTRATIVE
Resource Accounting/Chargeback
Data Center Reporting
Statistical Analysis/Report Generation

costs. If a system operates less efficiently, capacity requirements, and hence costs, can be substantially higher even if workloads are the same.

Consolidation, Rationalization, and Automation

Properly applied, the principles of consolidation, rationalization, and automation almost invariably reduce IT costs. Conversely, an organization characterized by diseconomies of scale, unnecessary overlaps and duplications of IT resources, and a prevalence of manual operating procedures will experience significantly higher IT costs than one that is efficiently managed.

For example, in many organizations, numerous applications perform more or less the same function. These applications have few users relative to their Central Processing Unit and storage capacity utilization, as well as to their license fee costs. Proliferation of databases, networks, and other facilities, along with underutilized operating systems and subsystems, also unnecessarily increases IT costs.

Requirements for hardware capacity can also be inflated by software versions that contain aged and inefficiently structured code. System loading will be significantly less if these older versions are reengineered or replaced with more efficient alternatives or if system, database, and application tuning procedures are used.

Automation tools can reduce staffing levels, usually by eliminating manual tasks. Properly used, these tools also deliver higher levels of central processing unit (CPU) capacity utilization and disk occupancy than would be possible with more labor-intensive scheduling and tuning techniques. A 1993 study commissioned by the US Department of Defense compared key cost items for more efficient best practice data centers with industry averages. Its results, summarized in Exhibit 4-3, are consistent with the findings of similar benchmarking studies worldwide.

It should be emphasized that these figures (which are based on used rather than theoretical capacity) compare best practice organizations with industry averages. Many organizations have cost structures much higher than the averages cited in this study.

Capacity utilization, along with the effects of consolidation, rationalization, and automation, suggest that efficiency is in fact the single most important variable in IT costs. Clearly, the best way to reduce IT costs for any platform is to increase the efficiency with which IT resources are used.

APPLICATION LIFE CYCLES

One of the major long-term IT cost items for any business is the staff needed to maintain applications. In this context, maintenance means ongoing changes and enhancements to applications in response to changing user requirements. Even organizations that use packaged software will need personnel to perform these tasks.

The typical software application experiences a distinct U-curve pattern of demand for changes and enhancements over time. Demand is relatively high early in the cycle as the application is shaken down. Change and enhancement frequency then decline, before increasing again at a later stage as the application becomes progressively less appropriate for user requirements.

The frequency of application change and enhancement is affected by change in such factors as organizational structures and work patterns. The level may remain low if the business operates in a reasonably stable manner. Because all applications age and eventually become obsolete, increases are inevitable. The main variable is how long this takes, not whether it occurs.

The application life cycle has important implications for IT costs. Once the shakedown phase is completed, a new application usually requires comparatively little application maintenance overhead. However, at some point maintenance requirements usually escalate, and so will the required staffing level.

Measuring application maintenance requirements for limited periods only gives a highly misleading impression of long-term costs. Application maintenance costs eventually become excessive if organizations do not redevelop or replace applications on an ongoing basis. Moreover, where most or the entire applications portfolio is aged (which is the case in many less sophisticated mainframe and minicomputer installations), the IT staff will be dedicated predominantly to maintenance rather than to developing new applications.

As an applications portfolio ages, IT managers face a straightforward choice between spending to develop or reengineer applications or accepting user dissatisfaction with existing applications. Failure to make this choice means an implicit decision in favor of high maintenance costs, user dissatisfaction, and eventually a more radical — and expensive — solution to the problem.

APPLICATIONS DEVELOPMENT VARIABLES

The cost of applications development in any business is a function of two variables:

- Demand for new applications.
- Productivity of the application developers.

Costs will decrease only if there is low demand and high productivity. In most organizations, demand for applications is elastic. As the quality of IT solutions increases, users' demands for applications also increase. This is particularly the case for interactive, user-oriented computing applications. Early in the cycle after a major system change, user demand for these applications can easily reach exponential proportions.

If this effect is not anticipated, unexpected backlogs are likely to occur. More than a few IT managers who committed to reducing IT costs have been forced to explain to users that t is not possible to meet their requirements.

Similarly, the productivity of applications development can vary widely. Some of the major factors affecting applications development productivity are summarized in Exhibit 4-4.

Development tools are an important part of the equation. Normally, third-generation languages (3GLs) yield the lowest levels of productivity, fourth-generation languages (4GLs) offer incremental improvements, and Computer-Aided Software Engineering tools, particularly those using Rapid Application Development methodologies, come out best. Visual programming interfaces and the use of object-oriented architecture can also have significant effects. Productivity, in this context, is normally measured in terms of function points per programmer over time.

Productivity gains are not automatic, however. Tools designed for relatively small, query-intensive applications may not work well for large, mission-critical Online Transaction Processing systems, and vice versa. Matching the proper tool to the application is thus an important factor in productivity. However, IT managers should be wary of vendor claims that the tools will improve productivity and reduce staff costs, unless it can be

Exhibit 4-4. Factors affecting applications development productivity.

- Proper Definition of Requirements
- Application/Systems Design
- Applications Characteristics
- Applications Structure/Size
- Underlying Applications Technologies
- Applications Complexity
- Functionality of Tools
- Development Methodology
- Match of Tools to Applications
- Degree of Customization
- Training/Documentation
- Programmer Skills/Motivation
- Project Management
- Management Effectiveness

shown that this has occurred for applications comparable to their own requirements.

Increases in productivity can be offset by increases in underlying software complexities (i.e., increases in the number of variables that must be handled during the programming process) and in degrees of customization.

Sophisticated user interfaces, complex distributed computing architectures, and extensive functionality at the workstation level has become common user requirements.

However, multi-user applications with these characteristics are relatively difficult to implement and require realistic expectations, careful planning, and strong project management skills. Failure to take these factors into account is the reason for most of the delays and cost overruns associated with client/server initiatives.

New development methodologies and tools may alleviate, but not remove, problem areas. Regardless of the tools and methodologies used, effective requirements definition and management of the applications development process are more likely to be the critical factors in productivity.

TRANSITION COSTS

Costs involved in switching applications and databases from one system to another are commonly underestimated. Many businesses treat transition costs as a secondary issue and give them less scrutiny than capital investment or ongoing operating costs. Even organizations that handle other aspects of the costing process with diligence often tolerate a great deal of vagueness as to the time and expense required for transition.

This imprecision also extends to many claims of cost savings. Most of the figures quoted by vendors, consultants, and the media refer to purported savings in operating costs, not to net gains after transition outlays. Moreover, operating costs may be artificially low early in the few years following a change precisely because major one-time investments have been made in new hardware and software, with applications that are relatively new and require little maintenance.

Initial Installation of New Hardware and Software

Costs of the initial installation of new hardware and software are comparatively easy to quantify, provided that capacity has been properly estimated using workloads, service levels, and other criteria. If this has not been done, the organization may experience a sharp increase in costs above projected levels during the first year as the new system comes into production and actual requirements become apparent.

One-Time Services Outlays

Some one-time services outlays are usually required as well. These may range from large-scale conversions of applications and data, to the recabling of data centers and end-user environments, retraining of IT and user personnel, along with the installation and assurance of system and applications software.

Many organizations use generic cost data supplied by consultants or vendors. This data can be highly inaccurate for the specific situation. Hard costs should be obtained to provide more precise data for planning purposes.

Length of the Transition Period

The length of the transition period has a major impact on costs. The actual time taken depends greatly on several factors. Organizations moving to new, relatively untried platforms and technologies need to allow for longer periods to shake down the new system and test its stability in the production environment. Depending on the size and requirements of the organization, as well as application workloads, transitions can take five years or more. A protracted transition period means that operating costs (e.g., software, hardware and software maintenance, personnel, cost of capital) are substantial even before a new system goes into normal operations. Parallel operations costs (i.e., maintaining the existing system in production) can also increase if the transition period is extended.

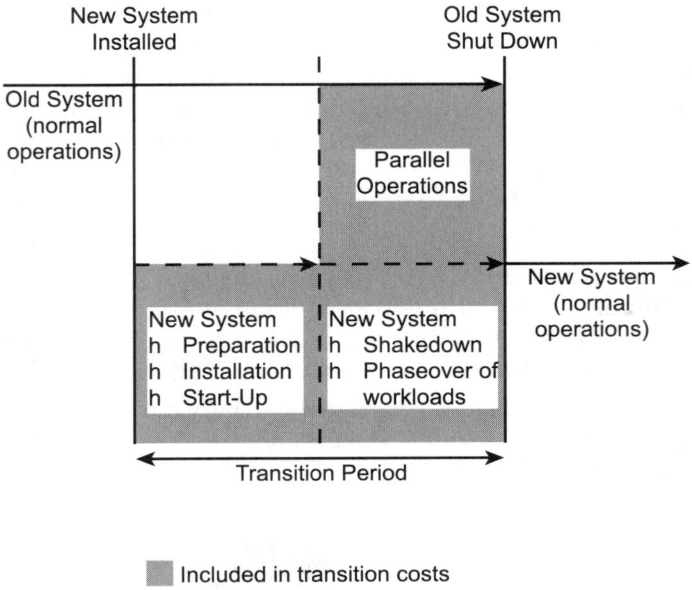

Exhibit 4-5. Measurement periods for comparative costing.

All these factors make it important that IT managers set precise dates for the transition process, beginning with the start-up of a new system in test mode and ending with the shutdown of the old system. This approach (shown in Exhibit 4-5) allows for more accurate five-year costing.

MEASUREMENT PERIODS FOR COMPARATIVE COSTING COMPANY-TO-COMPANY COMPARISONS

Reliability of Case Studies

For any business considering a major computing systems change, the experiences of others who have made similar changes should, in principle, provide useful input. However, few well-documented case studies exist, and those that do are not always representative. The lack of reliable information is most obvious for mainframe migration patterns.

Organizations that have replaced and removed mainframes entirely fit a distinct profile. In the majority of the cases, these organizations possessed older equipment and aging applications portfolios. Their IT organizations were characterized by lack of previous capital investment, poor management practices, inefficient manual coding techniques for applications development and maintenance, lack of automation, and just about every other factor that leads to excessive IT costs.

All this raises some major questions about comparisons based on case studies. Even where overall savings in IT costs are realized, the savings occur only under specific circumstances, usually because IT costs were abnormally high to begin with. Organizations with higher-quality applications, current hardware, efficient software, and different workloads will have an entirely different cost structure. Cost savings are particularly unlikely in an organization that uses system resources and personnel effectively.

Mainframe replacements are a relatively small percentage compared to the total volume of mainframe procurements. A survey of mainframe migration patterns in the US in 1993, compiled by Computer Intelligence InfoCorp of La Jolla, CA, is particularly revealing as depicted below in Exhibit 4-6.

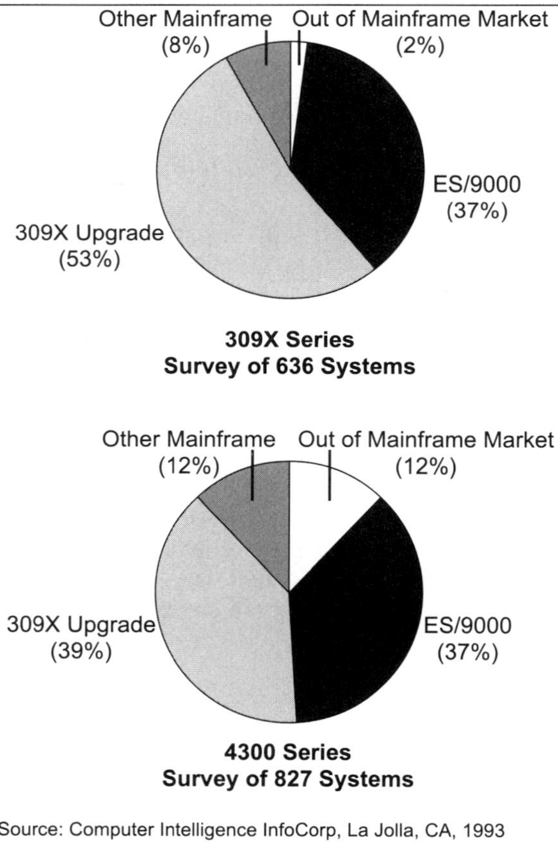

Exhibit 4-6. US mainframe migration patterns in 1993 for 309X and 4300 series.

US Mainframe Migration Patterns in 1993 for 309X and 4300 Series

According to the survey data, users of 309X-class systems who acquired new mainframe systems outnumbered those who moved to alternative platforms by more than 20 to 1. If 309X upgrades are included, the figure is 50 to 1. Among 4300-class users, new mainframe acquisitions outnumbered replacements by more than 8 to 1. This figure does not include users who upgraded within 4300 product lines.

The extent of real mainframe replacement appears to be relatively small. The majority of downsizing actions involve moving specific applications from mainframes to smaller platforms, not actually replacing mainframes. This affects the validity of cost savings claims. Although the cost of individual applications may be lower on new platforms, this does not necessarily mean that overall IT costs were reduced. In many cases, applications are either relatively small, or exploit mainframe databases, or both. In addition, transition costs are seldom included in calculations.

CONCLUSION

One of the computer industry's enduring ironies is that those who most uncritically and aggressively target IT cost savings are the least likely to achieve their goal. That is because unrealistic perceptions about automatic cost savings or inexpensive platforms often lead to inadequately managed planning and procurement. Preoccupation with technology may mean that major opportunities to achieve real, substantial cost savings through increased operation efficiencies are neglected. Even if real business benefits are achieved, the cost of realizing them is likely to be unnecessarily high.

Only by understanding IT cost structures, and targeting all the variables affecting these structures, can businesses ensure that they will obtain maximum cost effectiveness from their IT expenditures.

Chapter 5

Application Servers: The Next Wave in Corporate Intranets and Internet Access

Lisa M. Lindgren

A CORPORATION'S WEB PRESENCE TYPICALLY EVOLVES IN THREE STAGES. In the first stage, static information is published via Web pages. Information about the company, its products, and its services is made available to the general public via the Internet. In a more secure internal intranet, employees have access to company holiday schedules, personnel policies, company benefits, and employee directories.

While this first step is necessary, it is really only a substitute for other traditional forms of publishing information. The information can become dated, and there is no interaction with the user. Most organizations quickly evolve from the first step to the second — publishing dynamic information and dynamically interacting with the user via new scripts, applications, or applets that are written for the Web server or Web client. An example of this stage of Web presence is a newspaper that offers online news content and classified ad search capabilities. This stage offers realtime information, rather than static "brochure-ware," and presents the opportunity to carry out electronic commerce transactions. The second stage usually demonstrates to an organization the vast efficiencies and increased customer and employee satisfaction that can result from a well-designed and executed intranet and Internet presence. The challenge many organizations then face is how to rapidly deliver new services over their corporate intranets and the Internet.

0-8493-0893-3/00/$0.00+$.50

In the third stage of Web evolution, the focus is on offering new transactional services that communicate directly with the core IT systems. This allows companies to maintain a competitive edge and meet the unrelenting thirst for new and better ways to interact with an organization via the familiar Web interface. The transactional services are offered over the Internet for public use, over business-to-business extranets to allow business partners to more effectively do business, and over internal corporate intranets to offer employees new and better ways to do their jobs. Examples of this third stage of Web presence geared to the public over the Internet include home banking, package tracking, travel booking, stock trading, and the online purchase of consumer goods. Business-to-business examples include online policy sales and updates for insurance agents, manufacturing and delivery schedules for distributors, and direct order entry into suppliers. Intranet examples geared to employees include expense report submission, benefits calculation, and conference room scheduling.

The key emphasis of this third stage of Web presence is its transactional nature. This next level of services can only be achieved by tapping the vast and sophisticated systems and applications that have been built over a period of years. These mission-critical systems and applications represent the "crown jewels" of an IT organization, and include customer records, product availability and pricing, customer service databases, and the transactional applications that literally keep the business running. IT organizations must try to create a unified interface, leveraging a variety of existing systems. The problem is that the existing systems are usually very diverse. They differ in architecture (i.e., client/server versus hierarchical), operating system, programming language, networking protocol, interface (i.e., realtime, batch, programmatic), and access control. The application server is a new breed of product that unifies a variety of different systems and technologies in order to deliver new transactional services to a variety of clients.

OVERVIEW OF A WEB SERVER

To fully understand what an application server does, it is first useful to review the functions of a Web server. A Web server's primary function is to "serve" Web pages to Web clients. The protocol used between the Web client and the Web server is HyperText Transfer Protocol (HTTP). HTTP defines the valid operations between the Web server and the browser. For example, the Get operation is how the browser requests the download of a particular Web page or file. Exhibit 5-1 illustrates the sequence of events when a Web client requests the download of a particular Web page.

HyperText Markup Language (HTML) defines the contents and structure of the Web page. It is the browser, not the server, that reads and interprets the tags within HTML to format and display a Web page. Extensible Markup Language (XML) is the next-generation Web page content language that

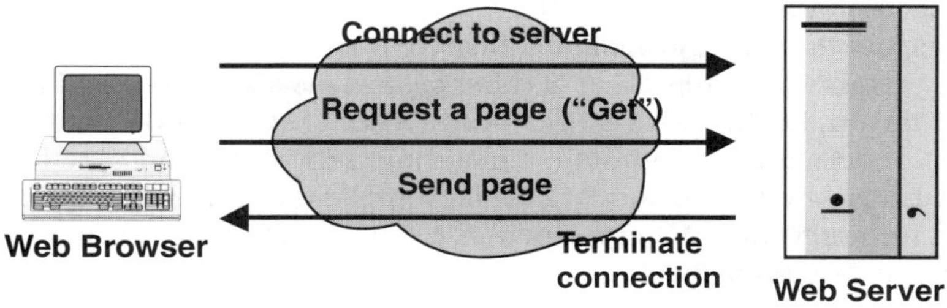

Exhibit 5-1. Sequence for download of a Web page.

allows programmers to define the tags in a page for better programmatic access to the page content. XML separates the definition of content from the presentation of that content.

The Web page can contain text, images, video, and audio. The Web server serves up the files associated with these different types of content the same. It is the Web browser that must display or play the different data types. As long as the request from the Web browser is valid, the file type is known, and the file exists, the Web server simply downloads whatever is requested.[1] The server behaves differently, however, if the page that the Web browser requests is actually a script.

A script, quite simply, is a program. It can be written in any language and can be compiled or interpreted. A script can be used to access non-Web resources such as databases, to interact with the user via forms, and to construct documents dynamically that are specific to that user or that transaction. The Web server executes the script and the results are returned to the user in the form of a Web page. Scripts interface to the Web server using either a standard or a vendor-proprietary application programming interface, or API2. The base standard API is the Common Gateway Interface (CGI). Some Web server vendors offer proprietary APIs that extend the capability beyond what is possible with CGI. For example, Netscape and Microsoft both defined proprietary extensions in their products (NSAPI and ISAPI, respectively). Microsoft's Active Server Pages (ASP) technology is an alternative scripting technology for Microsoft Web servers.

A Web server, then, serves Web pages to users but also executes business logic in the form of scripts. The scripts can gather data from databases and applications on various systems. The result is returned to a single type of user, the Web browser user.

OVERVIEW OF AN APPLICATION SERVER

An application server is an extension of a Web server running scripts. Like Web servers, application servers execute business logic. The scripts that execute on a Web server can be written to integrate data from other systems, but there are no special tools provided with the Web server to do so. In contrast, this integration of other systems is a key focus and integral part of the application server. It includes a set of "back-ends" that handle the job of communicating with, extracting data from, and carrying out transactions with a wide variety of legacy applications and databases. And while a Web server only accommodates a single type of user, an application server can deal with several types of end users, including Web browsers, traditional desktop applications, or new handheld devices.

Some application servers are sold bundled with a Web server. Others are sold independently of a Web server and will communicate with a variety of different Web servers running on the same physical server or across the network to a Web server on a different machine. However, most application servers can function without a Web server. An IT organization could implement an application server that only communicates with in-house PCs over an internal network without using Web servers or Web browsers at all. Nonetheless, the strength of the application server, compared to other types of middleware, is its ability to form a bridge between the existing legacy applications (including traditional client/server applications) and the new, Web-based applications driving what IBM calls "E-business." Exhibit 5-2 depicts the basic architecture of an application server.

At the core of the application server is the engine that ties all of the other pieces together and sets the stage for application integration. In many application servers, this engine is based on an object-oriented, component-based model like the Common Object Request Broker Architecture (CORBA), Enterprise Java Beans (EJB), or Microsoft's (Distributed) Component Object Model (COM/DCOM). Each of these architectures supports

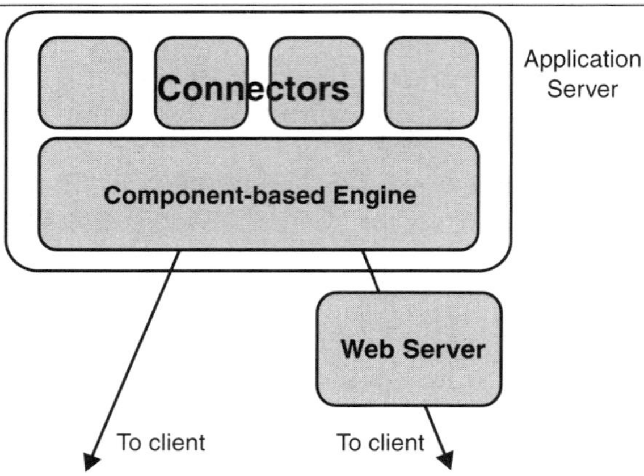

Exhibit 5-2. Basic architecture of an application server.

the development, deployment, execution, and management of new, distributed applications.

- CORBA: Defined over a period of years by the Object Management Group (OMG), a vendor consortium of approximately 800 members, CORBA is a component framework that is language-neutral and supported on a wide variety of platforms. At the heart of the CORBA framework is the Object Request Broker (ORB). Communication between objects is achieved with the Internet Inter-ORB Protocol (IIOP).
- Enterprise Java Beans: EJB is a Java-based component framework defined by Sun Microsystems. Once potentially at conflict with CORBA, the two frameworks have begun to complement one another. The EJB specification defined the Remote Method Invocation (RMI) as the method for components to communicate across Java Virtual Machine (JVM) and machine boundaries. RMI-over-IIOP is becoming common as the two frameworks begin to more explicitly support one another.
- COM/DCOM: The vendor community positions COM/DCOM as yet another Microsoft proprietary architecture meant to lock customers in to Microsoft-specific solutions. Microsoft positions it as the most widely implemented component model because COM/DCOM has been an integral part of all Windows systems since the introduction of Windows 95. A number of UNIX system vendors have indicated they will support COM in the future.

The definition of standards and architecture for creating stand-alone components, or objects, allows application developers to combine previously developed components in new ways to create new applications. The developer is then able to focus on the business logic of the problem at hand rather than the details of the objects. With the combination of object technologies and the new visual development tools, new applications are more easily built and more stable than the monolithic, built-from-the-ground-up applications of the past. It is because of this flexibility that most application servers are based on a core component-based engine.

Application servers offer "back-ends" that provide an interface into data and applications on other systems. These back ends are often called connectors, bridges, or integration modules by the vendors. These connectors can interact with an application or system in a variety of different ways and at a variety of different levels. The following connectors are available on some or all of the commercially available application servers:

- Web server interfaces
- message queuing interfaces for Microsoft's MSMQ and IBM's MQSeries
- transactional and API interfaces to the IBM CICS or the Microsoft Transaction Server (MTS)

- structured query database interfaces (e.g., SQL, ODBC, DRDA)
- component connectors to Java applets and servlets, ActiveX components, CORBA objects, Enterprise Java Beans, and others
- terminal interfaces to legacy applications on mainframes and midrange systems (e.g., 3270, 5250, VT220, HP, Bull)
- application-specific interfaces to Enterprise Resource Planning (ERP) applications, such as those from SAP, PeopleSoft, and BAAN
- custom connectors for custom applications

Downstream from the application server to the client, the protocol can vary, depending on the type of client and the base technology of the application (i.e., CORBA, EJB, COM). A common and basic method of exchanging information with end users will be via standard Web pages using HTTP, HTML, and possibly XML. Another option that involves some local processing on the part of the client is to download Java or ActiveX applets to the client. This thin-client approach is desirable when some local processing is desired but the size of the client program is sufficiently small to make downloading over the network feasible. When a more traditional fat-client approach is required, in which the end user's PC takes on a larger piece of the overall distributed application, a client-side program written in Java, C, C++, or any other language is installed. In this case, the client and the application server will utilize some communication protocol, typically over TCP/IP. In the case of CORBA, the standard IIOP is used. In Java environments, the standard scheme is Remote Method Invocation (RMI). Microsoft's COM/DCOM specifies its own protocol and distributed processing scheme. Exhibit 5-3 illustrates an example of an enterprise that has application servers, multiple back-ends, and multiple client types.

A final but important piece of the application server offering is the support for visual development tools and application programming interfaces (APIs). Because application servers are focused on building new applications that integrate various other systems, the ease with which these new applications are developed is key to the viability and success of the application server. Some application servers are packaged with their own integrated development environment (IDE), complete with a software development kit (SDK), that is modeled after the popular visual development tools. Other vendors simply choose to support the dominant visual development tools, such as the IBM VisualAge, Microsoft's InterDev, or Symantec's Visual Café.

The number of application servers available on the market grows each day. Vendors offering these products come from a wide variety of backgrounds. Some have a solid background in providing client/server integration middleware; others were early adopters of standards-based component technology like CORBA; and still others have evolved from the Web server space. Exhibit 5-4 lists some of the application servers available, along with some of the key points of each of the products.

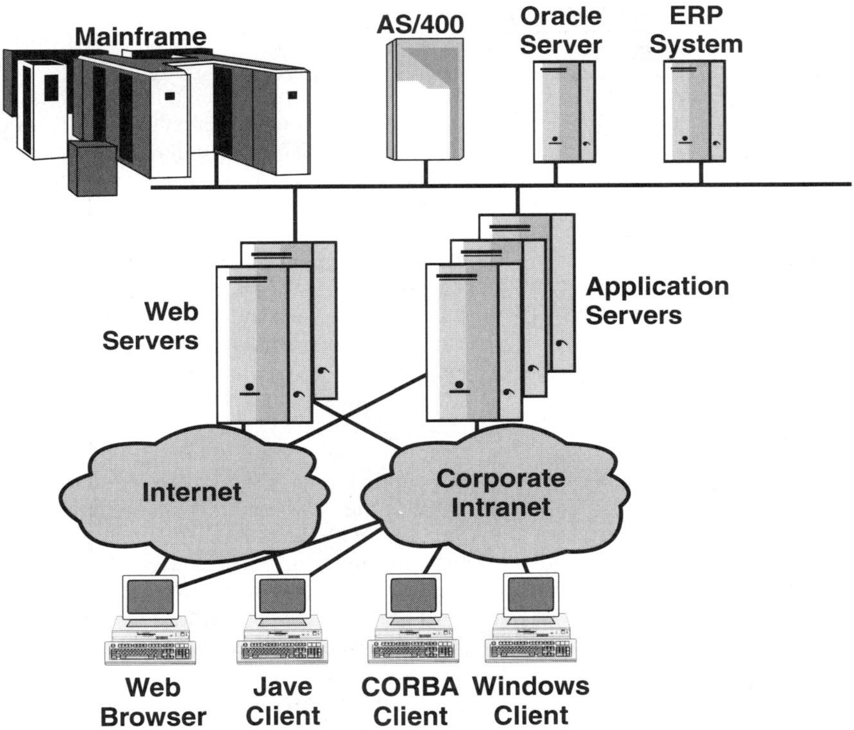

Exhibit 5-3. Example of an enterprise with application servers.

DEPLOYMENT IN THE ENTERPRISE

When deploying application servers in an enterprise environment, there are some very important and key capabilities of the application server that must be considered above and beyond its component architecture, protocols, and back ends. IT organizations that have made it through the first two steps of Web integration and Web presence and are now ready to embark on this third phase realize how quickly Web-based systems become mission critical. Once new services like online catalog ordering, home banking, Web-based trading, and others become available, new users rapidly adopt the services and become reliant on them. If the Web-based

Exhibit 5-4. Application servers available.

Vendor	Product	Key Points
BEA	WebLogic	Family of products offering different levels; based on Java but CORBA support comes in at the high end; built on common base of the BEA TUXEDO transaction monitor; includes support for Microsoft's COM
Bluestone Software	Sapphire/Web	Java-based solution; includes integrated development environment for application development; large number of integration modules for back-end access to systems; state management and load balancing
IBM	WebSphere Application Server Enterprise Edition	Includes Web server; focused on high-volume transactions and high reliability; core technologies are CORBA, EJB, XML; common IIOP infrastructure
Inprise	Application Server	Built upon Inprise's VisiBroker, a dominant ORB in the CORBA market space; integrated solution with Web server, IDE (Jbuilder), and management (AppCenter)
Microsoft	Babylon (avail. 2000)	Successor to Microsoft's SNA Server; built around Microsoft's COM/DCOM model; integration of UNIX, NetWare, and IBM mainframe and midrange systems; COMTI integrates transaction systems; includes direct access to mainframe/midrange data, DRDA for IBM database access, and MQSeries bridge
Novera	Integrator	Integrator includes the component designer back-ends with Novera's Integration Server, the runtime environment; Integration Server runs in a Java Virtual Machine; communication to objects and other servers is based on the CORBA IIOP

systems of a company fail, consumers are likely to go elsewhere and never return. Therefore, it is essential that the application servers be designed and implemented with ample security, scalability, load balancing, fault tolerance, and sophisticated management capabilities.

SECURITY

Security is even more critical in an application server environment than in a stand-alone Web server environment. This is because an integral part of the application server is the integration of existing data and applications. Often, these data and applications reside on mission-critical systems like IBM mainframes and midrange systems and high-end UNIX platforms. These are the systems that house the most important and sensitive information in an enterprise, including customer records, historical sales information, and other material that would be valuable to the competition or to the malicious hacker.

An overall security plan and architecture must accomplish three things. First, it must ensure that the data flowing in the network and on the wire is not legible to prying eyes. Second, it must ensure that the identity of the user is verified. Third, it must ensure that a particular user can only access the resources for which he or she is authorized.

A number of different technologies and products can be leveraged to accomplish these three goals. For example, Secure Sockets Layer (SSL) is a popular security protocol that accomplishes the first two goals by using encryption on the wire and digital certificates for user authentication. Secure HTTP (HTTPS) is also used to protect Web transactions. Application-specific user ID/password schemes as well as centralized servers, such as those based on the Lightweight Directory Access Protocol (LDAP) standard, provide user authorization.

Application servers must also take into account the notion of session persistence as a facet of security. There is a fundamental mismatch between the Web paradigm of user-to-server interaction when compared to client/server or traditional hierarchical applications. In the Web paradigm, each individual page interaction or request is a stand-alone transaction. The Web server does not maintain state information for each user. Session state information must be maintained by an application server to prevent the possibility of one user gaining access to an existing, active session. This is a security issue because, without session persistence, user authentication and user authorization security schemes are compromised.

SCALABILITY, LOAD BALANCING, AND FAULT TOLERANCE

Scalability refers to the ability of a system to grow seamlessly to support an increasing number of users. Systems that are scalable are able to add users in such a way that the consumption of resources is linear. The system should not hit a bottleneck point or barrier beyond which the addition of another user dramatically impacts session resources or overall response time. Systems that are scalable can grow to accommodate a particular maximum number of concurrent users in such a way that the response time is roughly equivalent for all users. For many organizations, the design point for scalability will be thousands — or even tens of thousands — of concurrent users.

This level of scalability is usually only achieved by implementing multiple, load-balancing servers. In this design, there are multiple application servers, each supporting the same services and presenting a portion of the total pool of available servers. End users, either fat-client PCs or thin-client Web-based users, should all have a common view to the pool of application servers. That is, one should not have to configure each device or session to use a specific server in the pool. The load-balancing front end (which may be a separate unit or integrated into the application server) should load-balance sessions across all available servers in an intelligent manner based on system capacity, current load, and other metrics.

High availability is provided by the load-balancing front end through its awareness of the availability of the application servers. If a server fails, it obviously should be removed from the pool of servers to which new sessions are allocated. Existing sessions that are active at the time of the failure of an application server will usually be disrupted, although some systems, like the IBM mainframes with Parallel Sysplex, can avoid even session disruption.

MANAGEMENT

Because an application server environment encompasses a variety of different types of users, back ends, and distributed processing technologies, it can be a very complex environment to manage. Most application server vendors provide tools that are supported using one or more of the common management platforms, including IBM TME 10/NetView, CA UniCenter, and HP OpenView.

The management tool should include the ability to manage the pool of application servers as a logical entity. The operator should be able to view and control all of the resources, objects, and sessions from an application viewpoint. A visual display of all elements with current status should be an integral capability. The management tool should be able to assist with the deployment and tracking of new applets and applications. The ability to specify actions based on certain events can help to automate some of the routine management functions. Additional information for capacity planning and modeling is helpful.

CONCLUSION

Application servers allow organizations to evolve to the third phase of Web presence, in which the focus is on providing realtime transaction-based services to both internal and external users. The integration of the wealth of existing data processing systems, applications, and data is essential to the ability to deliver new transactional services quickly and efficiently. Application servers unify the existing systems with the Web-based infrastructure, allowing IT organizations to leverage their vast investment in systems and applications to deliver new services to their employees, business partners, and the public.

Notes

1. *Web Server Technology: The Advanced Guide for the World Wide Web Information Providers,* Nancy J. Yeager and Robert E. McGrath, Morgan Kaufmann Publishers, Inc., pp. 37–41.
2. *Ibid.,* pp. 58–59.

Section II
Data Architecture and Structure

CIO PROFESSIONALS RECOGNIZE THAT UNDERSTANDING THE RELATIONSHIP OF THE DATA ARCHITECTURE IS CRITICAL TO KNOWING WHAT IS AVAILABLE AND FOR EVALUATION PRIOR TO ANY STRUCTURE CHANGES. A trade-off is frequently needed to determine whether the enterprise profits more by putting the data closer to the end users or by keeping the data centralized for management and security. If an enterprise has selected distributed systems, then distributed where and how becomes the next important decision.

The question of what data is to be distributed brings up a whole series of questions. What does distributed multimedia do to the responsiveness of the overall data system? Does one continue to increase the amount of bandwidth so the free-for-all across the campus or wide area network (WAN) environment continues to run properly, or does one employ policy servers to throttle and prioritize data traffic?

A key issue in every data networking environment is data standards. These data standards often require difficult decisions by the CIO. Can data management staff support a distributed environment if everything is unique and "one-of," or do data standards require a level of conformity for the good of the enterprise? When taken down to the data elements, should standards also apply? Can the concept of data-handling standards and uniformity be achieved in a distributed environment? Data standards often apply in other facets of the enterprise, but are often lacking in the IS world, typically because it is rapidly changing.

Enterprises spend a tremendous amount of money on collecting, assembling, and storing data. This is often done without regard to the data usage requirements. Relegating data to tape or other media also requires standards after understanding the end-user needs. Determining if the data is safe, maintainable, and accessible is critical to making decisions regarding distributed data or centralized data management. In the real-world application of data management, an alternative may be necessary that provides the best of technology integration based on the needs of the Enterprise and the experience of the CIO.

If the orientation is to provide distributed data architecture to the end users, then pushing data closer to the data consumers is an implied commitment. Then the methods to maintain data integrity and reliability must be the focus of the data management staff. Decisions affecting the profitability of the enterprise often find their source based in the data available. While the accuracy of the data is not the responsibility of the data management department, the integrity of the data is; therefore, choice and standards must be realistic as well as distributed to all data handlers.

As part of every CIO professional's career, there will come a time when a data management system becomes obsolete or needs to be migrated to another platform. It is too bad that enterprises cannot buy an insurance policy against poor data migration. However, the next best thing is a good map for staying out of trouble while converting critical data. If a CIO is committed to a distributed data architecture, then some day soon plans to convert a legacy database will be required.

For those responsible for data operations support in a distributed data environment, life is a constant battle with departments and end users who buy what they want and insist on data management support. It does not have to remain that way. Standards for the LAN/WAN environment help reduce support costs and, if implemented properly, do not crush the spirit of distributed data architecture. This section discusses the distributed environment, database structures, standards, and tips for surviving data conversions. Most CIO professionals will relate to one or more of the problems outlined within the chapters contained in this section and come away with methods to improve their data management environments going forward:

- The Importance of Data Architecture in a Client/Server Environment
- Business Aspects of Multimedia Networking
- Using Expert Systems Technology to Standardize Data Elements
- Managing Data on the Network: Data Warehousing
- Ensuring the Integrity of the Database
- A Practical Example of Data Conversion
- Legacy Database Conversion
- Design, Implementation, and Management of Distributed Databases—An Overview
- Operating Standards and Practices for LANs

Chapter 6
The Importance of Data Architecture in a Client/Server Environment

Gary Lord

CLIENT/SERVER TECHNOLOGY CAN BE THOUGHT OF AS A TECHNICAL ARCHITECTURE that is a mix of personal computers and midrange systems with middleware connecting them so that they work together to perform a process. Within this environment, the distribution of data is just as important to a successful implementation as is the distribution of processes.

The concepts of data architecture and technical architecture are defined as follows:

- The data architecture depicts the distribution and access mechanisms associated with data for one or more applications. It defines the standards and procedures needed to create consistent, accurate, complete, and timely data. It defines a process for rationalizing data needs across applications and determining its appropriate distribution and placement. It defines the methods for the collection and distribution of all computerized information.
- The technical architecture represents various components and services that make up a suite of applications or a specific application. It describes the classes of technology required to support data storage, application access, processing, and communications and how they fit together. It defines the standards, guidelines, and infrastructure necessary to meet the requirements of the application. The technical architecture encompasses the hardware, operating systems, network facilities, and tools that enable the implementation of systems.

0-8493-0893-3/00/$0.00+$.50

The data and technical architectures are highly integrated in that the technical blueprint includes the classes of technology necessary to support the implementation of the data blueprint.

CREATING A DATA ARCHITECTURE

Significant issues are associated with the creation of a data architecture in a client/server environment. Among these issues are

- Data metrics: Determinants include the size of data, the frequency that data is needed, and the cost associated with getting it, as well as the frequency with which the data changes.
- Data access: Challenges in this area concern whether access is to be ad hoc or controlled and whether it will be for update or read-only purposes.
- Data harvesting: One of the challenges with defining the data architecture is the formulation of appropriate harvesting strategies — that is, how to manage data from transaction systems to data warehouses to departmental servers and, in some cases, to the desktop.
- Data replication: Another challenge is to define under what conditions data should be distributed or replicated.
- Data ownership and security: Issues to resolve include determining who will take responsibility for owning the data and who will have what type of access to what data.

Architecture Definition: High-Level to Lower-Level Design

As with traditional data modeling, the technical architecture and data architecture definition can begin at a high level early in a development effort and progress to more detailed levels throughout the development life cycle. A certain degree of rigor must be applied to develop both the data architecture and the technical architecture concurrently. One approach is to follow the time-tested data modeling concept of conceptual, logical, and physical representations.

The Conceptual Layer. The conceptual layer includes requirements or objectives. This layer describes the "what" in terms of business-linked objectives. The conceptual data architecture is the distribution of conceptual data stores across the technology framework at a very high level. For example, sales data resides in the data warehouse. Edit rules related to sales data reside both in the repository and on the desktop.

The conceptual technical architecture includes application components and services positioned across the various technology platforms. For example, the user interface resides on the desktop. The calculation engine resides on the server. A process resides on the desktop to down-load the edit rules data from the repository when the data changes.

The conceptual layer of the data and technical architectures should be defined during the requirements definition phase of the development project.

The Logical Layer. The logical layer represents design. It describes the engineering specifications and strategies required for implementation at a lower level of detail.

The logical data architecture should include data at the entity and attribute level distributed across the various technology platforms. For example, the sales data that is to reside in the data warehouse includes the sales order master and sales order detail file.

The logical technical architecture should further define the various services and components that make up the application. For example, the graphical user interface (GUI) on the desktop may be made up of seven screens and 12 reports, each referenced by name. The service necessary to propagate the edit rules data from the repository to the desktop actually consists of two services, one on the repository machine and one on the desktop. The service on the repository machine is responsible for processing a request for update. The service on the desktop is responsible for making the request depending on the time of last update.

The logical technical and data architecture should be defined during the high-level design phase of the project. In fact, there may need to be multiple iterations of the logical layer at increasingly more detailed levels of specification.

The Physical Layer. The physical layer describes the products and environments needed for systems implementation. The physical data architecture includes the specific physical environments used to implement the data architecture. For example, the repository may include a relational database; the edit rules data residing on the desktop may be implemented in C tables.

The physical technical architecture would include the specific hardware, software, and middleware needed to implement the technical architecture. For example, the seven user interface screens may be developed in C++ running on a Macintosh. The calculation engine may be developed in VMS C running on a DEC VAX.

The physical layer should be defined at the end of high-level design.

MULTITIER DATA ARCHITECTURES

Data architectures in a client/server environment should be defined according to a four-tier architecture:

- Tier 1: Transaction data: The first tier of the architecture is the transaction data itself. This is the raw data that actually is captured by production systems. An example of production data would be the header and detail accounts receivable transactions captured in a financial system.
- Tier 2: Data warehouse: The data warehouse consists of a subset of data that has been extracted from the transaction systems and placed in the warehouse for use by a variety of information consumers.
- Tier 3: Departmental/functional data extracts: These extracts consist of data sourced from the warehouse but restructured from a relational perspective to meet the needs of a specific information consumer. An example of the data in the departmental extract might consist of a subset of the accounts payable.
- Tier 4: Local data extracts: The local data extracts represent semi-static data that has been downloaded to the desktop. An example of local access data would be lookup data, such as units of measure codes or user interface constraint data.

Separating Users and Providers of Data

A multitier data architecture defines the topology and organization of the data according to the different types of users and providers that access it.

From an access perspective, consumers of the data captured by transaction systems should not be accessing the transaction database directly. From the perspective of consolidation of the data so that it can be harvested, information required by consumers is held in the data warehouse. The information providers thus are separated from the information consumers.

From a concurrency perspective, it makes sense to consolidate and denormalize certain views of the warehouse data into departmental or functional extracts for those consumers with specialized needs.

From a data ownership perspective, again, information consumers are separated from the information providers. Tier 1 databases are owned by the data capture function; tier 2 by the custodians of the warehouse; tier 3 by the groups of consumers; and tier 4 by individual consumers.

Security also is addressed by separating the providers from the consumers. Consumers are only allowed access to the views of the data that are appropriate for their use.

KEY CONCEPTS OF SERVICE-BASED ARCHITECTURES

As the name implies, service-based architectures specify the topology of a system in the form of discrete services and components. They provide a framework for information systems that is user-centric, highly modular, seamlessly integrated, easily shared, platform-independent, and network-oriented.

Apple Computer Inc.'s Virtually Integrated Technical Architecture Lifecycle (VITAL) is an example of a service-based architecture. This environment is discussed to illustrate the concepts of service-based architectures and to show how data and processes can be distributed in a data architecture.

Fundamentals of the VITAL model include desktop integration (i.e., user interface, navigation, information synthesis, training, and consulting); data access (i.e., the information consumption and sharing process); data capture (i.e., the data production/creation process); repository (i.e., definitions of the data, processes, and controls that manage the information as a corporate asset); and infrastructure (i.e., the operating systems software, hardware, and support organization).

Data Capture

The data capture environment supports and promotes the data production functions of the enterprise. Its purpose is to manage the transaction update systems of the business, maintain the accuracy and integrity of business data, manage any direct interfaces required between transaction update systems, and create data snapshots as needed.

The key component of the data capture environment is a suite of modular software services. Taken together, these services handle all of the functions of a major transaction update system. Their modular design and client/server approach increase adaptability while improving performance.

From a multitier data architecture perspective, data capture includes tier 1 (transaction databases).

Data Access

Whereas data capture governs data production functions, the data access environment directly supports information consumers in the organization. The primary duty of data access is to manage the acquisition and distribution of all shareable data throughout the business and to provide access to consistent data that may originate from diverse functions within the organization.

The key component of data access is a shared data warehouse network. The services in this network manage a system of read-only databases that can be distributed globally, regionally, or locally, depending on the needs of the business. Data in the network is replenished regularly from the data capture environment, thus separating information management from transaction update functions, allowing both to be managed optimally.

From a multitier data architecture perspective, data access includes tier 2 (data warehouse) and tier 3 (departmental/functional data extracts).

Repository

The repository contains a uniform set of business rules, data definitions, and system usage rules for the organization. The repository also provides an encyclopedia of metadata or data about all of the software services, data, and other components contained in the enterprise information systems. Repository services manage this metadata, which in turn is used by services in the other environments.

The repository supports the other environments with three classes of services: definition, navigation, and administration. Repository services manage access to metadata. Examples of the types of metadata include standard data definitions, location and routing information, and synchronization management for distributing shared data.

Desktop Integration

The desktop integration environment's purpose is to enhance the role of the desktop in the larger enterprise system. It provides the user interface, personal application support, and interconnection to the enterprise computing network. Essentially, it works as an agent on behalf of knowledge workers, buffering them from the information bureaucracy.

In the VITAL environment, the key component of desktop integration is an integration services manager that coordinates a set of modular software services linking desktop applications to other enterprise tools and software services. The manager works with other VITAL environments to increase the use of desktop computing power. It frees users from the burden of having to remember protocols and log-on strings when accessing data.

From a multitier data architecture perspective, desktop integration includes tier 4 (local data extracts).

Infrastructure

The infrastructure environment is essentially the glue that holds the other environments together. Systems infrastructure is more than just the connectivity required for global enterprise systems. It includes a set of software utility services that support and integrate the other environments so that the services in the other environments do not have to know routing or protocol details.

Systems infrastructure has three main elements: computing resources, network resources, and interface resources. Computing resources include the operating systems and hardware of all devices within the enterprise system. Network resources also include messaging, security, and data transfer services. These and other network services provide the key interfaces between software on separate platforms.

CASE STUDY

To illustrate a data architecture as it relates to technical architecture in a client/server environment, this section examines a specific application. The Insurance Underwriter's Workstation was developed by KPMG Peat Marwick for one of its client companies — a major provider of worker's compensation insurance products. The primary function performed by thr application was to allow underwriters to prepare insurance premiums quotations and produce a report that could be filed with state and federal regulatory agencies.

Problem

The client was using an IBM mainframe-based application for the calculations of insurance premiums. The Rating Plan Quote System (RPQS) performed well and produced rating plan quotes that were acceptable for filing with regulatory agencies. However, the system allowed only a limited number of concurrent users. When the threshold was reached, other users were locked out of the system until someone logged off.

In addition, most of the data reference tables were hard-coded in the program, so when changes needed to be made the programs had to be modified. Finally, users were unable to save quotes. If users needed to rerun a quote because of an error, they had to retype the policy information into the system again.

Opportunity

The client was required by the National Council to support a new calculation for its retrospectively rated policies. This presented an opportunity for the client to evaluate the current application and to decide whether to modify it or create a new application. The client company was committed to using the Macintosh development platform for client/server environment interaction. After evaluating the advantage of the client/server environment, the company opted to discontinue its mainframe stovepipe application and pursue a more strategic alternative for implementing the new calculation for the retrospective rating plan quote system.

In this case, a client/server solution was found using Macintosh as the client interface and the DEC VAX as the host. The approach allowed reference data to be modified without modifying the code. In addition, the user could save the input necessary to calculate a quote, which eliminated the need to retype information, and the user would never be locked out of the system because of concurrent user limitations.

The application also can be examined from a service-based architecture perspective, dividing the application's technical architecture and data architecture into the five environments used in the VITAL architecture. Exhibits 6-1 through 6-4 illustrate the distribution of data and processes in this architecture.

Data Capture. The data capture component of new Rate Plan Workstation (RPW) application supports the creation, reading, update, and deletion of the reference-table data. The VAX-based relational database gateway provides the infrastructure for the capturing of reference-table data. The data then was mapped into an operational database.

Referential integrity checks on the data occur based on the metadata associated with the operational database. Once the application is loaded into the operational database, users can run a custom application to propagate their modification to the development database and to the production warehouse immediately or set up a batch job for that night. They also have the option of just propagating the development database so they may test their modifications before putting them into production. When the production propagation occurs, the operational database is copied to the development database and to the production warehouse; then the production warehouse is distributed to the local access databases for users to access through the RPW user interface. Exhibit 6-1 shows the data capture environment for this application.

Data Access. The data access component (see Exhibit 6-2) receives the reference table data from the data capture environment and provides the constraint information for data input. The data access component also provides access to the reference-table data for performing the calculation process, passing the completed calculation data to the RPW user interface for storage.

The VAX/relational-based data warehouse provides a central repository from where the local access databases have been populated. The warehouse allows for on-demand update of local access databases. Once the reference-table data is available in the local access databases, a custom application called the calculation manager receives all user requests for system access and calculations. This application handles software validation and, using DecMessage Queue, distributes the calculation requests to a set of VAXs designated to handle parallel calculations.

Desktop Integration. Once the data was available on the local access databases, a MacApp Application was developed to collect valid plan information to perform the calculations for the quote or filing report. Once a plan has been saved, the user can send it to another user through a mail

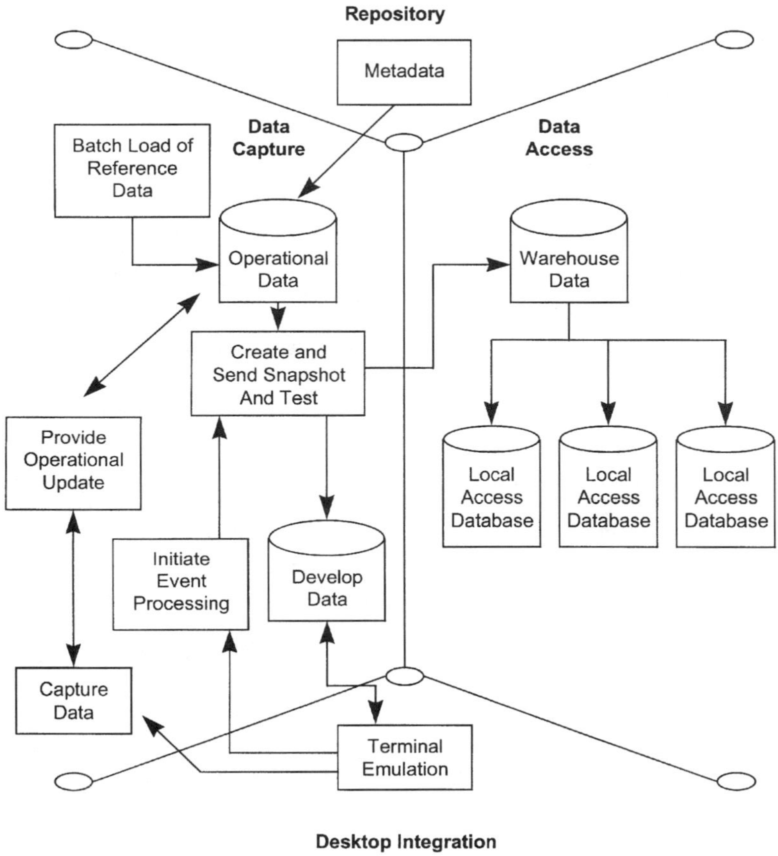

Exhibit 6-1. Data capture environment for RPW application.

system and they would be able to make modifications, provided their Macintosh was configured so they could run the application.

The RPW user interface subsystem is built around a Macintosh front end. The subsystem requests information from the host at different times during user interaction. When a user launches the system, the workstation requests that the host validates the application software version number running on the Mac and validates the versions of the constraint files

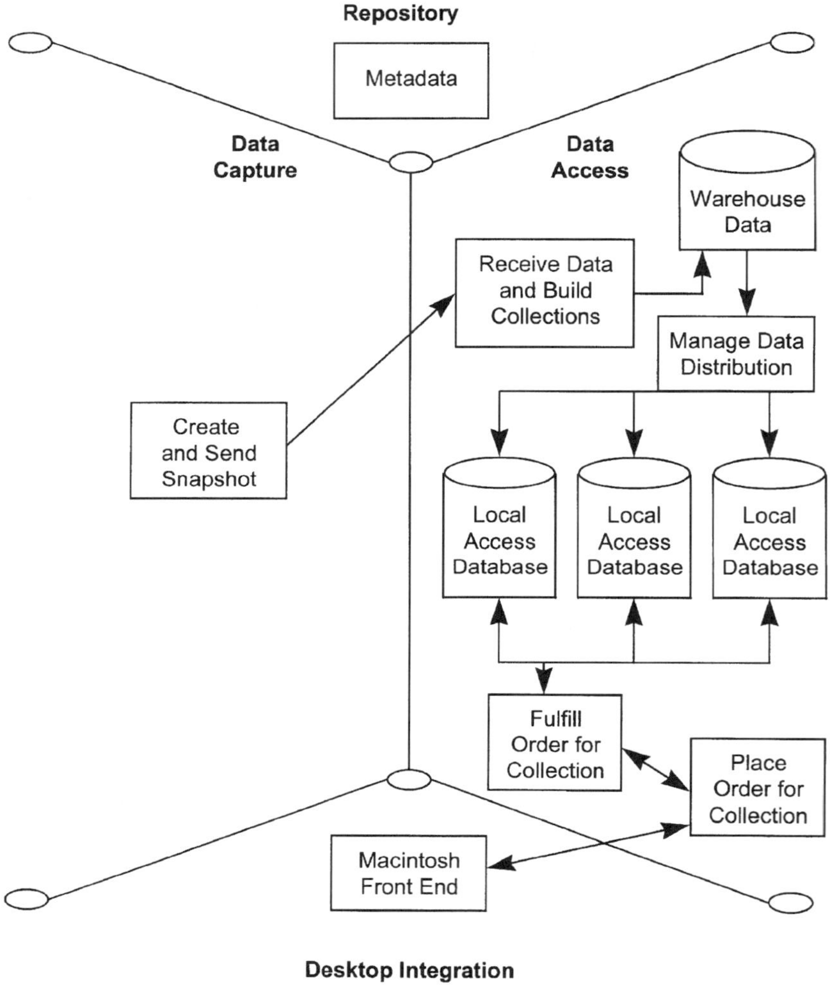

Exhibit 6-2. Data access in RPW application.

existing on the Mac. If the user opens a plan that has previously been calculated, the workstation requests that the host verify that the last time reference-table maintenance was performed so that the workstation can inform the user that the plan may have to be recalculated. The user can request the host to perform the calculation on demand. Local data on the desktop is updated and accessed based on changes to the local access databases and user interaction with the front end. The data integration environment is shown in Exhibit 6-3.

When new calculation reference tables are issued by the National Council or state change constraint values used in calculations, the production

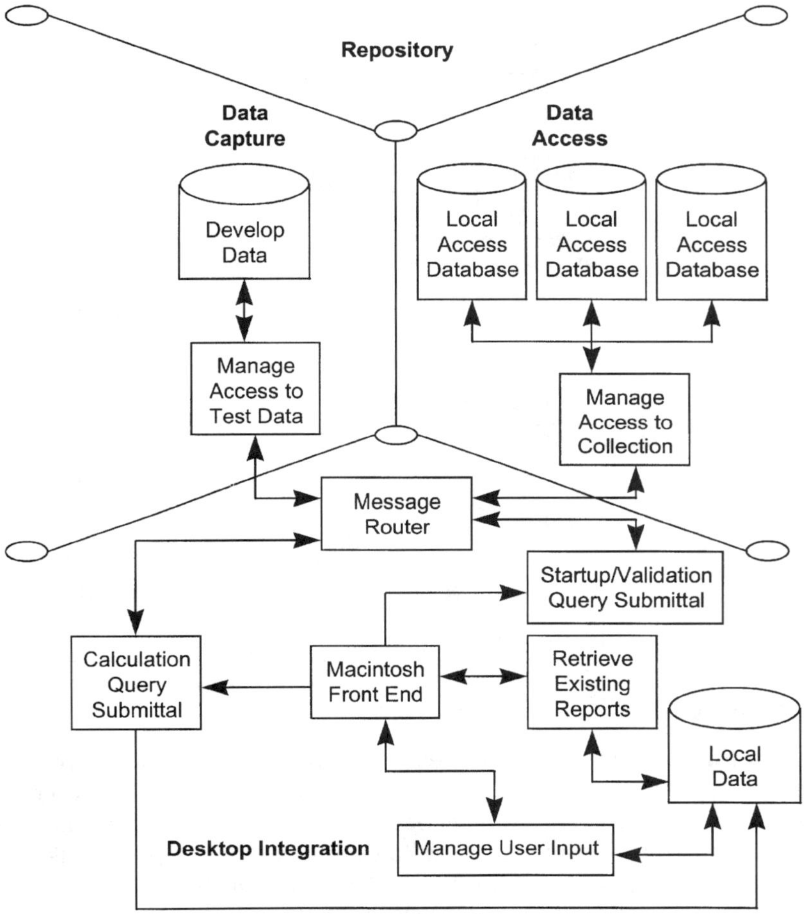

Exhibit 6-3. Desktop integration in RPW application.

support person has the ability to make such changes without requesting a coding modification. This is accomplished by using the file maintenance user interface.

The file maintenance user interface subsystem was developed on the VAX using an Ingres DBMS to manage the user input screens. A shell was developed around the Ingres application using DCL, which is Digital Equipment Corp.'s connectivity language. This shell creates captive system access when the user logs in, allowing only one user access to table maintenance at a time and providing the user with options for data propagation (Exhibit 6-4). This desktop component lets the user maintain the reference-table data stored in the operational database and allows the user to control the triggering propagation of the operational database to the development or production environments.

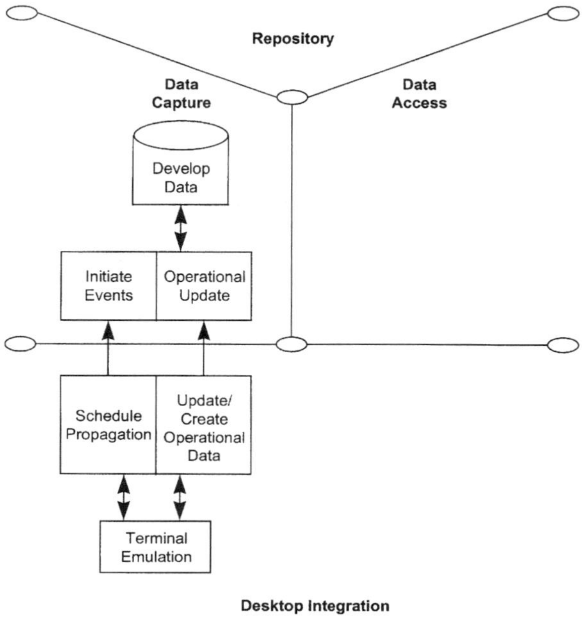

Exhibit 6-4. File maintenance user interface.

CONCLUSION

This actual case study illustrates how data can be located physically where it is most economically practical in terms of propagation and collection and where it supports an acceptable user response level. One of the best ways to define and validate a data topology that supports this objective is to develop a data architecture using the underlying concepts associated with service-based architectures, a multitier data strategy, and conventional conceptual, logical, and physical data modeling.

Processes, data, and technology can be defined concurrently in a highly integrated development effort. During the requirements definition phase, the relationships between data and the processes it supports should be documented at a very high level. During the high-level design phase, both the data architecture and the technical architecture must be drilled down to lower levels of detail. Finally, during the detail design phase, the data and technical architectures should be defined at the lowest level of detail, including the specific products to be used.

Chapter 7
Business Aspects of Multimedia Networking

T.M. Rajkumar
Amitava Haldar

AS A HIGHLY EFFECTIVE METHOD OF COMMUNICATION THAT SIMULTANEOUSLY PROVIDES SEVERAL FORMS OF INFORMATION TO THE USER—audio, graphics and animation, full-motion video, still images, and text—multimedia offers a departure from the communication confines present in other singular-media applications. Advances in multimedia technology and widespread acceptance of the technology in the business community are driving the need to effectively and efficiently distribute multimedia applications.

Users today have easy and inexpensive access to multimedia-capable equipment. The explosive growth of the CD-ROM applications such as multimedia databases, and the World Wide Web indicate the ease with which multimedia applications proliferate in an organization. Despite this ready availability, however, most multimedia applications are currently not distributed and work on single desktop computers. Most organizations have been unable both to keep up with the requirements to distribute multimedia information and to realize the goal of network computing—to build an infrastructure that supports a cooperative enterprise environment. This chapter identifies common multimedia applications and business considerations in effective distribution of multimedia information.

BUSINESS DRIVERS OF MULTIMEDIA APPLICATIONS

The primary function of multimedia in most applications is as an interface; it allows an unhindered and manageable flow of information to the user that is consistent yet flexible in design and enables the user to accommodate varied workflows. Multimedia must therefore not be a barrier to information transfer; it must be conducive to it.

0-8493-0893-3/00/$0.00+$.50

The following several technology advances have improved multimedia ability to effectively transfer information and are driving the development of multimedia applications:

- Availability of multimedia-authoring applications.
- Continuously decreasing cost/memory of computer systems.
- Sustained improvements in microprocessor designs that enable multimedia-compression algorithms to be committed to silicon.
- Availability of network and communications equipment that facilitates the storage, management, and transfer of multimedia objects.
- Availability of improved input/output devices such as scanners, voice- and handwriting-recognition systems, and virtual reality.

The most important business driver of multimedia applications is teleconferencing, which saves organizations travel costs by enabling geographically dispersed individuals and groups to communicate in real-time. Multimedia applications development is also driven by the need to access information on the World Wide Web, demand for information and training systems, improved customer services such as advertising and public advice systems, and improved enterprise effectiveness such as correspondence management.

APPLICATIONS OF NETWORKED MULTIMEDIA

For the purposes of this chapter, the applications of networked multimedia are divided into two categories:

- People-to-people applications, which assist in interpersonal communication.
- People-to-information server applications, in which the user generally interacts with a remote system to receive information or interact with a server. For example, in a WWW application, clients interact with a web server to provide information to the user.

In addition, networked applications are also classified on the basis of time; they are either immediate or deferred. Immediate applications, in which a user interacts with another person or computer in real-time, must meet latency or delay requirements. Deferred applications imply that the user is interacting with the other user or server in a manner that does not have latency or delay requirements. Messaging applications such as E-mail and voice mail are people-to-people applications in the deferred category.

A useful test for determining whether an application is immediate or deferred is whether the user is only working on the one application (which would make the application immediate) or can move to other applications during its use (making the application deferred). Exhibit 7-1 depicts the categories of networked multimedia applications.

Exhibit 7-1. Categories of networked multimedia applications.

	Immediate	Deferred
People-to-People	Telephony, Multimedia Conferencing	E-Mail, Voice Mail
People-to-Information Server	WWW Browsing, Video-on-Demand	File Transfer

Messerschmitt, "The Convergence of Telecommunications and Computing: What are the Implications Today," IEEE Communications 84, no. 8 (1996)

The following sections examine multimedia applications and their networking requirements. The focus is on immediate applications, because they place greater demands on the network system than do deferred applications.

PEOPLE-TO-SERVER APPLICATIONS

Video-on-Demand

Video-on-demand applications let users request a video from a remote server. In a business setting, this approach is applicable for downloading training videos and viewing them on the desktop. If the videos are stored on a server, video-on-demand can be used for just-in-time training.

Because the disk requirements to download and store a video (before presentation) are expensive, video-on-demand has strict real-time requirements on transmissions but tolerates an initial delay in the playback of the data. Transmission guarantees require that the bandwidth be available for the entire duration of the video. The delay requirements are not stringent, because some data can be buffered at the receiving end.

WWW Browsing

The World Wide Web is a system that allows clients to retrieve and browse through hypertext/hypermedia documents stored on remote servers. Currently most material on the Web is text- or graphic-based; the data storage and transmission requirements associated with audio and video, allow only a few users to add these features. Video access is also awkward because the video player that supports the video format (i.e., software plug-in) must exist on the client.

Many businesses, however, use the Web to provide organizational information and to support access to databases (mostly internal to the company). The Web creates different challenges for business organizations, which must conduct comprehensive capacity planning (i.e., of bandwidth, types of applications, and security) before roll out. It is bandwidth and the number of simultaneous users accessing the service that play a critical role in Web site management. Applications providing multimedia data require greater bandwidth that supports transmission-delay requirements.

PEOPLE-TO-PEOPLE APPLICATIONS

Two common people-to-people applications are multimedia conferencing and groupware.

Multimedia Conferencing

Multimedia conferencing is used by many businesses to support the collaborative efforts of growing numbers of virtual groups and organizational teams. The benefits of multimedia conferencing include:

- Reduction or elimination of costly business trips
- Facilitation of collaborative work such as computer-aided design/computer-aided manufacturing CAD/CAM
- Increased productivity resulting from the ability to meet deadlines and less chance for miscommunication

Types of Multimedia Conferencing Systems

There are three main types of multimedia conferencing systems: point-to-point, multipoint, and multicast.

Point-to-Point Systems. Point-to-point systems involve two persons communicating interactively from the desktop or groups of people communicating from a conference room. Point-to-point desktop conferencing systems are becoming popular because of the availability of inexpensive, low-overhead digital cameras such as the Quickcam and associated videoconferencing software. These systems let users share screens of data, text, or images.

Multipoint Systems. Multipoint conferencing involves three or more locations that are linked either through a local area network or a wide area network and can each send and receive video. Such systems have several unique characteristics, including presentation of multiple media, management and transport of multiple media streams, distributed access to multiple media, high bandwidth requirements, and low-latency bulk data transfer and multipoint communications. Because desktop systems quickly run out of screen space, multipoint conferencing is more effectively conducted in conference rooms with video walls.

Multicasting Systems. Multicasting involves the transmission of multimedia traffic by one site and its receipt by other sites. Rather than sending a separate stream to each individual user (i.e., uni-casting) or transmitting all packets to everyone (i.e., broadcasting), a multicasting system simultaneously transmits traffic to a designated subset of network users. Many existing systems use broadcasting and let the receivers sort out their messages. This inefficient practice fails to maximize use of network bandwidth and poses potential security problems.

Groupware

The notion of conferencing is changing to include such features as shared windows and whiteboards enabled by distributed computing. In addition, the use of computer mediation and integration is increasing.

A shared application or conferencing system permits two or more users at separate workstations to simultaneously view and interact with a common instance of an application and content. With such applications, users working on a report, for example, can collectively edit a shared copy. In general, documents used in groupware are active (i.e., the document displayed on the screen is connected to content in a database or spreadsheet).

Groupware provides such features as support for group protocols and control, including round robin or on-demand floor-control policy, and both symmetric and asymmetric views of changes. In symmetric view, a change that is made is immediately shown to other users. In asymmetric view, applicable in applications involving teacher-student or physician-patient interactions, the changes made in one window may not be shown in another window. Groupware systems also support such issues as membership control (i.e., latecomers) and media control (i.e., synchronization of media).

TECHNICAL REQUIREMENTS FOR NETWORKED MULTIMEDIA APPLICATIONS

The immediate multimedia applications discussed (i.e., video-on-demand, multimedia conferencing, groupware, and web browsing) have several technical requirements.

Latency. Latency refers to the delay between the times of transmission from the data source to the reception of data at the destination. Associated with delay is the notion of jitter. Jitter is the uncertainty of arrival of data. In the case of multimedia conferencing systems, practical experience has shown that a maximum delay of 150 milliseconds is appropriate. Synchronous communications involve a bounded transmission delay.

Synchronization. Existing networks and computing systems treat individual traffic streams (i.e., audio, video, data) as completely independent and unrelated units. When different routes are taken by each of these streams, they must be synchronized at the receiving end through effective and expeditious signaling.

Bandwidth. Bandwidth requirements for multimedia are steep, because high data throughput is essential for meeting the stream demands of audio and video traffic. A minimum of 1.5M bps is needed for MPEG2, the emerging standard for broadcast-quality video from the Moving Picture Experts Group. Exhibit 7-2 depicts the storage and communications requirements for multimedia traffic streams.

Exhibit 7-2. Storage and communications requirements for multimedia applications.

	Storage	Communications
Text	2K bits per page	1K bps
Graphics	20K bits per page	10K bps
Audio	20K bits per signal	20K bps
Image	300K bits per image (20 Kb compressed)	100 Kbps
Motion		
Video	150K bps (compressed) for MPEG1 0.42 M bps for MPEG2 27 Mbytes for NTSC quality	150K bps
Animation	15K bps	15K bps

Reliability. The high data- presentation rate associated with uncompressed video means that errors such as a single missed frame are not readily noticeable. Most digital video is compressed, however, and dropped frames are easily noticeable. In addition, the human ear is sensitive to loss of audio data. Hence, error controls (such as check sums) and recovery mechanisms (i. e., retransmission requests) need to be built into the network. Adding such mechanisms raises a new complexity, because retransmitted frames may be too late for real-time processing.

GUARANTEEING QUALITY OF SERVICE

Quality-of-service guarantees aim to conserve resources. In a broad sense, quality of service enables an application to state what peak bandwidth it requires, how much variability can it tolerate in the bandwidth, the propagation delay it is sensitive to, and the connection type it requires (i.e., permanent or connectionless, multipoint). The principle of quality of service states that the network must reliably achieve a level of performance that the user/ application finds acceptable, but no better than that. Network systems can either guarantee the quality of service, not respond to it, or negotiate a level of service that they can guarantee.

Quality of service has several components, which are depicted in Exhibit 7-3 and described in the sections that follow.

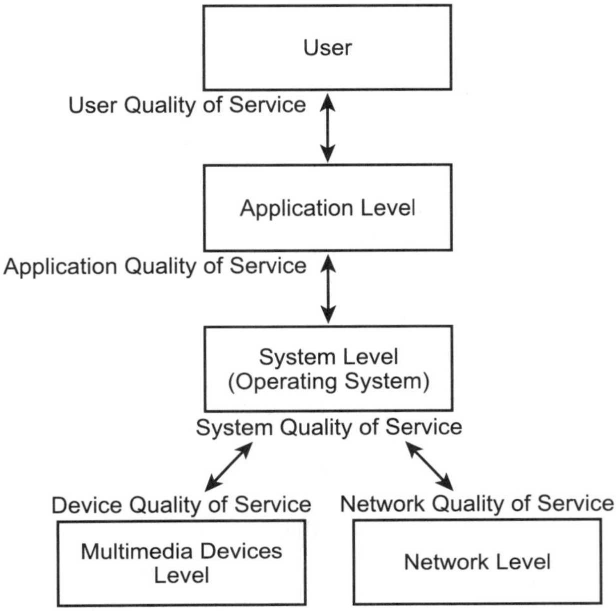

Exhibit 7-3. Quality-of-service components in networked multimedia applications.

Application Parameters

Application quality-of-service parameters describe requirements for applications, such as media quality and media relations. Media quality refers to source/sink characteristics (e.g., media data-unit rate) and transmission characteristics (e.g., end-to-end delay). Media-relations specifies media conversion and inter-and intra-stream synchronization.

System Parameters

System quality-of-service requirements are specified in qualitative and quantitative terms for communication services and the operating system. Qualitative parameters define the following expected level of services:

- Inter-stream synchronization, which is defined by an acceptable skew relative to another stream or virtual clock
- Ordered delivery of data
- Error-recovery and scheduling mechanisms

Quantitative parameters are more concrete measures that include specifications such as bits per second, number of errors, job processing time, and data size unit.

Network and Device Parameters

Network quality-of-service parameters describe requirements on the network, such as network load (i.e., ongoing traffic requirements such as inter-arrival time), and performance or guaranteed requirements in terms of latency and bandwidth. In addition, traffic parameters such as peak data rate, burst length or jitter, and a traffic model are specified. Traffic models describe arrival of connection requests or traffic contract based on calculated expected traffic parameters.

Device quality-of-service parameters typically include timing and throughput demands for media data units.

Determining Service Levels

Several different types of service levels can be negotiated, including:

- Guaranteed service, which establishes quality of service within deterministic or statistical bounds
- Predictive service, which estimates quality of service from past behavior
- Best-effort service, which is used in the absence of available quality parameters

SYSTEM CONSIDERATIONS

Designing networks to support multimedia applications involves more than just networking requirements; attention must also be paid to the entire system. Network configurations, for example, do not treat how the bandwidth is handled once it reaches the desktop. Bus speeds and input/output operation throughput are part of the link between the data source and the users' screen. There are two possible approaches to handling bus speeds and throughput:

- Faster bus and I/O hardware
- Desktop LAN that eliminate the workstation bus altogether and replace it with an internal packet switch linking the motherboard and peripheral system

Bandwidth is also handled through compression techniques for images and video that radically reduce the amount of data transmitted and consequently lower bandwidth requirements. Multimedia information bursts, meaning that some parts of it require higher bandwidth than others. Dynamic bandwidth allocation is useful to lessen the network burden.

Another consideration involves the accommodation of real-time requirements by the operating system. For example, the jitter and slowdown of a movie player may not be due to availability of resources but to a lack of proper scheduling. A music play program often pickups speed when contending programs terminate. Principal requirements for multimedia-capable operating systems are as follows:

- Operating-system resource management must now be based on quality of service and respond to a new class of service that satisfies time constraints and negotiable service levels
- Real-time CPU scheduling, memory buffer and file management policies to support real-time processing, and support for real-time synchronization
- Support for standard applications in addition to real-time multimedia applications
- Low-overhead task management resulting from the need for frequent switching

BARRIERS TO MULTIMEDIA NETWORKING

The extensive bandwidth and storage required to transmit multimedia streams coupled with the insufficient bandwidth of existing networks pose one of the major barriers to multimedia networking. The tendency of existing networks to treat individual streams as independent and unrelated units underscores the challenge of and need for effective synchronization.

Another major roadblock in networking existing applications is caused by proprietary development environments, data formats, and runtime environments, and by incompatible proprietary client-server models. The tight coupling among existing devices, data formats, and application program interfaces API makes it even more difficult to devise a standard.

Heterogeneous delivery platforms pose networking challenges even when multimedia applications are not involved. Other related concerns that aggravate existing problems associated with networked multimedia applications result from the lack of uniform standards in the following areas:

- *Data capture and recording.* Uniform data formats for graphics, sound, music, text, video, animation, and still images are needed
- *Data compression and decompression.* Although there is no predominant standard, several organizations have proposed data compression and decompression standards. Among them are MPEG2 and Joint Photographic Experts Group (Joint Photographic Experts Group).
- *Media storage and retrieval.* In the case of CD-ROMs, digital videodiscs are needed for portability across platforms.
- *Edit and assembly.* Content description and container standards are either specified as universal object types or through the conventional method of surrounding dissimilar information types with wrappers. Scripted, structural tagging, identification tagging, and other language constructs have emerged as the conventional tools for cross-platform applications development and parameter passing.

- *Presentation.* Uniform customizable presentation standards are needed for maintaining a common look-and-feel across platforms.
- *Transfer or networking.* Asynchronous transfer mode Asynchronous Transfer Mode and TCP/IP-NG are emerging standards in this area.
- *Multimedia signaling.* Setting up a multimedia conference automatically, without being routed through a common conference bridge, requires a sequence of signaling events, such as call setup/connect and messages. New approaches are needed to support the capability of originating, modifying, and terminating sessions in a network.

ISSUES IN MULTIMEDIA SYSTEMS PLANNING

The challenge in networking applications is to develop a strategy that works with existing technology and enables management to provide gradual enhancements to the existing infrastructure. Both scalability and integration must be considered during the planning process. In terms of network management support, the technology chosen should support the entire infrastructure.

Scalability

The network must be capable of scaling smoothly when new nodes, or applications are added; the goal is to simply add resources to the system rather than change the technology. A desirable form of scalability is that resource costs be linear in some measure of performance or usage.

Integration

Networked applications are designed along the principles of either vertical or horizontal integration. In vertical integration, a dedicated infrastructure is designed for each application so that, for example, the telephone network is kept separate from the computer network.

In contrast, horizontal integration is based on open standards and provides for complexity, management, and portability. It has the following characteristics:

- Use of integrated networks that handle data, audio, and video and are configured to meet application requirements.
- Use of middleware software to provide, for example, directory and authentication services. Although the underlying network may be heterogeneous, middleware services provide a set of distributed services with standard programming interfaces and communication protocols.
- The user is provided with a diverse set of applications.

Application/Content Awareness

In general, vertically integrated networks are application-aware (e.g., videoconferencing networks in general know the media type), and horizontal networks are application-blind (e.g., the Internet). Networks are also sometimes content-aware (e.g., a video-on-demand network knows what video is being downloaded).

PLANNING STRATEGIES

Several approaches to multimedia systems planning are available. Assuming that network resources will grow to meet the demand of the most-stringent combined user-applications, best-effort schemes are sufficient as currently used. Examples include low profile, low-cost videoconferences, multimedia E-mail, and downloadable files. This approach, however, does not take the entire multimedia system into account.

Another alternative is to over-engineer the networks, making bandwidth shortage a rare problem and access to services almost always available. This approach entails providing the user with the latest technologies and a high cost. In addition, leapfrogging computer power and applications resource requirements makes this approach highly susceptible to problems.

A third and generally more effective approach is to use either quality-of-service parameters or resource reservation, or both. For example, high-profile users (e.g., users of investment banking and medical applications) require that some form of resource reservation occur before the execution of multimedia applications.

CONCLUSION

As networking evolves and voice, video, and data are handled together, networking systems are expected to handle data streams with equal efficiency and reliability from the temporal, synchronization, and functional perspectives. Technology advancements have made users less tolerant of response delays, unreliable service, and loss of data occurring either at the network or at the desktop system.

For these reasons, it is essential that multimedia networks be designed with all computing resources in mind and provide some resource reservation or quality-of-service guarantee. The task before organizations is to find the most flexible, cost-effective method for delivering multimedia applications over networks while also providing for guaranteed quality of service.

Chapter 8

Using Expert Systems Technology to Standardize Data Elements

Jennifer Little

EXPERT SYSTEMS CAN HARNESS THE EXPERTISE OF TALENTED SYSTEMS ANALYSTS. This expertise can be leveraged to help an organization accomplish its goals more quickly and at a lower cost. Similarly, expert system can be applied to data element standardization to improve the efficiency of the process. This article describes how an organization can develop an expert system that can be used as a tool to achieve optimum data element standardization. The examples used in this article were taken from the Department of Defense (DoD) because they have selected the best available data administration components (e.g., definitions, rules, policies, and concepts).

VALUE OF EXPERT SYSTEMS

Most data element standardization programs use an automated tool to assist the process. Data modeling tools, data dictionary tools, repository tools, off-the-shelf tools, and in-house developed tools are used. Because these tools were not designed to tackle the specific problem of data element standardization, they do not adequately support the standardization process. The tools are somewhat helpful, however, in standardizing data elements because of the expertise of the human analysts in linking, contorting, or forcing the tools to give them what they need to perform the bulk of the analysis. Several data element standardization efforts have probably resulted in the development of a partial expert system.

Expert systems can accelerate the standardization process and produce higher-quality products at a lower cost. Expert systems perform repetitive

0-8493-0893-3/00/$0.00+$.50

processes rapidly. Expert systems can also assist users with the complex semantic analysis required by standardization programs. It is important, however, that standardization be performed consistently, otherwise teams or groups within an organization working independently from other groups will achieve inconsistent results.

THE DATA ELEMENT STANDARDIZATION PROCESS

To understand the process, it is important to understand the meaning of the terms data, data element, and standard data element. Exhibit 8-1 contains the Department of Defense's definitions of these terms.

Exhibit 8-1. Definitions of terms.

Data. A representation of facts, concepts, or instructions in a formalized manner suitable for communication, interpretation, or processing by humans or by automatic means.

Data Element. A named identifier of each of the entities and their attributes that are represented in a database.

Data Element Standardization. The process of documenting, reviewing, and approving unique name, definitions, characteristics, and representations of data elements according to established procedures and conventions.

Standard Data Element. A data element that has been submitted formally for standardization in accordance with the organization's data element standardization procedures.

Source: From the Office of the Assistant Secretary of Defense (Command, Control, Communications, and Intelligence), Department of Defense Data Element Standardization Procedures, Department of Defense, Washington DC, 1993.

Standard data elements aid many data information management objectives, including ensuring the quality of the data. Because standard data elements define customers' requirements, they specify the quality standards to be used in measuring the quality of that data. When the quality of data can be measured against the standard data element, it can be improved when necessary. When the data meets all the requirements, then it is the highest quality data. When the data does not meet the requirements, the quality can still be quantitatively measured and improved.

Why Organizations Standardize Data

Organizations standardize data because they want higher-quality data that is reusable. Standard data elements provide an accurate and consistent definition of the data to users. They also provide information systems developers with consistent raw materials from which to build databases more quickly and easily.

The data element standardization process is complex. It is partly influenced by the technology used to implement automated information systems (e.g., database management systems employing the relational model and flat file), the semantic differences among specialty management functions (e.g., finance, inventory, and personnel), and the political power held by those different functions. Experts are required if an organization wants to successfully standardize data elements. There are, however, very few experts.

Types of Expertise in Standardizing Data Elements

The process of standardizing data elements requires technical expertise (i.e., the knowledge and skill in how to standardize data elements well, also referred to as the syntactical characteristics) and functional expertise (i.e., knowledge of the content and context of the data elements, also referred to as the semantic characteristics). Data element standardization criteria typically address the syntactical characteristics but only indirectly address the semantic characteristics because the content and context of each data element will be different.

Data Element Requirements

A data element is standard if it complies with a set of standardization rules and is approved within an organization's standardization program. No two organizations' rules are exactly alike. However, they all include some general principles—for example, standard data elements must be unique, defined, and well named.

A few of the standardization policies and procedures for the Department of Defense are shown in Exhibits 8-2 and 8-3. These policies and procedures contain many requirements for data element design, definition, and naming. The requirements can be implemented easily in an expert system, but are extremely difficult to implement consistently without one.

For example, a core requirement for standard data elements is that an element must not have more than one meaning. A data element should reflect a single concept to promote shareability and data independence from applications using the data element. This is a critical requirement for data elements, and it is complex to fulfill. Data elements can be examined and compared with other elements for analysis. heuristics may be used for performing this analysis, although their results are not always consistent, they take a long time to achieve, and they must be developed by human experts.

Potential Difficulties with Standardization

The difficulties organizations have with data element standardization are usually related to:

Exhibit 8-2. Considerations for data element quality.

The quality of the data element is the key to the sound foundation for all data structures. Proper emphasis on the creation, naming, and definition of data elements will improve the quality of the entire data structure. Standard data elements should be based on the data entities and data entity attributes identified in the DoD data model, or recommended for expansion of the DoD data model from a lower-level data model, to ensure maximum share ability and interoperability of data throughout the Department of Defense. Several considerations are important to the quality of the data element.

1. Data elements must be designed:
   a. To represent the attributes (i.e., characteristics) of data entities identified in data models. A model-driven approach to data standards provides a logical basis for, and lends integrity to, standard data elements.
   b. According to functional requirements and logical, not physical, characteristics. Physical characteristics include any connotations regarding technology (e.g., hardware or software), physical location (e.g., databases, records, files, or tables), organization (e.g., data steward), or application (e.g., systems, applications, or programs.)
   c. According to the purpose or function of the data element rather than how, where, and when the data element is used or who uses it. This function indicates what the data element represents and ensures common understanding.
   d. So that it has singularity of purpose. Data elements must not have more than one meaning. A data element should reflect a single concept to promote share ability and data independence from applications using the data element.
   e. With generic element values (domain) that are mutually exclusive and totally exhaustive when the class word "Code" is used.
2. Data elements should not be designed with:
   a. Values (domain) that may be confused with another value in the same domain. For example, avoid mixing similar numbers and letters such as: 0/O, 1/l, 2/Z, U/V, and 5/S.
   b. Values (domain) that have embedded meaning or intelligence within part of the code when the class word "Code" is used. For example, do not develop a multiple-character code where in the value of one or more of the characters own the code have special meaning (i. e., a benefits plan code such as "201," "202," "204," or "205," where the last digit identifies a particular option within the benefit plan).
   c. Overlap or redundancy among the purpose or use of different data elements (e.g., "Birth Date," "Current Date," and "Age")

Source: From the Office of the Assistant Secretary of Defense (Command, Control, Communications, and Intelligence), Department of Defense Data Element Standardization Procedures, Department of Defense, Washington DC, 1993.

Exhibit 8-3. Excerpt from a written policy for data element definition and naming.

Data Element Definition

The definition and naming of a data element is an iterative design process with the data element definition often being modified as the data element is being developed.

1. Data element definitions must:
   a. Be based on the definitions of data entity attributes established in the DoD data model or established in an approved data model linked (mapped) to the DoD data model.
   b. . . . .
   c. . . .
   Consist of the minimum number of words that categorize the data element. Fewer words may be too general whereas more words may be too narrow or restrictive. Modifiers may be used with class words, generic elements, and prime words to fully describe generic elements and data elements. Modifiers are often derived from the data entity attitude names and the entity names identified in the DoD model or an approved data model linked (mapped) to the DoD data model.
   d. Include only alphabetic characters (A-Z, a-z), hyphens (-), and spaces ().
   e. Have each component of the name separated by a space.
   f. Have multiple word prime words connected with hyphens. Examples of multiple prime words might be "Purchase-Order," "Medical–Facility." Or "Civilian Government."
2. The following are not permitted in data element names:
   a. Words that redefine the data element or contain information that more correctly belongs in the definition.
   b. Class words used as modifiers or prime words.
   c. Abbreviations or acronyms. (Exceptions to this rule may be granted in the case of universally accepted abbreviations or acronyms. The DDRS contains a list of approved abbreviations and acronyms.)
   d. Names of organizations, computer or information systems, directives, forms, screens or reports.
   e. Titles of blocks, rows, or columns of screens, reports, forms, or listings.
   f. Expression of multiple concepts, either implicitly or explicitly.
   g. Plurals of words.
   h. The possessive forms of a word (i.e. a word that denotes ownership).
   i. Articles (e.g. a, an, the)
   j. Conjunctions (e.g. and, or, but)
   k. Verbs
   l. Prepositions (e.g. at, by, for, from, in, of, to).

SOURCE: From the Office of the Assistant Secretary of Defense (Command, Control, Communications, and Intelligence). Department of Defense Data Element Standardization Procedures. Department of Defense, Washington DC, 1993.

- *Time.* For example, an organization may not have the data elements standardized in time to use them in a new information system being developed so the system is developed without them and plans are added to retrofit to the standards later.
- *Quality.* For example, an organization expends resources to standardize their data elements in their accounting system and is appalled with the resulting accounting specific data elements because they expected the data elements to reflect their entire organization's understanding of their financial data.
- *Cost.* For example, an organization hires several analysts to standardize their data elements during a multiyear project, but the resources are diverted in the middle of the project and the standardization remains unfinished and unusable because it was done with a monolithic perspective.

There are likely many causes of these difficulties that are unrelated to the data element standardization process, such as changes in organizational strategies or changes in the marketplace. However, some of the difficulties may be caused by standardization criteria that are conflicting or overly stringent.

Data administrators have been accused at times of being perfectionists and of sacrificing practical results for the perfect data element. Some organizations have eased their standardization requirements after initial attempts to implement them resulted in resistance from the people responsible for implementing the standardization criteria.

Another characteristic of the standardization process that may cause difficulties is inexperienced personnel. A lack of adequate tools to support the process is also problematic. Some of the tasks to be performed as part of the standardization process cannot possibly be performed by humans alone and, in fact, were not intended to be (e.g., searching numerous existing data elements for similarities and linking data elements to attributes in data models).

There are other characteristics of a task that need to be analyzed to determine whether applying expert systems technology is appropriate. The following questions are relevant for determining whether an expert systems is necessary:

- *Is symbol manipulation required?* If the answer is yes, then an expert systems would be helpful in the data element standardization process. Most problem-solving tasks require symbol manipulation (the exceptions are usually mathematical problems).
- *Are heuristic solutions required?* Again, if the answer is yes, an expert systems would be helpful.

- *What is the complexity of the task?* The more complex the task, the more helpful an expert systems would be.
- *What is the practical value of the task?* If practical, usable results rather than theoretical results are sought through the standardization process, an expert system would be a helpful tool.
- *What is the size of the task?* The task of standardizing all the data elements of an organization can be performed much more quickly with the help of an expert system.

DEFINING EXPERT SYSTEMS

Expert systems do not have a definition that all the experts agree on. However, even without an accepted and precise definition, expert system can be grouped into six major types: procedural, diagnostic, monitoring, configuration/design, scheduling, and planning.

The characteristics of diagnostic expert systems most closely describe the type of expert systems needed for the data element standardization process. As the name implies, a diagnostic expert systems diagnoses the situation and provides advice for the next course of action. It is the most common type among expert systems developed.

Another way to group expert systems is by the role they serve. The type of problem domain needs to be taken into account when choosing the role of the expert systems, and the role in which the expert systems will serve must be decided before the design process begins. The relationship between users and the system also strongly influences the choice of the role for the expert systems. An expert systems must be accepted by the users in the role that it is developed to fill; otherwise it will be ineffective. The resources available to develop the expert systems must also be taken into account when selecting the role of an expert systems. The more technically sophisticated roles demand more technically sophisticated development processes.

Expert Systems as Advisers. The least demanding role expert systems can play is as an adviser. This is the role that data element standardization expert systems would fill best. In this role, the expert systems help ensure consistency among many analysts performing the same task. The advisory expert systems help train analysts who have general experience with the functional area (i.e., data administration, data management, or information resource management) but are not skilled in implementing the specific detailed requirements.

The expert systems that performs in this role is not expected to perform on par with the human experts that perform this task; it is expected to provide guidance and act as a sounding board. Advisory expert system are well suited for domains that demand human decision making, such as those that address potentially life-threatening situations or that put large amounts of valuable resources at risk.

Expert Systems as a Peer or an Expert. The other two roles expert systems may fill—acting as a peer and an expert—require a higher degree of trust in the system for it to be productive. In the peer role, the expert systems perform as an equal to human analysts. The analysts fully investigate the suggestions that the expert systems provides, even when the suggestions differ from their own. The expert systems provide the reasoning it has applied to explain why its conclusions may be different from those of the human analysts.

The most technically sophisticated role for an expert systems is as the expert. In this role, analysts who have minimal experience performing the task use the system. The expert systems, in this role, are the decision maker.

THE EXPERT SYSTEMS DEVELOPMENT PROCESS

Once the choices of type and role have been made, the systems development process can begin. Developers will find that expert system development is similar to traditional systems development in some ways.

The Initial Phase: Specifying Requirements. Specifying the requirements and identifying the problem, scope, participants, and goals of the system are done during the initial phase of the development process, similar to traditional systems development. The selection of participants is slightly different from traditional systems development because the human experts at the current task need to be involved so their expertise can be captured, whereas traditional systems development tends to involve representative users of the proposed system.

Phase Two: Selecting a Problem-Solving Strategy. The next phase includes choosing the basis for the problem-solving strategy to be used by the expert systems. expert systems shells are commonly used for this task.

Expert systems shells are empty programs that include only the basis for solving the problem and for building the actual expert systems. Rule-based expert systems shells are set up to have rule sets or knowledge bases loaded into them that can be used to perform the expert analysis. These rules are not simply a series of consecutively preformed procedures. They are heuristics that are applied to the problems presented. The Heuristics and the problems are merged, and the contradictions are reconciled. There are also domain-specific, inductive, and hybrid types of expert systems shells.

Choosing an expert systems shell focuses the rest of the development tasks, but it may also limit the flexibility of the solutions to be provided.

The limitations caused by selecting a rule-based expert systems shell for developing a data element expert systems are offset by the choice of the advisory role for the data element expert system, which is the least demanding role for an expert systems.

Phase Three: Translating the User's Job for the System. The next phase of expert systems development translates what human experts do into components that the expert system shell can understand. It might not be possible to use one diagramming and documentation technique to achieve this explanation process. In addition, a model of the process human experts use may already exist. In either case, a translation between two or more models may be necessary to accomplish this phase. Many detailed conversations with the people expert in data element standardization may be necessary to establish how they do what they do.

The Final Phase: Loading the Rules and Operating the System. The next phase results in a working system. The rules are loaded into the expert system's knowledge base and testing begins.

Data elements that have already been standardized by the human experts can be used to test the advice provided by the expert systems. When the results do not match, the differences will point to the rules that were not discovered during the previous phase. These new rules need to be documented and added to the knowledge base.

This version of the expert systems can be thought of as a prototype because it only implements the performance of a small group of the human experts. It may need to be expanded to reflect a larger set of situations and relevant rules or it may be appropriate that it reflects only the small group of human experts, since they may be the only real experts that exist. The purpose of the system may be to assist the rest of the people performing the task to produce consistent results.

CONCLUSION

Although expert system technologies have been available for years, there are no commercially available data element standardization expert systems. Perhaps systems developers are too busy developing systems for their clients to stop and develop systems they can use themselves. Commercial software developers need to be made aware of the need for this technology.

A more important question may be, what will it take to create data element standardization expert systems? A collaborative partnership is needed. A consortium consisting of a research institution (i.e., a government or university), a client with a need for standard data elements, a technology expert, and data element standardization experts should be assembled to jointly tackle the problem.

Chapter 9

Managing Data on the Network: Data Warehousing

Richard A. Bellaver

THE PRACTICAL APPROACH TO DATA WAREHOUSING REQUIRES REVIEW OF THE ENTERPRISE AND BUSINESS REQUIREMENTS. This covers the challenges that use of data warehousing can present and methodology for implementing the best solution for the environment presented. It discusses the storage, identification and quality of data in the network. New opportunities to develop corporate databases and share data across companies are technologically feasible, and many companies are starting to evolve data processing systems to take advantage of networking and other new technologies under the name of data warehousing.

These phenomena and the obsession with "quality" in American industry are having profound effects on company data processing (DP) planning. The practicality of distributed DP and the desire to take advantage of the latest technology have led many companies to concentrate on cleaning up the databases and restructuring the processing. This twofold approach provides a challenge to both corporate DP and business planning communities. The difficulty for planners lies in an apparent inconsistency in the "quality" definition in DP. Are the advertising-type descriptions of processing (e.g., new, improved, faster) in conflict with the historical descriptions of data (e.g., identifiable, complete, accurate)?

In those companies undergoing mergers or acquisitions, bringing together diverse DP systems, organizations, and methodologies provides an even more challenging opportunity. Even some of the large, more stable DP organizations have experienced the accordion effect of centralization vs. decentralization leading to a similar "clean it up and make it better situation." A look at an evolution of the strategies concerning system architecture can be an aid to meeting such a challenge. By definition, a computer system architecture is the logical structure and relationship of the data and

0-8493-0893-3/00/$0.00+$.50

application functions used to satisfy a company's business requirements. This chapter describes a practical architectural evolution that can lead to quality-based DP and that includes both definitions while emphasizing the data aspects of quality. It will also go into the nontechnical problems in sharing data that may be more severe than the technical ones.

Data can be a most valuable asset to a business, and technology can allow access to that data faster than ever; however, there must be a logical approach to the establishment of data quality procedures before the benefits of warehousing can be attained. At a minimum, interdepartmental battles about ownership of data must be fought, new chargeback algorithms must be accepted, and managers will probably have to learn at least new coding structures if not new languages. An examination of the present systems of many companies will establish a base for comparison.

CURRENT ARCHITECTURE

Even with the advent of client/server and unbridled growth in the use of personal computers (PCs), the current architecture of many large computer systems can generally be defined as mainframe oriented, stand alone, and data redundant. This situation did not happen by accident. The early approach to DP for most large companies was to search for projects based on economy of scale. For example, companies looked for large, team-sized applications. Usually, for order clerks or bill investigators, manual training methods and procedures had been standardized to achieve the last measure of efficiency. Computer mechanization followed the model of these standard operating procedures.

Very large, procedurally (organizationally) oriented systems were built based on the need to increase operational productivity. Generally, the systems used for ordering, dispatching, billing, inventory control, financial control, and many other business functions have been developed using the most efficient technology for both hardware and software. That technology in the past was basically large mainframes.

In many cases, a total systems approach to mechanization was implemented with that organizational orientation. All the data needed to solve a business problem was isolated. The workgroups that needed access to the mechanized process were identified, and the rules of the data, the processing, and the communications to solve the specific problem were defined and implemented into one system.

As depicted in Exhibit 9-1, if data A were necessary to support process 1, they were acquired, edited, and stored. If the same data were needed for process 2, they were also acquired, edited, and stored. At best, the data was passed off-line from I to N, then still edited according to process N rules, and stored again (usually in a new format). As a result of the

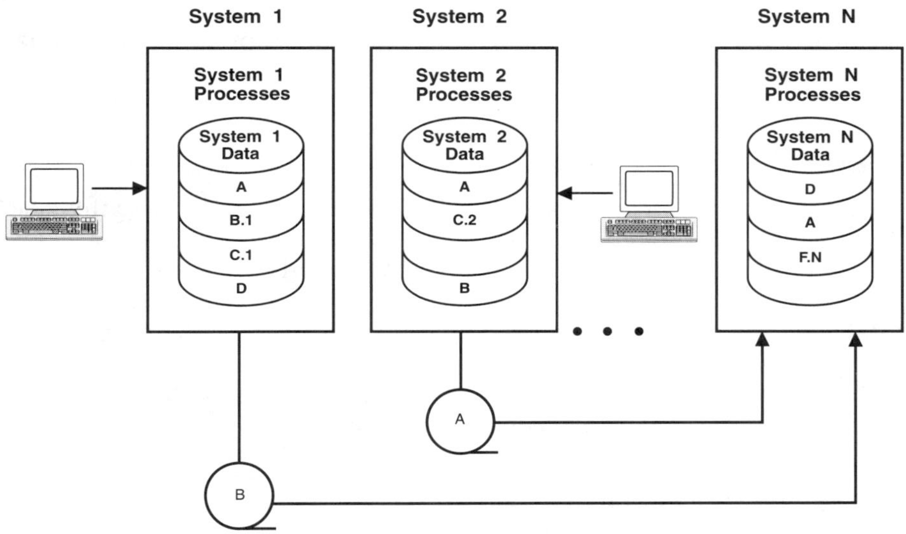

Exhibit 9-1. Current architecture.

magnitude of the process, the large volume of data, or the limitation of hardware and software capabilities, all aspects of each system were tightly integrated to ensure efficiency of processing time and data storage charges. The cost justification of the project was usually based on increasing human productivity. User departments that paid for the development and the use of the systems reduced cost by reducing human resources. User departments had a very proprietary interest in both the data and the supporting processing system.

The state of the art, especially the limitations of database management systems and communications software, also left its mark on the current architecture. In many cases, systems developed were efficient, monolithic, inflexible, end-to-end special-purpose procedure "speeder-uppers" owned by various departments. The computer implementations matched the work, the work matched the organizations, and a degree of stasis was obtained. However, over time, most organizations are subject to significant change.

To contain costs as a corporation moves forward (especially toward centralization or integration), there is a need to increase partnering of organizations while sharing resources and data are required. Technology cost structure changes and user needs become more sophisticated. Unfortunately to meet this change, most current architectures are characterized by:

- Many large stand-alone systems
- Individual communications networks
- Data configured differently for each process

- Redundant functionality and data
- Inability of organizations and systems to access other organizations' systems and data
- A nonquality situation

THE OPPORTUNITIES AND THE CHALLENGES

The current architecture picture looks pretty bleak. Must everything be thrown out and started over to clean up and restructure? Economics answers that question. Not many companies have the resources to rearchitect their systems from scratch. Cost-effective ways must be found to establish targets for architectural migration. System architecture strategies must provide a transition from the current status to a more flexible architecture that supports organizations and systems working together. These strategies must also maximize the advantage of:

- Increasing capabilities of large and small processors
- Networking capabilities
- Less complicated programming techniques
- Concentration on quality data

The latter point should be emphasized for a simple reason. Data is more permanent than processing. Data is also what ties the corporation together. Some organizations would not talk to each other at all if they did not have to exchange data. Business functionality, although basic, can usually be handled in a variety of ways, but the data needed is usually stable. (After all, humans ran the business before computers.) Improvement of the processing aspects of data processing cannot make up for the lack of historically defined quality of the data. The emphasis of quality for data can be achieved by trapping required data as close to its source as possible and leaving it in its barest form. The long-range goal must then be to have systems designed around the provision of quality data. There are several interim targets that can be used along the way.

An analysis of existing vs. long-range target systems architecture yields the following steps for maximizing productivity of existing resources while building target system architectures:

- Search and destroy—eliminating redundancy of functionality and data
- Surround—adding flexibility to present systems
- Quality data—designing, planning, and implementing architecture for data quality and long-term flexibility

SEARCH AND DESTROY: ELIMINATE REDUNDANCY

The first architectural strategy is to eliminate functional duplication and redundancy on an application-by-application basis. Financial and administrative systems are normally a high priority because of the need for common bookkeeping processes, payroll, and personnel systems. In merged companies, whole systems of the current architecture are subject to elimination. However, usually, under the pressure of time requirements, systems are patched together and new feeder systems are created. Pure duplication in the systems that support operations is usually more difficult to find because the organizations coming together do not quite perform exactly the same tasks.

In some cases, a company is still determining which operations should be merged and which should be kept separated during DP consolidation. Usually, not a great number of whole systems can be eliminated or can much major functionality be disabled, but costs can be reduced by eliminating any duplication of less-than-whole systems or major functions. That is difficult because the current architectures are normally quite inflexible and costly to modify. Therefore, it is ordinarily determined at merge time that the largest part of the current architecture be continued for some period of time.

This determination seems quite appropriate at the time. However, company operations start to change. Some of the work done by separate organizational entities starts to be done by consolidated groups. People then do work that requires them to get data from multiple systems in the current architecture. A strategy has to be developed that can allow users to get to multiple old systems from the same terminal to do their work functions.

DEFINING CORE DATA

The first of the new traumas facing the convert manager is the definition of corporate or "core" data. Core data in the smallest component (usually third normal form) is that essential to the functionality of the business. It is not financial report data, organizational data, or even necessarily previously defined customer data (that data with which the manager is familiar). It may not be the previously most used data or most redundantly stored data, although the later is probably good indicators. Core data cannot be defined until the company's business functions are well-defined.

This is a difficult task that must involve interdepartmental or corporate planners. The task is too important to be left to DP planners. Business functions are distinct from departmental goals or even business objectives. Business functions are the detail of what the business does and how it does it. Hard looks at business functions result in strange new descriptors for the work of the organization generally under the headings of management control, operations, support, and planning. Only after these overall functions are broken down can planners really determine what data is necessary to perform the functions and determine where to find the source of highest quality data.

The science of data analysis is becoming better defined each day, but the art of agreement as to what data belong to departments and what is core is ill-defined. The practice of charging back the costs of DP to the user has reduced DP budgets over the years while bringing in more hardware and software, but it has also engendered a very proprietary feeling toward systems and data on the part of the users. Individual departments say because they paid for the conversion, processing, and storage, they own the data. Upper management intervention is usually required to settle many arguments and establish the general rules for the shared use of data. As if upper management intervention was not traumatic enough, the reason for defining core data is to share it. This is not always recognized by all participants, which leads to psychological manifestations such as sibling rivalry or who has the biggest ego (or budget).

THE DATA ENGINE

Once it is agreed what should be core or shared, that data must go through three steps before storage (Exhibit 9-2):

1. The one source of the smallest component of the data must be identified. Basically this step determines from where and how the basic data will enter the storage system. This step is essential in establishing the quality framework of the system. The rules for data integrity must be established here.
2. Standard identification and the catalog structure must be determined. The user must understand and identify the data. The use of "directories" seems to be a way to solve this problem. (see below.)
3. A standard output interface must be defined. The calling terminology and the access rules to the data must be spelled out fully.

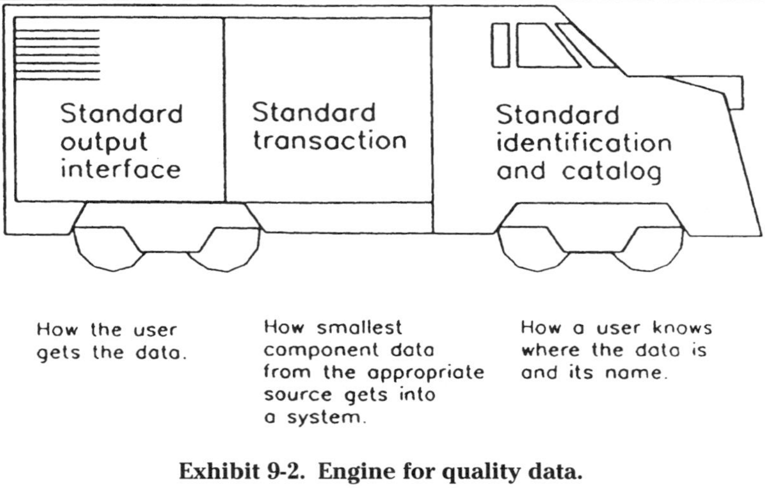

Exhibit 9-2. Engine for quality data.

The preceding three steps are usually performed by technicians, but the result generates some syntax that must be understood by managers to get the full benefit of core data. Learning new language and codes has great psychological ramifications.

WHAT IS A DIRECTORY?

A directory is a specialized repository that contains lists of system users and their access rights. It also functions as a kind of network white pages, giving users a simple way to locate applications, print services, and other computing resources. The directory also plays a role in system administration, providing information technology (IT) managers a listing of all the hardware and software assets in a far-flung enterprise. Most important, a directory is a tool to integrate applications and business units that have functioned as stand-alone systems in the past.

The first widely adopted directory technology was based on the X.500 standard developed by the Consultative Committee on International Telephone and Telegraph's (CCITT) international standards organization. X.500 is a directory service that includes a model for naming users and system resources, a method for computer systems to exchange directory information, and a way of authenticating users. Although a number of information systems (IS) shops adopted X.500 products, the service failed to live up to its potential largely because it was difficult to implement.

In 1994, the Internet Engineering Task Force issued the first version of the Lightweight Directory Access Protocol (LDAP) standard, a smaller, more efficient version of X.500 (developed at the University of Michigan) that lets clients access and manage information in a centralized directory service. Some 40 vendors have decided to support LDAP since 1996, and the standard is now in its third generation. The primary reason behind its growing acceptance is that LDAP takes up less memory and uses fewer processing resources than X.500.

Today, directories exist in a multitude of applications ranging from a network operating system and asset management system to e-mail and database applications. The cost of implementing and administrating these disparate and often proprietary directories is great. That is why many companies are moving to implement a single, master directory that can integrate these diverse systems. The business value of a unified directory is compelling: It is the elimination of redundancy and the automation of business processes across an entire enterprise.

SURROUND-INCREASE FLEXIBILITY OF PRESENT SYSTEMS

In addition to accessing multiple systems functionality from the same terminal to increase flexibility, there is a desire to distribute the data of

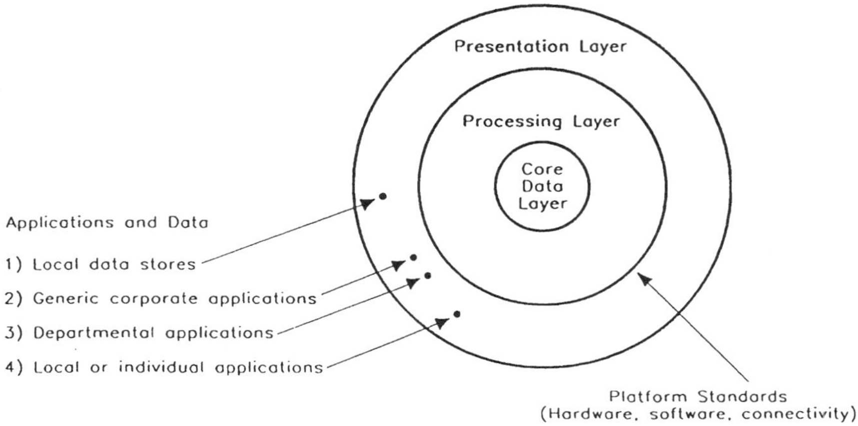

Exhibit 9-3. Conceptual model.

those systems for the users to add their own functionality. The Gartner Group has developed a rather complex seven-stage model depicting the evolution to a client/server architecture. Exhibit 9-3 shows a more simplified model indicating the shift from a single-purpose DP system (in many cases, that is a current corporate architecture on a mainframe) through a separation of some processing (which may include a minicomputer or smart terminals) leading to a networked system with the possible use of all the processing tools with access to data that could be stored almost anywhere in the network.

Currently available computer hardware, software, and network products can be used to accomplish a partial distribution of DP on a step-by-step basis. Large mainframe systems can be accessed without renetworking every terminal and without multiple log-on and log-off procedures. A minicomputer can be programmed to emulate the current terminal and mainframe interface. Data can be accessed using the current data management schema. This can be done with the same or enhanced security requirements with little additional communications time. In addition, with the use of different communications and database management software, file segments or whole files can be downloaded for different local processing.

The surround approach can be implemented with minimum complications to present mainframe processing or database software. The present application programs require modest modifications; some "add-on" programming is required to meet interface standards. Local area networking (LAN) technology helps resolve communication delays. The distribution of minicomputer and storage devices can provide resources for local development and capability for additional centrally developed systems such as electronic mail (e-mail) and office automation. With the use of a tightly controlled standards process for software distribution and data security, there is potential for departmental reports processing, site-oriented database administration, or other user-generated programming at each site or from a combination of sites. However, this would mean additional costs.

The great advantage to the surround approach is that it decreases the need for mainframe program modification. It leaves the current mainframe databases as they are. New user functionality can recreated using minicomputer-based programming that can be generated faster and cheaper than mainframe programs can be enhanced. By not having to get into mainframe languages or database management systems for every change required by users, analysts and programmers can have more time to apply their knowledge and experience to developing a long-term view of systems architecture.

QUALITY DATA STRUCTURE

The "search" portion of search and destroy takes a detailed look at the processing and data of the current architecture. Surround uses what is learned in search and links data and processing and attempts to meet changed business needs. The long-term view should introduce the concept of a functional orientation as opposed to the traditional organizational approach to doing business. The theory is to examine what functions are required to best serve the needs of the corporation's customers and then to determine how best to accomplish those functions. A functional model of the corporation should be constructed. When the functional model is understood, the data needed to support the business functions must be defined and the source described. The data must then be standardized and a corporate data catalog built to ensure that the data is of the highest quality and stays that way.

SEPARATE THE DATA FROM THE PROCESSING

Close examination of the data in most current system architectures indicates several potential barriers to data quality. The search to eliminate functional redundancy usually identifies significant data redundancy or apparent redundancy. There are multiple systems storing the same data (see Exhibit 9-1) but coming from different sources. There are multiple systems storing different data from the same source. There are systems deriving and storing summarized data from detail for one business purpose and other systems deriving and storing a somewhat different summarization to be used by a different business function.

Although data editing and quality checking were stressed when individual systems were built, the combination of data that may be used for new organizations for different business purposes was not preplanned or coordinated. An obvious problem with the current architecture is the cost of resources for processing and storage for the redundant data. The more serious problem, however, is the lack of confidence generated when a user confronts nonmatching data while trying to solve a customer problem. Redundant data or apparent redundancy is not quality data. Use of poor quality data causes slow reaction to customer needs and poor customer satisfaction. Resolution of the data redundancy and quality problem is simple—separate the data from the processing and build a data engine as mentioned earlier.

CONCEPTUAL MODEL

Thinking about data separated from processing leads to a layered approach. This approach is feasible only through well-defined, strictly enforced standards dealing with hardware, software, and connectivity. These rules form a standard operating environment that must be in place to allow access to shared data. A conceptual systems model depicts three layers:

- The core data necessary to accomplish business functions
- Processing of transactions necessary to get core data into and out of databases
- Presentation or other manipulation of core or local data required by the user (Exhibit 9-3)

SUPPORTING TECHNOLOGY

The conceptual model does not imply any specific hardware implementation, but certain inferences can be derived based on changing technology. In the current architecture, terminals connected to mainframes are used to gather, edit, and store data (see Exhibit 9-4). Mainframe programming formats reports and rearranges data on terminal screens. Mainframes summarize and restore data. All DP and presentation are done by mainframe programming. With capabilities of new technology, opportunities are available to use mainframes, minicomputers, and PCs to greater advantage through networking.

To store core data in the smallest logical component, find the data, and provide all the required derivations, it will be necessary to use complex relational data structures and the directories mentioned earlier. The processing power required (even with special database machines) indicates that mainframes may be required to build and maintain large shared databases. However, the processing of that data, or the manipulation of the transactions that get the data into and out of the system, could be done with minicomputers.

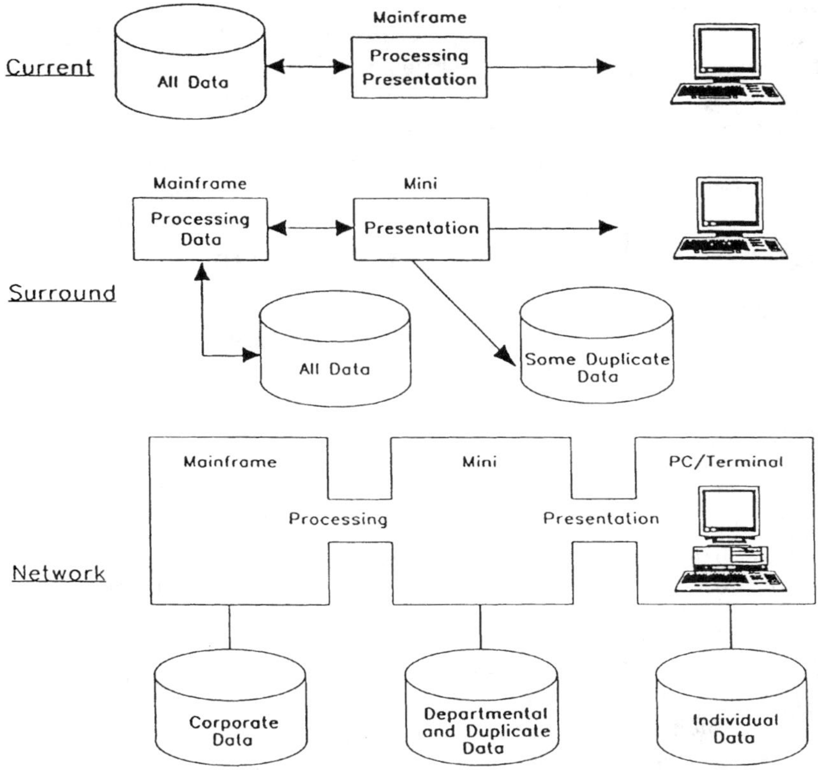

Exhibit 9-4. Technological Architecture

THE STEAK OR THE SIZZLE?

Once consistent quality data is available, presentation—the way data looks on output can be driven closer to the user to provide flexibility. All the formatting of the data can be done outside the mainframe, thereby reducing the load on the communications facility. (Terminal emulation mode requires that all screen format characters, as well as data, be exchanged with the mainframe. Studies indicate that by sending only data, communications requirements can be cut by orders of magnitude.) The programming could be done in a minicomputer for a group of users to analyze data in the same manner or in a networked PC if the display is for an individual.

Although this new technological approach (the processing definition of quality) is important to architectural planning, it is more important to analyze functions and data required for functions before jumping to the technology. The surround approach and the uses of new technology will produce some better efficiencies and add some flexibility at a reasonable cost (if local enhancement capabilities are very carefully accounted for), but the quality roadblock cannot be eliminated unless corporate data is standardized and made available for all processing. In the long run, a redesign of major systems around the use of quality data is required. A combination of moving to new technology while achieving quality data is ideal.

IMPLEMENTATING DATA WAREHOUSING STRATEGY

The idea of redesigning major systems around quality data or anything else seems to be an anathema in these days of cutbacks. A greater problem is that data planning is difficult on a corporate scope. The whole is too big even for the best corporate and DP planners. However, planning done on an organizational basis will bring about another generation of new, improved, faster nonquality systems. It is possible to identify clusters of data to single source and start sharing. Search will identify data that is currently being shared. Savings achieved in elimination of redundancy in the reduction process can be used to pay for extra hardware needed for the surround process.

Each of these strategies refines the data sharing process until it becomes practical (either through cost justification or some less tangible value judgment) to separate certain specific data and build a data engine. It is impractical to reimplement most operational support systems at one time to make a great leap forward. The better plan is to move from the current architecture to a series of interim architectures, each becoming more quality data oriented (Exhibit 9-5).

Search and destroy should be pursued not only to save money but also to identify and to start the elimination of redundant data. A logical separation can begin with implementation of the surround approach for specific functions. Most of this hardware can remain in place to transfer to processors in the conceptual model. Concentration on quality data can begin by examining each new mechanization project in light of its use of standard core data.

As practical clusters of data are identified, data engines should be designed that provide the storage structure and distribution of corporate data using the presently installed mainframes. All present database systems should be examined to determine modifications needed for interim data systems and methods for converting and merging data into the next generation of engines. Over time, with new systems and high priority modification required by present systems, the goal of quality data can be reached.

All aspects of quality are important to DP, but data quality is essential. Current systems architectures do not support economical data sharing or

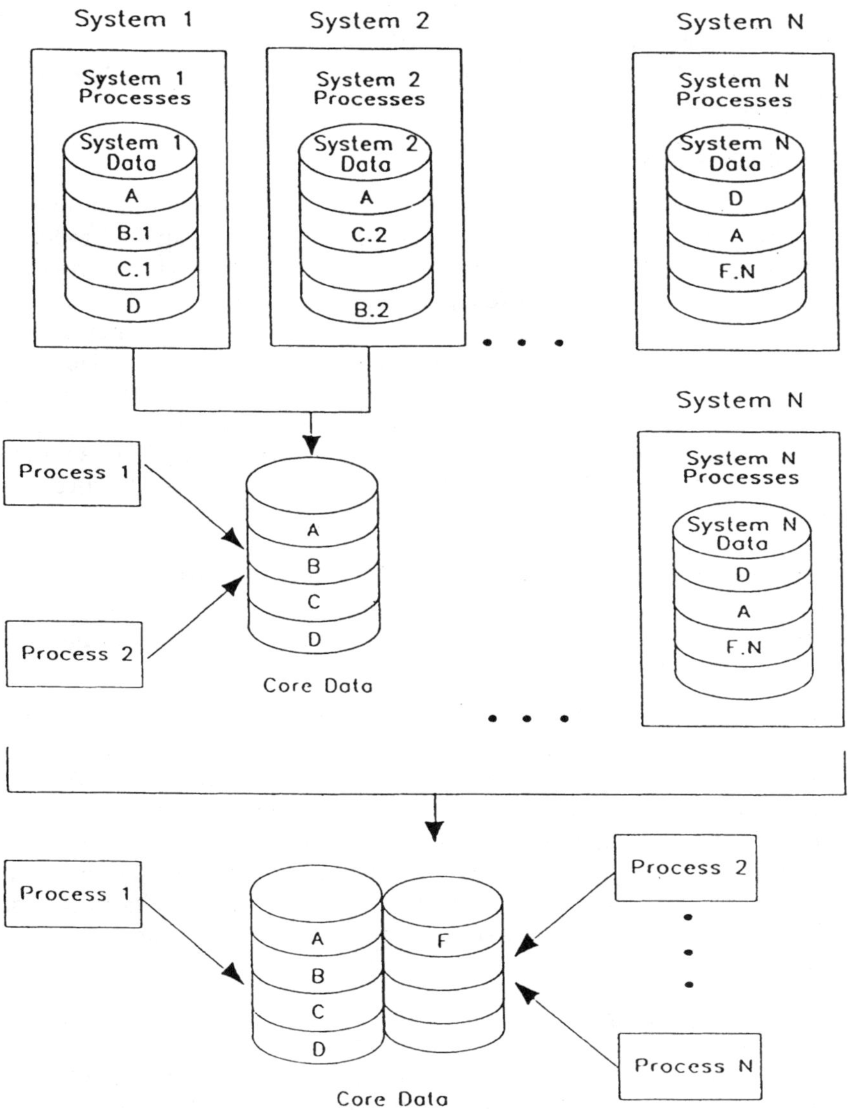

Exhibit 9-5. Architectural Evolution

take advantage of new technology. Future systems will be designed around the use of quality data stored in the smallest component and available for all processing. Networking will provide the advantages of the best properties of mainframes, minicomputers, and PCs. Surround structures are an interim approach, providing continuing use of the current architecture while laying the hardware base for the transition to transaction and presentation processing of the future. A plan of migration can be developed targeting an ever-increasing sharing of data until the future design can be realized.

UNDER WHICH SHELL IS THE PEA?

The technical architecture of the evolved storage structure shows the repository of core data, but it also implies that core data can be duplicated so that departmental and individual data can be defined. This means that after definition of core data there must be further definitions of the storage structure. Core data will be used for traditional corporate DP, that is, turning the data into information for corporate reports, payroll, etc. However, the data in this information (output or presentation format) will never be kept in a corporate information base. Only the data will be kept. Summarization will never be retained in the corporate database, but just generated on output. Customer bills will never be found in bill format in the corporate database. Storage backup will be less data-intensive and cost less, but users must now address that database with the proper language to retrieve year to date or quarterly results or to create a bill status when handling customer inquiries. A hard copy of a customer bill will never be retained. Archiving, if the media is cheap enough (microform or laser storage technology), can be on an information basis.

"What if..." games will now be done outside the mainframe on departmental processors (if the data must be shared) or all the way out on individual PCs. Departmental data, not needed for corporate processing (i.e., team sales results, training information, bowling scores, etc.), can reside only at the departmental level. Corporate data can be duplicated and reside at the departmental level if aging information is applied by the departmental processors when the data are downloaded. (Warnings that the data was downloaded at a certain time or the data is valid only until a certain time must be applied.)

MORE COMPLICATIONS

Individual or private data and individual programs will be stored only in PCs with the tightest security precautions to avoid upward contamination. Mail or announcement services will originate at the PC and can still be hubbed on mainframes, depending on the communications networking scheme, but any storage on mainframes will be physically separated from corporate data. Formatted data such as expense vouchers will be input from the PC, but only corporate required data will be passed up the line. Other data will be kept in departmental files or even locally. If it is appropriate to disburse from the departmental level, the check creation or an electronic funds transfer can take place there (hopefully speeding up the process) with only financial data going to corporate. Decentralization with centralized quality data will gain a new meaning.

The psychology of change impact of such a data and information processing hierarchy as described is traumatic. Besides the knowledge of the standard identification of data needed (new codes and language) for sharing, an understanding of the storage hierarchy must be in place. Individual managers must understand what data will be shared and where to find it. They must also understand how to legitimately avoid the sharing of data. Auditors, as will the managers, will no longer be able to pull hard copies of vouchers from departmental files. They must know how to navigate to the farthest ends of the storage structure to get all the comments added by originators.

Storage pricing structures will vary greatly, depending on the location and utilization of data. New chargeback allocations will have to be developed. All this takes place after the trauma of core data definition with all its internecine battles and, yes, even the need for top management involvement in really determining the functions of the business, have been faced. These factors must be understood by all before it is appropriate to move ahead.

CONCLUSION

The concept and data warehousing create a new set of promises of quality, strategic impact, and even cost savings available to potential users. If managers are not interested in these promises, the paper glut will force them finally to use new systems. The need to prepare users for the psychological aspects of the great opportunities has never been so important. Companies must be prepared to face the challenges and the time required to do all the interdepartmental planning work required to gain the potential advantages.

Chapter 10

Ensuring the Integrity of the Database

William E. Perry

A DATABASE IS A REPOSITORY FOR DATA, BOTH BETWEEN AND DURING PROCESSING. In traditional business systems, transactions constitute an organization's data. Data can include such items as product prices, messages, status of processing, and error or diagnostic data. Data can also be processing modules, or objects. When stored in a Computer-Aided Software Engineering (CASE) technology environment, databases are often referred to as repositories. This article considers all of these database environments.

In a database environment, data management is separate from data processing. Data management functions that were performed by application programmers in non-database systems may now be performed by people independently of the application project team. Therefore, the application project team, and thus the user, must rely on the integrity of data managed by others.

A database environment in its simplest from (i.e., in which a single application or a series of closely related applications is the only user of the database) is not much more complex than an environment in which some other indexed access method is used. This type of environment may not pose any more integrity problems than a non-database environment.

A more sophisticated database, however, can involve multiple users. A loss of integrity in this type of database environment can be catastrophic to the organization as a whole.

The increased use of microcomputers has created a need for vast amounts of data. Much of that need is satisfied by downloading segments of data from corporate databases. This poses a new audit risk because many microcomputer users are unskilled in data integrity and methods of ensuring integrity.

0-8493-0893-3/00/$0.00+$.50

The way that computer systems are constructed is changing radically. CASE technology has introduced an engineering discipline into system development. One of the key concepts in CASE is the repository, a database that stores system components (subroutines or modules) until they are assembled into programs. IBM's Application Development/Cycle (AD/Cycle) is a CASE methodology that improves the quality and productivity of new computer systems. Its repository contains subroutine and design specifications generated during system design; these are later tied together and implemented to build the system.

Data stored in a repository differs from that stored in a traditional database. Although the database typically contains business transaction data (e.g., accounts receivable and payroll), a repository contains data that defines data elements, processing modules, and their relationship. Despite this fundamental difference, the risks associated with repositories and traditional databases are similar; therefore, the concepts presented in this article are applicable to both. The article explains how to audit a traditional database and describes how the same approach can be used to audit a repository.

CUSTODIAL RESPONSIBILITY

Databases are usually managed by a database administration (DBA) function. In large organizations, this may be an independent group staffed by many individuals; in smaller organizations, however, the function may be performed on a part-time basis by a systems programmer or by computer operations personnel. In a client/server environment, the server facility has data management responsibility.

Although the DBA function is responsible for safeguarding the data delivered to the database, it cannot assume responsibility for the accuracy, completeness, and authorization of transaction that access the database. Thus, the responsibility for ensuring the integrity of a database is a custodial responsibility. This responsibility is fivefold:

- To safeguard the data delivered to the database.
- To protect the system from unauthorized access.
- To ensure that the database can be reconstructed in the event of technological problems.
- To establish an organization structure that provides necessary checks and balances.
- To provide and users with controls that ensure the integrity of actions and reports prepared using all or parts of a database.

DATABASE INTEGRITY CONCERNS

Databases involve several audit concerns. They include:

- *More reliance on integrity.* Users often do not enter their own data and thus rely on others for ensuring integrity. In addition, multiple users may access the same data element, thereby increasing the magnitude of problems should data integrity be lost.
- *Data managed independently of programs.* The people who use data are normally not those who manage it.
- *Complexity of database technology.* To be effective in designing, operating, and using databases requires different (sometimes higher-level) skills from those required for non-database technology.
- *Concurrent use of data.* Two or more users can access and use the same data item concurrently. Without proper controls, improper processing of data may occur.
- *Complexity of database structure.* There are three general types of data structure: hierarchical, network, and relational. All three types currently require a series of indexes and pointers that permit users to view the data from their individual perspectives. The more options available to the users, the greater the complexity of the data structure. In complex data structures, it is not uncommon for half of the total space allocated to the database to be used for indexes and pointers. The addition, deletion, and modification of data can literally require hundreds of these indexes and pointers to be changed. Improper data structure can thus make a database unresponsive to user needs.
- *Complexity of database recovery procedures.* The sophisticated use of databases can involve multiple users accessing, modifying, entering, and deleting data concurrently. Some of these processes are complex and occur in stages. Thus, at any time, various transactions are in various stages of processing, making database recovery difficult.
- The database environment can fail for a variety of reasons, including hardware failure, application system failure, operating system failure, database management system (DBMS) failure, loss of integrity of database, and operator failure. Adding to the complexity of recovery is the size of the database and the time required to recover. In large, sophisticated databases, recovery may require many hours or even days.
- *Extensiveness of backup data.* Databases can encompass many billions of bytes or characters of data. Stored on magnetic media, such data is often susceptible to loss. Thus, two factors must be considered in providing database backup. The first factor is the time frame in which recovery must occur. (The need for quick recovery requires frequent copies of the database.) The second factor to be considered is the volume of data in the database. (Large databases require large amounts of time to copy.)
- *Nonstandard DBMs.* The file structure, access methods, and operating characteristics of DBMSs can vary from vendor to vendor and even within a single vendor. Because there is little uniformity between the operations of various databases, it is not always possible to pull out

one database and plug in another. Individuals trained in one DBMS sometimes require additional training to deal effectively with another. The lack of standardization creates difficulties for auditors who have audit responsibilities for DBMSs from more than one vendor.

- *Segregation of new responsibilities.* Managing data independently of the application system requires a new organizational structure. In this reorganization, responsibilities should be adequately segregated to ensure the appropriate checks and balances in the database environment.
- *Increased privacy risk.* The concentration of personal data in a single place increases concern over privacy. This concern involved the accessibility of online database information and the fact that a greater concentration of data about an individual permits more analysis at a given time.
- *Increased security risk.* The greater concentration and accessibility of data in a database increases the need for security over that data. Although it is possible to intermix data of different security classifications, this should not be done in a way that gives users access to more data than they need.
- *Improper use of data by microcomputer users.* Improper processing of interpretation by microcomputer users of downloaded data from corporate databases can result in inconsistent reports, improper management actions, and misuse or loss of funds due to misinterpretation of data. For example, erroneously assuming that monthly data is weekly data and ordering inventory accordingly can result in the misuse or loss of funds.
- *Portability risk between multiple processing platforms.* In client/server environments and some Computer-Aided Software Engineering technology environments, various processing platforms are used (i.e., hardware and software from different vendors or different hardware and software from the same vendor). Data moving from one platform to another can be inadvertently altered unless adequate controls are in place. Field lengths may be changed, or data elements lost in movement.

THE DATABASE CONTROL ENVIRONMENT

Before conducting an internal control review, the auditor must understand the control environment in which the database operates. Such an understanding is also helpful in conducting tests of the control environment. The database control environment is illustrated in Exhibit 10-1.

The center of the control environment is the DBMS. As the name implies, it manages the environment, as opposed to reading and writing data to the database. In this management process, the DBMS interfaces with the operating system to perform the actual read and write instructions to the disk

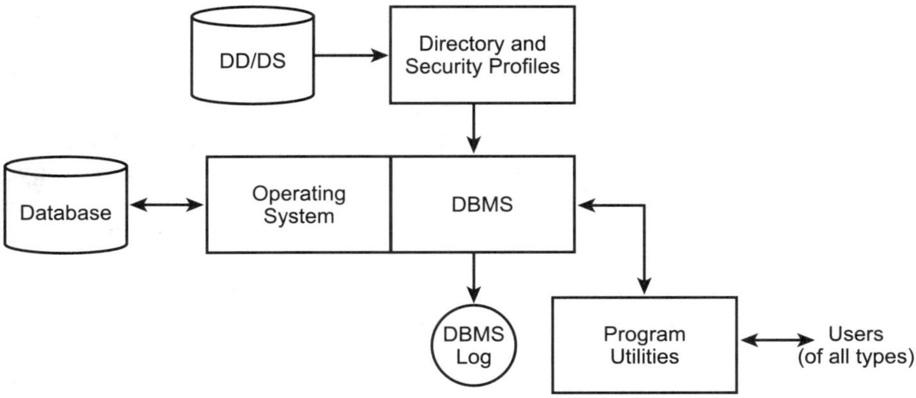

Exhibit 10-1. Database control environment.

file. The users' interface to the DBMS is through their application program, or both. (Most DBMSs come with a query or interrogation language utility.)

There are three categories of database users. The first category includes users who need data for day-to-day operation. Second are the systems analysts and programmers who build and modify computer applications. Third are such technical personnel as operators, database administrators, and systems programmers who keep the database operational.

The DBMS has two components-the directory (including security profiles) and the DBMS log-that are crucial for control. The directory may be generated from a data dictionary or may be incorporated directly into the DBMS. the purpose of the directory is to match data on the database with user needs. The security profile defines access to data. The DBMS log is used to record events in the database; such information is used primarily for database recovery.

PLANNING CONSIDERATIONS

Because of the technical complexity of the database environment, the following considerations should be included in the audit planning process:

- *Use of database utilities.* Whether the use of database utilities affects the auditors independence in verifying the integrity of the database should be considered. These tools are quite powerful and can provide capabilities unavailable with other tools.
- *Depth of technical involvement by auditors.* Although databases are relatively easy to understand conceptually, they can be very complex technically. One organization estimated that a skilled systems analyst would require three months of training to use its database effectively.

The auditor needs to develop a comparable level of skill to correctly assess the technical components of a database technology.

- *Database audit tools.* Of the database audit tools and the techniques available to auditors, the most prominent audit technique is called conversion to a flat file. With this technique, the data on the database is converted to a sequential file and then evaluated independently, through the use of audit software.
- *Skill of the auditor.* Effective auditing in a database environment requires skills that most auditors do not have. Unless the auditor understands database risks, concepts, and approaches, the auditor can neither access the adequacy of control nor obtain and evaluate the new forms of evidence available in a database environment. At a minimum, the auditor must understand the concepts of terminology of database technology.
- *Scope of the audit.* The database is normally independent of the applications that use that data. Thus, the database should be audited first, and the applications that use the data audited second. After the database is audited, conclusions of that audit can be applied to all of the application audits that follow. The integrity of the application normally depends on the adequacy of the controls in the database. Thus, without evaluating the database the auditor may not be able to conclude that controls in a specific application are effective.
- *Lack of standard audit approach.* There is no generally accepted approach to auditing databases; therefore, auditors must develop new audit approaches and identify audit tools that aid in the verification of database integrity.

AUDIT OBJECTIVES

The audit of database integrity is, in large part, an audit of the custodial responsibility of the group administering the database. Thus, the audit objectives addressing data integrity address he custodial aspects of data integrity. For example, accuracy deals with the ability to retain and return data accurately, as opposed to ensuring that the data included in the transaction is accurate from a business perspective, the following objectives are both operational and financial and encompass the concerns associated with ensuring database integrity.

Balancing of Data Items. The auditor should verify that the individual groupings of data balance to the control totals for those groupings. The data in a database belongs to, and is used by, multiple users. In the more sophisticated DBMSs, the access path to retrieve data can be created dynamically. Even with less sophisticated DBMSs, the DBA may not know how individual users use and control data. Therefore, the database controls may not maintain totals on groupings of data used by applications.

The database system normally keeps counts of items in various paths and of total data items or segments within the database, which the auditor can use when balancing data items.

Accounting Period Cutoff Procedures. Because data need not be entered tin the database on the effective data of the transaction, the auditor should verify that data is properly identified so that users will include it in the proper accounting period. For example, in many banking systems the depositor can request the transmittal of funds up to 30 days before the execution date of that transaction. Those unexpected transactions that reside in the database must be properly handled.

Completeness of the Database. The auditor should endure that all data entered into the database is retrievable. The complexity of retrieving data depends on the data structure; that is, the more complex the structure, the greater the number of indexes and pointers required in the database. If these indexes or pointers are no constructed and used properly, the DBMS may inform a user that all of a grouping of data has been delivered, while in face it has not.

Recovery of the Database. The auditor should verify that the integrity of the database can be restored in the event of problems. This is one of the most complex tasks in a database, the organization may not have developed or practiced the procedures for some of them.

Reconstruction of Processing. The auditor should verify that the process creating the current status of data in the database can reconstructed. This audit objective is particularly important in an online environment because processing can occur in an interactive mode and involve multiple users. In such a situation, no single application may have an audit trail capable of reconstructing all of the processing.

Adequacy of Service Level. The auditor should verify that the service level provided by the database is adequate to meet the needs of all users. With multiple users vying for a single resource, one user may monopolize too large a segment of the database capacity. In addition, a poorly constructed data structure or an inadequate computer capacity can lead to the degradation of service levels. In a non-database environment, service usually degrades slowly. Because of the complexity of data structure in a database, environment, however, degradation can occur quickly. It is not uncommon, for example, for response rates to double in a few hours or days.

Access to Data is Restricted to Authorized Users. The auditor should verify that access to data is restricted to those individuals and programs authorized to access that data. Access controls should apply to end users, computer operators, DBAs, database technicians, vendor personnel, and other individuals using the system; no one should be excluded to access controls. These controls can be as restrictive as the organization or the DBMS permits.

The Data Definitions Are Complete. The auditor should verify that data Definitions are complete. Database users may depend on these definitions for the correct interpretation of the data. When the definitions do not contain the needed information, erroneous decisions may be made or the data may be modified in a manner unfamiliar to the other users of the data. From an audit prospective, a complete definition includes the name of the individual responsible for that data element, the data validation rules, where the data originates, who uses the data, and what individuals and programs have access to that element.

Security is Adequate. The auditor should verify that the security procedures are adequate to protect the data. Control over access to data is only one aspect of security. Adequate security includes protection from physical destruction, fraud, and embezzlement and from such acts of nature as floods.

Individual Privacy is Protected. The auditor should verify that procedures are adequate to ensure that data about individuals is protected according to law and good business practice and that the data is destroyed at the appropriate time. Privacy requirements are defined in federal and state laws. In addition, many organizations assume a moral obligation to protect information about their employees and customers.

Data Items Are Accurate. The auditor should verify that the accuracy of individual data items in the database is protected. With multiple users accessing data concurrently, two users can update the same data items concurrently, resulting in the loss of one of the updates. In addition, procedures should protect against loss of accuracy in the case of hardware or software failure.

Downloaded Data is Properly Utilized. The auditor should verify that there are controls, procedures, and training sessions to assist end users with ensuring the integrity of downloaded database data. Users should have a means to validate the integrity of data received and instructions for applying the validation method. End users should also be instructed on adequately protecting data from unauthorized access.

Assignment of Responsibilities is Adequate. The auditor should verify that no individual can cause and conceal a problem. Segregation of duties should be sufficient to prevent this.

Multiple platforms Are Compatible. The auditor should verify that the interfaces between platforms have been tested and are working. The risk of incompatible platforms is closely associated with the client/server environment. Software currently under development for managing client/server systems should deal with these problems better then today's software does. However, until these systems are available, the auditor should address the risk of incompatible platforms.

INTERNAL CONTROL REVIEW

To ensure that these objectives are met, the auditor should review internal controls and conduct tests on the basis of the results of this review. These tests should indicate whether internal controls are effective and whether they verify the integrity of data within the database environment.

For the database integrity audit, the auditor should be concerned about the custodial, security, and organizational controls over the database. Exhibit 10-2 lists the internal control questions recommended for assessing these controls. The auditor can access the adequacy of internal controls by applying information obtained from these questions. If the controls are strong, the auditor can perform minimal tests. The assessment is therefore important in determining the scope of the audit tests.

AUDIT TESTS BY OBJECTIVE

After the adequacy of the internal controls have been assessed, the auditor must design tests to verify the integrity of the database and to help achieve the stated audit objectives. Descriptions of these test follow. (Exhibit 10-3 presents a checklist of audit tests with there corresponding audit objectives.)

Review the Data Dictionary. Information about responsibility, verification, and access to key data elements must be extracted from the data dictionary. The auditor does this by examining data dictionary printouts or by analyzing the information in an automated data dictionary, using audit software. The test should then verify whether all needed information is contained in the data dictionary, whether it is correct, and whether the information can be used to perform other audit tests.

Verify the Database Pointers. It should be determined whether the pointers and indexes in the database are complete. Utility programs, commonly called database verifiers, can be used for this purpose. These verifiers, which may run for several hours or even days in large databases, verify that all access paths are complete and that all data in the database can be accessed by at least one data path.

Exhibit 10-2. Internal control questionnaire.

Question Number	Question	Response			Comments
		Yes	No	NA	
	Traditional Database Control Concerns				
1.	Is the database managed independently of the application programs that use that database?				
2.	Is the operation of the database organizationally separate from the administration of the database?				
3.	Is the definition of the data organizationally separate from the application systems that use that data?				
4.	Is the data policy of the organization established by senior management (i.e., normally done through a data administrator)?				
5.	Is one individual responsible for the accuracy, completeness, and authorization of each data item used in the database?				
6.	Is each programmer's knowledge of the database restricted to his or her view of the data in the database?				
7.	Is each data entity (called segments and elements in various DBMSs) password protected?				
8.	Is the database administration function restricted from accessing data in the database?				
9.	Are technical interface personnel restricted from accessing data in the database?				
10.	Can data be deleted only by application programs (i.e., administrative and technical personnel cannot delete data through procedures such as reorganization)?				
11.	Are counts of each different kind of data entity (e.g., segments, elements) maintained?				
12.	Is the completeness of the pointers verified immediately following each database reorganization?				
13.	Are database reorganization controls sufficient to ensure that the completeness and accuracy of data are maintained during the reorganization process?				

Exhibit 10-2. Internal control questionnaire. (continued)

Question Number	Question	Response			Comments
		Yes	No	NA	
14.	Do users maintain independent control totals over data used in financial and other key applications?				
15.	Is sufficient backup data maintained to recover the database within the specified time interval?				
16.	Are standards established for database performance levels?				
17.	Can each data item be associated with the accounting period in which it belongs?				
18.	Is sufficient information maintained in the DBMS log to reconstruct transaction processing?				
19.	Is a log maintained of invalid attempts to access data and other potential security violations?				
20.	Is follow-up action taken on potential security and access violations?				
21.	Are mechanized tools (e.g., database modeling programs) used by the database administration function to aid in optimizing database performance and need satisfaction?				
22.	Is data defined in a data dictionary?				
23.	Is the data dictionary integrated into the DBMS so that the definitions and access rules can be enforced?				
24.	Are all adjustments to data in the database made through application systems, and not entered directly by technical or administrative personnel?				
25.	Are controls included with downloaded data to enable users to verify the integrity of the data?				
26.	Are end users trained in exercising data integrity controls, and do they use those procedures?				
27.	Are the CASE tools compatible?				
28.	Has a plan been developed to integrate all of the applications that will use the repository?				
29.	Do all of the applications using the repository employ the same definition for the data included in the repository?				

Exhibit 10-2. Internal control questionnaire. (continued)

Question Number	Question	Response			Comments
		Yes	No	NA	
30.	Have standards been established to ensure that all hardware components to the client/server system are compatible?				
31.	Have standards been established to ensure that all software packages for the client/server system are compatible?				
32.	Are all databases under the control of the server facility?				
33.	If there are multiple databases, are common data definitions used throughout all of them?				
34.	Does the server facility perform the DBA function?				

Audit Objectives \ Audit Tests	Review Data Dictionary	Verify DB Pointers	Review Vendor Documentation	Test Password Procedures	Analyze DBMS (Query/Utilities)	Analyze DBMS Log	Analyze Security Log	Perform Disaster Test	Verify Details to External Control Totals	Review DB Operational Procedures	Count/Foot Database	Verify Ent-User Control over Downloaded Data	Platforms are Compatible
The detailed data items balance to the control totals.					✔				✔		✔		
Data is recorded in the proper accounting period.					✔								
The database is complete.		✔							✔		✔		
The database can be recovered.			✔					✔		✔			
Processing can be reconstructed.						✔		✔					
The service level is adequate.			✔			✔							
Access to data is restricted to authorized users.	✔			✔								✔	
The data definitions are complete.	✔											✔	
Security is adequate.				✔			✔			✔		✔	
Individual privacy is protected.							✔			✔		✔	
Data items are accurate.					✔				✔		✔	✔	
Assignment of responsibilities is adequate.	✔									✔		✔	
Downloaded data is properly utilized.												✔	
Verify that multiple platforms are compatible.													✔

Exhibit 10-3. Audit tests by objective.

Review the Vendor Documentation. DBMS vendors supply information on achievable ranges of performance for their DBMS as well as on operational and recovery procedures. This information can be used to assess actual service levels and to determine whether organizational recovery and operational procedures are adequate.

Test the Password Procedures. The auditor should verify that password procedures are adequate and that the procedures are enforced in the operating environment. When used, passwords can restrict data access to authorized individuals. By operating a terminal, the auditor can access the adequacy of password procedures by attempting to enter invalid passwords, by using valid passwords for invalid purposes, and by discovering passwords through repetitive attempts.

Analyze the DBMS. Query languages and other utilities that search and print selected data items can help the auditor verify database integrity. query language contain most of the facilities found in an audit software language, and in some cases, they contain additional capabilities. The one audit software feature usually not found in query language is statistical sampling.

Analyze the DBMS Log. The DBMS log contains the equivalent of a motion picture of the activities occurring in a database operation. Although this log is typically used to help recover database operations, it also contains information that can be valuable for audit purposes. The auditor can use this information to reconstruct Transaction Processing as well as to analyze the types of activities that occur during database operations.

Analyze the Security Log. The security log records who accessed what item in the database. In addition, the security log should list the frequency and type of invalid accesses that were attempted. The auditor can sort this log by individuals accessing data to determine what data they accessed, or by key data items to determine who is accessing key data items. This information can be used for both security and privacy analyses.

Perform a Disaster Test. The auditor can simulate a disaster to verify whether operations personnel can recover the database and substantiate processing, should a real failure occur.

Verify Details to External Control Totals. Using the audit software or DBMS utilities, the auditor can accumulate the value of detailed data elements and then verify the accumulated total to that maintain independently by the application systems.

Review Database Operational Procedures. The auditor should determine whether the organization has procedures for designing, organizing, reorganizing, recovering, and performing other operational activities related to the database. The procedures should then be reviewed to determine if they are adequate and if actual procedures match the documented ones.

Verify Database Control Totals. A total of the number of data entities (e.g., segments or items)within the database should be accumulated and verified to the accounts maintained by the DBA. If the DBA function also maintains hash total or other accumulated totals, the auditor can verify those totals by using audit software or database utilities.

Verify End-User Control over Downloaded Data. The methods for controlling downloaded data should be determined, and the use of those controls at the end users' sites should be verified. The auditor should determine whether reports and decisions made by end users on the basis of downloaded data are consistent with the content of that data.

Verify Platform Compatibility. This test is normally too complex for the auditor to perform, but the auditor should verify that platform compatibility tests have be performed. The auditor can review the test plan and test results to verify compatibility. Many audit software languages cannot access a database. In such an environment, the auditor must either use database utilities or have the DBA function convert the database to a file that can be accessed by the auditor.

AUDITING A CASE TECHNOLOGY REPOSITORY

The major component of a Computer-Aided Software Engineering environment is the repository, where all common data and processing modules are stored. The upper CASE tools specify the attributes of the repository. The lower CASE tools use the repository to produce operational code. The repository is similar to the database in that the major components of the database are also components of the repository and the risks associated with loss of integrity are similar. Traditional databases and repositories differ in the following ways:

- Databases contain transaction data, where as repositories contain data about the processing characteristics of data.
- Databases are subject to more financial risk, where- as repositories are subject to more processing integrity risks.
- Errors and manipulation of databases pose an immediate threat, whereas errors and manipulation in repositories can usually be detected during testing and evaluation.
- Improper or unauthorized processing is a greater risk in a repository then in a database because once such processing is introduced into the production environment, it can occur repeatedly over long periods of time.

- Repository problems can lead to loss of processing integrity, whereas database problems lead to loss of data integrity.

A CASE environment can be audited using the database integrity audit program presented in this article, but the auditor must follow the three-step process described in the following sections.

Step 1: Define Repository Characteristics

The auditor should first determine what type of database is used in the repository (i.e., traditional or unique database architecture). In addition, the auditor should establish the following:

- The repository's size.
- The indexing method used to access repository data.
- How the repository is secured.
- How the repository is used (i.e., is the primary purpose to reuse already developed capabilities throughout the organization?)
- Who generates, maintains, and controls the repository.

Step 2: Review the Database Integrity Program

On the basis of the information contained in step 1 and the similarities and differences between databases and repositories listed in this repository audit section, the audit program presented in this article should be reviewed to determine whether the differences between a database and a repository would alter the audit approach. For example, when reviewing the section on database integrity concerns, the auditor should evaluate each concern by asking the following questions:

- *Is this concern affected by a difference between databases and repositories?* For example, a concern regarding loss of data affects both databases and repositories, whereas a concern regarding the integrity of financial data involves only databases.
- *Is this concern affected by the repository's architecture or structure?* For example, if the architecture's naming or selection capabilities are limited in their ability to differentiate among program modules with similar names, an incorrect module may be selected.

Step 3: Modify the Audit Program

The audit program should be modified on the basis of conclusions drawn in step 2. For example, if a risk is increased because of a difference between databases and repositories, the audit program should be adjusted.

CASE software tools are usually available with repositories. The auditor may be able to use these tools to access the repository, list data contain in the repository, or perform repository analyses.

AUDITING CLIENT/SERVER DATABASES

Client/server databases and traditional databases are similar in the following ways:

- Both contain data.
- Both use the same basic storage and access approaches.
- Both contain indexes to access their data.
- Both are accessed by multiple users.

Traditional databases and client/server databases differ in the following ways:

- Transactions updating client/server databases move between multiple platforms, subjecting the data to greater processing integrity risks.
- Uses of data in a client/server system are less predictable then in a traditional database environment.
- Because testing methods in client/server systems are not as sophisticated as those in traditional database systems, they subject data integrity to more risks.
- Management of the server component of client/server systems may be less sophisticated in data processing technologies than in a traditional database environment.

A client/server environment can be audited using the database integrity audit program presented in this article, if the following four steps are added.

STEP 1: Define Client/Server Technology/Platforms

The auditor should determine the variety of platforms and technology used in a client/server environment. The more diverse the environment, the greater the risk to process integrity. Therefore, the auditor must establish the following regarding the client/server environment:

- The hardware vendors involved.
- The software vendors involved.
- An inventory of hardware platforms.
- An inventory of software systems.
- An assessment of the incompatibility of the platforms(The auditor may need to perform this step with the manager of the client/server environment.)

STEP 2: Review the Potential Usage of Data by Clients

The auditor should identify the potential uses of data in a client/server environment by talking to a representative number of system clients. The objective of this step is to determine the level of risk to data integrity due to the high-risk usage of data. To perform this step the auditor should ask the following questions:

- Will the client add, delete, or modify data before producing reports that may need to be reconciled by other uses of data from the same database?
- Is the client processing data with unproven software and then using the results to make business decisions?

STEP 3: Determine the Number of Databases in a Client/Server Environment

Having a single database in a client/server environment involves a similar risk relationship as with a traditional database. If additional databases exist, the auditor should ask the following questions:

- Will the databases be used independently or with one another? (If used together, the data integrity risk is increased.)
- Are the additional databases subsets of the main database? (If so, the auditor should explore how the integrity of the extracted database will be maintained.)

STEP 4: Modify the Audit Program

The audit program should be modified on the basis of conclusions drawn in steps 1 through 3. If multiple platforms pose additional risks, user-processing characteristics pose additional risks, or multiple databases exist, the audit program should be adjusted.

The auditor should view himself or herself as a client of the client/server system. In this way, the auditor can perform the needed audit processing to evaluate the client/server risk.

RECOMMENDED COURSE OF ACTION

The proper functioning of application systems in a database environment depends on the ongoing integrity of the database. Without verifying the integrity of the database, the auditor may be unable to rely on data used by an application. It is therefore recommended that the auditor verify the integrity of the database before auditing individual applications that use that database. This article has provided an approach to verifying the integrity of the database, using several automated audit approaches.

Chapter 11
A Practical Example of Data Conversion

Charles Banyay

CONVERSION — THE WORD IS ENOUGH TO DIM THE ENTHUSIASM OF MOST SYSTEMS DEVELOPERS. The word instills fear in some, trepidation and loathing in others. Regardless of the nature of the project with which an individual is involved, if there is any conversion effort involved, the reaction is the same. Exclude it from project scope! Let someone else do it! While some might suspect that there may be some religious connotation here, and rightly so, the topic of this chapter, however, is not about converting from one religion to another. Nor is the topic software conversion, although this would be closer to the mark. This chapter deals with the various forms of the conversion of data.

Even if the project promises to be primarily development or implementation, which is usually the dream of most developers; even if it involves some of the latest state of the art technology, the word "conversion" immediately throws a pall over all the luster and glitter, and hopes of an interesting endeavor. Most systems implementations involve some form of conversion. When the software changes, the data model or the data itself often changes with it.

For some reason, conversions have come to be associated with the mundane, boring, and tiresome aspects of systems implementation. Most developers would consider conversion efforts as boring, tiresome, and devoid of interesting challenges, when compared to the implementation of state-of-the-art technology.

This is a misconception in many instances. Conversion efforts can be as challenging as any state-of-the-art technology. They can exercise the most creative abilities of technology professionals. An entire chapter could probably be devoted to discussing the possible reasons behind the general lack of enthusiasm for the conversion effort. This chapter, however, will focus on examining:

0-8493-0893-3/00/$0.00+$.50

- some of the different types of conversion efforts that one encounters during systems implementation projects
- the taxonomy of the conversion effort
- some common pitfalls that can have rather detrimental effects on the overall effort if one is not aware of them and does not take the necessary precautions beforehand

CLASSIFYING DATA CONVERSIONS

There are a number of different ways of classifying a data conversion. One of the most common ways is to classify it by what is involved in the conversion effort. This could be one or more of the following:

- converting from one hardware platform to another; for example, a host system upgrade (on PCs, this is done on a matter-of-fact basis almost daily)
- converting from one operating system to another; for example, UNIX to NT
- converting from one file access method to another; for example, converting from an indexed or flat file structure into a DBMS
- converting from one coding structure or format to another; for example, from EBCDIC to ASCII
- converting application software, such as upgrading versions of an application or replacing one application with another as in replacing an outmoded payroll application with a state-of-the-art pay benefits system

One of the most common pitfalls of conversions is to combine into one conversion effort, a change of too many variables. For example, changing hardware, operating system(s), file access method(s), and application software all at once. Sometimes, this cannot be avoided. Ideally, however, as few as possible of the variables should be changed at once. With only one variable changing, error detection and correction is the simplest. Any problem can be attributed to the change of the single variable and can thus be rectified by analyzing the single variable. With combinations and permutations, the effort increases exponentially.

Unfortunately, as often happens in life, the ideal state is the exception. In general, it is a rare conversion that does not have some combination of the above variables changing at once. The taxonomy of each, however, can be explored individually, as can most of the pitfalls. Some combinations will have unique pitfalls simply due to the combination of changes in variables.

CHANGE IN HARDWARE

In general, the simplest conversion is upgrading hardware assuming that all of the other variables remain constant (i.e., operating systems, file access method, coding structure and format, and application software). This can best be illustrated in the PC world. PCs have been upgraded continuously with relative ease from one configuration to another for the past ten years. As long as the operating system does not change, the upgrade in hardware usually involves nothing more than copying the files from one hard disk to another. This migration of files is usually accomplished with the assistance of some standard utilities. Using utilities rather than custom-developed software lowers the amount of effort involved in ensuring that the files have migrated successfully. Most utilities provide fairly good audit trails for this purpose. Even files on the same floppies can be used in a 286, 386, 486, or a Pentium machine. Data on floppies does not require any conversion.

In environments other than personal computers, the same simplicity of conversion generally holds true. Upgrading from one configuration of mainframe to another is relatively easy. Changing configurations of a minicomputer, such as from one AS/400 to a more powerful configuration of the same, or from one HP/3000 to a more powerful HP/3000, generally does not require significant effort. These kinds of conversions are generally imperceptible to the users, and are done without much involvement from the user community. There usually is no requirement for any user testing or programmer testing. This cannot be said for the more complex conversions such as changes in the operating system.

MIGRATING FROM ONE OPERATING SYSTEM TO ANOTHER

Changes to the operating system are generally more complicated from a conversion perspective than changes to hardware. The complexity, however, is usually more pronounced at the application software rather than at the data level. There is considerable insulation by the operating system, of the application software and associated data from the hardware. In general, there is little to insulate the application software from the operating system. Object-oriented approaches are slowly changing this fact; but for now, it is safe to say that a change in operating system requires a more complex conversion effort than a change in hardware.

For individuals who have primarily limited their involvement with technology to the WINTEL world, conversion complexity due to changes in operating system may come as a surprise. In the WINTEL world, one can generally change from DOS, to Windows 3.x, to Win/95, with little or limited problems. In fact, most users do this on a regular basis. This may imply that changes in the operating system are as simple as changes in hardware. This is a misconception. The people at Microsoft and, to a limited extent, at Intel have spent innumerable hours to ensure that there exists a degree of compatibility between these operating systems that does not exist in any other environment.

Even in the WINTEL world, this compatibility is breaking down. As the move to NT accelerates, this is becoming evident. Users moving to NT have discovered that many of their favorite software programs are not functioning as they would like them to or the programs are not functioning at all.

Although some form of conversion effort is usually involved when operating systems are changed, the changes in operating system more definitely impact the application software than the data. The impact on any of the data is usually from indirect sources, such as from a change in one of the other variables (e.g., as data format or file access method). Different operating systems may only support different data coding structures or different file access methods.

CHANGES IN FILE ACCESS METHOD

It is not often that one changes a file access method while leaving the operating system and the application system the same. The reasons for doing this in general would be suspect unless the current file access method was being abandoned by whomever was providing support. Another valid reason for changing the file access method may be if a packaged application system vendor released a new version of its application. This new version may offer a new data architecture such as an RDBMS. There may be valid reasons, such as better reporting capability using third-party tools, for upgrading to this new version with the RDBMS. Whatever the reason, a change in file access method usually requires some form of change in data architecture.

A simple illustration of this change in the underlying data architecture would be in converting a flat file sequential access method to an indexed file access method. Some form of indexing would have to be designed into the file structure, resulting in a change in the underlying data architecture. A more complex example would be in changing from a sequential access method to a database management system.

This change, at a minimum, would involve some degree of data normalization and a break-up of the single segment or record structure of the file. The resultant change in data architecture would be quite substantive. This type of conversion generally is not simple and requires a comprehensive conversion utility. In the case where it is a packaged application that is being upgraded, the vendor would probably provide the conversion utility. In the case where a custom-developed application is being converted, the conversion utility would probably have to be custom-developed as well.

In either case, the tasks are straightforward. All of the data must be converted. Every record must have a corresponding entry or entries in some table or tables. Each field in the source file needs to be transferred to the target database. Field conversion is not required. There is only a limited degree of selection involved. The conversion utility is run against the source data to create the target data store. Often there are a number of intermediate steps. Different tables or segments of the database may be created in different steps. The resultant data is verified at each step. Taking a step-by-step approach, one can minimize the number and extent of the reruns of the conversion. This is another example of minimizing the number of variables that can change at once.

There are a number of approaches for ensuring that the resultant data store has the required integrity. These approaches are identical to the ones used to ensure the integrity of data that is converted due to a change in the application software.

The extent of the effort depends on the degree of reliability required. The effort has an obvious cost. The lack of data integrity also has a cost. A financial system requires a high degree of data integrity. It can be argued that the data controlling the operation of a nuclear power station requires an even higher degree of integrity.

MIGRATING FROM ONE APPLICATION SYSTEM TO ANOTHER

Changing or upgrading applications always requires converting data from the old to the new application. These conversions are generally the most complex and require the most effort.

One of the first steps in the conversion process is to decide which is the driving application. What is most important in the conversion process? Being exhaustive in converting the data in the old application or ensuring that the new application has the required fields which it needs to operate effectively? This may not be intuitively obvious. This is not to imply that the decision as to which data to convert is at the whim of the person designing the conversion programs.

There is always a base amount of data that must be converted. Many old applications, however, accumulate various codes and indicators over the years that either lose meaning over time or are particular to that application and are not required in a new application. This situation is more particular to operational applications such as payroll, materials management, etc. In converting data in an operational application, the emphasis is on converting the minimum amount of current data, in order for the new application to fulfill its role and be able to operate. The data requirements of the new application drive the conversion design.

Recordkeeping applications, on the other hand (e.g., document management systems) and pension administration systems need to retain almost all of the information within the current database. These applications generally hold a tremendous amount of history, which needs to be retained. Recordkeeping applications as a rule require that the emphasis be on being exhaustive in converting all of the information within the current database. The data requirements of the old application drive the conversion design.

Generally speaking, converting operational applications is considerably easier than converting recordkeeping applications. Populating fields necessary for the operation of a particular piece of software can be performed in various ways. New information required for the effective operation of the new application, which is not available from the old application, can be collected from other repositories. This is generally the most time-consuming and complex way of meeting the data requirements of the new application. On the one extreme of the conversion continuum is the possibility of disregarding the old application completely and satisfying the data requirements of the new application by collecting the data from original sources. This approach is particularly useful when the data integrity of the old application is very suspect.

New information can also be provided as defaults based on other data, which is available from the old application; for example, in classifying employees for payroll purposes, giving each employee the same classification based on the department where that employee works. In some instances, new information can be fudged if the new data is not critical to the output required. For example, if source medium for an invoice is a required field in a new accounts payable application and it is not a current business requirement to keep source medium, then it could be assumed that all invoices are on paper and the information fudged with that indicator.

Being exhaustive and ensuring that all the data in an old application is converted to a new application, as a rule, is more complex than meeting the data requirements of a new application. The complexity is not just in the conversion. The old application must be analyzed much more thoroughly in order to ensure that all the data is understood and put into proper context. The converted data must be screened much more thoroughly to ensure that everything has been converted appropriately and is in the proper context within the new application. In addition, there are still the data requirements of the new application to consider.

Converting historical information often requires shoe-horning existing data into fields that were not designed for that data. Very often, field conversions are required. For various reasons there may be an array of information in the old application, for which there is only one field in the new application. Pension administration systems are notorious for this. For example, it is not uncommon to have numerous pension enrollment dates, depending on the prior plans of which an individual was a member. The new application, especially if it is not sophisticated, may only provide one pension enrollment date.

Acquisitions, mergers, and changes in union agreements and government legislation can cause havoc with historical recordkeeping systems. These then result in a conversion nightmare when one of these applications needs to be converted to a new application system. A very common experience is that the conversion routines often approach the complexity of artificial intelligence applications. These are the conversions that tax the abilities of even the most experienced developers. These conversions are also the ones that are potentially the most interesting and challenging to complete.

Once the driving application is determined, the next decision that is basic to any conversion is whether an automated conversion is the most effective way of transferring the data to the new application. In certain instances, an automated conversion may not even be possible. For example, if the source data architecture or the data format is not known and cannot be determined, and there is no export utility provided by the application, then it would be very difficult to develop an automated conversion utility. In some instances, it is simply not cost effective to develop an automated conversion utility. If the volume of source data is relatively low and the complexity of the data requires conversion routines approaching the complexity of artificial intelligence routines, then a manual conversion effort may be more cost effective.

The next conversion decision that must be made is how to get the data into the new application. For some reason, many application system designers never think of the initial population of their application with the relevant data. It is as if this was supposed to occur by magic. There are four basic ways of populating the new application. In order of relative complexity, these are:

- using a bulk load facility if one is provided by the target application
- generating input transactions into the new application if the application is transaction based and the format of the transactions is known
- realtime data entry through keystroke emulation
- creating the target database so that it is external to the application

Bulk load facilities are often provided by most packaged application system vendors. If a bulk load facility is not provided, then the vendor often provides the necessary APIs in order that a bulk load facility can be developed. Bulk load facilities are the most effective tools with which to populate a new application. The bulk load facility generally provides the necessary native edit and validation routines required by the application, while providing the necessary audit capabilities with which to determine the degree of success of the conversion.

If a bulk load facility is not provided and cannot be developed from vendor-provided APIs, then the next best thing is to generate the transactions that would ordinarily be used to enter data into the system. In this way, the data is cleansed by the application-provided routines and one is assured that the resultant data has the required integrity from the application perspective and is appropriately converted. This approach generally requires multiple conversion routines, possibly one per transaction type, and multiple iterations of the conversion as the transactions are loaded.

If neither of the above methods for converting the data is available, then one can explore using keystroke emulation as a method of entering the data. There are numerous keystroke emulation or screen scraping utilities available that can assist in this endeavor. The trick here is to generate flat files from the source application and then to assemble screens of information that are ordinarily used by the application for data entry. The application is, in essence, fooled into behaving as if a client was communicating with it for data entry.

There are some technical limitations or challenges associated with this approach. With large volumes of information, multiple clients with multiple client sessions may have to be established. This is dependent on the efficiency of the client application. The slower the client application and the higher the volume of data, the greater the number of clients that need to operate simultaneously. The more the client sessions, the higher the risk of malfunction. Auditing this type of conversion effort is usually quite challenging. The audit process needs to be very thorough to ensure that all of the data is converted. As with the previous approaches to conversion, using this process one is still assured that the data that does make it to the new application has been validated and edited by the application-provided routines.

As a last resort, if it is determined that none of the above alternatives are feasible or available, then one can attempt to use the following approach. The tool of last resort is to convert the data from the source application by constructing the target database from outside the application. In the past, when applications and application data architectures were relatively simple (i.e., a flat file structure), this approach was used quite frequently. The trick here is that the conversion designer must have an intimate knowledge of both the application design and the underlying data architecture and the context of the data. With a simple application and a simple data architecture, this is not a daunting requirement. With today's complex application packages, however, this approach is almost not supportable. For example, creating the application database for an SAP implementation outside of the application would be out of the question.

Once the decision is made as to which approach to use for the conversion, the actual conversion routines need to be written and tested just like any other piece of application code. There usually is no user testing required at this point. When the routines are ready and thoroughly tested, the time comes for the actual conversion. This is the trickiest part of the entire effort. It is rare to have the luxury of ample time between running the conversion and certifying the resultant database for live operation. The planning of the actual conversion, checking the resultant database, and certifying the data must be planned with military precision.

Checking the data is usually done using multiple independent audit trails at least providing the count of data records converted and some hash totals on certain fields. The amount of effort expended is usually commensurate with the cost and impact of an error. The users of the data must be involved and have the final sign-off. Whatever audit trails are used, the results and associated statistics must be kept in archives at least for the first few years of operation of the new application. A copy of the source database used for the conversion should also be archived, together with some application code that can access the data for reporting purposes. If questions with regard to the conversion process arise at a later date, then one has something to go back to for verification.

After a successful conversion, the last step involves decommissioning the old application. This sounds much simpler than it actually is. It is not unusual, in fact; it is often absolutely mandatory that the old and new applications be run in parallel for some specified time period. Weaning users from the old application, however, can sometimes be a major challenge. That, however, is not a subject for a chapter on conversions, but is more in the realm of change management.

CONCLUSION

As the preceding discussion illustrates, conversions are not as boring and lacking in challenges as most professionals assume. Neither are conversions as frightening as they are made out to be. Most systems implementations involve some form of data conversion. When the software changes, the data model or the data itself often changes with it. Conversion software design and development can challenge the most creative juices of the most skilled developers. Conversions can be interesting and fun. One should keep this in mind the next time the word "conversion" is heard.

Chapter 12
Legacy Database Conversion

James Woods

THE MATERIAL PRESENTED IN THIS ARTICLE AIDS THE DATA CENTER MANAGER IN PLANNING THE MOVE TO A RELATIONAL DATABASE SYSTEM. Encompassing more than the traditional information (e.g., table normalization and project organization), the article examines managerial, political, and other considerations and identifies and discusses the more technical considerations.

Before any project is begun, certain questions must be answered. Why is the organization going to a relational database? What are the benefits that managers hope to gain? Now, if the list of benefits comes solely from the vendor's representative, the organization may not get a complete and accurate representation of what is to be gained. Instead, managers need to consider what new capabilities mean specifically to the way the organization does business, for example, how the new system will make it easier or faster to do business, thereby lowering overhead?

One of the things to be considered is the capability of the old system as opposed to the capabilities of the new. If the abilities of the new system are drawn as a circle or a set, and the abilities of the old system are likewise drawn, the two should have an area where they overlap, representing the union of the two sets. If project managers target this union to be the result of the conversion, they are losing many of the advantages of the new system. The most desirable objective, therefore, is to gain the whole second set, rather than just the union of those sets. Project managers should not limit the new system by thinking only in terms of the old system.

The legacy system was thought of in terms of applications. The new system should be thought of in terms of models. There is a paradigm shift involved. The most severe shift is to be expected at the technical level. As far as the end user is concerned, there should not be a great difference in the content of the information at the first stage. There certainly may be, after the initial conversion, because at that point, it will be possible to

0-8493-0893-?/00/$0.00+$.50

implement the wonderful features that have been talked about for years but were never cost-effective to add.

Generally, one of the benefits of moving to a modern database system is the facility of the tools. They are better, faster, and more complete. COBOL, for example, may indeed be the mainstay of business, because of the legacy systems, but it is not more powerful than a visually oriented diagramming tool that will automatically set up the users' screens, filter the data, and so forth.

PRECONCEPTIONS AND MISCONCEPTIONS

The announcement of an implementation of a legacy-conversion project gives rise to certain predictable reactions within an organization, and the data center manager needs to be aware of the preconceptions members may hold. Two common expectations are:

- There will be no problems with the new system, or at least the new system will present fewer problems than historically encountered with the legacy system. Human nature is such that staff will expect the new system to be without challenges. Everyone hopes to move from the old, patched system to the new, improved system, one that will not have any problems. This, however, is seldom the case. Whereas the likelihood is that the new system will offer many advantages over the old system, those advantages do not exhibit themselves without effort.
- The new system will be more efficient. On the contrary, database performance could very well be lowered when performing the same tasks using a relational system. A database that must make access path decisions at query time is inherently slower than a system that is preconfigured only to retrieve data in a particular way; such decision-making takes time. However, if a computer hardware upgrade is also involved in the conversion project, the increased demand for Central Processing Unit (CPU) cycles is more than compensated for by the increased power of the new machines. The data center manager should note that if the organization is changing only database systems, rather than changing database systems as well as moving to a new, more powerful computer platform, users could most likely suffer a performance hit for at least part of the system, perhaps even a major part. This, of course, depends on the efficiency of the existing system. A broad rule is that generalized solutions cost more CPU cycles than specific solutions do. The system does, however, gain great flexibility in return for the additional CPU cycle cost.

To identify and isolate the potential problem areas, the safest route is to perform benchmarks for both the old and new systems. In fact, many organizations make it a condition of sale. The managers can choose samples of transaction data and run them on both systems. At least one of the sample sets should be large, because the response of a database system is seldom linear. Managers should also be sure to include critical applications in the benchmark set. These are the applications that must fly in order for the new system to be a success.

BEYOND NORMALIZATION

Any thorough textbook on relational databases outlines clear instructions on applying standard normalization rules to non-normalized data. (Normalization refers to a procedure used to ensure that a data model conforms to standards that have been developed to avoid duplication of data and to minimize create, update, and delete anomalies of data. Normalization involves the decomposition of a large relation into smaller relations; this process generally improves data integrity and increases the effectiveness of a database system's long-term maintenance.) Textbook instructions on applying normalization rules generally do not cover some of the difficulties that can be encountered in the conversion of a legacy system. The information content must be reverse-engineered from the legacy database, at which point the actual normalization can begin. The exceptions that are almost never examined within the textbooks fall into two categories:

- *The Data-Definition Shift.* The definition of the data originated, at one point in the system's history, in one form and has evolved into another. One reason is that the data usage is subject to change over the course of many years. For example, what used to be a facility location may now really be labeled "Material Storage Location." This type of shift has important ramifications when deciding how to represent this data in a relational database.
- *Incognito Data.* In this situation, the data's name is not necessarily indicative of its function. It is, instead, a statement of the data's original intent. In fact, the name of a data item reflects the understanding of the programmer involved at the time that the first program using that data was written.

DATA REDUNDANCY

On occasion, the conversion process uncovers two, or more, items of data that conflict. Possibly, they have different names, but they serve similar functions. Under the old system, these two or more items do not come into contact, but they may in the new. The function of each piece of data must be clearly understood before a correct model of that data can be made in the relational database.

Summary Data Redundancy

Many systems store summary data, because the cost, in terms of time/CPU cycles, is too high to perform the calculations in real time. However, this stored summary data may not match the actual counts or sums. This causes a difficult and embarrassing situation: The first report on the new system does not balance with the report on the old system. This can be distressing because, if the new system is correct, the old system has been wrong for an undetermined amount of time. In any case, the summary data should be discarded in favor of direct calculations from the database.

Data Conflicts

It is not unusual to have redundant data conflict. For example, in one system, the vendor record was duplicated for each product line that was supplied by that vendor. There was a bug in the update program that caused the system to update the records of only the active products. During the conversion project, when the data was brought over, sometimes one of the old records was picked up and the demographic data was taken from there. There must be a standard decision reached, to apply to all redundant data within the system, as to which data will be considered true. The other data must be discarded during the transfer. However, the data center manager should be advised that this could cause the users to see differences between their old reports and new.

HISTORICAL ERROR TRACKS

A scenario common to organizations going through a conversion project is the existence of hidden, damaged data. What very often has happened is this: At one time in a company's history, an error occurred in an update program; the program was fixed, and the data was corrected. However, some of the damaged data still lingers in the system. It may never actually show up in user reports, but it will stop the new systems' data transfer cold because it violates the very rules that were culled from the program that was supposed to guard that data.

The precaution is simple: Programs must be audited; so must data. For example, a certain field is supposed to contain the groupings of letters INC or SER, which indicate the type of record. Before any transfer attempt is made, a simple program should be written to look at all the records including historical records, if they are to be transferred to the new database, to ascertain that indeed those are the only two codes embedded in the data.

If the database involved employs dictionaries, staff members can use them as a source for the data item name and function, depending on how well the code has been documented. However, if the legacy file or database system does not have a centralized dictionary, then staff members are dependent on the program code to provide the name and function and thereby the implied function of the data item.

AVOIDING HIDDEN PITFALLS

The larger the number of programs, and the more extended the lifetime of the system, the more likely it is that the data items involved conflict in intent and purpose and perhaps even form and function. At this point, it might be time to start thinking about the planning of the conversion. Even though the legacy system is presumably well understood and the relational database is thought to be well understood, no manager should assume that the translation from the legacy system to the relational database would be the simple matter of applying normalization rules to the legacy system.

The first assumption that leads to numerous problems is that the current staff understands the intricacies of the legacy system. Unless their numbers include at least a few members who originally helped to build the system, the assumption should be otherwise. Each staff member working on the conversion has a specific, applications-oriented view of the data, as opposed to a system-wide view, and the conflicts and the anomalies that staff members in systems development have lived with and accommodated within the application code over the years will not be able to be tolerated easily within the new system. The situation calls for a solution to be found, finally.

The second assumption is that relational databases are well understood. In academic and theoretical circles, this is a true assumption. It is not, however, necessarily true of the organization's staff, and this staff must be able to support the system. Sending them to the vendor's school is a starting point, but it is not a finish line. They must understand relational databases, but they must also see the need and understand the benefits for the organization.

THE COMPONENTS OF THE CONVERSION PROCESS

The conversion is not a technical process; rather, it is a managerial process with major technical components. The following sections describe two key considerations in the project.

Defining Documentation

Certain preliminary decisions have been made, so the project has loosely been defined. For example, the organization is determined to move to a relational database; managers have chosen which database is to be the replacement system, and a clear picture of the current system has been created. The staff training has been arranged for and the project is set to go in a couple of months. At this point, what is the procedure?

The first step is to document the current legacy system. If the system has inadequate documentation, the project will be besieged by last-minute surprises during the conversion process and while bringing up the new system. If the system is over-documented (if, indeed, such a thing is possible), the project will be assured of no surprises and a smooth transition. Therefore, logic would dictate that, if the staff does err, they should err on the side of too much documentation.

The term documentation requires some definition, because what the manager means by documentation and what the programmer means are not necessarily the same things.

To the programmer, documentation means materials that answer such questions as, "When I get ready to make an application that asks for the insured's middle name, what data item, in what file, will give it to me?" and "Is there an index on that item?"

What managers mean when they ask for documentation is material that answers such questions, as, "When I ask you to modify a particular application, is there some documentation that you can use to find out what that application currently does and what the factors are that will be involved in your modification of that process?"

What end-users mean when they ask for documentation, of course, is how they "drive" that application. In the context of this article, users could include either the end user for terminal systems or the operator for batch systems.

At least three different definitions exist for documentation. For the purposes of the conversion, the term actually refers to a combination of all three, to some degree. Technically, yes, the programmer-level documentation must be complete. The interrelationships that the manager wants must be completely documented. The user information, however, does not need to be complete for the purposes of the conversion, but it still needs to be noted and understood.

One of the determinations to make in the labyrinth of management decisions for a conversion effort of this type is estimating the desired degree of impact on the current organization and end users? Questions to consider are: Will applications look the same? Will they act the same? It may be a highly desirable motive, politically and even sociologically, to keep the impact as small as possible. However, minimizing the effects is not a desirable goal, technically. That would mean the project is simply putting new milk in an old bottle, limiting the benefits of the new system by trying to make the system appear as it always did.

One of the things that users usually insist on, of course, is accurate paper reports. Those reports have, over the years, become a definition of their work. Even though there has been much crowing about the benefits of the paperless office for some time now, it has not yet materialized. This does not mean, however, that the office has to be one or the other, entirely based on paper reports or entirely paperless; it is not an all-or-nothing kind of deal. The new system can reduce the amount of paper and still come out way ahead, and the biggest deterrent to being able to achieve great savings in information acquisition and turnaround is the end user who may be emotionally tied to the reports. It has been their private database; they have been able to mark it up, highlight it, and in general own it. Now, all of a sudden, the new system threatens to take that away from them, and the new database is in a magic box that the end user does not yet know how to access.

Managers must sell the benefits of online information as opposed to printed information. It is to the corporation's benefit to head in this direction, as many of the modern database systems are oriented toward online information retrieval, as opposed to printed information. True, the new system can be created to replicate the old reports, but this approach misses one of the major benefits of an online database.

DATA HISTORY IN THE NEW SYSTEM

Legacy systems typically have a particular way of trapping the data's history. Some remove the record, or a copy of it, to another file. Others record the history within the record itself. A relational database, however, is designed to model the current data flow. It is a model of the current data within the organization. The model reflects the data as it is rather than as it was. Usually, the plan should be to trap the information in a number of historical tables, which must be designed at the outset.

CONCLUSION

In general, time for planning is crucial. Conversions succeed or fail in the planning stage. The management challenge is most often seen as technical, but there are many areas to manage in such an endeavor. The technical planning is a critical activity, but so are managing expectations of the new system, selling the capabilities of the new system, and providing a plan to implement those capabilities into company strategic tools that help put the organization ahead of the competition.

There has never been a conversion that was "over planned"; however, many that not been planned in sufficient detail to succeed.

Chapter 13 Design, Implementation, and Management of Distributed Databases— An Overview

Elizabeth N. Fong
Charles L. Sheppard
Kathryn A. Harvill

A DISTRIBUTED DATABASE ENVIRONMENT ENABLES A USER TO ACCESS DATA RESIDING ANYWHERE IN A CORPORATION'S COMPUTER NETWORK, without regard to differences among computers, operating systems, Data Manipulation Language, or file structures. Data that is actually distributed across multiple remote computers will appear to the user as if it resided on the user's own computer. This scenario is functionally limited with today's distributed database technology; true distributed database technology is still a research consideration. The functional limitations are generally in the following areas:

- Transaction management.
- Standard protocols for establishing a remote connection
- Independence of network topology

Transaction management capabilities are essential to maintaining reliable and accurate databases. In some cases, today's distributed database software places and responsibility of managing transactions on the application

0-8493-0893-3/00/$0.00+$.50

program. In other cases, transactions are committed or rolled back at each location independently, which means that it is not possible to create a single distributed transaction. For example, multiple site updates require multiple transactions.

TODAY'S TECHNOLOGY

In today's distributed database technology, different gateway software must be used and installed to connect nodes using different distributed database management system (DBMS) software. Therefore, connectivity among heterogeneous distributed DBMS nodes is not readily available (i.e., available only through selected vendor markets). In some instances, distributed DBMS software is tied to a single Network Operating System. This limits the design alternatives for the distributed DBMS environment to the products of a single vendor. It is advisable to select a product that supports more than one Network Operating System. This will increase the possibility of successfully integrating the distributed DBMS software into existing computer environments. In reality, distributed databases encompass a wide spectrum of possibilities including:

Remote terminal access to centralized DBMSs (e.g., an airline reservation system)

- Remote terminal access to different DBMSs, but one at a time (e.g., Prodigy, CompuServe, and Dow Jones)
- Simple pairwise interconnection with data sharing that requires users to know the data location, data access language, and the log-on procedure to the remote DBMS
- Distributed database management with a generic Data Definition Language and a Data Manipulation Language at all nodes
- Distributed update and transaction management
- Distributed databases with replication that support vertical and horizontal fragmentation
- "True" distributed DBMSs with heterogeneous hardware, software, and communications

The definition of distributed DBMSs lies anywhere along this spectrum. For the purpose of this article, the remote terminal access to data as discussed in the first two bullets in the preceding list is not considered a distributed DBMS because a node in the distributed DBMS must have its own hardware, central processor, and software.

MANAGEMENT MOTIVATION

Some of the problems that currently frustrate managers and technicians who might otherwise be interested in exploring distributed database solutions include:

- A distributed database environment has all of the problems associated with the single centralized database environment but at a more complex level.
- There is a lack of basic step-by-step guides covering the analysis, design, and implementation of a distributed database environment.

A distributed database management system offers many benefits. However, there are also many architectural choices that make the application design for distributed databases very complex. To ensure an effective and productive distributed database environment, it is essential that the distributed environment be properly designed to support the expected distributed database applications. In addition, an effective design will depend on the limitations of the distributed DBMS software. Therefore, implementing today's distributed database technology requires identifying the functional limitations of a selected commercial product. Identification of these limitations is critical to the successful operation of an application in a distributed database environment.

DISTRIBUTED DATABASE DEVELOPMENT PHASES

Effective corporation wide distributed database processing is not going to happen overnight. It requires a carefully planned infrastructure within which an orderly evolution can occur. The four major development phases are: planning, design, installation and implementation, and support and maintenance.

The Planning Phase

The planning phase consists of the very high-level management strategy planning. During the planning phase, an organization must consider whether it is advantageous to migrate to a distributed environment. This article assumes that migration to a distributed environment is desirable and feasible and that the corporate strategy planning issues and tasks has been identified. The result of this phase is the total management commitment for cost, resources, and a careful migration path towards a distributed database environment.

The Design Phase

The design phase is concerned with the overall design of the distributed database strategy. The overall design task involves the selection of a distributed DBMS environment in terms of the hardware, software, and the communications network for each node and how these elements are to be interconnected. The design of the distributed database environment must incorporate the requirements for the actual distributed database application. The overall design divides into two main tasks: the detailed design of the distributed database environment and the detailed design of the initial distributed database application. In certain cases, the initial application may be a prototype that is intended to pave the way for the full-production distributed database application.

The Installation and Implementation Phase

This phase consists of the installation and implementation of the environment that provides basic software support for the distributed DBMS application. The task of developing the distributed database application could occur in parallel with the installation of the environment.

The Support and Maintenance Phase

The support and maintenance phase consists of support for the distributed DBMS environment and the support and maintenance of the application. Although the same people can perform these support and maintenance tasks, the nature of the tasks and responsibilities are quite distinct. For example, the distributed application may require modification of report formats, while the distributed environment may require modification to add more memory.

CORPORATION STRATEGY-PLANNING

The main task during the strategic planning phase is to obtain the commitment of senior management. The measure of this commitment is the amount of resources—both personnel and equipment—necessary for the development of a distributed DBMS. The factors that must be considered during the strategy-planning phase are as follows:

- What are the objectives of the organization's next five-year plan?
- How will technological changes affect the organization's way of doing business?
- What resources are needed to plan for the development of, and migration to, a distributed DBMS?
- What tools or methods can be employed to develop and implement the plan?
- How will outcomes be measured relative to the impact on the organization's competitive position?

The corporate strategy plan must include detailed specifications of the total system lifecycle. It must also include a realistic timetable of schedules and milestones. Important consideration must be paid to the allocation of cost for new acquisitions, training of personnel, physical space requirements, and other tangible items.

During the strategic planning phase, information must be gathered on the organization's business functions and goals, related constraints and problem areas, and the organization's user groups. Only after the needed information has been gathered is it possible to develop high-level information categories and their interrelationships.

The process of developing the distributed database plan is iterative. Data administrators or information resource managers often perform the activities involved. Although these individuals often have the vision to recognize the long-term benefit of a distributed DBMS environment to an organization, they must rely on the participation and input of those in the organization who are directly involved with the business functions and use information to make decisions and manage operations. There must be considerable interaction among many different people in the organization, each of whom provides feedback to validate and refine the plans.

Strategic planning must first provide a sufficient justification for the expenditure of resources necessary to migrate to a distributed environment. Only after this justification has been accepted and fully approved by senior management can the task of initiating projects to design, develop, and implement a distributed DBMS environment and applications start.

OVERALL DESIGN OF DISTRIBUTED DATABASE STRATEGY

A distributed database environment consists of a collection of sites or nodes, connected by a communications network. Each node has its own hardware, central processor, and software that may, or may not, include a database management system. The primary objective of a distributed DBMS is to give interactive query users and application programs access to remote data as well as local data.

Individual nodes within the distributed environment can have different computing requirements. Accordingly, these nodes may have different hardware, different software, and they may be connected in many different ways. Some of the variations possible in the distributed database environment are discussed in the following sections.

Client/Server Computing

The most basic distributed capability is Remote Database access from single users at a node. A node may be a mainframe, a minicomputer, or a microcomputer (personal computer). The node that makes the database access request is referred to as a client node, and the node that responds to the request and provides database services is referred to as the server node. The association is limited to the two parties involved—the client and the server.

Exhibit 13-1 represents several different configurations available under a client/server-computing environment. The following are descriptions of the different configurations shown in the exhibit.

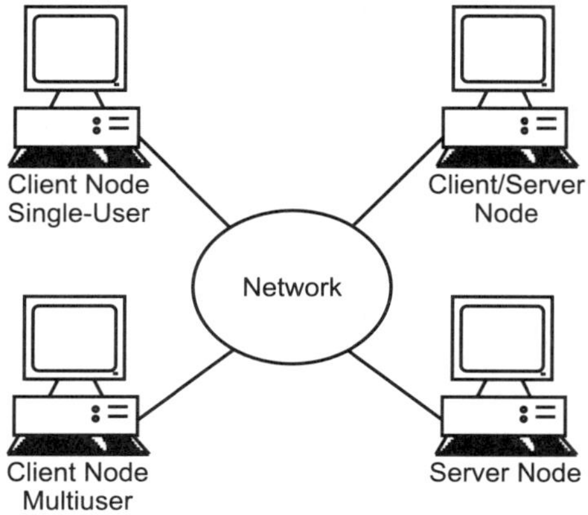

Exhibit 13-1. Client/server computing.

Client Single User Node. The operating environment of an individual node can be single-user or multi-user, depending on the operating system of that node. In a single-user operating environment, a node can be only a client. Such a node may or may not have databases. For non-database client nodes, the software typically consists of front-end application programs used to access remote database server nodes. This front-end software is generally in the form of end-user interface tools (e.g., a query language processor, a form processor, or some other application-specific program written in a third-Generation Language).

The front-end software formulates and issues user requests. It processes user requests through its established links with appropriate communications software. The front-end software only captures a user's request and uses communications software to send that request to a remote database node requesting its database management system to process the request. In addition to the capabilities outlined, single-user nodes with databases allow local data to be included in the same query operations specified for remote data. Therefore, operationally, the query results will appear as if all data is coming from a single central database.

Client Multi-User Node. The functional capabilities outlined for the client single-user node are expanded in the client multi-user node, because of the presence of a multi-user operating system at the user node. Such a configuration generally has several user processes running at the same time. At peak use time, the presence of several user processes can cause slower response time than is experienced in a client single-user node. The client multi-user node is more cost-effective, however, because it can allow multiple remote database accesses at different sites by different users at the same time. This is made possible through an identifiable list of remote server node locations. In addition, as with the client single-user node, the client multi-user node can include local database accesses in conjunction with accessing remote database.

Server Node. The server node is capable of providing database services to other client requests as well as for itself. It is a special multi-user node that is dedicated to servicing Remote Database requests and any local processes. This means that incoming requests are serviced, but it does not originate requests to other server nodes. The functional capabilities of a server node are as follows: this node must be included in the server list of some remote client node, there must be an operating DBMS, and there must be a continuously running process that listens for incoming database requests.

Client/Server Node. A node with a database can be a client as well as a server. This means that this node can service remote database requests as well as originate database requests to other server nodes. Therefore, the client/server node can play a dual role.

Homogeneous Distributed DBMS Environment

A completely homogeneous distributed DBMS environment exists when all the nodes in the distributed environment have the same DBMS but not necessarily the same hardware and operating system. However, the communication software for each node must use the same protocol to send or receive requests and data.

Design and implementation of a homogeneous distributed DBMS environment need involve only a single vendor. Any database request issued at a client node does not require translation, because the database language and data model are the same across all nodes in the network.

Heterogeneous Distributed DBMS Environment

In a truly heterogeneous distributed DBMS environment, the hardware, operating systems, communications systems, and DBMSs can all be different. Different DBMSs may mean different data models along with different database languages for definition and manipulation. Any database request issued at a client node would have to be translated so that the server node responding to the request would understand how to execute the request.

Various degrees of heterogeneity can exist. For example, within the distributed environment, different DBMSs can still be compatible if they all support the relational data model and understand SQL, a relational query language that is an American National Standards Institute and International Standards Organization standard. Presently, however, even among SQL conforming systems, there is no general communications software that will accept generic SQL statements from any other SQL conforming DBMS. This is an area in which the pending remote data access (RDA) standards are needed.

DISTRIBUTED ENVIRONMENT ARCHITECTURE

The design of a distributed database environment can be evolutionary — by incremental interconnection of existing systems, or by developing a totally new distributed DBMS environment using the bottom-up approach. Some of the design issues in adopting either approach are described in the following sections.

Interconnection of Existing Systems

Not all organizations have the luxury of developing the distributed database environment from scratch. Already existing database management applications are costly investments that are not likely to be replaced all at once by new distributed systems. The existing environment, including hardware, software, and databases, can be preserved by providing a mechanism for producing federated systems (i.e., systems composed of autonomous software components).

The federated approach is a practical, first-step solution toward a distributed database environment. It accommodates a legacy of existing systems while extending to incorporate new nodes. Therefore, it is important to select distributed DBMS software that supports existing computing hardware and allows for expansion. Within a federated system, pairs of nodes can be coupled in ways that range from very loose (i.e., each node is autonomous) to very tight (i.e., each node interacts directly with the other). The various forms of coupling affect the design, execution, and capability of the distributed applications.

The mode of coupling affects the number of translations required to exchange information between each site. Zero translations are needed when both components use the same representations. Some systems may choose to translate the data produced by one site directly to the format required by the other site. A more common method is to translate the data into a neutral format first, and then translate into the target format.

Loose Coupling. Loosely coupled systems are the most modular and in some ways are easier to maintain. This is because changes to the implementation of a site's system characteristics and its DBMS are not as likely to affect other sites. The disadvantage of loosely coupled systems is that users must have some knowledge of each site's characteristics to execute requests. Because very little central authority to control consistency exists, correctness cannot be guaranteed. In addition, loosely coupled systems typically involve more translations that may cause performance problems.

Tight Coupling. Tightly coupled systems behave more like a single, integrated system. Users need not be aware of the characteristics of the sites fulfilling a request. With centralized control, the tightly coupled systems are more consistent in their use of resources and in their management of shared data. The disadvantage of tight coupling is that because sites are interdependent, changes to one site are likely to affect other sites. Also, users at some sites may object to the loss of freedom to the central control mechanisms necessary to maintain the tight coupling of all the systems.

Cooperation Between Sites

For a truly distributed DBMS environment, a variety of methods are available to specify cooperation between sites. One way of classifying the distributed environment is to define the amount of transparency offered to the users. Another way is to define the amount of site autonomy available to each site, and the way sites interact cooperatively.

Degrees of Transparency. Transparency is the degree to which a service is offered by the distributed DBMS so that the user does not need to be aware of it. One example of transparency is location transparency, which means users can retrieve data from any site without having to know where the data is located.

Types of Site Autonomy. Site autonomy refers to the amount of independence that a site has in making policy decisions. Some examples of policy decisions include ownership of data, policies for accessing the data, policies for hours and days of operation, and human support. In addition, the cooperating federation of data administrators must approve all modifications to the site's data structures.

Interconnection of Newly Purchased Systems

An organization will have much more freedom if it decides to establish a distributed database environment from scratch. Currently, vendors are offering homogeneous distributed DBMSs with a compatible family of software. Specific details on how to configure the hardware, software, and communications equipment are discussed in the second article of this series. This approach, however, can lock the organization into a single vendor's proprietary distributed database products. Other approaches in selecting distributed architecture choices are as follows:

- Identical DBMS products at each node, with possibly different hardware environments but a single proprietary communications network to interconnect all sites.
- Standard conforming DBMS products at each node that rely on standard communications protocols

- Different DBMSs, using the same data model (e.g., relational), interconnected by a single or standard communications protocol
- Different DBMSs, using different data models (e.g., relational or object-oriented), interconnected by a single or standard communications protocol

Some distributed DBMS vendors offer a bridge (gateway) mechanism from their distributed database software to any foreign distributed database software. This bridge (gateway) may be obtained at additional development cost if it has not already been included in the vendor's library of available software.

In the design of a totally new distributed DBMS product, it is advisable to consider a mixture of standard conforming DBMSs and communications protocols. Because the technology and products are changing quickly, the designed architecture must be continuously reviewed to prevent it from being locked into an inflexible mode.

CONSIDERATION FOR STANDARDS

As the trend towards distributed computing accelerates, the need for standards, guidance, and support will increase. Application distribution and use will be chaotic unless there is an architectural vision and some degree of uniformity in information technology platforms. This is particularly true in client/server and workstation environments. To achieve this goal, a systems architecture incorporating standards to meet the users' needs must be established. This architecture must isolate the application software from the lower levels of machine architecture and systems service implementation. The systems architecture serves as the context for user requirements, technology integration, and standards specifications.

The benefits of standardization for both the user and the vendor are many. The number and variety of distributed DBMS products is increasing. By insisting that purchased products conform to standards, users may be able to choose the best product for each function without being locked into a specific vendor. Therefore, small to mid-sized vendors may effectively compete in the open marketplace. For effective planning and designing of a distributed DBMS environment, it is important for the designers to consider what standards already exist and what standards will be emerging to be able to incorporate standardized products.

There are many areas of a distributed DBMS environment in which standards should be applied. Some of the standards relevant to the design of a distributed DBMS include: communications protocols, application programming interfaces, data languages for DBMSs, data representation and interchange format, and remote data access.

Communications protocol standards are necessary so that systems from different products can connect to a communications network and understand the information being transmitted. An example of a communications protocol standard is the Government Open Systems Interconnection Profile (GOSIP).

The application programming interface standard is directed toward the goal of having portable applications. This enables software applications developed in one computing environment to run almost unchanged in any other environment. An example of an application programming interface standard is the Portable Operating System Interface for Computer Environments (POSIX).

The data languages commonly supported by a DBMS are the Data Definition Language, the Data Manipulation Language, and the data Control Language. An example of a standard data language for the relational DBMS model is SQL.

To exchange data among open systems, a standard interchange format is necessary. The interchange format consists of a language for defining general data structures and the encoding rules. An example of a standard data interchange language is Abstract Syntax Notation One (ASN.1).

An important standard for the distributed processing environment is the remote access of data from a client site to a database server site. A specialized remote data access protocol based on the SQL standard is currently under development.

CONCLUSION

To start the overall design process, a review of the organization's existing facilities should be conducted. This review is done to determine whether the new distributed database environment can use some or all of the existing facilities. In the decision to move into a distributed environment, requirements for additional functionalities must be identified. Such organizational issues as setting up regional offices may also be involved. The distributed architecture must take into consideration the actual application to be operating and the characteristics of the user population and the workloads to be placed on the system. Such architecture must also incorporate standardized components.

Chapter 14
Operating Standards and Practices for LANs

Leo A. Wrobel

THE FOLLOWING SCENARIO IS COMMON IN MANY ORGANIZATIONS: There are 200 local area networks (LANs) located across the country, in everything from small sales offices with a handful of people to regional distribution centers. The company does not know if these outlying locations handle mission critical data or not. The company does not know with certainty who is running these LANs, because it ranges from office managers and clerical employees right up to seasoned IS professionals. A site that once had 10 salespeople now has 9 salespeople and a LAN administrator. The company does not know how these sites are buying equipment, yet it is reasonably sure that they are paying too much, because they are not buying in bulk or enjoying any economies of scale in equipment purchases.

Locations are beginning to lean on IS for help desk support because there is no way they can keep up with the rapid proliferation of hardware, platforms, software, and special equipment being installed in the field. The telecommunications department is worried about connecting all of these locations together.

Although some attempts at standardization of these locations may be made, invariably, LAN managers in the field consider standards to be an attempt by the IS department to regain control of the LAN administrators environment. Because LAN managers seldom have had any input into what these standards would be, they were soundly rejected.

Today, there are literally thousands of companies fighting this same battle. This article gives some solutions to these problems. First, however, it is important to understand why standards are required and how IS can implement standards without stifling productivity or adversely affecting the organization.

0-8493-0893-3/00/$0.00+$.50

WHY LANS REQUIRE STANDARDS

Exhibit 14-1 compares two distinctly different operating environments: mainframes and LANs. To illustrate a point, Exhibit 14-1 uses the same adjectives that LAN and mainframe people use to describe each other.

Exhibit 14-1. Operational and maintenance characteristics.

Operational Characteristics	
MAINFRAME	LAN
"Stodgy"	"Seat-of-Pants Approach"
"Stoic"	"Close to Business"
"Regimented"	"Happy, Productive Users"
"Inflexible"	
"Stifles Productively"	
Maintenance Characteristics	
MAINFRAME	LAN
"Highly Advanced Support Systems"	"Evolving Support Systems"
"High-Level Help Desk Support"	"Difficult Help Desk Support"
"Reliable and Well-Proven"	"High User Involvement in Routine Problems"
"High Support-to-Device-Ratio"	"Low Support-to-Device Ratio"
"High Maintenance"	

In an ideal environment, the LAN administrator can select exactly the type of equipment best tailored to do the job. LAN managers are historically close to the core business. For example, if the company is involved in trading stock, the LAN operations department can go out and buy equipment tailored exactly to trading stock. If the organization is engaged in engineering, the LAN administrator can buy equipment exactly tailored to engineering.

From the standpoint of operational characteristics, LANs are far more desirable than mainframes because they are closer to the business, they empower people, and they make people enormously productive by being close to the core business. This is not the whole story, however. It is equally important to support LANs once they are in place. This is where the trade-offs come in.

Lessons from Mainframe Experience

Because mainframes have been around so long, there is a high degree of support available. When users in the mainframe environment call the help desk with a hardware or a software problem, the help desk knows what they are talking about. Help desk staff are well trained in the hardware and the software packages and can quickly solve the users problems.

As another example, in an IBM 3070 terminal environment, a single technician could support 100 terminals or more. When those terminals became PCs, the ratio perhaps dropped to 50 PCs per technician. When those PCs became high-end workstations, the ratio dropped even further. The value of a mainframe level of technical support cannot be underestimated.

Mainframe professionals had 20 years to write effective operating and security standards. These standards cover a number of preventive safeguards that should be taken in the operational environment to assure smooth operation. These range from:

- How often to change passwords
- How often to make backups
- What equipment should be locked up
- Who is responsible for change control
- Defining the standards for interconnecting between environments.

In the mainframe world it was also easy to make very large bulk purchases. Because the mainframe has been around for so long, many advanced network management systems currently existing provide a high degree of support and fault isolation.

Balancing Productivity and Support Requirements for LANs

To the LAN administrator, the perfect environment, productivity-wise, is one which any LAN administrator anywhere in a large company can go out and buy anything at any time—flexibility to buy equipment that is exactly tailored to the core business and that has the maximum effect in the way of enhancing productivity is highly desired in LAN environments. However, if someone calls the help desk, the help desk staff will not really be sure what they have out there, let alone how to troubleshoot it. In many ways, if the users buy an oddball piece of equipment, no matter how productive it makes them, they are on their own as far as supporting that equipment.

LANs have a characteristically high ratio of technologists required to support the environment. Today, sophisticated boxes sit on the desktop that demand a much higher level of maintenance. Human resources with information base knowledge sills are such a valuable commodity and so difficult with the trends for downsizing or rightsizing. Consequently, LAN administration is usually relegated to a firefighting mode, without a lot of emphasis on long-range planning.

Because LAN platforms are relatively new, in comparison to mainframes, there has not been as much time to develop operating and security standards. This is especially irritating to auditors when mission critical applications move from the traditional mainframe environment onto LANs and the protective safeguards around them do not follow. Something as simple as transporting a tape backup copy of a file between LAN departments can be extremely complicated without standards. What if everyone buys a different type of tape backup unit? Without standards on what type of equipment to use, bulk purchases of equipment become difficult or impossible.

Even though major improvements have been made in network management systems over the past five years, the management systems associated with LANs often lag behind those associated with mainframe computers. Again, this causes the company to pay penalties in the area of maintenance and ease of use.

One answer, of course, is to force users into rigid standards. While this pays a handsome dividend in the area of support, it stifles the users productivity. They need equipment well suited to their core business purpose.

An alternative is to let users install whatever they want. This may increase productivity greatly, though it is doubtful that a company could ever hire and support enough people to maintain this type of configuration. Worse, mission critical applications could be damaged or lost altogether is users are not expected to take reasonable and prudent safeguards for their protection.

It is the responsibility of both users and technologists to find the middle ground between the regimented mainframe environment and the seat-of-the-pants LAN environment. Through careful preplanning, it is possible to configure a set of standards that offers the advantage of greater productivity that is afforded by LANs, but also the advantages learned through 20 years of mainframe operations in the areas of support, bulk purchases, and network management.

The remainder of this article concentrates on exactly what constitutes reasonable operating and security procedures for both LANs and telecommunications.

STANDARDS COMMITTEES

One method is through the formation of a communications and LAN operating and security standards committee. An ideal size for a standards committee would be 10 to 12 people, with representatives from sales, marketing, engineering, support, technical services, including LANs, IS and telecommunications, and other departments. It is important to broaden this committee to include not only technologists, but also people engaged in the core business, since enhancement of productivity would be a key concern.

The actual standards document that this committee produces must deal with issues for both the operation and protection of a company s automated platforms. Subjects include:

- Basic physical standards, including access to equipment rooms, where PBX equipment is kept, what type of fire protection should be employed, standards for new construction, standards for housekeeping, and standards for electrical power
- Software security, change control, which people are authorized to make changes, and how these changes are documented
- The security of information, such as identifying who is allowed to dial into a system, determining how to dispose of confidential materials, determining which telephone conversations should be considered private, and the company's policy on telecommunications privacy
- Weighing options with regard to technical support of equipment
- Resolving issues regarding interconnection standards for the telecommunications network.
- Disaster backup and recovery for both LANs and telecommunications, including defining what users must do to ensure protection of mission critical company applications.

Defining "Mission Critical"

Before all of this, however, the committee is expected to define and understand what a mission critical application is. Because standards are designed to cover both operational and security issues, the business processes themselves must be defined, in order to avoid imposing a heavy burden with regard to security on users who are not engaged in mission critical applications, or by not imposing a high enough level of security on users who are.

Standards for equipment that is not mission critical are relatively easy. Basically, a statement such as, "The Company bought it, the shareholders paid for it, the company will protect it," will suffice. In practice, this means securing the area in which the equipment resides from unauthorized access by outside persons when there is danger of tampering or theft. It also includes avoiding needless exposures to factors that could damage the equipment, such as water and combustibles, and controlling food items around the equipment, such as soft drinks and coffee. The most one would expect from a user engaged in non-mission critical applications would be something that protects the equipment itself, such as a maintenance contract.

Mission critical equipment, however, has a value to the company that far exceeds the value of the equipment itself, because of the type of functions it supports. Determination of what constitutes a mission critical system should be made at a senior management level. It cannot be automatically assumed that technical services will be privy to the organization s financial data.

LAN and telecommunication equipment that supports an in-bound call center for companies such as the Home Shopping Club, would definitely be mission critical equipment, because disruption of the equipment, for whatever cause, would cause a financial hit to the company that far exceeds the value of the equipment. Therefore, mission critical equipment should be defined as equipment that, if lost, would result in significant loss to the organization, measured in terms of lost sales, lost market share, lost customer confidence, or lost employee productivity.

Monetary cost is not the only measurement with regard to mission critical. If an organization supports a poison-control line, for example, and loss of equipment means a mother cannot get through when a child is in danger, it has other implications. Because financial cost is a meaningful criterion to probably 90% of the companies, it is the measurement used for purposes of this discussion.

There is not necessarily a correlation between physical size and mission criticality. It is easy to look at a LAN of 100 people and say that it is more mission critical than another LAN that has only 4 people. However, the LAN with 100 people on it may provide purely an administrative function. The LAN with four people on it may have an important financial function.

WRITING THE OPERATING AND SECURITY STANDARDS DOCUMENT

In the following approach, it is recommended that two distinct sets of standards be created for mission critical versus non-mission critical equipment.

Network Software Security and Change Control Management

One item that should be considered in this section is, Who is authorized to make major changes to LAN or telecommunications equipment?

There is a good reason to consider this question. If everyone is making major changes to a system haphazardly, a company is inviting disaster, because there is little communication concerning who changed what and whether these changes are compatible with changes made by another person. Standards should therefore include a list of persons authorized to make major changes to a mission critical technical system. It should also have procedures for changing passwords on a regular basis, both for the maintenance and operation functions of LANs and telecommunications. Procedures should be defined that mandate a backup before major changes in order to have something to fall back on in case something goes wrong.

Procedures should be established to include Direct Inward System Access (DISA). Unauthorized use of DISA lines is a major cause of telecommunication fraud or theft of long-distance services. Automated attendants, for example, should also be secured and telephone credit cards properly managed. As a minimum, establish a procedure that cancels remote access and telephone credit to employees who leave the company, especially under adverse conditions.

Physical and Environmental Security

There should be a set of basic, physical standards for all installations, regardless of their mission critical status. These might include use of a UPS (uninterruptible power supply) on any LAN server. A UPS not only guards against loss of productivity when the lights flicker, but also cleans up the power somewhat and protects the equipment itself.

There should be standards for physically protecting the equipment, because LAN equipment is frequently stolen and because there is a black market for PBX cards as well. There should be general housekeeping standards as far as prohibitions against eating and drinking in equipment areas and properly disposing of confidential materials through shredding or other means. No-smoking policies should be included. Standards for storing combustibles or flammables in the vicinity of equipment should also be written.

Physical standards for mission critical applications are more intensive. These might include sign-in logs for visitors requiring access to equipment rooms. They may require additional physical protection, such as sprinkler systems or fire extinguishers. They may require general improvements to the building, such as building fire-resistant walls. They should also include protection against water, since this is a frequent cause of disruption, either from drains, building plumbing, sprinklers, or other sources.

Technical Support

The standards committee ideally should provide a forum for users to display new technologies and subject them to a technical evaluation. For example, a LAN manager or end user may find a new, innovative use of technology that promises to greatly enhance productivity in their department. They can present this new technology to the standards committee for both productivity and technical evaluations. The technologist on the committee can then advise the user of the feasibility of this technology; whether it will create an undue maintenance burden, for example, or whether it is difficult to support.

If it is found that this equipment does indeed increase productivity and that it does not create an undue maintenance burden, it could be accepted by the committee and added to a list of supported services and vendors that is underwritten by the committee. Other issues include what level of support users are required to provide for themselves, what the support level of the help desk should be, and more global issues, such as interconnection standards for a corporate backbone network and policies on virus protection.

CONCLUSION

The LAN operating and securities standards document is designed to be an organization s system of government with regard to the conduct and operation of technical platforms supporting the business. A properly written standards document includes input from departments throughout the organization, both the enhance productivity and to keep expenses for procurement, maintenance, and support under control. Standards also ensure that appropriate preventive safeguards are undertaken, especially for mission- critical equipment, to avoid undue loss of productivity, profitability, or equity to the company in the event something goes wrong. In other words, they are designed to prevent disruptions.

Use of a LAN operating and security standards committee is advised to ensure that critical issues are decided by a group of people with wide exposure within the company and to increase ownership of the final document across departmental boundaries and throughout the organization. If properly defined, the standards document will accommodate the advantages of the mainframe environment and needs of LAN administrators by finding the middle ground between these operating environments. By writing and adopting effective standards, an organization can enjoy the productivity afforded by modern LAN environments while at the same time enjoying a high level of support afforded through more traditional environments.

Section III
Data Access

ENTERPRISE METHODS OF DATA ACCESS HAVE SIGNIFICANTLY CHANGED OVER THE LAST TEN YEARS. A competitive edge is often based on the availability of reliable information at a moment's notice. The CIO is the final decision-maker for most of the standards for data availability and the methods to access data. Faced with that responsibility, the reality by data management staff is that more and more enterprise workers rely on the instant availability of accurate information within the structure of the enterprise's databases to perform daily activities.

Today's CIO and the associated data management staff are increasingly concerned about where the electronic information is stored and how readily enterprise knowledge workers gain access. The methods for gaining access to the data, whether in the office or from remote locations, present different challenges to internal data management staff than previously considered for many of the systems designed over the last 25 years. Coupled with the need for knowledge workers companywide to locate current data information is the need to maintain a secure environment for inbound and outbound information. Enterprise management is often lacking in realizing the complexity of the data available and the difficulty in changing access methods during adaptation of technology.

In addition, tracking the software usage of a more remote workforce also plays a significant role in planning data access. Establishing standards for software used enterprisewide as well as data access methods requires IT staff to look at deciphering which of the hundreds of available software programs are needed and by whom within the organization. The legal requirements to comply with the differing licensing rules imposed by software manufacturers are a necessary control point that is more difficult to manage in a network configuration, as compared with mainframe configurations.

The primary method of transmitting information to and from staff is via e-mail methods. Configuring the proper e-mail system to provide the level of service and security necessary to conduct business inter- and intracompany may require migration to a more suitable platform. As with any data migration effort, it is imperative that any change of this magnitude is coordinated and justified throughout the enterprise. As a mainstay to office intercommunications, this subject is dealt with in detail to help avoid the pitfalls that plague many migration efforts.

As more information regarding an enterprise is collected and available in electronic formats, providing useful access to the data residing in dissimilar databases becomes an even larger task. How enterprise knowledge workers require presentation of the data information available will often determine the structure that is needed to organize data warehousing standards and provide tools to successfully mine for data in a simple user-friendly manner. Data management needs are also expanding to include methods of storage and access to multimedia data sources, including video and audio, information without over-taxing the data management network resources utilized enterprise-wide. This requires consideration of network bandwidth and decisions with regard to the methods to gain access to the information.

A growing concern by data management staff is the synchronization process of remote data, subsets. This is key to ensuring accurate and current PC-based data, regardless of the user access point. The framework needed to support data synchronization is discussed for application by data management staff to a wide range of client and server database platforms and open enough to permit the needed degree of customization.

Information, regardless of its sophisticated context in the enterprise, is useless if it is not available when users need data to fill the responsibilities of their daily job. With network configurations, this suggests up-to-the-minute data be available on demand; hence, the need for advanced technology to insure data availability. Critical data systems, such as those required to service customers, may require special care to maintain highly available resources to access data on demand. Rarely can an enterprise operate without telephone services. So it becomes with data to achieve the same level of reliability enjoyed by telephone systems.

This section helps the CIO, separate the methods and standards that might provide a technology plan to ensure reliable data access required by the enterprise. The following chapters explore the types of data that may be needed, standard practices that may require expansion or incorporation to the corporate culture, transition from one kind of data repository to another, and application of the technology available to help maximize data access in an increasingly demanding enterprise data management systems environment.

- Using Database Gateways for Enterprisewide Data Access
- Remote Access Concepts
- Software Management: The Practical Solution to the Cost-of-Ownership Crisis
- Enterprise Messaging Migration
- Online Data Mining
- Placing Images and Multimedia on the Corporate Network
- Data Subsets — PC-based Information: Is It Data for the Enterprise?
- Fail-over, Redundancy, and High-Availability Applications in the Call Center Environment

Chapter 15
Using Database Gateways for Enterprisewide Data Access

Martin D. Solomon

WHENEVER CLIENT/SERVER OR INTERNET-BASED SYSTEMS ARE DEVELOPED AND INTRODUCED INTO EXISTING LARGE-SIZE INFORMATION SYSTEMS ENVIRONMENTS, the need to have bidirectional access to legacy data is inevitable. Few developers have the luxury of building these systems without first having to inquire against or update to other databases or files somewhere else in the organization's infrastructure.

There are many software options for communicating with the various platforms. Primary choices include masking and screen scraping, advanced program-to-program communications (APPC), database gateway software, messaging software, and file transfer techniques.

This chapter is intended to help database managers understand how database gateways work, whether these products can provide effective solutions for their organizations' business issues, and how to choose and set up the gateway software, hardware, and support infrastructure.

DATABASE GATEWAY SETUP

All database gateways provide a translation stop or box hop so that the data being shipped can be manipulated for arrival at the destination stop (see Exhibit 15-1). This stop takes the form of a gateway server and provides varying degrees of service, including data translation, resource governing software, and load balancing or connection management tools. This server also manages the communications links and options between the data resources on the host and server platforms. This software is installed and coupled on its host and server counterparts in the enterprise at the

0-8493-0893-3/00/$0.00+$.50

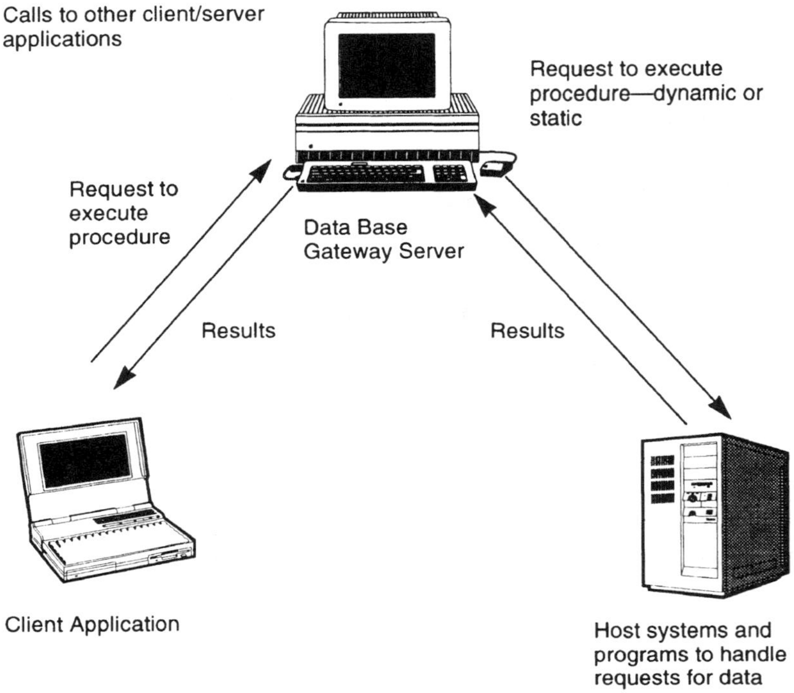

Exhibit 15-1. Client initiated remote procedure call (RPC) to host.

location of the user's choice. Frequency and size of the requests coming through this stop determine performance and whether multiple gateway servers are required.

DATABASE GATEWAY CAPACITY PLANNING

Several variables must be considered when choosing database gateway hardware and operating system software. Variables include maximum expected number of concurrent user connections to the gateway server, estimated daily and peak amounts of data to be passed through the gateway server, and the network protocols to be used in gateway access.

Concurrent User Connections

Concurrent user connections are a key determining factor in capacity planning because each user connected to the gateway hardware reserves memory on the server for address space, as much as 256K bytes per user, depending on the gateway software. To determine this parameter, it is important to know what types of applications are traversing the gateway and to gather information pertaining to performance expectations and the types of functions exploited on the gateway.

SQL Access. Many database gateways also support dynamic SQL access for updates to the host data store. Depending on the type of front-end tool used to perform these accesses, data integrity in DB2 for example, may only be assured by carrying a conversational transaction into the transaction processing (TP) monitor (e.g., customer information control system [CICS]). This usually forces the client running the application to remain connected to the gateway and to the TP monitor for extended periods of time to ensure the integrity of the data. Therefore, a moderate-size departmental application performing data access in this manner could end up maintaining a relatively large number of gateway and TP monitor resources throughout the day if the gateway connections are allocated when the user opens the application.

Static Remote Procedure Calls. In applications performing static remote procedure calls (RPCs) to the host, performance requirements become the key issue. Assuming that the application RPCs are constructed with stable, single-transaction units of work, the client application has no inherent need to maintain a continuous connection to the gateway server to preserve data integrity once the unit of work or transaction is completed. Each access, however, requires the establishment of a new address space on the gateway and a possible security-check exit routine. This can take anywhere from 50 to 500 milliseconds, depending on the processing speed of the gateway server and network configuration. The additional time spent on reestablishing a connection should be carefully evaluated when designing the application.

Low- and High-Volume OLTP. Low-volume processing, which can be loosely defined as fewer than 2500 online teleprocessing (OLTP) transactions per day, does not usually justify the tradeoff of using more memory and incurring the associated costs for the gain of about 200 milliseconds per transaction. High-volume OLTP type systems with upwards of 25,000 transactions per day generally require continuous connectivity to provide high-level response times for users.

In both cases — and especially if the expected use of the system cannot be clearly predicted as being at either end of the spectrum — it is worthwhile to invest the short amount of time it takes to code the system for either option. Any number of simple techniques can be used to develop a dynamic switch-type function to toggle the application between a continuous stay-connected mode and that of reestablishing a connection with each cross-platform request. This capability is even more valuable if several applications are expected to share a common database gateway server.

Amount of Data Passing Through the Server

The second determining factor in choosing the gateway hardware and operating system is the amount and frequency of data passed through the gateway server. The limits of technology still dictate that high-volume OLTP-type applications using the gateway should only send a relatively small amount of data for the average transaction, probably on the order of 1 to 2K bytes to ensure acceptable response time.

Frequently, however, database gateways are shared with other applications and ad hoc query users. With regard to multiple stable applications using static RPC calls, if the hardware requirements have been met for user connections, and the 1 to 2K bytes data-per-request maximum is adhered to, the amount of data being transported can also be managed adequately, provided the transaction workload is evenly distributed throughout the processing time periods.

Planning for ad hoc use and large data transfers (scheduled or otherwise) to and from the host and client/server DBMS poses a larger problem. Some database gateways can transfer large amounts of data across platforms (often to and from the host) using bulk copy functions. Nearly all gateways allow for ad hoc access to the host DBMS through user-friendly query tools. Either of these activities performed during peak processing times could severely impact response times for static applications or even affect host performance in unrelated applications.

For ad hoc query use, user education and tight control through the use of DBMS resource monitors and governors can go a long way in preventing gateway performance problems and maintaining an equally shared resource. If large queries and bulk copy functions must move an excess of about 100K bytes of data more than several times a day, then consideration must be given either to moving these functions to off-hours or acquiring a separate gateway server for those needs.

Network Protocols

Because most database gateway products are available for nearly all protocols, it is logical to remain consistent with the network architecture of the organization. A brief investigation into which protocols are supported by the vendor should be undertaken; but for the most part, performance of database gateway accesses are determined by the application design. If the database gateway applications or users request that large amounts of data be shipped across the network, a brief check should also be made with the network support area to ensure that the infrastructure is in place to support that requirement.

Hardware

Because the hardware choice for a database gateway server is fully dependent on transaction volumes, the amount of data shipped across the gateway, and the number of expected concurrent user connections, the remaining issue will be whether to choose Intel-based or RISC-based processors. In general, the latest Intel processors can comfortably handle at least 1000 moderate-sized (defined as less than 2K bytes each) gateway transactions per hour, with some room to spare for some ad hoc query activity. For higher volumes, or in anticipation of a significant ad hoc query component, it is recommended that a low-end RISC-based unit be acquired so that potential bottlenecks are avoided. In cases where transaction volumes may be low but a high number of concurrent connections (i.e., more than 300) are expected, the memory needed to support this requirement may tip the scales in favor of the RISC platforms, which can support more memory capacity.

In cases where usage is underestimated, adding additional gateway servers is an option, but load balancing between multiple servers in addition to maintenance and disaster recovery considerations could add substantial "hidden" costs to the effort. Disk space should be of no concern in either case, because entire gateway software packages and any logs that are required will not take up more than 200MB. Also, it is recommended that in production, gateway software be installed on dedicated computers.

GATEWAY-TO-HOST SECURITY

Gateway security is often not considered until after the product is in-house and already being used for development. Ideally, the gateway security exits and processing should fit in with the existing security software infrastructure. However, this is almost never the case.

Most standard mainframe-based security packages can interrogate LU6.2-based transaction processing for valid logon IDs and passwords. Delivery of the resulting messages from the attempted logon back to the workstation executing the applications is a much more complicated issue. The application generally requires customized code to decipher the message received from the host security package and must know how to react to any number of situations, including a combination of incorrect or expired IDs or passwords. In addition, the application is likely to be accessing other systems and software on other platforms that have their own security logic.

For gateway-specific applications, the user may also be accessing other systems and products directly through an unrelated application or tool and traverse the same proprietary security system at the same time. As a result, the user might on occasion log on to the gateway application with a given password, then at some point later, log on to another application system and be informed that his/her password has expired in the interim. If the system includes an E-mail system and an additional RDBMS on different platforms, for example, the potential for frustration is even greater.

Most security packages included with the gateway software are not robust enough to handle even the gateway-to-host security issues involved. A better method, and one that requires the most effort, is to standardize a custom-built front-end security application that automatically reviews and synchronizes user IDs and passwords across all products and platforms when users boot up their workstation. To minimize the inconvenience of this undertaking, the gateway security issues between client and host software could be the first to be addressed in a phased-in approach. Front-end security software could be developed or modified in concert with implementing the test gateway instances and continued through production.

Other alternatives include setting up unsecured gateway access to the host, or having the individual application support personnel code routines. Both of these methods, however, can lead to much larger problems and security risks in the long run.

TECHNICAL SUPPORT

Because they are one of the most complex software products to support, database gateways require coordinated efforts from several system support groups (see Exhibit 15-2). Without the ability to quickly access experts from the database (e.g., mainframe and client/server), OLTP (e.g., CICS), network, workstation, and operating system support areas, resolving gateway problems can prove troublesome.

As with most distributed client/server systems, locating the problem is usually the most time-consuming and difficult part. If the application that uses the gateway solution is not functioning properly, the problem could be purely a workstation health issue or it could indicate network problems

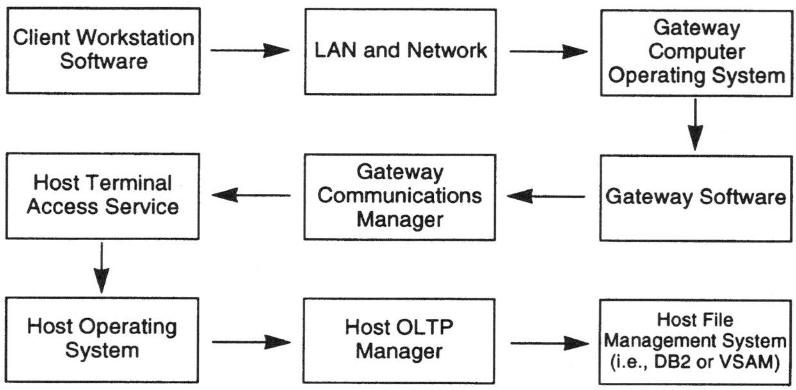

Exhibit 15-2. The path of database gateway access requests.

to the host processor and related software and hardware experiencing an outage. The potential for loss of valuable time is great if, for example, the problem is the unavailability of a particular mainframe database table, yet the individuals who are working to locate the problem are not familiar with or are not in the notification chain for such issues.

The Help Desk. To streamline the process as much as possible, it is recommended that if an information systems help desk is available, the help desk staff should be trained to filter as many gateway-related problems as possible. This means giving help desk personnel documentation that relates how each database gateway instance is connected to each network address, OLTP system, and mainframe database subsystems. Therefore, if DB2 is unavailable, the support staff knows that any gateway traffic using that system is potentially impaired or may not be functioning at all. Because most database gateways rely on the proper functioning of other software products, the alternative to not having a help desk could be longer work interruptions and incorrect support personnel being notified to investigate problems.

Usage Considerations

Most database gateway software is relatively easy to use from a developer and end-user perspective. Nearly all of the complexities of cross-platform and heterogeneous data access are resolved during software installation and setup. Systems programmers handle maintenance and other access requirements behind the scenes. In most cases, the programmer only has to provide a few lines of source code plus minor modifications to a couple of client workstation files to provide access to the desired database or file. Once a few minor modifications are made and the proper drivers are installed, ad hoc users only need to start the desired front-end software program and host access to any number of host databases and files is possible.

The gateway solution may not provide the best fit for every situation, however. One example is an application that provides the client with all of the updates to a particular file unique to that user since the request was last made. Although coding this access using the gateway may be simple, the actual access is relatively time-consuming and resource intensive. A better choice may be a messaging solution where those updates are delivered at regular intervals in the background so that when the request is made, the results are essentially fully in place and quickly available. Similar examples can be found for other types of middleware connectivity choices.

DISASTER RECOVERY

The database gateway server should be placed in a restricted access area, just like any other critical LAN server in the IS shop. The only case to be made against this recommendation is if remote systems management of the gateway software is not possible and maintenance is scheduled frequently. Except for a departmental-type test gateway, this is usually not recommended.

Because the gateway server does not contain any client data, only the customized software to provide a conduit to it, maintaining a hot spare locally or off-site is relatively easy. The cost of the hardware may be a limiting factor for an off-site unit, but local hot or warm spares can be set up on the test servers for emergency use. This can usually be accomplished by setting up and maintaining all of the production software, information, and the required customization on the designated test or development machine. If a major problem arises, the development server can be quickly switched to production mode until the problem is resolved. Depending on the stability of the test environment and the size of the machine, testing may have to be curtailed or discontinued during the outage.

ADD-ON SOFTWARE

Host as Client Processor. In most cases, the database gateway traffic consists of requests from the workstation or client/server database to the host, whether it be to query large mainframe data stores or to perform required updates to those files or databases. In some cases, however, it is necessary for a host-based process to initiate access to server-based data during the course of processing. Some gateway vendors offer additional software that can be installed for this process. Although this type of processing can also be accomplished with native-based code, it may be desirable to have these processes performed through this controlled software with built-in features similar to those used when processing client requests. In either case, it is something that should be considered.

Joins Across Engines and Files. Many database gateway vendors offer products in addition to the core gateway software that allows dynamic joins across platforms and data file systems. This could range from joining host and client/server relational data as well as host files (e.g., virtual storage access method [VSAM] or sequential). To have such capabilities, a careful watch must be kept on ad hoc queries to prevent CPU resource overuse.

For cases of reasonable ad hoc use where the business requires limited data multisource data access, however, this piece of add-on software could be quite beneficial. As with the core gateway software, these products require complex systems support and maintenance in the background. The relatively steep cost of these products may also play a role in evaluating the need for the additional capabilities provided.

Other Options. Although database gateways provide a great range of functionality for access to disparate data platforms and data stores, the relatively high cost of purchase and deployment may not be justified. This is especially true when just a few small applications require data access across platforms. In these cases, the two primary alternatives are the use of Open Database Connectivity (ODBC) drivers and the TCP/IP File Transfer Program (FTP). Virtually all GUI front-end software is ODBC-compliant. When examining this option, it is important to keep in mind the cost of purchasing an ODBC site license or individual driver for each client. ODBC transactions frequently incur significant overhead, causing them to run slower than those run across gateways.

The FTP process, on the other hand, allows the best performance for data transfer, but requires additional resources to code the data transfers required at each location. Depending on application requirements, this effort can be very complex and require a fairly large commitment of skilled resources to develop.

Web Connectivity

On the tails of the rapidly increasing use of the Internet is the need to integrate HTML and Java Web page scripting languages to back-end databases and files. Because gateway software already provides the analogous access from front-end GUI tools to back-end data stores, this added functionality is the next logical step for this middleware component. Several leading gateway software vendors are beta testing this functionality in terms of gateway add-on components and ODBC drivers to accommodate Web page languages.

At this early stage, issues regarding capacity, performance, and security are similar to those already discussed. Again, extra careful consideration must be given to dynamic calls and front-end application security.

CONCLUSION

With a small investment in research and analysis, database gateway software can be quickly implemented and provide relatively straightforward and efficient access to disparate data stores across the enterprise. It is, however, important to carefully consider usage and support requirements before acquisitions begin. Among the key issues to remember:

- The software is best suited for light to moderate OLTP-type processing to and from the host platforms, as well as for enabling controlled ad hoc access to mainframe RDBMSs.
- Although use of the software is simple, background support is complex and usually involves several areas of expertise within the organization. Building and orchestrating an efficient line of support for the

gateway product is essential in providing continuous availability through the different platforms.

- Security requirements and routines should be provided concurrently with gateway deployment.
- Because the gateway provides easy access to many environments, it is crucial that the actual use of the tool for specific applications is carefully reviewed to ensure that it is the correct technology for the situation.

Chapter 16
Remote Access Concepts

Gerald L. Bahr

INTRODUCTION

AS WE BEGIN THE NEW CENTURY, MY CRYSTAL BALL TELLS ME THAT WE ARE SOMEWHERE IN THE MIDDLE OF THE INFORMATION AGE. With not only the ability, but the need to have ready access to all sorts of information from anywhere on the globe, we have come to expect that we will have ready availability to any information that we need, day or night. Whether we are in the office, telecommuting, or temporarily mobile, we naturally expect to have access to the resources necessary for us to do our job efficiently and accurately.

This chapter will discuss two different approaches — remote node and remote control — with variations on remote control for accessing data, whether we are temporarily mobile or hardly ever seen in the office, building on the resources of Microsoft's Windows NT 4.0.

DRIVING FORCES

With the advent of the Internet, intranet, telecommuting, email, and voice mail, we have come to expect that we can have ready access to any data warehouse that will make users more productive, entertain, or make our lives more productive.

It is estimated that many large corporations are spending between $500,000 to over $1,000,000 per year to support remote access for their employees. This does not include the costs for the laptops that are used in the office as well as on the road. It is directed only toward server hardware and software and supporting equipment and dial-up access lines.

TWO APPROACHES — REMOTE NODE VS. REMOTE CONTROL

The remote node approach lets the remote client act just like another computer on the network. All files that are accessed by the remote client are transferred across the line. The responsiveness that the remote client

0-8493-0893-3/00/$0.00+$.50

experiences depends on the size of the file and speed of the line transfer session during access.

The remote control approach has two variations. These two variations use a computer as the "server" located at the central site to provide all the computational power and ability to communicate with all local resources. Remote control sends only key strokes from the remote client to the server, and screen updates from the server come across the line to the remote client. This can easily increase the responsiveness to the remote client by two to four times or more than that of the remote node approach.

Both the remote node and remote control hardware configuration and topology are essentially the same. What makes the difference in operation is the software on the Windows NT Access Server. Each of them has advantages and disadvantages.

Remote Control — Two Variations

Variation 1. Software is loaded on a dedicated "server" computer running Windows NT. This software supports someone calling in and taking control of that computer. Literally, anything that can be done from the local keyboard can be done from the remote client. This method requires a dedicated computer for each simultaneous caller. If remote clients are using different operating systems, you will most likely need to have different telephone lines directed to a specific server supporting that operating system.

Variation 2. This variation of remote control runs software that allows many simultaneous users (primarily determined by the applications being accessed and the configuration of the computer) to call into the same computer. Each remote client runs in its own environment within Windows NT; thus each remote user looks like a separate entity on the operating system and the network.

Since neither one of these methods requires serious computing power on the remote client side (all computational work is done on the server), the user might get by with a 286 running DOS or Windows 3.1 or a 386 or higher class machine running Windows 3.1, Windows 3.11, Windows 95, or Windows NT 4.0 Workstation. This can allow some companies to take advantage of the capital investment that has not been depreciated yet.

Advantages

- Client workstations generally do not require upgrades very often.
- Deploying a new application is simplified because it is handled at the central office.
- Upgrades are centrally administered.

- Even though the application is running on the central server, users can normally still load or save files to local drives, print to locally attached printers, cut and paste information between a remote and a local application, or drag and drop to copy files in the background.
- The look and feel of the applications is the same on the road as in the office.
- The remote application performs as fast as it would when running directly on the LAN.
- Users have access to the same database, along with all other productivity applications they are familiar with.
- Large databases are left intact; they do not have to be segmented.
- Sensitive information is not replicated to laptops; it can remain within the secured boundaries of the LAN.
- Remote workstations, which lack sufficient processing power, are able to run workgroup applications on-line from almost anywhere.

Disadvantages

- Normally there is a large up-front cost.
- It does not fit well into small systems.
- If a server fails, all of the users on that server are not serviceable.
- It is potentially a large network traffic generator.
- May need to be placed on a separate network segment.
- Requires a powerful computer for the server.
- Requires the purchase of additional software for the server.
- Some applications, like email, are more difficult to use in the off-line mode, because remote control does not automatically download the files needed to work off-line.
- If the single session option is selected, it might require different telephone numbers for each remote client operating system.
- Off-line work is more difficult, because files are not available on the local workstation.
- May require more support lines because on-line time may be longer (some off-line functions not supported).

Remote Node

With the introduction of LANs (Local Area Networks) the philosophy of shared wiring, high data transmission rates, and local computing (smart devices) came into being. This approach uses the LAN wiring system to download executable files as well as large image and database files to the local desktop computer.

Remote node access mirrors this same approach. Since you must transfer all files across the modem line (those which you are using to gain access), you must have all of your applications loaded on the remote client. Even with the applications loaded locally, the user may get discouraged with the responsiveness of the system if the file accessed is more than 50kB to 100KB.

Advantages

- Smaller up-front cost.
- Look and feel (visual) of being locally connected to the network.
- Might be able to use an older, less costly computer for server.
- Packaged with Windows NT.
- All commands, either command line or Windows, work just the same as if you were in the office.

Disadvantages

- Replication with several large databases takes too long and consumes a lot of disk space on the client system.
- To make replication more effective, large databases may have to be segmented into smaller databases. This can dramatically complicate the management of these databases.
- Because of the replication architecture, laptops carry sensitive corporate information. If your laptop is lost or stolen, security breaches can (and often do) occur.
- The client component requires a workstation with a minimum of a 486 processor, 8MB of RAM, Windows 3.1, or Windows 95, and a minimum of 500MB of disk space.
- Could generate some serious network traffic, depending on the number of users per server.
- Remote users often get discouraged waiting for large files to load.

Both remote control and remote nodes have been developed to support remote users. The one which is best for you depends on your computing environment and the method you use to provide the most features, functionality, ease of use, and security. Luckily, products are available that will support either approach on Windows NT 4.0 Server operating system.

NT REMOTE ACCESS SERVER

Dialing In

Determining the Number of Lines Required for Support. When considering the number of hunt lines you will need to support the number of remote users you have in your organization, keep in mind both the number of users and the type of applications which your users will be accessing. The telephone companies typically use a 1:10 ratio for the number of lines required vs. the number of subscribers. Keep in mind, however, that statistically the phone is only used for about 3 to 5 minutes at a time and usually with long periods of time in between.

This ratio may be reasonable for remote users who only access their email; however, if users will be using the network for on-line file updates or any heavy office work, the line usage rate will go up considerably. Local virtual office users may tie up the line for 8 hours or more at a time, while other users who are traveling may very well tie up a line for an hour or more at a time.

Local users will probably use the lines more in the daytime, while those who are traveling will most likely use the lines more during the evening hours. If you are looking for nonblocking access, you will need to consider incorporating a high number of lines for users — conceivably even a 1:1 ratio. Most modem pool systems range from between 1:3 to 1:8 lines to accommodate the number of users needing remote support.

Be sure that the number of lines that you finally determine to incorporate are placed in hunt groups (rotary) into common servers so that one number will serve many common users simultaneously.

Methods of Access

Modem Pools. Modem pools allow you to share the expense of modem hardware as well as the number of dial-in lines necessary to support the number of users who will be calling into your system. A modem usually supports analog voice dial-up lines with speeds normally at 33.6 Kbps. Some modems support 56.6 Kbps today, but are still having problems in trying to establish a real link at that speed. Keep in mind that many times a 33.6 Kbps modem won't establish reliable communications even at 33.6 Kbps speed because of noisy lines. This problem gets worse as you try to establish an analog link across the country. Aren't we glad that ISDN (Integrated Services Digital Network) is coming?

A modem pool can be configured from stand-alone modems that are already available or can be rack mounted with modems that are built to fill specific slots within the rack cabinet. If you anticipate the need for more than 12 modems, it would be wise to look at a rack-mounted unit that will provide for better support and cleaner installation.

A Windows NT Server with RAS (Remote Access Service) can support up to 256 simultaneous users and provide you with a stable, secure environment for dial-in clients. Choosing hardware to support that many users is often not easy. Most interface devices provide access to multiple modems or ISDN terminal adapters; however, they are only available in four-, eight-, or possibly 16-port versions. This may be sufficient to get you started, but large systems will probably grow out of this configuration very quickly.

ECCI has a selection of devices that will allow you to provide from four-port ISA adapters to a rack-mounted modem pool unit that will allow you to reach or exceed Windows NT's limit of 256 sessions or beyond with port speeds up to 115kbs transfer rates. If you anticipate serving more than 64 dial-in devices from a single server, you need to consider using a SCSI interface to external support boxes. This will allow you to chain more than seven rack-mount type boxes that will support multiple modems. With this approach, you can physically support more than the 256 simultaneous sessions.

Be careful, however. Don't exceed the load demand that the server itself can handle. This will vary depending on the manufacturer, the number of CPUs, and the amount of memory and I/O bus that your server can handle. If you anticipate numerous lines being serviced by a single server, you will want to use I/O boards that support their own CPU on board. The boards will cost more, but they will help to offload the server CPU and will allow you to provide high performance with less expensive server hardware.

ISDN Access. With the advent of telecommuting and Internet access, ISDN for wide area access has grown considerably in the last two years. The advantages of ISDN are many.

Advantages

- With ISDN you have dial-up access just the same as with the POTS (Plain Old Telephone System) that we are all used to. The only caution is that it is not available in all parts of the country.
- Instead of being limited to the high end rate of 33.6 Kbps with the modems mostly in use today, you can get access at 128 Kbps. With compression, a realized throughput can be as high a 500Kbps.
- You get two telephone lines that can be used for either voice or data or a combination of both. If you are using the two B (bearer) channels for data, you will have a data rate of 128 Kbps.
- Without band signaling on the D channel you can see (using caller ID) who is calling, even when both B channels are being used. If you answer the phone, then the data automatically rolls back to 64 Kbps. When the call is completed, it will return to 128 Kbps data rate.
- ISDN will connect within three to five seconds vs. the 20/40 seconds for the POTS network we are used to.

Cautions

- Not all areas of the country support ISDN at this time, so be sure to check with your local telephone company to determine availability.
- Because it is fairly new, however, not all personnel are familiar with it so you need to be specific with the carrier as to what you want.

- Standards are not fully developed yet, so stay with vendors who are reputable and well established in the market. As in the early stages of modem usage, not all manufacturers support the same features, particularly compression technology. This is probably still the biggest problem between ISDN equipment manufacturers, so if you plan to use compression, it would be wise to use the same vendors and equipment on both ends. You may wish to verify that the manufacturers you are considering will support the same compression and will be able to communicate with each other.

FRAME RELAY — PUBLIC OR PRIVATE NETWORK

Frame relay is a technology that you will need to support if you have your own private network which you wish to use to connect remote offices together. It works well for bursty traffic and is typically found in computer WANs (Wide Area Networking). If your company is planning to connect to the public networks that are primarily dedicated to computer networking, it is almost certain that you will be using frame relay technology.

If you have your own WAN implementation, you will only need to know the technology being implemented when you purchase and configure equipment. In this case, you will want to use a router to interface between the WAN and the LAN side of the networks. If you connect to a public network such as the Internet, you will want to place a firewall between the WAN and LAN interfaces.

Routing

Windows NT Routing vs. an External Router. Windows NT 4.0 will support routing of various protocols. The most popular and the one I recommend is TCP/IP (Transmission Control Protocol/Internet Protocol). This protocol is extremely robust and has been designed and tested for the worst conditions in WAN applications. All WAN external routers support TCP/IP, so you are virtually guaranteed support. Windows NT 4.0 will support it in native mode and, unless you have a good reason to do otherwise, I would recommend that this be your protocol of choice.

Windows NT Server 4.0 supports MultiProtocol Routing as part of the operating system. This is an integral part of the operating system that lets Windows NT route a number of protocols simultaneously. This is fine for small applications, since the routing that Windows NT supports is not what you would call fast or fully functional.

If you are anticipating the server to support a small number of users connected to a small LAN (less than 25 nodes) and not connected to any other network, then you might consider using the routing services provided by Windows NT 4.0. It supports Novell's IPX/SPX transport, so you don't have to deploy TCP/IP on your internal network to give your enterprise Internet access. This provides some degree of security since IPX/SPX does not support client-to-client communications, thus preventing someone from the outside gaining access to any devices other than servers running IP. This configuration provides a good solution since it also negates the need for a firewall.

If, on the other hand, you have a lot of users that will be calling in and/or the remote access server is connected to a large LAN, then you will want to strongly consider an external, dedicated router as the interface between the LAN and WAN that you interface with.

An external router typically will support more protocols and be able to process them faster and in greater detail (i.e., filtering, routing, etc.) than would the routing features of Windows NT 4.0. Because an external router is dedicated to only one service, it can also handle the number of packets that are required of it much faster than the Windows NT server that you are asking to do double duty.

Keep in mind that if you want a speedy response and wish to reduce your possibility of failure, you may want to consider using more units to provide the functions that are critical to your organization's needs.

Firewall for Internet Connection. A router was originally used to provide firewall activities. Many people still use a router to serve that purpose as well. There is, however, a philosophical difference between a firewall and a router. In essence, a router is configured to pass all traffic unless explicitly told not to. A firewall is configured not to pass any traffic unless explicitly told to.

This makes a lot of sense since both can be a bit tedious to configure. You might not think of all the rules or ways in which you want to deny others access to your network; therefore, if they must go through a firewall you have had to take action to allow them in. Just make sure to be careful to whom you authorize access in your company.

The reason for this discussion will become clear when we discuss later another alternative for remote users to access your network via the Internet using PPTP (Point-to-Point Tunneling Protocol).

IP ADDRESSING (PPP FOR DIAL UP)

Dynamic IP Addressing

TCP/IP is the leading protocol for connecting dissimilar platforms and operating systems. It has been tested under virtually all adverse conditions, and because it has been around for a long time, it has developed into a very robust and routable protocol. It is based on a four octet address, however, which has limited its growth to the number of "hosts" (the name given to any computer that uses TCP/IP). TCP/IP has been divided into four classes of addresses. All the classes are assigned with, the exception of the class "C" address, and it is being "subnetted" to help give everyone reasonable access until the new numbering scheme called IPv6 can be effectively implemented.

Because all companies are faced with the same dilemma — running out of IP addresses — and because it provides easier maintenance of an IP network, many companies are implementing DHCP (Dynamic Host Configuration Protocol) servers.

DHCP Servers. If you have chosen to use TCP/IP as your primary protocol, then the protocol that you will use between the remote client and the server for dial-up access will be PPP (point-to-point protocol). This is the IP protocol that supports dial-up access. Since the number of IP addresses available is truly limited, you will want to use DHCP, which dynamically assigns IP addresses to users as they call in.

The main advantage of using DHCP is that it assigns addresses from a predefined pool of addresses, thus allowing users to share the same scarce set of addresses. It will also allow users to dial in via remote offices and use the company WAN (thus saving long distance charges) without worrying about the subnet class of address that the remote office might be using. In essence, it will give you and the user far greater flexibility.

Use of the DHCP relay agent will allow the server to relay DHCP messages to other DHCP servers. This allows your network to communicate with full-fledged DHCP servers on one network even if your network only has a DHCP relay agent.

DNS/WINS (Windows Internetworking Name Server). Because IP addresses are much harder for humans to remember than names, a system has been put in place that allows us to use names when we want to talk to other computing devices, while still allowing machines to talk to each other by numbered addresses.

This technology is referred to as DNS (Domain Name Service) for the Internet. Microsoft has developed another approach called WINS (Windows Internetworking Name Server) for networks that use Windows NT-type network operating systems.

The good thing is that Windows NT 4.0 supports both of them, either separately or simultaneously. Thus you can decide which is best for you and your particular environment.

USING THE INTERNET FOR REMOTE ACCESS

The Internet will soon provide us the ability to logon to the Internet from a local ISP (Internet Service Provider) in our local area and then gain access to our company data via the Internet. This obviously saves us long distance access charges, but can expose our company proprietary information to the world if we are not careful. Internet access adds an alternate method to gain access.

PPTP

Enter Microsoft's sponsored PPTP protocol. This specification is being jointly developed by 3Com Corp., Santa Clara, Calif.; Ascend Communications Inc., Alameda, Calif.; U.K.-based ECI Telematics; Microsoft Corp., Redmond, Wash.; and U.S. Robotics Inc., Skokie, Ill. This new specification will allow companies to establish virtual private networks by allowing remote users to access corporate networks securely across the Internet.

Once PPTP is widely supported, the remote user would simply dial into a local ISP and then his workstation wraps the data packets into an encrypted "tunnel" using PPTP. The data is then sent across the Internet into the corporate Windows NT 4.0 remote-access server. Once the PPTP packets reach the Windows NT server, they are routed, decrypted, and filtered (if internal routing is used) before being forwarded to the corporate LAN.

The advantage of this approach is not only the reduction of line charges, but the reduction in modem pools, and supporting equipment that must be maintained and upgraded.

Another nice feature is that PPTP requires few changes in client configuration. The ISP will need to make minor upgrades to their sites. Microsoft has also promised to make the specifications available to anyone. At this writing they are supposed to have submitted it to the Internet Task Force (a body that helps determine standards used on the Internet).

Scalability

Since Windows NT 4.0 and above support SMP (symmetrical multiple processors) and over 4 GB of memory with a wide variety of network interface adapters with over 256 modems, ISDN equipment, WAN adapters as well as LAN adapters — it is possible to start out small and allow your servers to grow with you as your needs grow.

If you use the server for remote node service, it will be able to handle more users with a given configuration than if it were providing remote control services. This is because it is much easier to route information than it is to run applications and then provide screen updates.

Although you could provide all the services on one server, there is a more important question. Should you? Keep in mind that the more you have on one piece of hardware, the more you have at risk when the hardware or software fails. Generally good engineering practice dictates that you spread your risk by having more than one way of routing or gaining access to the information that your users need access to.

Disaster Prevention

Backup/Restoration. When considering disaster recovery, disaster prevention is always the best policy. It has been proven many times that the cost of replacing the data (whether it be customer data or configuration data like that on a communications server) is almost always more than it is to replace the hardware and operating system software.

It is therefore imperative that a backup plan be developed and implemented. Next to enforcing security policies, this is probably the most important function that the network administrator can perform. The frequency with which the data will change will determine the frequency of backup. At the very least, two full backups should be made every month, with one copy maintained off site. This ensures that if one copy is destroyed by fire, flood, or theft you have another one that is no more than a month old. Obviously, if the data changes very frequently or involves a large number of changes, then weekly or even daily backup should be considered.

Also, make sure that you can restore the data that was backed up. Many people try to restore the data that was backed up, but don't have the proper drivers and/or procedures necessary to restore the data from a total system failure.

Power Protection/UPS

The other major area for prevention consideration is power protection. This means providing clean, isolated power running on a true UPS system. You should not employ the switched-type UPS systems that are typically used in the small LAN servers or workstations. The true UPS units provide better line regulation and lightning protection than the switched units. Also make sure the UPS will support the server for a minimum of fifteen minutes under full load, or longer if the rest of the servers/hosts are also on a UPS system. Remote users should have the same access time or notice to complete and logoff as the local users do.

Security

The best security you can have for your system is a well thought out security policy procedure which is consistently enforced. The proper use of passwords should make them expire after a period of time, and certain secure logoff procedures should be enforced. These are all part of providing security to business-critical information.

For users at virtual offices, dial-back procedures should be implemented. With the right equipment and caller ID, this can be made rather automatic. This, however, may require them to have two different logon names and passwords to support the times when they travel.

Fortunately, Windows NT 4.0 supports multilevels of C2 security. Encryption has been added to this multilevel security with multilevel passwords and privileges, roving callback, encrypted logon and data, and file level security to protect data privacy and network resource integrity. Dubbed CAPI (for Cryptography API), it supports all of the most common encryption methods, including Data Encryption Standards and public-key encryption. It can handle digital signatures and transactions — where one party is validated by a licensed third party, commonly referred to as certification authority.

EQUIPMENT REQUIRED — CLIENT

Remote Control

Manipulation of files and calculations are made on the server; the computer that is carried on the road does not need the power or application support that is needed in the remote node configuration. In many situations a remote user might very well get by with a 286 processor with 2MB RAM and a 40MB hard drive running DOS or Windows 3.1. The biggest problem you might have will be finding a laptop of this vintage with a UART fast enough to handle the speed of a 28.8 Kbps modem.

If Windows 95 is used, then you will need to support a 386-class machine with 16MB to 24MB of RAM and at least a 500MB hard drive in order to provide you with adequate service.

Remote Node

When you are using remote node operation, the client must have all applications loaded locally in addition to all of the files/databases that the user needs while away from the office. You need to have a minimum of a 486-class laptop with a large hard drive (today that means greater than 2 GB) a minimum of 16 MB of RAM (preferably 32 MB) as well as the other peripherals that you have determined the user needs.

Application Server Requirements

Remote Control Server

1. A minimum of 200 MHz Pentium or higher microprocessor with 64 MB of base memory (add an additional 8MB for each concurrent user) with an EISA or PCI bus architecture

2. 32-bit disk controller recommended
3. 1GB hard disk drive recommended, not including application and data storage
4. A high-density 3.5 diskette drive
5. SVGA (800 × 600 × 16) video adapter
6. Intelligent multiport adapter or SCSI adapter supporting differential SCSI (depending on your modem pool selection)
7. 32-bit network interface card.

NOTE: If you are going to use SMP in the server, depending on the application, a single four-processor SMP Pentium server could support 40 to 60 concurrent users — depending upon applications that are being accessed by the remote users.

SUMMARY

Windows NT 4.0 is an operating system that supports many applications. In this chapter we have looked at how it can support multiple forms of remote access. It can support small businesses with just a few remote users up to large corporations with hundreds of remote users.

The most cost-effective approach is to use the RAS (Remote Access Service) that comes packaged with the operating system. This approach will provide all the security supported by Windows NT and is fairly easy to set up. RAS will only support remote node access, which will provide many users access to their data warehouse. The negative side is that the files which are accessed will be downloaded across a rather slow 28.8 Kbps line (unless you are using ISDN) when compared to the interoffice LAN. The advantage is that you can work off-line with your laptop since you have all of your files on your local computer. When you get back to the office, you can use Windows NT's "My Briefcase" to synchronize the files that have been updated on your machine as well as those that were changed in the office while you were gone.

Remote control access provides the fastest access to your data back in the office. It will support multiple users simultaneously on the same hardware platform. It can provide all of the services you are familiar with in the office. Depending on the configuration, however, it may be slightly more difficult to work off-line on some applications, such as your email. It is more expensive to implement initially because of the additional software that you will need to purchase as well as a more powerful computer which you will want to use for the server. It might be offset, however, because you can very possibly get by with remote clients that are less powerful. Depending on the applications that your company uses, you might even be able to use some older 286 processor machines running DOS applications.

If you prefer the remote control approach, but have a limited budget to get started, you may want to look at the less expensive remote control system that still provides most of the advantages of the multisession system. This requires a dedicated computer for each simultaneous user, but if you have only a few users who need access for a reasonably short period of time, this is a good choice.

Microsoft Windows NT has many options, but one of its strongest suits is its built-in multilevel security. When it comes to providing access to remote users, you are providing an opportunity for unauthorized users to gain access to your company's confidential information. This is an area that cannot be underestimated. Windows NT permits you to have a good start on providing the level of security that your company expects.

Although Windows NT will support up to 256 simultaneous connections, for reliability reasons (unless you have a very powerful computer with excellent power and line protection), it is not recommended that you use it in this mode. You should spread the risk of failure among multiple platforms if you begin serving between 60 and 100 simultaneous users in your organization.

Chapter 17 Software Management: The Practical Solution to the Cost-of-Ownership Crisis

Paul Davis

SINCE THEIR INTRODUCTION IN THE LATE 1970S, PERSONAL COMPUTERS HAVE RESHAPED THE WAY EMPLOYEES SPEND THEIR TIME and redefined the role of the corporate information technology (IT) department.

Each year, as the power of PCs has increased, their purchase price has gone down. Corporations have been willing to spend on desktop hardware and software with the increasingly common conviction that the returns in user efficiency more than justify the investment.

But recent studies of the cost of ownership of desktop personal computers have brought to light a sobering truth: that the *real* costs of owning PCs are much greater than previously suspected. The Gartner Group estimates that each year "a networked PC costs about $13,200 per node for hardware, software support and administrative services, and end-user operations."[1]

These estimates have fueled concern among the people responsible for corporate networks, from system administrators to senior executives. They want to know whether these previously "hidden" costs are justified and how to reduce them. Many organizations are taking a closer look at their software expenditures. This is because software drives PC ownership

0-8493-0893-3/00/$0.00+$.50

costs — not only as an expense itself, but also as the main reason for hardware purchases and upgrades, support calls, etc. Until recently, however, the lack of a clear understanding of cost of ownership was exacerbated by the lack of effective tools to measure and evaluate software usage, so that informed decisions can be made.

This chapter will discuss how the emergence of software management tools is enabling IT managers to gain awareness of real software usage and to dramatically reverse the trend of rising costs of ownership. It will also suggest some ways to get started on implementing an effective software management program.

WHAT IS SOFTWARE MANAGEMENT?

Software management is a set of practices that optimize an organization's software purchasing, upgrading, standardization, distribution, inventory, and usage. Good software management means a company is using its software assets in a manner that optimally supports its business activities, without spending any more than necessary. It helps companies save money, comply with license agreements, and gain new levels of network control and efficiency.

While system managers have been performing more labor-intensive methods of software management for years, today the most effective way to achieve optimal performance is by using a new class of software applications that fall into the categories shown in Exhibit 17-1.

REDUCING OWNERSHIP COSTS, ONE-BY-ONE

With software management tools, IT managers can systematically address the key costs of managing a networked enterprise.

Cost #1: Software and Hardware Purchases and Upgrades

Manage Software Licenses for Optimal Efficiency. The advent of networks made it possible for hundreds of users to run applications stored on a server simultaneously . But single-user license agreements, which require that each piece of software run on only one PC, made the practice of sharing applications on a network illegal. Concurrent licensing was introduced to address this dilemma and soon became the industry licensing norm.

Concurrent licensing allows users to share applications over a network, and requires the purchase of licenses equal to the greatest number of people using a particular application at any given time. But since there has been no accurate way to determine usage patterns for any given piece of software, the simplest way to ensure license compliance has been to purchase a license for every potential user (see Exhibit 17-2).

Exhibit 17-1. The key activities of effective software management.

Activities	Advantages	The old way	The new way
Metering — the measurement of software usage and the cornerstone of software management. Metering reveals which applications are in use by which users and how often.	• Reduce software costs by more effectively allocating resources • Stay in compliance with license agreements • Plan for upgrades according to true user needs • Determine training requirements	Rely on user-supplied information about usage. In addition to the work involved, the problem with this method is that users may inaccurately report their usage.	Metering software provides a fast and ongoing profile of software usage across the enterprise. Better metering packages also reduce software expenses dramatically by optimizing the use of licenses.
Inventory — the assessment of how much and which software is installed at individual workstations.	• Reveal what software is installed on which machines • Ensure license compliance • Detect new installations of unapproved applications	Visit each workstation frequently to see which software components are in use. This method is labor intensive and impractical, as users frequently download new software from the Internet, from home, and from other remote sites.	Inventory software automatically gathers information over the network in the background, without interrupting users' work flow. (Inventory packages vary greatly in their ability to "see" all desktop applications.)
Distribution — the installation and upgrading of software across networks.	• Efficiently ensure that the right versions of software applications and information resources are available to designated users	Visit each desktop to physically install the new software.	Distribution software automatically copies and installs software over the network in the background from a server — and bases installation on what users really need.

(continues)

Exhibit 17-1. The key activities of effective software management. ***(continued)***

Activities	Advantages	The old way	The new way
Reporting — the collection, integration, and presentation of data on software usage, inventory, and distribution.	• Build a foundation for decision making and planning • Share software management information among collaborative groups • Compile data across multi-site enterprises for administrative efficiency and group purchasing discounts	Manually input data from various sources, integrate it, and organize it.	Good software management packages can generate a variety of reports on the use of information technology assets. By integrating reporting and control, they can automatically optimize many aspects of IT asset management, and can implement policies without manual intervention.

Exhibit 17-2. A show of hands — the cost of informal polling.

Consider the case of a large U.S. public utility that wanted to evaluate which users it should upgrade to a new version of a popular database program.

The system manager sent an email to all employees to find out which ones considered themselves "frequent" users of the current version of the software.

Eighty-three percent said they frequently use the application. To be safe, the decision was made to purchase the software upgrade for 100% of the utility's employees. They also planned to upgrade the RAM on every employee's PC, as the new version of the application required 8 megabytes more than the old.

Later, the organization was given the opportunity to perform an audit of actual software usage. They discovered that only 13% of employees were actually frequent users of the software. If they had known this before they made the purchase, they could have saved 87% of the upgrade costs.

Software management helps businesses realize the potential cost savings of concurrent licensing. With metering software, system managers can monitor usage over time and purchase the least number of licenses necessary to satisfy user demand. In many cases, companies can reduce the number of licenses they purchase by 40 to 80 percent or more through the use of metering software.

Another benefit of software management tools is their ability to monitor different types of licenses. A system manager may decide, for instance, that he's going to purchase dedicated licenses of Microsoft Word for the most active users of the application and concurrent licenses for the remainder of the user pool. The most effective software management tools allow him to clearly see which users should be assigned which license type. Establishing and maintaining an efficient license mix ensures that every user has access to the software she needs, when she needs it, and that software costs are kept to a minimum.

Plan Ahead for Software Purchases and Upgrades. The standard operating mode for today's system manager is reactive. The complexity of making a great variety of software and hardware elements work together — combined with ever-increasing user demands for assistance — leaves little time for active planning. At the same time, those who plan for software and hardware needs do end up saving time and money. By knowing usage patterns, a system manager can forecast needs, budget more accurately, and take better advantage of quantity discounts.

Today's software management tools provide the information needed to plan effectively with very little effort on the system manager's part. The result is that users are better served and resources are deployed more efficiently. Exhibit 17-3 illustrates how one large U.S. corporation used software management to cut software license expenditures by nearly 80 percent.

Stay Legal. While not typically associated with cost of ownership, audits of companies suspected of illegal software use can cost a great deal of time, money, and aggravation, not to mention bad publicity. Many company executives don't realize that they are responsible for all applications run on company equipment, regardless of whether the applications are launched from the server or from clients, or whether they are company-approved or not.

With the proliferation of networks, it became much more difficult to monitor and comply with software license agreements. At the same time, the penalties for not doing so have increased. For example, in the U.S. in 1992, Congress instituted criminal penalties for software copyright infringement. Violators of license agreements can now be fined up to $250,000 and sent to jail for up to five years. And according to the Software Publishers

Exhibit 17-3. How one large U.S. corporation used software management to cut software license expenditures by nearly 80%.

Application	Licenses required without software management	License cost without software management	Licenses required with software management	License cost with software management	Savings by using software management
Lotus Freelance	543	$171,045	95	$29,925	$141,120
Micrografx ABC Flowchart	36	$10,800	15	$4,500	$6,300
Microsoft Access	502	$147,588	95	$27,930	$119,658
Microsoft Excel	718	$211,092	140	$41,160	$169,932
Microsoft Project	297	$128,304	50	$21,600	$106,704
Microsoft Word	1,088	$319,872	280	$82,320	$237,552
Total	3,184	$988,701	675	$207,345	$781,266

Association (SPA), as of 1996 more than $16 million in fines had been levied against companies in violation of software licensing agreements.

Software management not only helps to ensure license compliance; the reports available with software management tools can act as proof of compliance if a company is ever questioned.

Cost #2: Training and Technical Support

Reduce Training Expenses. Appropriately directed training leads to more productivity and fewer help desk calls. This is the rationale that leads companies to make large investments in training resources. Software management can help make those investments pay off by revealing which users should be trained on any given application.

For example, if a large corporation has standardized on one spreadsheet application, software management can reveal small populations of employees using other products. IT can then train those employees on the company-approved software and reduce help desk support for the unapproved applications. This also reduces the expense of keeping support personnel and trainers up-to-date on seldom-used applications.

And software distribution allows the controlled rollout of software to only those users who have been trained. This also reduces help desk costs because the majority of help requests for a given piece of software occur when the user is first learning how to use it. Similarly, with software management, corporations can determine the most frequent users of any given application and train them first.

Cost #3: Network Administration

Control the Software Invasion. On any given day in a large corporation, employees may load hundreds of unapproved software applications onto their desktops. While many of these applications are from home, an increasing number comes from the Internet, where it's easy to download new software with the click of a mouse.

In addition to the obvious effects on employee productivity, for the system manager this influx of software is a nightmare. It often leads to frozen machines and embarrassed employee calls to the help desk. And at its worst, it causes serious problems on the network.

Software management tools constantly monitor which applications are loaded and allow system managers to respond quickly to installations of unapproved applications.

Monitor the Effectiveness of IT Applications. IT departments spend a lot of time and money developing custom internal applications. But they may not know how effective their software is in meeting their objectives. Software management reports can give system managers the information they need to either improve the applications or discontinue their development efforts. Software management not only saves development time, but also helps companies more effectively plan for hardware needs (which are often quite expensive for internally developed applications).

Putting License Agreements to the Test. Enterprise license agreements are a common way for organizations to purchase software. Manufacturers of popular business applications (word processors, spreadsheets, databases, etc.) and office suites offer discounts to companies that agree to purchase an individual license for each PC on the network. These agreements are touted for their ability to save the customer money and ensure legality. But without software management tools, they may be only partially successful in accomplishing either goal.

REAL COST SAVINGS REQUIRES REAL USAGE INFORMATION

When creating an enterprise license agreement, the software manufacturer uses its own formulas to determine how many licenses are needed for a given customer. These formulas are standards they use with all of their customers and are not based on actual software usage.

Through software management, system administrators can be more informed customers. They can find out exactly how many licenses they need, rather than depending on external formulas. With this information, they are in a much better position to negotiate the most advantageous license agreement and the best price possible.

Partial Legality Means Only Partial Peace of Mind

It's easy to believe that by signing an enterprise license agreement, an organization's license-compliance worries are over. This may be true for the one application or set of applications covered by the agreement. But today's enterprise employs a wide variety of applications from many different manufacturers. And employees have the ability to install any software on their desktops.

When it comes to staying legal, true peace of mind for the system manager is only possible with the certain knowledge that *all* of the applications being used across the organization are being employed legally. Software management can supply that knowledge.

The First Step in Establishing a Software Management Program — Measure Usage

The best way to start managing software assets more efficiently and to reduce cost of ownership is to measure current usage accurately. This can be done with a software metering application in what's known as a software audit. A software audit provides a snapshot of exactly how a company uses its software and where that company stands with regard to compliance.

An effective software audit goes far beyond a simple inventory (such as that provided by many audit tools). Rather, it continually tracks which workstations on a network access which applications over the course of the audit, to reveal usage patterns.

By tracking current usage, a system manager can assemble a wealth of previously unknown information, including:

- Unauthorized applications in use
- Versions of applications in use
- The locations of all software run on users' PCs
- The actual users of specific applications
- Peak usage levels of individual applications
- The optimal location(s) to install software
- Exactly how much software is needed

With the results of a software usage audit in hand, the next step in establishing effective software management is to set priorities and make decisions about how to structure access to the organization's software assets. One of the most important of these decisions is which software management tools offer the features to help implement an organization's strategies. Exhibit 17-4 illustrates the future of cost considerations.

Exhibit 17-4. Network computers: the ultimate answer to cost of ownership?

The network computer (NC), an intranet-based "thin client," is being widely touted as an answer to rising costs of ownership. It offers a lower initial purchase price, reduced support costs, and excellent extensibility. However, the cost-conscious system manager may choose to not standardize on the new machines exclusively. This is because doing so requires a large investment in changing the network infrastructure. Expanded network bandwidth, server upgrades, and new applications are just a few of the expenses involved in establishing a viable NC environment. And while many are attracted to the NC paradigm because of the promise of ease of management, effective tools have yet to be developed.

Software management applications can help the system administrator determine which users are the best candidates for NCs and which ones need the desktop processing power and storage available with a PC.

And no matter what mixture of PCs and NCs an organization chooses to deploy, software management tools will offer cost-saving benefits in the form of usage information, inventory, license management, and more.

Here are some questions to ask when evaluating a software management product:

- Does it measure usage of applications launched from both the desktop and the server?
- Does it provide universal metering — the ability to see software on any network operating system?
- Does it ensure legality by detecting launches of all applications, whether or not they have been designated for monitoring by the system administrator?
- How comprehensive is its database of recognized applications?
- Is it easy to install, administer, and support?
- Are its various components well integrated?
- Does it operate in the background, allowing users to remain productive?
- Are its available reports truly useful? Do they help you make good decisions?
- Does the manufacturer of the software offer not only products, but also the ongoing support and expertise you need to develop and ensure the success of your software management strategies?

SUMMARY

In today's technology-centered workplace, software is an essential employee tool. The way an organization acquires, uses, and manages software directly affects its short- and long-term success. Until now, however, there has been no way to effectively determine whether software resources are being used efficiently.

Thanks to the new class of software management applications, system administrators now have access to the information and control they need to significantly increase productivity and improve their bottom line.

References

1. *TCO: The Emerging Manageable Desktop,* The Gartner Group, October, 1996.

Note: WRQ, the WRQ logo, Express Meter, Express Meter Audit Kit, and Enhanced Command are registered trademarks, and Enterprise Optimization Module is a trademark of WRQ, Inc., registered in the U.S. and other countries. Other brand and product names are the trademarks of their respective owners.

Chapter 18
Enterprise Messaging Migration

David Nelson

THE GOAL OF THIS CHAPTER IS TO DISCUSS LARGE ENTERPRISE MESSAGING MIGRATION PROJECTS and help the information technology professional avoid many of the common pitfalls associated with these types of projects. Messaging migration is the process of moving users from one or more source e-mail systems to one or more destination e-mail systems. Large enterprise projects are those involving anywhere from a few thousand users to over 100,000 users.

The checklists and methodology in this chapter can save frustration, time, and money. For example, what does it cost an organization if enterprise e-mail directories are corrupted and e-mail is down for hours or days due to a migration? What happens in the middle of a messaging migration project if the gateways cannot handle the traffic load and e-mail is terminally slow? What's the impact if stored messages are lost? How about personal address books? What's the benefit of completing the migration sooner than planned?

E-mail, or messaging, is necessary for people to do their jobs. It is no longer a "nice to have" form of communication — it is mission-critical. A recent Pitney-Bowes study found that the average office worker sends and receives more than 190 messages per day. Even though much of this e-mail is superfluous, many messages concern important meetings, projects, and other information necessary to do one's job. Messaging is indeed a valuable resource and changing e-mail systems should be treated with care.

WHY MIGRATE?

There are many reasons why organizations are migrating to new messaging systems. New systems have more capabilities and attractive features. Older systems have become difficult to maintain. Some older systems will not be made Year 2000 compliant. An environment of 6, 12, or more different e-mail systems, which is common in large enterprises, is difficult and costly

0-8493-0893-3/00/$0.00+$.50

to manage. The basic idea behind messaging migration is to simplify, consolidate, and lay a foundation for future applications.

Current E-mail Systems

Over the years, large enterprises have "collected" many different e-mail systems. They may have started out using mainframe computers and implemented e-mail systems like IBM's PROFS, Fischer's TAO or EMC2, or H&W's SYSM. Engineering or manufacturing divisions may have used DEC VAX computers and implemented VMSmail or ALL-IN-1. Later on, sales and marketing groups may have implemented PC LANs with Microsoft Mail, Lotus cc:Mail, DaVinci, or a number of other PC-based e-mail systems.

Each different computing environment carries with it a proprietary e-mail system. Each e-mail system has its own method of addressing users and storing messages. Enterprises have overcome these differences with gateways, message switches, and directory synchronization products. Over time, many have discovered that a complex environment of many different messaging systems is not ideal.

Some of the problems associated with multiple e-mail systems include the following:

- Lost messages
- Long delivery times
- Complex addressing
- Corrupted e-mail attachments
- Inability to communicate with Internet mail users

Future Outlook

Which e-mail systems will enterprises migrate to? It's important to note that many enterprises will never be able to migrate to a single e-mail system. Mergers and acquisitions, different business division needs, and new technology will invariably introduce different e-mail systems over time. There is, however, a benefit in reducing the number of messaging systems and having the processes and technology in place to perform messaging migrations. In their report on messaging migration, Ferris Research stated, "Migration is a fact of life and is going to remain a fact of life."

Internet mail has had a tremendous impact on today's messaging environment. The ability to communicate with millions of people on the Internet is of great benefit. The Internet mail standard of RFC-822 addressing and SMTP/MIME format (simple mail transport protocol/multipurpose Internet mail extensions) has also become the *de facto* corporate e-mail standard.

New client/server messaging systems support SMTP/MIME and also add new functionality like:

- Group scheduling and calendaring
- Public bulletin boards
- Shared documents and databases
- Collaborative groupware applications
- Application development environments

Some of the leading client/server messaging systems include the following:

- Microsoft Exchange
- Lotus Notes
- Novell GroupWise
- Netscape Messaging Server

PROJECT SPONSOR(S)

Politics play a very large role in the success of enterprise messaging migration projects. A successful project requires a sponsor that can ensure a timely decision on the company's new e-mail standard and the process that will be followed to get there.

The main concern is that the new e-mail system has to be agreed upon by all of the key decision makers in the organization and the migration process cannot disrupt the business. Each business unit will have its own unique requirements and seasonality. While the CEO may not have time to sponsor the messaging migration project, it's important that he or she provides leadership and support for the project. Business unit managers are also key members of the leadership team. Some organizations go the other direction, forming "grass-roots" committees that span all the different business units so that consensus can be formed. Whatever the approach, it's critical to gain buy-in from the entire organization.

Do not underestimate the time that will be required to gain consensus for your messaging migration project. In some large enterprises, this first step can take months. Look at other large IT projects that have touched all business units within your enterprise to gauge what the consensus forming stage will be like.

USE CONSULTANTS

There are many reasons to bring consultants in on your messaging migration project. First of all, they've been involved in enterprise messaging migration projects and you can benefit from their experience. Second, they can augment your resources so that your staff can stay focused on other critical projects. Finally, they are viewed as having an objective opinion and can help you gain consensus across different business units.

Each of the messaging vendors (Microsoft, Lotus, Novell, Netscape, etc.) has its own consulting services organization. Some of the independent consulting organizations that specialize in messaging migration include:

1. Wingra Technologies
   1-800-544-5465
   http://www.wingra.com
   info@wingra.com
2. Control Data Systems
   1-888-RIA-LTO4
   http://www.cdc.com
   info@cdc.com
3. Digital Equipment Corp.
   1-800-DIGITAL
   http://www.digital.com
   info@digital.com
4. Hewlett-Packard
   1-800-752-0900
   http://www.hp.com
   info@hp.com

DEVELOP A MIGRATION PLAN

A well thought-out migration plan is the cornerstone of a successful enterprise messaging migration project. If you've hired a consulting organization, migration planning will be one of their services. You will work closely with them to define what's important for your organization. The checklist in Exhibit 18-1 shows the basics that should be included in your messaging migration plan.

Define the Current Environment

The first step in the planning process is to define your current messaging environment. One of the best ways to start is to develop a network diagram. This diagram should show the e-mail systems in your enterprise and how they're connected. A simplistic diagram is given in Exhibit 18-2 to illustrate what a messaging network diagram should look like.

The description of your messaging environment should include:

- Names and vendors of existing messaging systems
- Number of users on each e-mail system
- Geographic locations of existing e-mail systems
- Names and vendors of existing gateways and/or message switch
- Current Internet address standard

Exhibit 18-1. Migration plan checklist.

- Executive Overview
- Project Goals
- Current Messaging Environment
- New Messaging Environment
- Migration Infrastructure
- Message Switch
- Directory Synchronization
- Migration Technology
- Migration Timing
- Migration Policies
- Date range of stored messages
- Message and attachment size restrictions
- Personal address books
- Messaging-enabled applications
- Distribution lists
- Bulletin boards
- Service levels
- Delivery times
- Functionality
- Risk Analysis
- Gantt Chart/Timeline
- Budget

- Message traffic volume within systems, between systems, and external to the Internet or other networks
- Average message size
- Average message store size — number of messages and size in megabytes
- Network bandwidth between systems and different geographic locations
- Names and contact information for the people who manage each of the current messaging systems, gateways or message switch, and networks.

Choose the Destination System

The choice of destination system will depend on a number of things. Sometimes it's simply a matter of sticking with a preferred vendor. Other times the decision is driven by a particular application or fit with existing standards. Some of the market-leading client/server messaging systems and their relative strengths are listed below:

- Microsoft Exchange
  - — Good integration with Microsoft Office and Microsoft Outlook
  - — Good solution where the main need is for e-mail

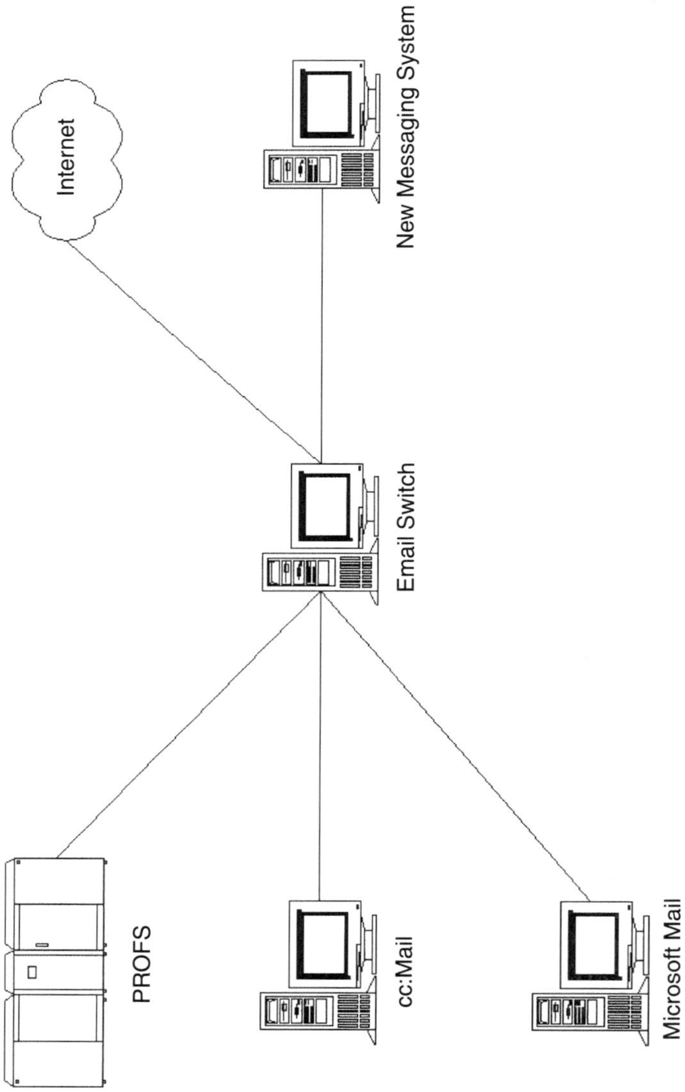

Exhibit 18-2. Simple enterprise messaging network diagram.

- Lotus Notes
  - —Wealth of third-party applications
  - —Strong groupware functionality
- Novell GroupWise
  - —Strong integration with Novell network servers
- Netscape Messaging Server
  - —Pure Internet standards

New System Requirements

Once you've decided on the destination system, you will need to define the requirements for that system. Some of the things you'll need to look at include the following:

- Standard messaging server configurations
- Standard desktop client configurations
- User training required
- Number of messaging servers required
- Geographic locations of messaging servers
- Network bandwidth requirements between servers

Migration Infrastructure

The messaging migration infrastructure includes technology to provide the following:

- E-mail gateway services
- Enterprise directory services, including directory synchronization
- Internet mail routing
- Message store migration

For enterprises with more than two different e-mail systems, an e-mail switch is required. The e-mail switch should be scalable so that it can handle the peak load when half the enterprise is on the old e-mail systems and half are on the new system. One large enterprise with more than 100,000 users found that they needed six to ten message switches to handle their peak loads. Several message switch vendors are listed below:

1. Wingra Technologies
   Product: *Missive*
   1-800-544-5465
   http://www.wingra.com
   info@wingra.com
2. Control Data Systems
   Product: *Mail*Hub*
   1-888-RIA-LTO4
   http://www.cdc.com
   info@cdc.com

3. Lotus Development Corp.
   Product: *LMS*
   1-800-343-5414
   http://www.lotus.com
   info@lotus.com

Migration technology should work with the message switch to ensure that addresses are translated correctly as message stores are migrated. Migration and integration, or coexistence, technology will also need to work together so that e-mail routing is updated as users switch to their new e-mail system. Migration technology should also make it easy to select a group of users to migrate, move their message stores and personal address books, create accounts on the new messaging system, and update the enterprise directory. It is also useful if message store migration can occur in a two-step process so that the bulk of stored messages can be moved two to three weeks ahead of the time and the remainder can be moved the weekend prior to the cutover date. This is an elegant way to deal with the large size of message stores, often measured in gigabytes.

Migration Timing

In this section of the migration plan, you will define which groups of users will be moved when. Usually it makes sense to approach migration on a business unit basis. Since 80 percent of e-mail is within a functional group, it makes sense to move each group at the same time. This approach will also allow you to take into account the seasonality of different business units. A retail operation, for example, will not want any system changes to occur during their peak selling season, often around Christmas time. Other business units may want to avoid changes around the time leading up to the end of their fiscal years. Migration timing will be negotiated with each business unit. Date ranges will need to be laid out for each business unit for installing new messaging servers and desktop hardware and software, training users, migrating message stores, and cutting over to the new system.

Migration Policies

There are several different philosophical approaches to messaging migration. One approach, often referred to as the "brute-force" method, advocates moving everyone at the same time and disregarding stored messages and personal address books. Another philosophy is to view messaging migration as a process and message stores as the knowledge of the enterprise.

Messaging migration technology is available to perform format and address translations between the old and new systems, preserve folder structures, and move personal address books and distribution lists. As mentioned earlier, it is critical that the migration technology you choose be integrated very tightly with your message switch and directory synchronization infrastructure. This integration will allow addresses to be translated properly so that stored messages can be replied to. Also, it's important that the migration technology feed into your directory synchronization and message routing processes so that e-mail will continue to flow properly as users are moved to the new messaging system.

Assuming your organization would like to retain the valuable information contained in stored messages and personal address books, the next step is to define your migration policies. Your migration policies will need to cover the following areas:

- Personal folders and stored messages — what will be migrated?
  - Restrictions on dates
  - Restrictions on message or attachment sizes
  - Preservation of status flags, i.e., read or unread
- International characters — for users in France, Quebec, Asia, or other parts of the world, will their folder names, message subjects, and e-mail addresses contain the same characters as they do in their current e-mail systems?
- Address translation as messages are migrated — will users be able to reply to stored messages from within the new e-mail system?
- Archives and laptops — will these message stores need to be moved to a server before they can be migrated?
- Internet mail addresses — will they change as users are migrated? What will the new standard be?
  - Personal address books
  - Distribution lists
  - Bulletin boards
- Personal calendars — is there a way to move appointments to the new system?
- Mail-enabled applications — often these have to be rewritten to work with the new messaging system
- Service-level agreements — what can users expect in terms of availability and e-mail delivery times during the migration?

Risk Analysis

The risk analysis section of your migration plan will define which elements of the migration process are reversible and what the backout plans are. If moving a group of users results in the corruption of all the e-mail directories in your enterprise, how will you back out those changes so that e-mail can continue to flow properly? Have current message stores and directories been backed up properly? What's the impact if the project timeline slips? These are some of the questions that need to be addressed in the risk analysis section of your migration plan.

Project Timeline

A project timeline is useful both as a means of communication and as a way to manage the overall project. The timeline should, at a glance, show the steps involved, their interdependencies, and the resources required to achieve your objectives. A high-level timeline is given in Exhibit 18-3 to illustrate the basic structure.

COMMUNICATE THE PLAN

Your migration plan will not have much meaning unless you communicate it within your organization and gain support for it. For your management, you should communicate the following:

- Why your enterprise is migrating
- What the new messaging standard will be
- When the migration will take place
- Benefits of migrating

Management in this case has a very broad meaning. Executive staff, business unit managers, and functional managers will all need to know about the messaging migration plan. Methods for communicating the plan include e-mail, formal meetings, or interoffice memos.

Of course, the rest of the organization will also need to know what's going to happen. E-mail users should receive information telling them:

- High-level view of the reasons the enterprise is migrating
- What the new e-mail standard will be
- When new hardware or software will be installed on their desktops
- Their new account name and initial password
- Training schedule
- What will happen to their stored e-mail, folders, and personal address books
- What their external Internet mail address will be
- When they should begin using their new e-mail system
- Who to contact with questions or issues

Because of the need to communicate individual account names and passwords, user communication will probably take the form of e-mail or interoffice memos with some form of mail-merge capability. For some of the more general information, you may consider developing a brochure or flyer describing the project and its benefits.

EXECUTE THE PLAN

You will need to decide who is going to perform messaging migration for your enterprise. Will it be internal IT staff, your migration consultant, or

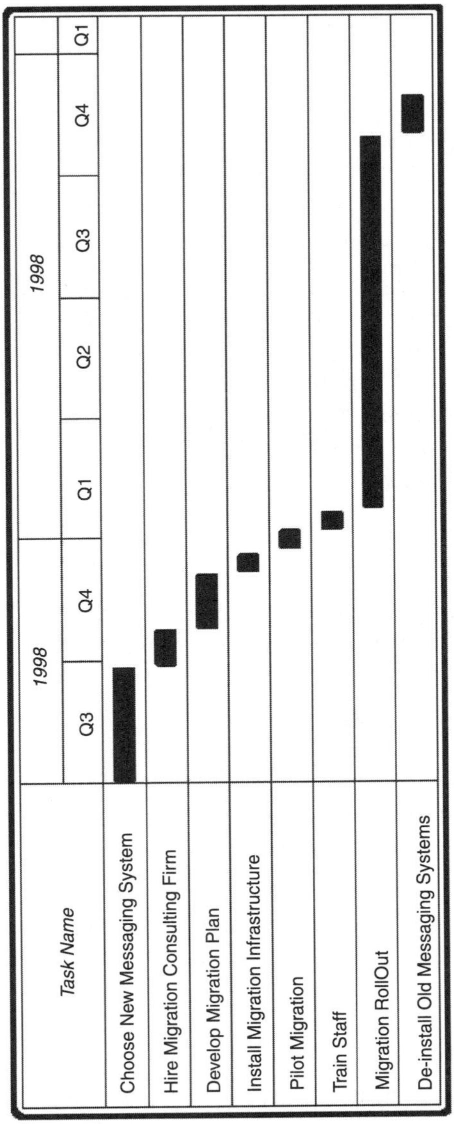

Exhibit 18-3. Sample migration timeline.

another third party? The key considerations are whether you have the resources and whether you want them devoted to messaging migration.

The first step in testing your migration plan is to perform a migration pilot. Set up a test lab that includes your primary e-mail systems, your messaging integration and migration technology, and your destination e-mail system. It's very important that this pilot be performed in a test lab environment. This is the stage where you will discover problems with your messaging migration plan. You will not want to introduce these problems into your production mail environment. Go through all of the steps of your migration plan and document your results. Change your plan as required.

The next step is to migrate the first business unit on the schedule. Communicate with the users what will be happening and how it will affect them. Again, document the results and adjust your migration plan as you go.

For the remainder of the project, which can often last 12 to 24 months, you will be repeating the migration process on a business unit basis. Standard project management practices should be followed to set milestones and make sure the process stays on track. Once complete, you can shut down and deinstall your old e-mail systems and wait for the next migration opportunity.

SUMMARY

The goal of this chapter was to describe enterprise messaging migrations and help the IT professional avoid many common pitfalls. The critical success factors for an enterprise messaging migration project include the following:

- Consensus and leadership
- Use of consultants
- Detailed planning
- Tightly integrated messaging migration and coexistence technology
- Communication with management and users
- Project management

Messaging migration is a complex process, but with careful planning an enterprise can deploy new e-mail systems on time and within budget.

References

1. *Pitney Bowes' Workplace Communications in the 21st Century*, May 18, 1998, Institute of the Future, 1 Elmcroft Road, 6309, Stamford, CT 06926-0700, http://www.pitney-bowes.com/pbi/whatsnew/releases/messaging_1998.htm
2. *Migration of E-mail Systems*, February 1998, Jonathan Penn, Ferris Research, 408 Columbus Avenue No. 1, San Francisco, CA 94133, telephone 415-986-1414, http://www.ferris.com

Chapter 19
Online Data Mining

John R. Vacca

CURRENTLY, MOST DATA WAREHOUSES ARE BEING USED FOR SUMMARIZATION-BASED, MULTI-DIMENSIONAL, ONLINE ANALYTICAL PROCESSING (OLAP). However, given the recent developments in data warehouse and online analytical processing technology, together with the rapid progress in data mining research, industry analysts anticipate that organizations will soon be using their data warehouses for sophisticated data analysis. As a result, a tremendous amount of data will be integrated, preprocessed, and stored in large data warehouses.

Online analytical mining (OLAM; also called OLAP mining) is among the many different paradigms and architectures for data mining systems. It integrates online analytical processing with data mining and mining knowledge in multi-dimensional databases. It is a promising direction due to the:

- high quality of data in data warehouses
- available information processing infrastructure surrounding data warehouses
- OLAP-based exploratory data analysis
- online selection of data mining functions

OLAM MINING BENEFITS

Most data mining tools must work on integrated, consistent, and cleaned data. This requires costly preprocessing for data cleaning, data transformation, and data integration. Therefore, a data warehouse constructed by such preprocessing is a valuable source of high-quality data for both OLAP and data mining. Data mining may also serve as a valuable tool for data cleaning and data integration.

Organizations with data warehouses have or will systematically construct comprehensive information processing and data analysis infrastructures surrounding them. The surrounding infrastructures include accessing, integration, consolidation, and transformation of multiple heterogeneous databases; Object-oriented Database Connectivity/Object Linking and Embedding Database (ODBC/OLEDB) connections; Web-accessing and service facilities; and reporting and OLAP analysis tools.

0-8493-0893-3/00/$0.00+$.50

Savvy organizations will make the best use of their available infrastructures, rather than constructing everything from scratch.

Effective data mining requires exploratory data analysis. Users often want to traverse through a database, select portions of relevant data, analyze them at different granularities, and present knowledge/results in different forms. Online analytical mining provides facilities for data mining on different subsets of data and at different levels of abstraction. It does this by drilling, pivoting, filtering, dicing, and slicing on a data cube and on intermediate data mining results. This, together with data/knowledge visualization tools, can greatly enhance the power and flexibility of exploratory data mining.

Users seldom know which kinds of knowledge they wish to mine. By integrating OLAP with multiple data mining functions, online analytical mining provides users with the flexibility to select desired data mining functions, and dynamically swap data mining tasks.

Because data mining functions are usually more computationally expensive than OLAP operations, organizations are challenged to efficiently implement online analytical mining in large data warehouses, and provide fast response. Various implementation methods and ways to perform online analytical mining are discussed below.

OLAM ARCHITECTURE

In a similar manner to how OLAP engine performs online analytical processing, an online analytical mining engine performs analytical mining in data cubes. Therefore, an integrated OLAM and OLAP architecture makes sense, whereby the OLAM and OLAP engines both accept users' online queries (or commands) via a user graphical user interface (GUI) application programming interface (API). Work with the data cube in the data analysis is performed through a cube API, and a metadata directory guides the data cube access. The data cube can be constructed by accessing or integrating multiple databases, or by filtering a data warehouse via a database API, which may support OLEDB or ODBC connections.

An OLAM engine can perform multiple data mining tasks, such as concept description, association, classification, prediction, clustering, and time-series analysis. Therefore, it usually consists of multiple, integrated data mining modules, making it more sophisticated than an OLAP engine. There is no fundamental difference between the data cube required for OLAP and that for OLAM, although OLAM analysis might require more powerful data cube construction and accessing tools. This is the case when OLAM involves more dimensions with finer granularities, or involves the discovery-driven exploration of multi-feature aggregations on the data cube, thereby requiring more than OLAP analysis.

Moreover, when exploratory data mining identifies interesting spots, an OLAM engine might need to drill through from the data cube into the corresponding relational databases for detailed analysis of particular portions of data; for example, in time-series analysis. Furthermore, a data mining process might disclose that the dimensions or measures of a constructed cube are not appropriate for data analysis. Here, a refined data cube design could improve the quality of data warehouse construction.

OLAM FEATURES

A well-thought-out design can help an organization to systematically develop OLAM mechanisms in data warehouses. The following features are important for successful online analytical mining:

- the ability to mine anywhere
- availability and efficient support of multi-feature cubes and cubes with complex dimensions and measures
- cube-based mining methods
- the selection or addition of data mining algorithms
- interaction among multiple data mining functions
- fast response and high-performance mining
- visualization tools
- extensibility

The OLAM process should be exploratory; that is, mining should be performed at different portions of data at multiple levels of abstraction. When using a multi-dimensional database and an OLAP engine, it is easy to carve many portions of data sets at multiple levels of abstraction using OLAP operations such as drilling, dicing/slicing, pivoting, and filtering. Such processes can also be performed during data mining, through interaction with OLAP operations.

Moreover, in some data mining processes, at least some of the data may require exploration in great detail. OLAP engines often provide facilities to drill through the data cube down to the primitive/low-level data stored in the database. The interaction of multiple data mining modules with an OLAP engine can ensure that mining is easily performed anywhere in a data warehouse.

Traditional data cube queries compute simple aggregates at multiple granularities. However, many data mining tasks require discovery-driven exploration of multi-feature cubes, which are complex subqueries involving multiple dependent queries at multiple granularities. This is the case, for example, when a user studies organizations whose growth rate in certain years in the 1990s was less than 60 percent of their average annual growth rate in that decade. The user could then compare the features associated with the poor performance years versus other years at multiple granularities, finding important associations.

Moreover, traditional data cubes support only dimensions of categorical data and measures of numerical data. In practice, the dimensions of a data cube can be of numerical, spatial, and multimedia data. The measures of a cube can also be of spatial and multimedia aggregations, or collections of them. Support of such nontraditional data cubes will enhance the power of data mining.

Cube-based data mining methods should be the foundation of the online analytical mining mechanism. Although there have been studies of concept description, classification, association, prediction, and clustering in relation to cube-based data mining, more research is needed on efficient cube-based mining algorithms.

Different data mining algorithms can generate dramatically different mining results — unlike relational query processing, which generates the same set of answers to a query with different processing efficiency. Therefore, it is important for organizations to provide alternative mining algorithms for a data mining function, giving users a choice.

Moreover, users might wish to develop their own algorithms in order to experiment with or customize a mining task. If they are given standard APIs, and the OLAM system is well modularized, sophisticated users can add or revise data mining algorithms. These user-defined algorithms could make good use of such well-developed system components as data cube accessing, OLAP functionality, and knowledge visualization tools, integrating them with the existing data mining functions.

One OLAM strength is the interaction of multiple data mining and OLAP functions; another is in selecting a set of data mining functions. For example, the steps may be to dice a portion of a cube, to classify the diced portion based on a designated class attribute, to then find association rules for a class of data so classified, and finally to drill down to find association rules at a finer granularity level. In this way, the organization can develop a data mining system that can tour around the selected data space at will, mining knowledge with multiple, integrated mining tools.

Because mining is usually more expensive than OLAP, OLAM may encounter greater challenges for fast response and high-performance processing. While it is highly desirable and productive to interact with the mining process and dynamically explore data spaces, fast response is critical for interactive mining. In fact, miners might choose to trade mining accuracy for fast response, since interactive mining might progressively lead them to focus the search space, and find ever more important patterns. Once users can identify a small search space, they can call up more sophisticated but slower mining algorithms for careful examination.

It is important for organizations to develop a variety of knowledge and data visualization tools, because an OLAM system will integrate OLAP and data mining, and mine various kinds of knowledge from data warehouses. Charts, curves, decision trees, rule graphs, cube views, and box-plot graphs are effective tools to describe data mining results, and can help users interact with the mining process and monitor their data mining progress.

An OLAM system communicates with users and knowledge visualization packages at the top, and data cubes/databases at the bottom. Therefore, it should be carefully designed, systematically developed, and highly modularized.

Moreover, because an OLAM system must integrate with many subsystems, it should be designed with extensibility in mind. For example, an OLAM system might be integrated with a statistical data analysis package, or be extended for spatial data mining, text mining, financial data analysis, multimedia data mining, or Web mining. Modularity allows easy extension into such new domains.

IMPLEMENTATION OF OLAM MECHANISMS

Because the OLAM mechanism requires efficient implementation, special attention should be paid to:

- modularized design and standard APIs
- support of online analytical mining by high-performance data cube technology
- constraint-based online analytical mining
- progressive refinement of data mining quality
- layer-shared mining with data cubes
- bookmarking and backtracking techniques

An OLAM system might well integrate a variety of data mining modules via different kinds of data cubes and visualization tools. Thus, highly modularized design and standard APIs will be important for the systematic development of OLAM systems, and for developing, testing, and sharing data mining modules across multiple platforms and systems.

In this context, OLEDB for OLAP by Microsoft, and multi-dimensional API (MDAPI)[1] by the OLAP Council, respectively, could be important initiatives toward standardizing data warehouse APIs for both OLAP and mining in data cubes. Sharable visualization tool packages could also prove useful here — in particular, Java-based, platform-independent knowledge visualization tools.

High-performance data cube technology is critical to online analytical mining in data warehouses. There have been many efficient data cube computation techniques developed in recent years that helped in the efficient construction of large data cubes. However, when a mining system must compute the relationships among many dimensions, or examine fine details, it might be necessary to dynamically compute portions of data cubes on-the-fly.

Moreover, effective data mining requires the support of nontraditional data cubes with complex dimensions and measures, in addition to the on-the-fly computation of query-based data cubes and the efficient computation of multi-featured data cubes. This requires further development of data cube technology.

While most data mining requests are query or constraint based, online analytical mining requires fast response to data mining requests. Therefore, the organization must perform mining with a limited scope of data, confined by queries and constraints. In addition, the organization must adopt efficient, constraint-based data mining algorithms. For example, many constraints involving set containments or aggregate functions can be pushed deeply into the association rule mining process. The organization should also explore such constraint-based mining in other data mining tasks.

There is a wide range of data mining algorithms. While some are fast and scalable, higher-quality algorithms generally cost more. Organizations can use a methodology that first applies fast mining algorithms on large data sets to identify the regions/patterns of interest, and then applies costly but more accurate algorithms for detailed analysis of these regions/patterns. For example, in spatial association rule mining, one technique first collects the candidates that *potentially* pass the roughly determined minimum support threshold, and then further examines only those that pass the rough test, using a more expensive spatial computation algorithm.

Each data cube dimension represents an organized layer of concepts. Therefore, data mining can be performing by first examining the high levels of abstraction, and then progressively deepening the mining process toward lower abstraction levels. This saves the organization from indiscriminately examining all the concepts at a low level.

The OLAM paradigm offers the user freedom to explore and discover knowledge by applying any sequence of data mining algorithms with data cube navigation. Users can often choose from many alternatives when traversing from one data mining state to the next. If users set bookmarks when a discover path proves uninteresting, they can return to a previous state and explore other alternatives. Such marking and backtracking mechanisms can protect users from being lost in the OLAM space.

ANALYTICAL MINING METHODS

There are other efficient and effective online analytical mining techniques.[1] These include the design of a data mining language, incremental and distributed mining of association rules, constrained association mining, mining periodic patterns, a wavelet technique for similarity-based time-series analysis, intelligent query answering with data mining techniques, and a multi-layer database model.

A good data mining query language will support ad hoc and interactive data mining. Such a language can serve as the underlying core for different GUIs in a variety of commercial data mining systems, and facilitate the standardization and wide adoption of the technology.

It is best to update data mining results incrementally, rather than mining from scratch on database updates — especially when a database contains huge amounts of data. And, while it is a straightforward process to work out incremental data mining algorithms for concept description, it is nontrivial to update association rules incrementally.

Ad hoc query-based data mining is best when users wish to examine various data portions with different constraints. Constrained association rule mining supports the constraint-based, human-centered exploratory mining of associations. By this process, too, user-specified constraints can be pushed deeply into the association mining process to reduce the search space.

Many patterns are periodic or approximately periodic in nature; for example, seasons change periodically by year, and temperatures change periodically by day. In some cases, while the whole sequence exhibits no periodicity behavior, some particular points or segments in the sequence could be approximately periodic. For example, while someone might watch a particular TV news show from 7:00 to 7:30 a.m. almost every morning, his TV-watching habit is *irregular* at other hours.

Using an OLAP-based technique for mining the periodicity of such patterns in large databases[1] can be explored via two cases: (1) with a given period, and (2) with an arbitrary period. For a user-specified given period, such as per day, per week, or per quarter, the organization can aggregate the potential activity patterns for the given period along the time dimension in a data cube. Similar OLAP-based methods apply for mining periodic patterns with arbitrary periods.

Similarity-based time-series analysis is similar to a stock market database. It is used to find similar time-related patterns such as trends and segments in a large, time-series database. In most previous analyses of similarity-based time series, organizations have adopted such traditional trend analysis techniques as Fourier transformation. More recently, wavelet transformation-based similarity mining methods have been used to discover trends or similar curves or curve segments. This method has proven efficient and effective at mining large time-series databases.

Database queries can be answered intelligently using concept hierarchies, data mining results, or online data mining techniques. For example, instead of bulky answers, a summary of answers can be presented, allowing users to manipulate the summary by drilling or dicing. Alternatively, related answers or rules can be presented in the form of associations or correlations, based on association mining results.

The autonomy and semantic heterogeneity among different databases present a major challenge for cooperating multiple databases. Tools to handle this problem use methods for schema analysis, transformation, integration, and mediation. However, because schema level analysis may be too general to solve the problem, the organization should consider data-level analysis, whereby the database contents are analyzed.

The organization can construct a multi-layer database model utilizing a common data access API, and using generalization-based data mining to generalize the database contents from a primitive level to multiple higher levels. A multi-layer database provides a useful architecture for intelligent query answering, and helps in information exchange and interoperability among heterogeneous databases. This is because the low-level heterogeneous data is transformed into high-level, relatively homogeneous information that can then be used for effective communication and query/information transformation among multiple databases.

OLAM AND COMPLEX DATA TYPES

It is challenging to extend the online analytical mining method to complex types of data. These include complex data objects, spatial data, and text and multimedia data.

Object-oriented and object-relational databases introduce advanced concepts into database systems, including object identity, complex structured objects, methods, and class/subclass hierarchies. A generalization-based data mining method can generalize complex objects, construct a multi-dimensional object cube, and perform analytical mining in such an object cube.

Here, objects with complex structures can be generalized to high-level data with relatively simple structures. For example, an object identifier can be generalized to the class identifier of the lowest class where the object resides. In addition, an object with a sophisticated structure can be generalized into several dimensions of data that reflect the structure, the generalized value, or other features of the object.

A spatial database stores nonspatial data representing other properties of spatial objects and their nonspatial relationships, as well as spatial data representing points, lines, and regions. A spatial data cube consists of both spatial and nonspatial dimensions and measures, and can be modeled by the star or snowflake schema, resembling its relational counterpart. Spatial data mining can be performed in a spatial database as well as in a spatial data cube.

Text analysis methods and content-based image retrieval techniques play an important role in mining text and multimedia data. By one method of online analytical mining of text and multimedia data, text/multimedia data cubes are built, whereupon the cube-based relational and spatial mining techniques are extended toward mining text and multimedia data.

Organizations can also mine the Web access patterns stored in Web log records. Web log records are preprocessed and cleaned, and multiple dimensions are built, based on such Web access information as page start time, duration, user, server, URL, next page, and page type. The process includes construction of a WebLog, and the performance of time-related, multi-dimensional data analysis and data mining.

CONCLUSION

The rapid development of data warehouse and OLAP technology has paved the way toward effective online analytical mining. Analysts anticipate that OLAM will become a natural addition to OLAP technology, which enhances data analysis in data warehouses.

Notes

1. The OLAP Council's proposed multi-dimensional API, now on version 2.0. The earlier, abortive version was called the MD-API (with a hyphen). Very few or no vendors are likely to support even the 2.0 version (which was released in January 1998), and no vendor has even announced a date for supporting it.
2. DBMiner is an intelligent data mining and data warehousing system. This educational release allows university teachers and research institutes to have a comprehensive data mining system to teach students and researchers the concepts and skills of data mining and data warehousing. Its first professional version has been released with enhanced data mining capabilities for professional users.
3. The traditional periodicity detection methods, such as Fast Fourier Transformation, find the periodicity of the whole sequence, but not the periodicity of a particular point/segment in the sequence.

Chapter 20
Placing Images and Multimedia on the Corporate Network

Gilbert Held

UNTIL RECENTLY, IT WAS RARE FOR A CORPORATE NETWORK TO TRANSPORT IMAGES, AND MULTIMEDIA WAS MORE TALKED ABOUT THAN ACTUALLY AVAILABLE. The primary use of images was for incorporation into word processing or desktop publishing applications, and most images remained local to the personal computer they were stored on.

Recently, the use of images has moved off the individual PC workstation and onto network servers and mainframes, making images available for retrieval by virtually any employee with a PC connected to a local area network or to the corporate network. In addition, the recent standardization of multimedia data storage has increased the ability of organizations to purchase or develop applications that merge audio, video, and data. Thus, there is a growing trend of organizations adding images, as well as multimedia data, to applications. This chapter discusses methods of restructuring an existing network to accommodate the transportation of images and multimedia cost-effectively.

MULTIMEDIA

The term *multimedia* is a catchall phrase that refers to the use of two or more methods for conveying information. Thus, multimedia can include voice or sound (both collectively referred to as audio), still images, moving images, and fax images, as well as text documents. This means that multimedia can be considered an extension of image storage. To understand how multimedia data storage requirements differ from conventional data storage requirements, this chapter focuses first on the storage requirements of images.

0-8493-0893-3/00/$0.00+$.50

Image Data Storage Requirements

Images are converted into a series of pixels or picture elements by a scanner. Software used to control the scanner will place the resulting pixels into a particular order based on the file format selected from the scanning software menu. Some file storage formats require the use of compression before the image can be stored. Compression typically reduces data storage requirements by 50% or more.

Text and image data storage requirements are significantly different. A full page of text, such as a one-page letter, might contain approximately 300 words, with an average of five characters per word. Thus, a typical one-page text document would require 1500 characters of data storage. Adding formatting characters used by a word processor, a one-page text document might require up to 2000 characters, or 16,000 bits of data storage.

When an image is scanned, the data storage requirements of the resulting file depend on four factors. Those factors include the size of the image, the scan resolution used during the scanning process, the type of image being scanned—color or black and white—and whether or not the selected file format results in the compression of pixels before their storage.

To illustrate the data storage requirements of different types of images, one example focuses on a 3" x 5" photograph. That photograph contains a total of 15 square inches that must be scanned.

A low-resolution black-and-white scan normally occurs using 150 lines per inch and 150 pixels per line per inch, where a pixel with a zero value represents white and a pixel whose value is one represents black. Thus, the total number of bits required to store a 3" x 5" black-and-white photograph using a low-resolution scan without first compressing the data would be 337,500 bits, which would result in a requirement to store 42,188 bytes of data. Thus, a 3" x 5" black-and-white photograph would require 42,188/2000,or approximately 21 times the amount of storage required by a one-page document.

Most scanners now consider 300 lines per inch with 300 pixels per line, per inch, to represent a high-resolution scan. However, some newly introduced scanning products now consider 300 lines per inch with 300 pixels per line to represent a medium- or high-resolution scan. Regardless of the pixel density considered to represent a medium- or high-resolution scan; the computation of the resulting data storage requirement is performed in the same manner. That is, storing the photograph would entail multiplying the number of square inches of the document—in this example, 15—by the pixel density squared. Exhibit 20-1 compares the data storage requirements of a one-page text document to the data storage required to store a 3" x 5" black-and-white photograph at different scan resolutions.

Exhibit 20-1. Document versus image storage requirements.

Type of Document/Image	Data Storage (Bytes)
Text document containing 300 words	2,000
3" x 5" B & W photograph scanned at 150 pixels/inch	42,188
3" x 5" B & W photograph scanned at 300 pixels/inch	84,375
3" x 5" B & W photograph scanned at 450 pixels/inch	126,563
3" x 5" B & W photograph scanned at 600 pixels/inch	168,750

To store an image in color, data storage requirements would increase significantly. For example, if a scanner supports color, each pixel would require one byte to represent each possible color of the pixel. Thus, a color image would require eight times the data storage of a black-and-white image when a scanner supports up to 256 colors per pixel. This means that the 3" x 5" photograph scanned at 300 pixels per inch would require 675,000 bytes of storage. Similarly, a 3" x 5" color photograph scanned at a resolution of 600 pixels per inch would require 1.35M bytes of storage, or 675 times the amount of storage required for a 300 word one-page document.

Without considering the effect of data compression, the transmission of images on a network can require from 20 to more than 600 times the amount of time required to transmit a one-page standard text document. Thus, it is obvious that the transmission of images by themselves or as a part of a multimedia application can adversely affect the capability of a network to support other users in an efficient manner unless proper planning precedes the support of the multimedia data transfer.

Audio Storage Requirements

The most popular method of voice digitization is known as Pulse Code Modulation, in which analog speech is digitized at a rate of 64K b/s. Thus, one minute of speech would require 480,000 bytes of data storage. At this digitization rate, data storage of digitized speech can easily expand to require a significant portion of a hard disk for just 10 to 20 minutes of audio.

Multimedia applications developers do not store audio using Plug-Compatible Manufacturer. Instead, they store audio using a standardized audio compression technique that results in a lower level of audio fidelity but significantly lowers the data storage requirement of digitized audio.

Today, several competing multimedia voice digitization standards permit speech to be digitized at 8K b/s. Although this is a significant improvement over PCM used by telephone companies to digitize voice, it still requires a substantial amount of disk space to store a meaningful amount of voice. For example, one hour of voice would require 2.8M bytes of data storage. Thus, data storage of audio is similar to video, in that a meaningful database of images and sound must either be placed on a CD -ROM or on the hard disk of a network server or mainframe computer that usually has a larger data storage capacity than individual personal computers.

Image Utilization

In spite of the vast increase in the amount of data that must be transported to support image applications, the use of imaging is rapidly increasing. The old adage "a picture is worth a thousand words" is especially true when considering many computer applications. Today, several network-compliant database programs support the attachment of image files to database records. Using a Canon digital camera or similar product, real estate agents can photograph the exterior and interior of homes and transfer the digitized images to the network server upon their return to the office. When a potential client comes into the office, an agent can enter the client's home criteria, such as the number of bedrooms, baths, price range, school district, and similar information, and have both textual information as well as photographs of the suitable homes meeting the client's criteria displayed on their screen. This capability significantly reduces the time required to develop a list of homes that the client may wish to physically view.

Audio Utilization

The primary use of audio is to supplement images and text with sound. Unlike a conventional PC, which can display any image supported by the resolution of the computer's monitor, the use of audio requires specialized equipment. First, the computer must have a sound board or specialized adapter card that supports the method used to digitize audio. Second, each computer must have one or more speakers connected to the sound board or speech adapter card to broadcast the resulting reconverted analog signal.

STORING IMAGES ON A LAN SERVER OR MAINFRAME

There are three methods for storing images on a LAN server or mainframe. First, images can be transferred to a computer's hard disk using either a personal computer or scanner, or, by connecting the PC to a digital camera. Another method for storing images involves forwarding each image after it is scanned or transferred from a digital camera or similar device. A third method for placing images on a file server or mainframe is based on pre-mastering a CD-ROM or another type of optical disk.

Transferring a large number of images at one time can adversely affect network users. To minimize the effect, images can be transferred from a computer to a server or mainframe after normal work hours. As an alternative, a removable hard disk can be used, permitting movement of the disk to a similarly equipped network server to transfer images without affecting network users.

Forwarding Images After Scanning

This method of storing images on the LAN has the greatest potential for negative impact on network users. Some document scanners are capable of scanning several pages per minute. If a large number of images were scanned, transferring the digitized images through a local or WAN connection could saturate a network during the scanning and transferring process. This happens because, as other network users are transferring a few thousand bytes, transferring images containing 20 to 600 times more data would consume most of the network bandwidth for relatively long periods of time. Thus, the effect of image transfer can be compared to the addition of 20 to 600 network users transferring one-page documents, with the actual addition based on the resolution of the images, and whether or not they are in black and white or color.

Pre-Mastering

Pre-mastering a CD-ROM or other type of optical disk permits images to become accessible by other network users without adversely affecting network operations. However, cost and ease of image modification or replacement must be weighed against the advantage of this method.

From a cost perspective, equipment required to master images on a CD-ROM will cost between $3,000 and $5,000. In comparison, the use of conventional magnetic storage on the server or mainframe can avoid that equipment cost as well as the cost of a CD-ROM drive connected to a file server.

Concerning ease of image modification or replacement, CD-ROM data cannot be modified once a disk is mastered. This means that a new CD-ROM disk must be mastered each time previously stored images or data must be modified or replaced.

If real-time or daily updates are not required, this method of image placement on a network server or mainframe should be considered. The time required to master a CD-ROM disk has been reduced to a few hours, when mastering occurs on a 486-based personal computer. Also, write-once CD-ROM disks now cost under $20. Thus, a weekly update of an image database could be performed for a one-time cost of between $3,000 and $5,000, and $20 per week for each write-once CD-ROM disk used. Since this method would have no negative impact on network operations, its cost would be minor in comparison to the cost of modifying a network.

The next section focuses on methods used to provide access to images stored in a central repository. Use of both LAN and WAN transmission facilities are examined, with several strategies for minimizing the effect of image transfers on network users.

ACCESSING IMAGES

Once a decision is made to add images to a database or other application, the potential effect of the retrieval of images by network users against the current organizational network infrastructure must be examined. Doing so provides the information necessary to determine if an existing network should be modified to support the transfer of images, as well as data.

To illustrate the factors that must be considered, this example assumes that images are to be added to a 50-node LAN server. The network server is attached to a 10M-b/s Ethernet network as illustrated in Exhibit 20-2a, with images placed on a CD-ROM jukebox connected to the server.

Based on an analysis of the expected use of the LAN, 15 stations were identified that are expected to primarily use the images stored on the CD-ROM jukebox. The other 35 network users are expected to casually use the CD-ROM jukebox, primarily using the LAN to access other applications on the server, such as workgroup software and other application programs, including a conventional text-based database and electronic mail.

One method of minimizing the contention for network resources between network users is obtained by segmenting the network. Exhibit 20-2b illustrates

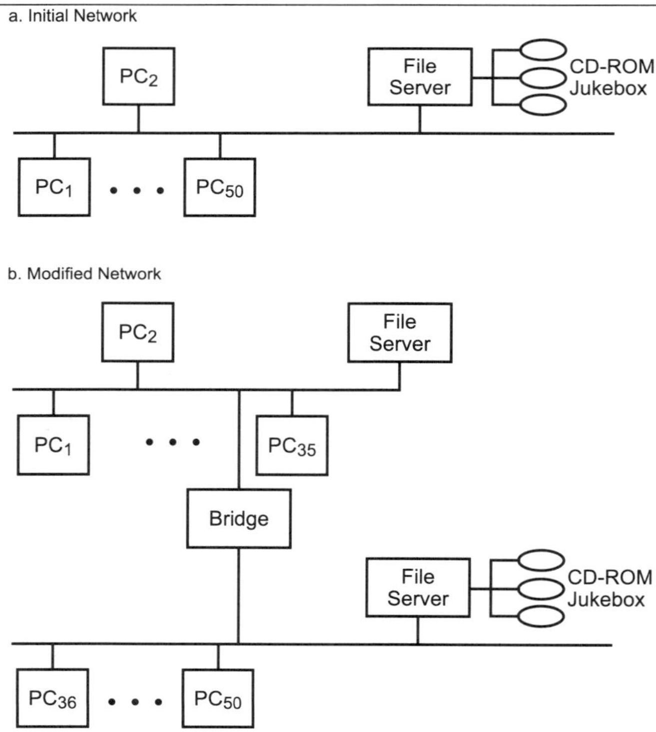

Exhibit 20-2. Modifying an Ethernet network.

the use of a local bridge to link separate networks. In this illustration the 35 network users expected to have a minimal requirement for image transfers are located on one network, while the remaining 15 network users that have a significant requirement to transfer images are placed on a second network. The use of the bridge permits users of each network to access applications stored on the file server on the other network. However, this new network structure segments network stations by their expected usage, minimizing the adverse effect of heavy image transfer by 15 users on what was a total network of 50 users.

INTERNETWORKING

The segmentation of an Ethernet LAN into two networks linked together by a local bridge created an inter-network. Although the network structure was created to minimize the effect of transporting images on a larger network, this method of increasing the volume of image traffic through bridges that directly interconnect separate LANs can produce a bottleneck and inhibit the flow of other traffic, such as client/server queues, E-mail, and other network applications.

Placing Images on Image Servers

When constructing a local inter-network consisting of several linked LANs within a building, one method to minimize the effect of image traffic on other network applications is to place image applications on image servers located on a separate high-speed network. Exhibit 20-3 illustrates the use of an FDDI backbone ring consisting of two image servers whose access is obtainable from workstations located on several Ethernet and token ring networks through local bridges linking those networks to the FDDI ring. By using the FDDI ring for image applications, the 100M-b/s operating rate of FDDI provides a delivery mechanism that enables workstation users on multiple lower operating rate LANs to simultaneously access image applications without experiencing network delays.

For example, one network user on each LAN illustrated in Exhibit 20-3 accesses the same image application on an image server connected to the FDDI backbone LAN. If each token ring network operates at 16M b/s, and each Ethernet operates at 10M b/s, the composite transfer rate from the FDDI network to each of the lower operating rate LANs bridged to that network is 52M b/s. Since the FDDI network operates at 100M b/s, it can simultaneously present images to network users on each of the four LANs without any inter-network bottlenecks occurring.

Another advantage associated with using an FDDI backbone restricted to supporting image servers and bridges is economics. This configuration minimizes the requirement for using more expensive FDDI adapter cards to one card per image server and one card per bridge. In comparison, upgrading an

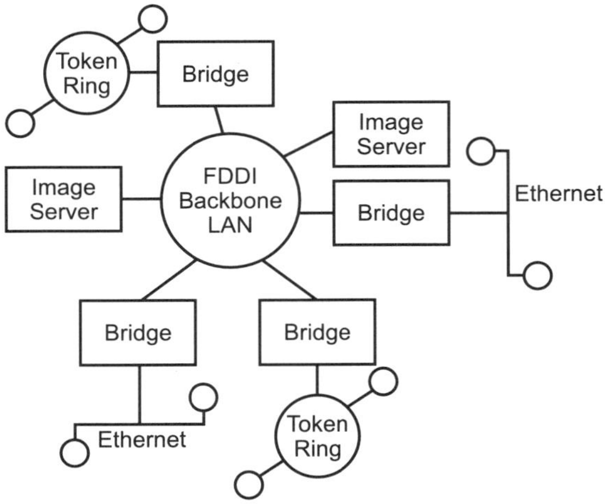

Exhibit 20-3. Using a high-speed FDDI backbone.

existing network to FDDI would require replacing each workstation's existing network adapter card with a more expensive FDDI adapter card.

To illustrate the potential cost savings, assume each Ethernet and token ring network has 100 workstations, resulting in a total of 400 adapter cards, including two image servers that would require replacement if each existing LAN was replaced by a common FDDI network. Since FDDI adapter cards cost approximately $800, this replacement would result in the expenditure of $320,000. In comparison, the acquisition of four bridges and six FDDI adapter cards would cost less than $20,000.

TRANSFERRING IMAGES THROUGH WIDE AREA NETWORKS

In the next example, a group of PC users requires the use of a WAN to access images database in a database at a remote location. Images are placed on a CD -ROM jukebox connected to a server on LAN A, which in turn is connected to LAN B through a pair of remote bridges operating at 64K b/s. This network configuration is illustrated in Exhibit 20-4.

If users on network A access several applications on network B and vice versa, in addition to accessing the images stored on the CD -ROM jukebox on network A, what happens when a user on network B attempts to access text data on network A during an image transfer? If another network B user requested an image transfer, the user requesting a text transfer is now contending for network resources with the user performing the image transfer. This means that alternate frames of data flow over the 64K-b/s transmission facility—first a frame containing a portion of an image, then a frame containing a portion of the text transfer. This alternate frame transmission continues until one transfer is completed, prior to all network resources becoming devoted to the remaining transfer.

Thus, not only is the 64K-b/s transmission rate a significant bottleneck to the transfer of images, but WAN users must contend for access to that resource. A 640K-byte image would require 80 seconds to transfer between remotely located LANs on a digital circuit operating at 64K b/s and devoted to a single remote user. If that remote user had to share the use of the WAN link with another user performing another image transfer, each transfer would require 160 seconds. Thus, transferring images through a WAN connection can result in a relatively long waiting time. Although the WAN connection could be upgraded to a T1 or a Fractional T1 circuit, the monthly incremental cost of a 500 mile 64K-b/s digital circuit is approximately $600. In comparison, the monthly cost of a 500 mile 1.544M-b/s digital circuit would exceed $4,200.

Localizing Images

One alternative to problems associated with the transfer of images through a WAN can be obtained by localizing images to each LAN to remove or substantially reduce the necessity to transfer images through a WAN. To do so with respect to the network configuration illustrated in Exhibit 20-4 would require the installation of either a single CD-ROM drive or a CD-ROM jukebox onto network B's file server. This would enable network users on each LAN to obtain the majority of the images they require through a LAN transmission facility that normally operates at 10 to 100 times the operating rate of most WAN transmission facilities. The placement

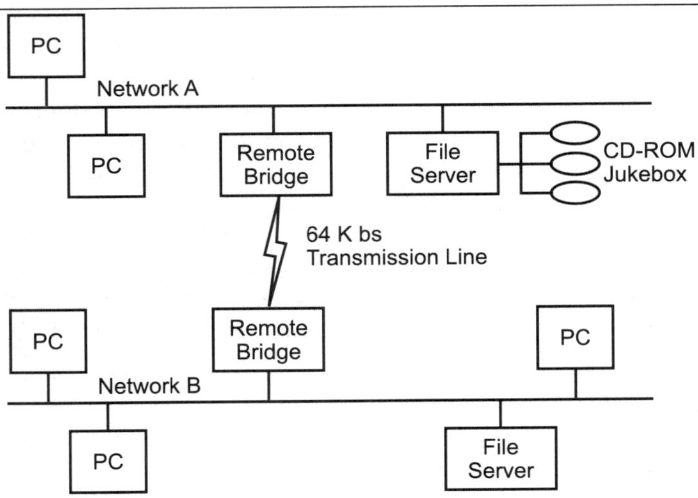

Exhibit 20-4. Image transfers using a WAN link.

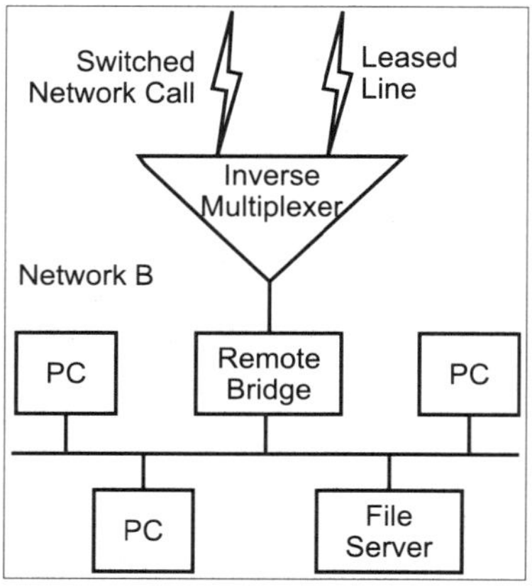

Exhibit 20-5. Using a bandwidth-on-demand inverse multiplexer.

of additional image storage facilities on each LAN can substantially reduce potential WAN bottlenecks by reducing the need to transfer images via the WAN.

Bandwidth-on-Demand Inverse Multiplexers

A second method of reducing WAN bottlenecks caused by the transfer of images is obtained by the use of bandwidth-on-demand inverse multiplexers. Several vendors market bandwidth-on-demand inverse multiplexers that can monitor the utilization of a leased line and initiate a switched network call when a predefined lease line utilization threshold is reached.

Exhibit 20-5 illustrates the use of a bandwidth-on-demand inverse multiplexer at the network B location shown in Exhibit 20-4. Under normal operating conditions, a 64K-b/s leased line connects network A to network B. When the transfer of images begins to saturate the use of the leased line, one inverse multiplexer will automatically initiate a call over the switched network to the other multiplexer. That call can be a switched digital call at 56/64K b/s or a call over the Public Switched Telephone Network, in which the data transfer operating rate depends on the type or analog call costs between 10 and 25 cents per minute, the use of inverse multiplexers can represent an economical alternative to the use of additional or higher-speed leased lines when image transfers only occur periodically during the workday.

CONCLUSION

Since multimedia includes either digitized images; digitized speech; or both, the methods and techniques described in this chapter for handling images are applicable for multimedia. Thus, the segmentation of a local area network, the use of a high-speed backbone network for providing access to image servers, or the addition of multimedia storage facilities on individual LANs to reduce WAN traffic are all applicable to the transfer of multimedia information.

Placing images and multimedia on the corporate network can be considered equivalent to the addition of a very large number of network users. When planning to add access to image and multimedia databases, network managers should use the same planning process required to support conventional access to file servers and mainframe databases. When data transfer requirements begin to adversely affect network performance, managers should consider transferring multimedia data to storage repositories and accessing it through the methods suggested in this chapter. The goal at all times is to avoid burdening network users while remaining able to support an organization's image and multimedia database access requirements in an efficient and cost-effective manner.

Chapter 21
Data Subsets—PC-based Information: Is It Data for the Enterprise?

John R. Vacca

IT AUTOMATION IS THE APPLICATION OF COMPUTERS, SOFTWARE, AND OTHER TECHNICAL COMPONENTS TO DEFINE AND MAINTAIN STANDARD IT PROCESSES, with the end result being a more efficient and productive IT enterprise. IT automation systems are typically used by enterprises to help IT users and managers better plan, organize, and execute the IT plan. These systems often allow users to analyze sales trends, schedule account calls, process end-user requests, communicate via electronic mail, keep track of end user and software and hardware product lists, generate price quotes, and plan end-user IT objectives, among many other IT applications. IT automation systems often incorporate portable notebook or handheld computers, remote database synchronization, and highly specialized software. To date, thousands of IT enterprises worldwide have implemented some form of IT automation.

Successful IT automation implementations commonly result in 20 percent productivity gains, and often as high as 50 percent or more. IT enterprises have realized significant and documentable cost savings with payback periods of 16 months or less. Falling technology prices, together with technological advances, make IT automation more attractive today than ever before. Total IT automation expenditures by U.S. IT enterprises grew by 50 percent in 1999 and are expected to total almost $700 billion in 2002.

Distributed IT users using laptop or handheld PC-based IT automation systems need access to up-to-date enterprise data. Remote data subset synchronization allows IT users to access the most current PC-based

0-8493-0893-3/00/$0.00+$.50

information, whether the data is entered or updated by remote IT users or the enterprise offices.

Successful IT automation implementations depend on an efficient, reliable data subset synchronization framework. For IT users and managers to effectively share end-user notes, activities, objectives, and IT data, the IT automation synchronization routines need to work without fail.

DATA SUBSET SYNCHRONIZATION FRAMEWORK

At the heart of data subset synchronization technology is ActiveX Data Objects (ADO),[1] the latest data access technology from Microsoft. ADO offers the following major benefits for IT automation subset synchronization:

1. *Universal data access:* Most IT enterprises employ multiple client and server database platforms. ADO is flexible enough to support any database platform that exposes an object linking and embedding Database (OLE DB)[2] provider or open database connectivity (ODBC)[3] driver.
2. *Performance:* Because ADO is a thin layer that sits between an application and its data, the performance of ADO is comparable to direct (often proprietary) database access methods.
3. *Future considerations:* ADO is an open technology that will continue to evolve as database technologies evolve.

Now, take a look at the following data subset synchronization topics:

- steps in the data subset synchronization process
- methods for tracking changes on the client and server
- generation and transfer of log files
- IT library documents
- log file application
- conflict resolution
- synchronizing data subsets
- cascading deletes on client database
- restoring a client database
- distribution of application and database changes

STEPS IN THE DATA SUBSET SYNCHRONIZATION PROCESS

The following are the high-level steps involved in the data subset synchronization framework:

1. Remote user databases are created as subsets of the master server database.
2. As updates, inserts, and deletes are made to remote client databases and to the central server database, the changes are flagged to

be included in log files created during the data subset synchronization process.

3. The remote user initiates an exchange of log files containing incremental data changes and IT library documents between the client and server.
4. After the successful exchange of log files, changes are applied so that each database contains up-to-date PC-based information.

TRACKING DATABASE CHANGES IN THE CLIENT

The client application, for example, uses the table structure (as shown in Exhibit 21-1) to track deletes and field-level updates as they occur. Each deleted row generates a new record in *tbl_Sync_Deleted* and each updated field generates a new record in *tbl_Sync_Updated.* Optionally, updates for any given table can be handled at the record level. This is often desirable for processing updates on very narrow tables. Both *tbl_Sync_Deleted* and *tbl_Sync_Updated* are later used to generate the log file to be sent to the server.

Inserts to the database are tracked with a simple True/False field in the base table. For example, if a record is added to *tbl_Contacts*, the new row will contain a column indicating that this is a new record.

By only tracking a flag in the base table for inserts, the overhead required to copy the transaction to a log table is avoided.

The data subset synchronization framework does not rely on the client computer clock time to track changes. This frees the data subset

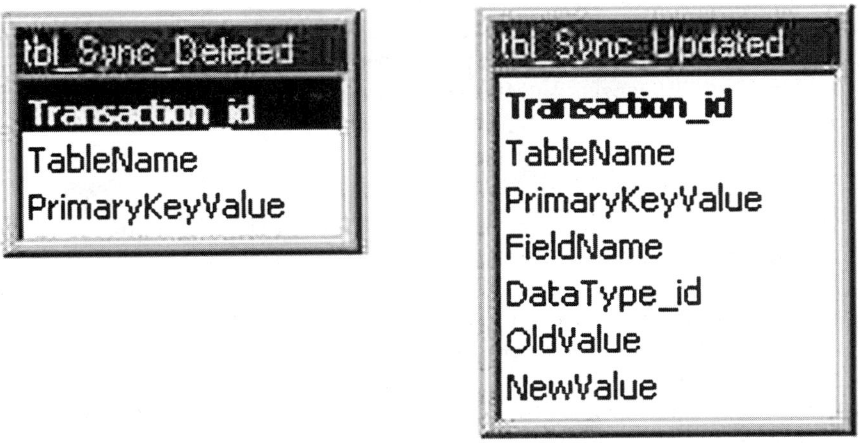

Exhibit 21-1. Table structure to track deletes and field-level updates as they occur.

synchronization process from problems related to unsynchronized clocks and varying time zones.

TRACKING DATABASE CHANGES IN THE SERVER

The server database tracks deletes, updates, and inserts in the same structure as the client, as shown in Exhibit 21-2. The only difference is the method of populating the sync tables. On the server side, it is often desirable to make mass updates to the data using an administrative application or structure query language (as opposed to using the IT application). When mass updates are made, many systems will not be able to track the incremental changes. Because the data subset synchronization framework uses server-side triggers, transaction tables will always be accurate. These database triggers offer extremely high performance and ease of implementation.

GENERATING AND TRANSFERRING LOG FILES FOR THE CLIENT

A client log file is generated each time the user initiates data subset synchronization, as shown in Exhibit 21-3. The log file contains only incremental changes tracked on the client. The user-initiated process creates the log file and initiates connectivity to the central database server. In the event that the process is interrupted before successfully connecting to the central database and transferring the log file, the log file will remain on the client to be transferred during the subsequent connection. To ensure transactional integrity, each transfer is either committed in its entirety, or backed-out, so that it is as if none of the operations took place.

In the event of an interrupted data subset synchronization process, the user can simply synchronize at a later time. At this point, another log file is created, capturing incremental database changes since the failed attempt. This new log file is saved with a sequenced number appended to the end of the file name. In each data subset synchronization, all waiting sequential sync files are compressed and then transferred once a server connection is established.

GENERATING AND TRANSFERRING LOG FILES FOR THE SERVER

A server process is needed that can be scheduled to run automatically at predetermined times, generating client-specific log files that remain on the server until downloaded by the user. The data for this log file is extracted from the server database by pulling out changes made since the time the previous log file was generated. If a user does not synchronize for several days, additional log files are created each time the process is run, with a sequenced number appended to the end of the filename. All log files are compressed after creation, or appended to an existing Zip file of logs. All client-specific log files are transferred to the client in a single compressed file when the user initiates synchronization. After the successful

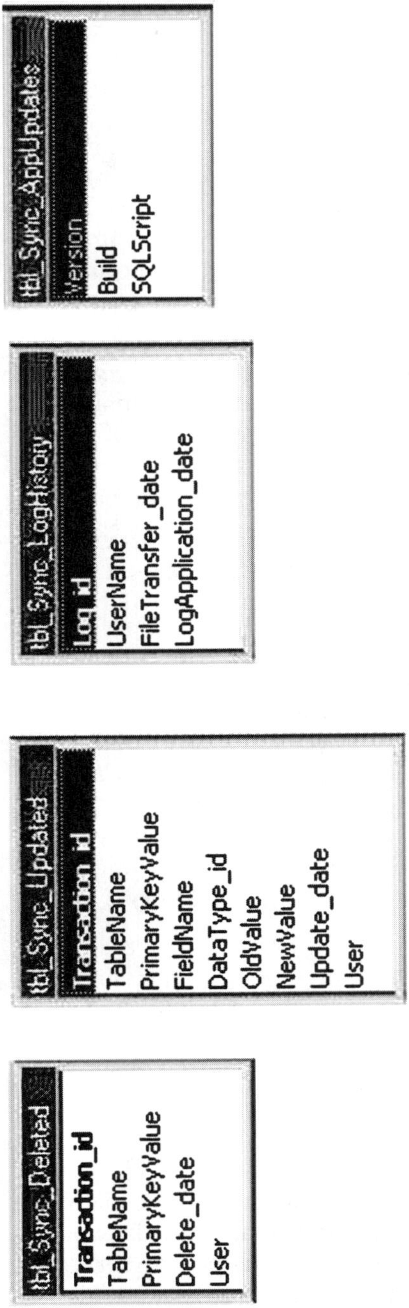

Exhibit 21-2. Tracking deletes, updates, and inserts in the same structure as the client.

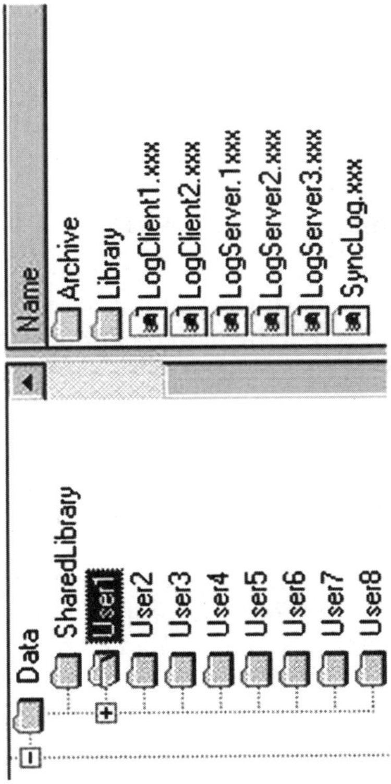

Exhibit 21-3. Generating a client log file.

Exhibit 21-4. Storing IT library documents by the data subset synchronization framework.

transfer of log files between client and server, an entry is made in *synclog.xxx* in the user's data folder, indicating the time of successful transfer (see Exhibit 21-3).

IT LIBRARY DOCUMENTS

The data subset synchronization framework stores IT library documents in the format shown in Exhibit 21-4. Documents that are user specific are stored in the path *UserName\Library*. Shared documents, which will be delivered to all users, are placed in *\SharedLibrary*.

When the server process is run, the last modified date for each library document is checked against the *LastModified_date* field in *tbl_Sync_SalesLibrary*. If a document has been modified, it is compressed and added to the *UserName\Library* path for download by the user upon the next data subset synchronization. The date comparison method makes it easy for an administrator to update documents in the library by simply copying the documents to the appropriate directory on the server. All documents are synchronized to the *ClientPath* specified in *tbl_Sync_SalesLibrary*

APPLYING LOG FILES

Log files contain the data necessary to process database deletes, inserts, and updates. Deletes are processed first, followed by inserts and updates. All database modification operations occur in a sequence that ensures referential integrity is not violated.

Client

Changes contained in the server log file(s) transferred to the client are applied after the remote connection is terminated. This minimizes potentially expensive connection fees. Before attempting to apply the server log file(s), the sync process checks for a *Commit Flag* to verify that the file was transferred successfully. Each record that was added, updated, or deleted in the client database, as the result of applying the server log, is flagged for inclusion in the client application's *What's New* module the next time the application is opened.

Server

When the scheduled server process is run, all client log files sitting in each of the user directories are applied to the central database server. Each log file applied represents a transaction. If for any reason an error occurs while applying a single log file, all changes are rolled back.

After successful application, the log file is transferred to an archive directory and kept for a specified number of days. The *tbl_Sync_LogHistory* is updated with user log file transfer and log file application time-stamps.

CONFLICT RESOLUTION

In the data subset synchronization framework, conflicts are resolved at the field level. Conflicts are detected by storing the *OldValue* and *NewValue* of a field in *tbl_Sync_Updated*. For example, if a contact phone number is 111-1111 and the remote user changes it to 222-2222, the client database *tbl_Sync_Updated* will have a record that has *OldValue* = '111-1111' and *NewValue* = '222-2222.' In the meantime, if another user has updated the same phone number field for the same contact to 333-3333, during the data subset synchronization, the client database will see that the current value on the server ('333-3333') is not equal to the *OldValue* ('111-1111") stored on the client. Because the values are different, a conflict needs to be resolved. This resolution is handled through the server data subset synchronization process.

The default conflict setting applies a *last-in-wins* rule. If this rule is not acceptable, the data subset synchronization framework is open enough to allow highly customized conflict rules to be created, such as *record owner wins*, *remote wins*, *server wins*, etc.

SYNCHRONIZING DATA SUBSETS

Because rules for partitioning data are seldom exactly the same from one system to another, the data subset synchronization framework defines subsets of the master server database on a per-table basis. For each synchronized table, a custom structured query language (SQL)[4] WHERE clause can be implemented so users are given the data that is relevant to them.

This is illustrated using a very simple example that synchronizes *tbl_Contacts* as shown in Exhibit 21-5. Implementing the following WHERE

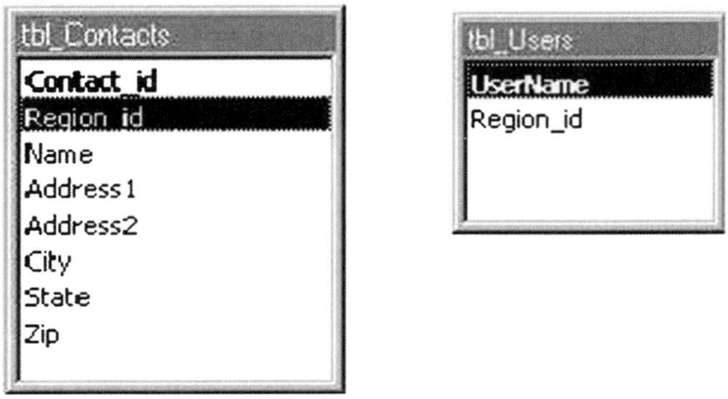

Exhibit 21-5. Data subset synchronization framework.

clause will partition the data so that each user only receives contacts in his/her region:

```
Where tbl_Contacts.Region_id = tbl_Users.Region_id AND
tbl_Users.UserName = SUSER_NAME()
```

CASCADING DELETES ON CLIENT DATABASE

It is often necessary to remove large subsets of data from the client database. IT users are often reassigned to different regions, records become outdated, and security access to data changes. If the client database platform does not support cascading deletes, *cleaning up* a client database can involve specifying individual records for deletion. The data subset synchronization framework includes methods to cascade the deletion of child records on database platforms that do not support cascading deletes.

For example, an IT user is reassigned and will no longer cover IT in France. With cascading deletes, this *cleanup* process only requires an administrative tool to create a single entry in this users log file that deletes the parent record. All child records will be removed and unneeded data will no longer sit on the client.

RESTORING A CLIENT DATABASE

Invariably, there will always be a situation where a hard drive crashes or a database file is inadvertently deleted. When this happens, the client database must be restored from data in the server database. Because the creation of server log files is based on a time-stamp parameter, this time-stamp simply needs to be reset and the user will receive data to rebuild the client database from scratch. An option can even be given in the client application to perform a complete refresh of data. This allows the user to get up and running in the shortest possible amount of time.

DISTRIBUTION OF APPLICATION AND DATABASE CHANGES

A remote application must provide a way to distribute application updates, fixes, new reports, etc. There are two common approaches to updating remote applications: (1) copying new application component files to the client and (2) packaging program logic and form changes as part of the database. The latter, although an efficient way to distribute changes, often has a negative impact on application performance, especially when processing power on the client is marginal.

A remote application must also provide a way to change the structure of the client database (add fields, tables, relationships, etc.). The data subset synchronization framework handles database structure modifications through transact SQL scripts. SQL scripts make database structure modifications without transferring new database files and rebuilding data.

At the time of data subset synchronization, if a user is running a version older than the version number in *tbl_Sync_AppUpdates*, new application files and transact SQL script files are transferred to the client. The *tbl_Sync_AppUpdates* stores version PC-based information and contains a memo field that holds the SQL script required for each update. After the needed files are transferred to the client, an upgrade process is initiated that closes the IT application, copies new application files to their proper locations, runs all SQL scripts against the client database, and reopens the application.

Finally, this is accomplished through the use of a light, secondary application—the application controller—that executes SQL scripts and updates application files. The controller is stored in a location accessible to the IT library. Should modifications be required to the controller application itself, a new application executable is simply transferred via the standard IT library update process, replacing the original controller application.

CONCLUSION

Remote data subset synchronization is the key piece in any remote IT application. It allows IT users to share accurate and up-to-date PC-based information while away from the central office.

Finally, it appears that the data subset synchronization framework is a robust and highly flexible solution for remote IT users. The framework supports a wide range of client and server database platforms and is open enough to allow a high degree of customization.

Notes

1. Abbreviation for ActiveX Data Objects, Microsoft's newest high-level interface for data objects. ADO is designed to eventually replace Data Access Objects (DAO) and Remote Data Objects (RDO). Unlike RDO and DAO, which are designed only for accessing relational databases, ADO is more general and can be used to access all sorts of different types of data, including Web pages, spreadsheets, and other types of documents. Together with OLE DB and ODBC, ADO is one of the main components of Microsoft's Universal Data Access (UDA) specification, which is designed to provide a consistent way of accessing data, regardless of how the data, is structured.
2. Microsoft's OLAP API, effectively the first industry standard for OLAP connectivity. Used to link OLAP clients and servers using a multidimensional language (MDX).
3. A widely adopted Microsoft standard for database connectivity.
4. Abbreviation for structured query language, and pronounced either *see-kwell* or as separate letters. SQL is a standardized query language for requesting information from a database. The original version called SEQUEL (structured English query language) was designed by an IBM research center in 1974 and 1975. SQL was first introduced as a commercial database system in 1979 by Oracle Corporation. Historically, SQL has been the favorite query language for database management systems running on minicomputers and mainframes. Increasingly, however, SQL is being supported by PC database systems because it supports distributed databases (databases that are spread out over several computer systems). This enables several users on a local area network to access the same database simultaneously. Although there are different dialects of SQL, it is nevertheless the closest thing to a standard query language that currently exists. In 1986, ANSI approved a rudimentary version of SQL as the official standard, but most versions of SQL since then have included many extensions to the ANSI standard. In 1991, ANSI updated the standard. The new standard is known as SAG SQL.

Chapter 22
Failover, Redundancy, and High-Availability Applications in the Call Center Environment

Charles V. Breakfield

HOW DOES A COMPANY BUILD A HIGH-END CALL CENTER (for 250 agents and up) USING THE HIGHLY RELIABLE AND PROPRIETARY PBX SWITCH IN CONJUNCTION WITH THE HIGHLY OPEN AND VULNERABLE COMPUTER TELEPHONY INTEGRATION (CTI) AND CALL CENTER SERVER TECHNOLOGY? Today's call centers inter-mesh voice applications with data applications, so each area must have the same level of high availability as the other. PBX switches have had decades to evolve and are built as proprietary solutions for voice handling. PBX outages are measured in units of minutes per years (in some cases, decades). CTI data systems of today are not built as closed proprietary systems, but open systems running operating systems (OS) with hooks for a multitude of third-party vendors. The openness of data systems, coupled with the youth of server technology, leaves these systems far more fragile and more vulnerable to failure.

Leading-edge call center equipment manufacturers have placed the convergence of voice and data technology to meet the expected growth explosion. Each manufacturer, especially those with PBX historically, has specifically positioned its product line to impact a huge market segment worldwide. Therefore, end-user expectations for the reliability of products and services are extremely high. For this and many other reasons, it is critical that CTI products and services live up to the end-user expectations that the telecom companies have developed.

0-8493-0893-3/00/$0.00+$.50

Current technology is available to ensure that the call center product suite—including skills-based routing capability, CTI screen-pop at the desktop, interactive voice response (IVR), and Web response for Internet users—works together. This convergence of voice and data provides the high-end technology solutions that also bridge the telecom and information systems (IS) groups within an enterprise. Current product offerings have not met neither the telecom, nor IS groups expectations for reliability.

Management expects voice and data to be at the same robust level of availability, but the data side does not yet have the years of experience to compete with the reliability of voice. The question then becomes one of reviewing the technology available to determine the architecture structure that might compensate for the lacking within the products offered.

Call center experience currently resides with the main PBX manufacturers. With a long relationship with many businesses, the user community naturally expects the PBX manufacturers and telecom support for products that not only play well together, but also contain zero tolerance for failure. Telephony manufacturers have positioned products to positively impact the enterprise—but with a huge encroachment into the IS environment. The associated CTI solution vendors must be fluent in both telecom and IS to be successful, long-term suppliers to the call center environment. The first step is to ensure that the products fit the primary expectations of reliability.

TERMINOLOGY

To move forward, the premise is that the availability of the data side of the CTI environment must be as high as on a PBX. There are several approaches to building "high-availability" applications. Each approach has a different strength and weakness to offer, depending on the scenario in which it is placed, in conjunction with the needs of the enterprise.

It is important that the understanding of the technology available be coupled with the definitions of some basic terms.

- *Redundancy* is used here to refer to duplicate hardware—either component level—or server level, that can be brought online in an automated or semi-automated manner.
- *High-availability* is used to qualify an application's readiness to fulfill a task or user request.
- *Failover* is used when a failed server's processing is transferred to another server.

Redundancy is then hardware based, and high-availability is software in orientation. The software's high availability is dependent on hardware functioning correctly. High availability is not just having all the hardware turned on and the lights flashing; it must be fulfilling user requests. High availability is really from the end-users' perspective and is judged to be "up" if a standard transaction or request can be completed in a timely manner.

Redundancy and high availability should not just be the focus of the hardware or the application, but also the operating system (OS). Thus, the proper solution(s) must address CTI hardware redundancy, high availability of the OS, and high availability of the CTI application, which includes skills-based routing, CTI screen-pops, IVR, and Web response. As a further criterion, the solutions to the problems are best accomplished with only minor modifications to the available off-the-shelf products to better position the enterprise for future technology growth or expansion.

A further consideration to be included is scalability. How well a highly available solution can be expanded to accommodate additional users and additional hardware is a function of the solution's "scalability." Solutions that are dependent on a static environment or too rigid to grow with end-user demands will not last in the marketplace. Scalability is an important corollary to high-availability systems. Without scalability, the implementation team is faced with replacing an entire high-availability system to achieve the next plateau of functionality for service to the new user population. Today's corporations are only interested in growing larger, having more customers, and servicing a larger installed base. Scalability, whether implied or stated, is a necessary feature of any voice or data purchase and high-availability systems are no different.

UNDERSTANDING THE TECHNOLOGY

By building redundancy into the call center components, the environment can offer the same uptime to the various CTI solutions that voice offerings take for granted.

The current focal point of convergence begins with the call center server. All components downstream from this server depend on information from this device to correctly handle the calls. All downstream components would require the same attention, although the focus will remain with this one critical server for discussion purposes. It is appropriate then to discuss the basic hardware components that can be used to improve the basic reliability of the call center server. A call center server should be built on a hardware platform that will support dual processors (or better), error control and correction (ECC) memory, redundant power supplies and internal fans, RAID array server storage that can take advantage of "hot-swappable" disks, redundant network interface cards (NIC), and a software-driven UPS that permits graceful server shutdown during a power loss. This internal, redundant component approach to building a server is similar to that used in building a high-availability PBX. Exhibit 22-1 is a typical call center configuration.

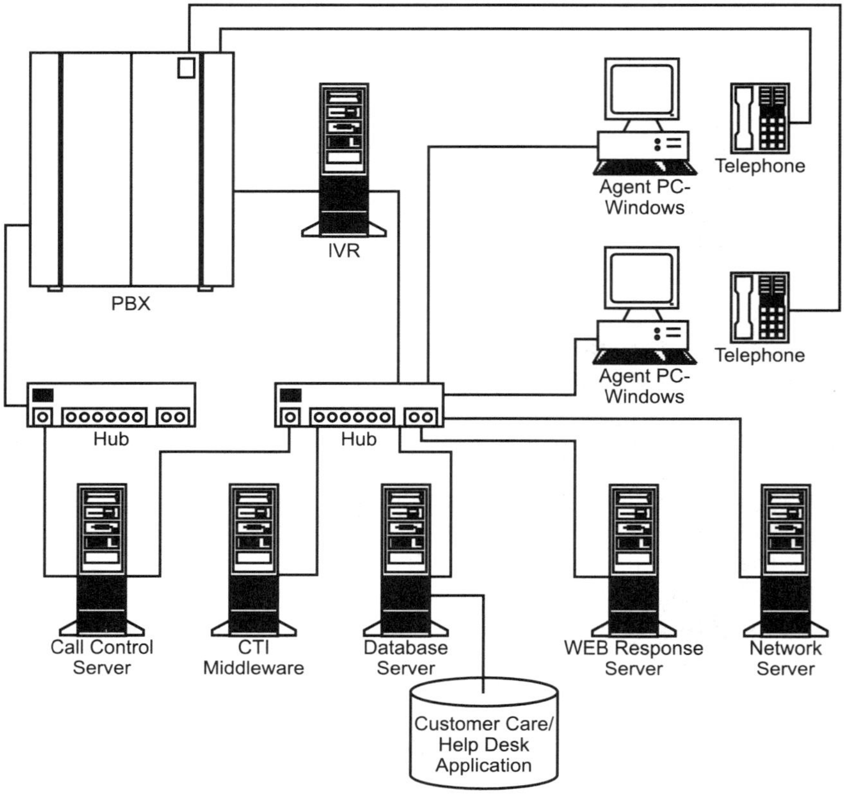

Exhibit 22-1. Call center components.

When each component in a CTI solution contains redundant hardware, there is still an issue when a CTI server has to be taken off-line for backups or device driver updates, or if the application "goes-to-sleep." Even with a highly redundant hardware platform, these systems require more maintenance (translated: downtime) time than that required by the PBX. Call center server offerings are built on various operating system (OS) platforms, and solutions are needed to improve the availability of the applications.

There are two distinct approaches to building a high-availability CTI server that are readily recognized within the IS environment. Again, each has its strengths and weaknesses as well as cost differentiators.

1. The first approach is to run the operating system and application on a single, highly redundant server and replicate the pertinent data to a "warm standby" server. This approach still relies on a single box and thus has the potential of a single point of failure. In the event of component failure, the user community would experience downtime

while the warm standby server is brought online. The implementation uses the relatively primitive technique of copy commands inside batch files and is really designed for data protection, not a real-time application. Still, this technology should be explored as a solution offering, as it is OS independent.

2. The second way is to use a second server in a hot-standby solution. This method requires building an identical second CTI server, giving it a high-speed link to its master, and then mirroring all activity. In the event of a failure of the master, the slave assumes the identity of the master, a brief pause is detected throughout the user community, and then activity resumes. This approach is often referred to as fail-over technology. It takes redundancy of the internal hardware components onestep further by having a redundant system mirrored external to the master server. While this approach offers a good solution for a failed server component or for a failed server, it does not provide for scalability or the kind of transparency to the user community that is desired. This technology is incorporated into Windows 2000 and has good potential, again depending on the needs of the enterprise.

A higher-end solution is to have the application served by multiple servers in a virtual mode. The application processes would service requests made of it on processors located on different CTI servers. An IP load balancer is used to "disguise" the multiple CTI servers from the PBX and the user community and deliver service requests to one of the processors supporting the call center application. Single point of hardware failure is eliminated as different tasks are distributed and multiple processors run multiple instances of the application. The user community would not typically notice a component failure, as the requests would continue to be seamlessly processed from another source.

In keeping with this "virtual application," if the application and the database are placed not on a single server or duplicated on several servers, but on a storage area network (SAN), then the availability of the data is increased to other technology such as hierarchical storage management (HSM) for data archival. Ideally, as the number of users and calls increase, additional processors (translates as more servers) are added to provide scalability to *n* users. In this manner, servers and associated processors can be added or removed based on load demand and maintenance needs. With this type of plug-and-play of server components into the environment, the solution provides scalability discussed earlier. The application just described is at the heart of the "clustering" technology that has been used in the UNIX world for years.

Clustering of servers, using IP load balancing to front-end the requests and SANs for data storage, make for the right combination for supporting

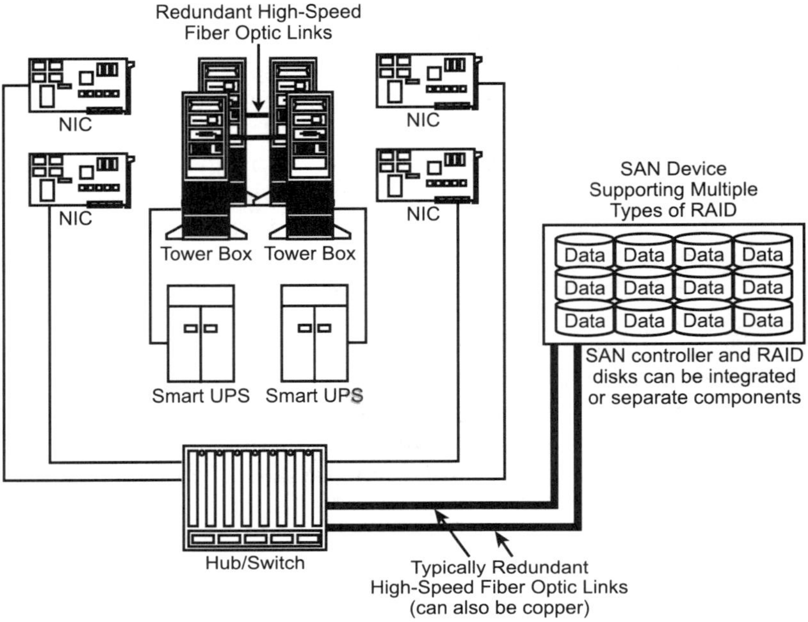

Exhibit 22-2. CHOMP diagram.

a critical application in a virtual mode. The Clustered High-availability Optimum Message Processing (CHOMP) configuration in Exhibit 22-2 would be the proper solution and provides the high availability and scalability necessary for message processing in growing call centers with large call and data volumes.

TECHNOLOGY SCENARIOS

Each of the solutions listed above can be used to fit the needs of any given enterprise and the critical level of support required. It is important that an enterprise characterize internal and external requirements for systems availability to ensure that the correct solution is employed. The following scenarios may help determine where an enterprise fits during its evolution.

Scenario 1

An enterprise has several small- to medium-sized call centers connected via WAN links. In this scenario, calls are redirected from one site to another in the event of a site emergency closure or based on call overflow to another site. Each of the call centers could do real-time data recovery (RTDR) to the central site or main data center to protect the site data. An up-to-the-minute historical data archive would be maintained at a remote location in the event of a server failure or site disaster. Typically, in this type of scenario, calls would be rerouted until the call center server could be restored to pre-disaster conditions.

This type of server availability is a low-end solution that would allow a failed server to be restored quickly, although it requires manual intervention. It would not provide a rules-based, automated failover from one server to another, nor would the reporting on calls necessarily differentiate between originally requested locations. The advantages are that this solution would be cost-effective and OS independent. It only works, however, because the enterprise has more than one location available to route callers.

Scenario 2

An enterprise company has one main call center of medium size, running 24 hours a day, 7 days a week. It cannot afford to have the call center go down except during monthly scheduled maintenance, such as backups and software version modifications. Any additional maintenance activity outside of that window is problematic and presents potential lost revenue to the enterprise. Due to the customer demands for service, the call center server cannot afford to have an unscheduled outage or failure during these production periods.

The call center would best be served by using failover technology to mirror the call center server right on-site. The call center server would have full hardware redundancy and, in the event of a failure of the master server, the slave server take over with minimum (if any) downtime. Internal staff agents may have to log-in again to re-establish sessions, but the application would be available immediately. Failed components could be replaced on the down call server without impacting the call center itself. Additional processes would ensure that the correct responsible parties were notified in a timely manner to respond to such events.

This solution is considered the middle-of-the-road solution and would be more expensive, requiring more hardware (servers), and be more OS dependent. However, the CTI applications would be available because of greater uptime. Typically, this solution is implemented in a one-to-one server relationship. Failover from one server to another is usually an all-or-nothing proposition based on server availability.

Scenario 3

An enterprise consolidates multiple call centers into one center to take advantage of economies of scale or because it is already a large volume call center. The call center is available to critical-need customers 24 hours per day, 7 days a week. Maintenance windows are not available, so backups and upgrades are done in conjunction with the applications processing. Multiple servers are set up to run the call center server application in a cluster server arrangement. An IP load-balancing server takes call center agent requests and distributes the IP conversations across *n* server processors. Data is stored on a SAN server connected to a fiber-optic ring using hot-swappable drives in a RAID array system. Data protection of the SAN server can be done using either RTDR technology or conventional backup technology that will back up open files.

The granularity available within this configuration would allow for just failover of an application—not the entire server. This would provide for shorter time periods of application "outages," and would work and scale across *n* servers, not just in a one-to-one relationship. The costs to establish this type of system vary, depending on the number of servers needed to achieve the necessary level of support. This is the high-end, high-availability solution that would scale for a company's most important clients. Rules to determine what takes over and how routing is performed are established in advance to optimize uptime and application availability.

CHANGE DRIVERS

An enterprise needs to critically review the needs of the call center to determine when is the best time to make a change. Factors for change include costs, staff resources, and corporate mergers. Many corporations are taking a different approach to customer call centers. Instead of treating it as cost centers, a necessary but evil expense, customer care centers are being turned into profit centers with responsibility for turning a profit.

As call centers become revenue generators, the infrastructure requirements start evolving. Call centers no longer get the company's castoff equipment, but instead get to install state-of-the-art technology with an expectation of servicing callers in real time 24 × 7, with cross-sell and upsell components. Profitability requirements drive the need for high-availability applications in the call center environment. When a service is chargeable or a call center is trying to sell, the CTI solution must be up for profits to go up. No globally competitive company is willing to invest internally in technology only to see systems off-line and unavailable. This downtime is viewed as alienating customers and forfeiting profitability. Business investments yield corporate profits. Poor business investments or declining profits have ended more than one corporate career.

SYSTEMS RECONFIGURATIONS

When viewing call center data systems, the issue of disk storage, redundancy (RAID), and backups (disaster recovery) are usually grouped together or interchanged. Several questions are often asked. How much disk storage does this server need? What type of RAID configuration is needed? Does every CTI server, or every server for that matter, need the same standard configuration, or should SAN technology be deployed that

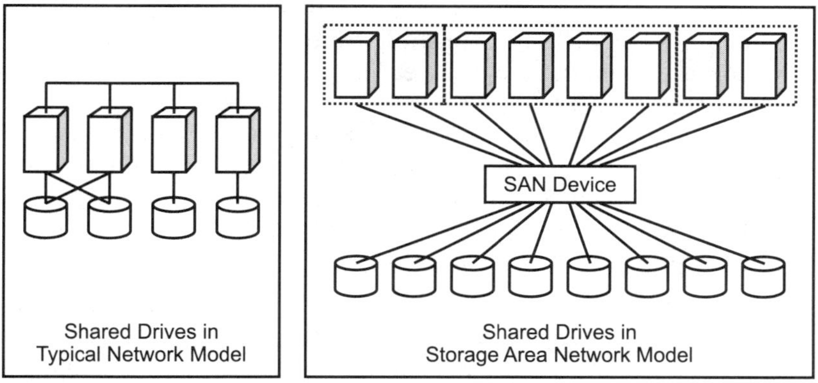

Exhibit 22-3. Storage area network to complement the CTI server.

will allow for a centralized storage area? Is adding more disk space to these configurations easier than the other choices? Will the tape backup system of the data center support both types of data storage? Rather than trying to build a large-enough CTI server to hold all the data of each specialized application, an IS group can consider two alternative solutions.

The first alternative would include an external disk expansion chassis that could hold additional RAID drives. This solution requires a SCSI card in the server itself and a cable running to the external disk drive unit. Using this configuration, drives are added on demand, under the right conditions. Generally speaking, to add more disk space to an existing volume means that the whole partition must be restored from tape once the drive is added, which means that mirrored volumes must be broken as well. This approach does not work easily for field upgrades and is prone to human error as well as excessive downtime.

The second alternative is a SAN to complement the CTI server, as shown in Exhibit 22-3. Organizations that want to do extensive data warehousing can archive data from the CTI server, but still have it available on the SAN server. There are several vendors that currently offer this type of product, including EMC and XIOtech.

A combination of HSM (hierarchical storage management) and SAN technology could also be employed together with this type of solution. HSM allows data to be transparently "migrated" to standby disk drives located in a SAN server, thus freeing valuable disk space on the primary CTI server. A pointer to the location of the actual data is left behind on the primary server so that when the data is accessed, HSM simply completes the request of the OS by going to the actual data location, and retrieves the data for the requesting transaction.

A follow-on benefit of this type of solution is that clustering of servers is greatly facilitated in this configuration. By unbundling the disk storage from the actual server, the stage is set for multiple CTI servers, including skills-based routing, CTI screen-pop, IVR, and Web response server to access a centralized database. Clustering of application servers to support the critical-need center activities is much more attainable in this configuration. Two or three call center servers could be set up to access one SAN server, highly RAID-ed of course, thus improving the availability and increasing the disk storage necessary for archival purposes.

Clustering servers and using SAN servers for data storage make for the right combination for supporting critical-need applications. This modularity provides the scalability to call center solutions currently lacking. The costs for adding components are incremental based on the growth of the organization.

COST ASSOCIATIONS

There are a couple of ways to look at costs. Lost customer satisfaction, while very important, is a little subjective to measure in this document and so will only be referenced. There is the obvious cost associated with acquisition and implementation for high availability solutions and with each type of solution a different cost consideration.

The other way to view costs is from the viewpoint of what are the costs to not implement high-availability solutions a call center? The simple spreadsheet shown in Exhibit 22-4 provides some perspective on downtime and service outages in a typical call center that is dependent on CTI.

A proper cost justification to the ultimate decision-maker would include not only the acquisition and implementation costs, but also the lost opportunity cost shown above. Obviously, the numbers are tailored to fit each scenario by varying the number of agents, the earnings potential, etc., as well as the chosen solution proposed to guard against this unplanned downtime.

Exhibit 22-4. Cost analysis.

Cost of call center downtime	$ 10,000	(per hour)
(100 agents @ $15 per hour)		
(100 agents billable @$75/hour)		
(5 engineers @ $195/hour)		
(lost customer satisfaction?)		
Failure recovery time	4	(hours)
Cost of failed CTI server	$ 40,000	

CONCLUSION

For businesses involved in global competition (and what company is not?), the key to ongoing survivability—and if executed correctly—is systems availability. Customers and affiliated businesses are in contact with an enterprise for only one thing: reliable servicing of customer needs. All the marketing efforts, name-branding costs, and product offerings of a company are wasted efforts if an enterprise is not available to take a call or process an order. If the infrastructure supporting the call center, whether phone, Web, fax, or e-mail, is not online and available, the company is out of business because there is always a competitor to take the order.

Technology can and should be used to increase the availability of applications that are used to service/maintain customers and increase profits. High-availability solutions have a further requirement to also be scalable to grow with an enterprise company. Enterprises competing in the global marketplace must position for growth along with competitive edge. High-availability systems are a part of maintaining a competitive edge.

Section IV
Data Management

CIO PROFESSIONALS LOOK AT ALL ASPECTS OF DATA MANAGEMENT FOR THE ENTERPRISE ENVIRONMENT. The processes required to store, access, secure, and protect data for the enterprise must embrace not only technology, but also apply long-standing rules to maintain data integrity. A primary foundation is ensuring valid methods of data storage and data retrieval. This portion of data management is primarily a balance of good existing data structures and updating processes. Promoting data availability by use of software agents is a method for optimizing access to data by keyword and Boolean techniques.

Determining the level of security needed for various types of enterprise data suggests a review of classification of data throughout the enterprise and minimization of risk to the corruption of the data by outside factors. One method for securing data requires an understanding of data encryption methods available, points for potential data comprise, and how to incorporate that into a comprehensive security plan for enterprise data management. With the increases in access to internal data information by enterprise staff and outside sources, securing data from outside attacks by viruses is also detailed for consideration. Encryption methods coupled with virus protection offers an increasingly secure environment for enterprise data that is able to keep up with constant data management changes.

When processes are incorporated for data security, methods to plan, design, and use an archives repository will minimize loss of enterprise memory. A CIO is provided with material and business rationale to construct long-term data archives. Although similar in nature to data warehousing, data archives and long-term secured environments for enterprise historical data are not the same. Because all enterprise data is not needed for the enterprise memory, this section also covers the tedious process of identifying data candidates for archiving.

Open systems and user availability are easy targets for the cyber-thief. Data access across the Internet is vulnerable. Can the CIO provide ease-of-use and a secure transaction to end users? There are two chapters in this section that discuss available Internet security technologies such as encryption and firewalls and how to use them to guard against the potential of attacks. Each provides significant protection for the enterprise, and both are needed. They are not mutually exclusive technologies—but instead, complement each other.

As the CIO, one is also expected to protect the corporate data not only from cyber-thieves, but also cyber-illnesses: the ever-present computer virus. Choosing and implementing computer virus protection differs from platform to platform and company to company. This section discusses some of the decision criteria for choosing virus protection and provides a primer on how viruses have evolved from their early beginnings to the present day. A futuristic look as to where viruses might evolve is also explored.

Selection of the end-user computing support services is needed to operate data management strategies for data retrieval in a diversified data environment. Therefore, a plan for how to best select vendors that are both cost-effective and strategically fit the needs of the enterprise are a critical function of data management staff. This section explores TCO (total cost of ownership)—the rational that can lead to outsourcing non-core areas.

The last proactive measure that CIO professionals typically review is the long-term plans for disaster recovery. A written plan is critical for an enterprise to come back quickly when faced with disaster conditions. Key staff deification and planning for the enterprise to return to business as usual as rapidly as possible is centered on data management planning during the aftermath of a disaster.

Data management practices are therefore the core responsibility of a data center. It is in the best interest of the CIO to become as familiar as possible with core data management aspects. Certainly, data storage, security, and access must look to all points of entry into the enterprise that touch data. Data management departments need to understand the technology available and how to apply use of the right technology to data handling. The following chapters in this section provide the CIO with insight into positioning the evolution of the data management systems environment.

- Software Agents for Data Management
- Selecting a Cryptographic System
- Data Security for the Masses
- Firewall Management and Internet Attacks
- Evaluating Anti-virus Solutions Within Distributed Environments
- The Future of Computer Viruses
- Strategies for an Archives Management Program
- Managing EUC Support Vendors
- Organizing for Disaster Recovery

Chapter 23
Software Agents for Data Management

David Mattox
Kenneth Smith
Len Seligman

THE STUDY OF AGENTS IS THE STUDY OF AUTONOMY. To be more precise, it is the study of how to implement autonomous software systems that can independently navigate and analyze the vast array of online data sources in order to produce the information required by a user.

Agents are autonomous software entities that use existing data management systems in order to perform tasks on behalf of a user. Because of their autonomy, agents are able to provide a level of abstraction between the high-level information goals of users and the concrete realities of data management systems.

However, agents are not data management systems. The task of efficiently storing and retrieving data (of all types) is best left to the vast array of tools that already exist for that purpose. Agents simply exploit those tools on behalf of the user.

Interest in software agents has increased over the past few years, primarily because of the popularity of the Internet as a source of information and services. The exponentially expanding amount of information has underscored the need for tools to help users locate what they need in an environment that is vast in scope, constantly changing, and poorly structured. Research in software agents shows promise in providing autonomous software systems capable of acting as surrogates for users to perform tasks that users either do not know how to or simply do not want to do. This chapter describes what software agents are and how they compliment traditional data management systems.

AGENT DEFINITIONS: INTELLIGENT AND OTHERWISE

The word *agent* has been used (or overused) to describe many things in the past few years

0-8493-0893-3/00/$0.00+$.50

The idea of a computer-based agent has been around since the early years of artificial intelligence (AI). Much of AI research works toward software that can exhibit enough independence to be considered autonomous. Agent research originates in work in multi-agent systems, which are part of distributed artificial intelligence (DAI). One of the first multi-agent models was Carl Hewitt's Concurrent Actor model (ca. 1977), which described the concept of actors — concurrently executing self-contained objects with the ability to interact with one another.

One of the popular terms for agents is *intelligent agents*. But are agents intelligent? Agents are as intelligent as any other software. The term *intelligent* is in the eye of the beholder and until such time as a rigorous definition of intelligence is agreed upon, there is no sense in arguing whether agents, or any other software, are truly intelligent. Therefore, for purposes of this chapter, the authors simply refer to agents and leave the intelligence to the perceptive systems of the beholding entity.

So, What Is an Agent?

Unfortunately, the term *agent* is nearly as ill-defined as the term *intelligent*. Rather than try to provide a precise definition of autonomous software agents, it is simpler to start with the dictionary definition: "one that acts as the representative of another."

This definition captures the essence of what an agent should be — an entity that represents the interests of another. This definition applies equally well to all types of agents, whether they are biological (e.g., secretary, travel agent), hardware (e.g., robot), or software.

Exhibit 23-1 shows the very top level of the agent taxonomy. Agents can be broken down into biological, hardware, and software agents. Artificial life agents are similar to taskable software agents in construction, but are entirely different in purpose.

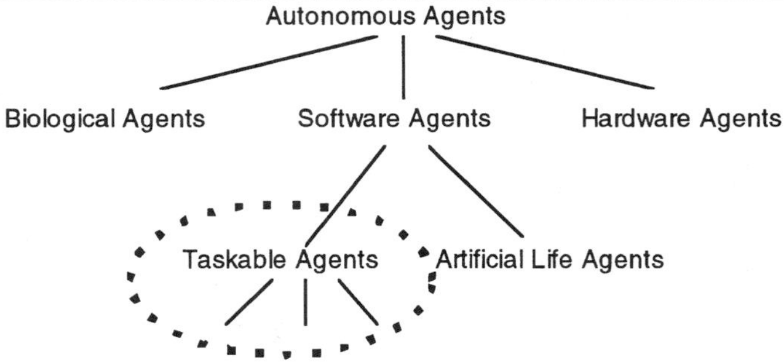

Exhibit 23-1. Agent taxonomy.

The goal in constructing taskable agents is to create a software entity that is able to accomplish a specific task. To the user, how that task is accomplished is of secondary importance. The goal in artificial life, however, is to construct software agents that behave as much like real-life entities as possible. How they go about accomplishing the 'task" given them is of primary importance, and whether they successfully achieve their goal is secondary.

This chapter interests itself only in software agents and, specifically, taskable software agents and how they can help in data management tasks.

Agents as Metaphor. For the moment, imagine agents as a metaphor for describing the interaction among processes and between humans and computational processes. In the past, humans interacted with programs in much the same way that they interact with physical objects such as cars — that is, by direct manipulation.

Driving a car to the restaurant to get a pizza or locating a reference through a card catalog can be accomplished through the direct manipulation of physical or logical constructs. Another way to accomplish such tasks is to ask for the pizza to be delivered or ask a reference librarian to find the right book. With this latter approach, one could say that the pizza delivery person and the librarian are acting on behalf of the person's needs (i.e., their agent). Other obvious examples are real estate agents and "secret" agents.

Upon closer examination, it seems that the human is still manipulating physical or logical constructs in order to accomplish his or her objective. However, by tasking the agent, the interaction between the human and the world has been raised to a more abstract level.

So, are agents simply more sophisticated processes? If so, what is the threshold that separates an agent from a simple process or machine? The answer to the first question is yes, and the second question is irrelevant. The critical observation to make is that an agent captures the notion of autonomous taskability.

One could argue that pressing a key while in a word processor is "tasking" the computer, and therefore the key must also be an agent. Rather than deny this argument, it should be embraced.

Agents are a metaphor — a computing paradigm — for designing and building systems. In this case, it is possible to look at everything as an agent, each with its own level of sophistication. Under this approach, however, it quickly becomes boring to spend time considering taskability of a key stroke agent or the gas peddle agent.

If everything is an agent, how does that change the way you are going to write the next line of code or the way you interact with your computer? The answer is that it will not change the next line of code, but it should begin to change the way that you think about interacting with computers and change the way you approach the creation of the next program.

To this point, the chapter has discussed the semantics of agents and what they represent philosophically. We recognize that the term *agent* has become encumbered with much hype and misinformation and, as a result, any argument on the definition of the term will never be won. Therefore, rather than focus on the agent part of the issue, attention is focused on the useful portion of the agent metaphor — namely, one of taskability or *autonomous taskable computation*. The next section discusses what taskable computation is.

CHARACTERISTICS OF AUTONOMOUS SOFTWARE AGENTS

The utility of the agent-centric view arises from the focus on the objective more than the tools necessary for accomplishing the task. For example, if the task is to plant a tree, one needs a hole in the yard. The objective is a hole of a proper dimension in the proper location. It is realized that as soon as one asks, "How will the hole be created?", one moves into a finer-grained view of the task and the objective.

It is the purpose of an agent to accomplish tasks. Agents manage the details of the task, tasking other agents if necessary, and hide the details from the user. In essence, an agent in the agent-oriented programming metaphor encapsulates a task in much the same way that an object (in the object-oriented programming metaphor) encapsulates data and procedures.

To support this advanced notion of taskability, an agent must posses a certain degree of autonomy. It is the degree of autonomy that makes an agent useful and interesting to study. It is thus beneficial to describe the various characteristics that support autonomy — namely, goal-directed behavior, reactivity, learning, cognizant failure, communication, cooperation, tool use, and mobility.

Goal-Directed Behavior

If agents are a level of abstraction between a user and a set of low-level tasks, an agent must be able to create a mapping between the high-level goal and the available tools such that it can use the tools effectively to achieve the goal. In other words, the agent must be able to plan.

For example, a U.S. Army Colonel may task a Major to move several items of equipment from a base in the U.S. to a forward staging area in Europe. The subordinate needs to:

1. Break the high-level goal into subtasks (e.g., package equipment, load onto some vehicle, move it to the new location, and unload it).

2. Decide what order to perform the tasks (e.g., package → load → ship → unload).
3. Decide on the best available tools for each task (e.g., should this equipment be transported by plane or ship?).

The Major may handle all subtasks himself, but could also delegate them to yet more subordinates. How the equipment is moved is immaterial to the Colonel since all he is interested in is that it gets to the right place in a timely manner. This is exactly what a user would expect from a software agent as well — to be able to provide it with an abstract goal and have the agent take care of the details. The ability of an agent to exhibit goal-directed behavior typically comes from incorporating AI planning techniques into the agent code.

Cognizant Failure. An important (but often neglected) component of goal-driven behavior is cognizant failure. Cognizant failure is the idea that once tasked, the agent either completes the task and returns, or recognizes that it cannot complete the task and reports a failure.

While this issue may seem innocuous on the surface, there are some important issues. First, it is simply bad practice to have processes that do not terminate. This is more subtle than an inadvertent infinite loop. An agent is expected to recognize that it is not making progress on the given task. This is critical because if the agent is not able to do this, then the taskor must constantly monitor the agent. The taskor must then know all about the means and resources that the agent uses to accomplish its task. For the taskor to have such an omniscient view of the taskee's world, the taskor would also have all the knowledge necessary to do the agent's job. This defeats the purpose of having an agent perform the task in the first place.

Cognizant failure is an important component of a taskable system. It provides the basis of raising the level of abstraction for the taskor and makes modularity and reusability possible. But while it must be possible for the taskee to detect that it is failing to accomplish its task, it may not know why nor what to do about the failure. This is the inverse of a previous concern that the taskor not be omniscient to the taskee's failure monitoring. If the taskee were to know how to recover from all failures, then it would need to have the ability to know the greater purpose behind the choice to execute that task. To continue this example, if the Major cannot complete his task (perhaps there is no available transportation), then he had better let the Colonel know as soon as possible.

Reactivity

For the concept of taskable computation to support the uncertainty of real-world operation, each taskable element must accomplish its given task under a robust range of situations. *Reactivity* is the ability of an agent to alter its intended course of action based on an unplanned circumstance. This is crucial when operating in an unpredictable environment containing a large number of data sources scattered over a wide area network. In this type of environment, machines go down, data becomes inconsistent, and connections break unexpectedly. If an agent queries an information source and finds no answers to its query, it would then try alternate sources of information until it could come up with a reasonable number of answers.

From the perspective of the user, this adaptation to the situation should be transparent. Information on how the agent accomplished its task may be important for accountability later, but how it gets done is not the primary concern of the user. Usually, the reactivity is implemented as a set of condition-action rules that embody knowledge about the particular domain in which the agent is operating.

Learning

Another important characteristic of autonomous behavior is the ability to enhance future performance as a result of past experiences. *Machine learning* techniques allow an agent to learn new methods or refine existing ones to meet specific needs.

For example, an agent that uses Internet search engines to accomplish its task may learn that some engines consistently return more hits for the same query than the others and alter the order in which it uses these tools. Learning is especially valuable in the case of interface or personal assistant agents. This class of agents provides an intelligent interface to assist the user in interacting with computer tools.

The purpose of a news filtering agent is to only show articles that a particular user would really want to see. Learning plays a big role in this class of agents because it is difficult and tedious for a user to specify precisely what he or she would like. The NewT information filter (reported by B. Sheth and P. Maes in the *Proceedings of the Ninth Conference on Artificial Intelligence for Applications '93*) is an example of how an agent can use learning to improve performance. The NewT news filtering agent uses a genetic algorithm to customize the behavior of the agent based on user feedback. This allows for the creation of an information filter that is more accurate than a typical Boolean keyword approach.

Communication and Cooperation

In software as in life, cooperation between agents allows a greater range of tasks to be accomplished. Agents can specialize and cooperate with others to perform more complex tasks than could be accomplished alone. This section considers cooperative collections of agents.

Cooperation between agents can be seen in two different contexts:

- Cooperation to achieve a common goal
- Cooperation to achieve individual goals

An example of the first is a set of specialized agents collaborating to design an artifact. Each agent is tasked with developing a particular subsystem, but must cooperate with the other agents to produce an overall design. Each agent has local goals that it must achieve, but each of those goals must support the achievement of the global goal. This is the same problem addressed by blackboard systems.

The second mode of cooperation is when two or more agents in some common environment have complementary local goals but no common global goal. For each to achieve its own goal, it may have to cooperate with the others. An example of this is a personal assistant agent sent to purchase merchandise on the Internet from a selling agent. The goal of the assistant agent is to locate a suitable product at the lowest price. The selling agent has the goal of advertising all of its products, and selling them at the highest possible price. The agents then negotiate a reasonable price that satisfies both local goals.

The ability to communicate is important to any group of agents that must cooperate. In the previous example, it would be difficult to reach an agreed-upon price without the ability to communicate. The inherent difficulty in developing communications strategies for agents is that agents are intended to operate on a higher level of abstraction than say, a client/server database system. This means that the type of information communicated is qualitatively different.

Beyond insulating users from the peculiarities of specific computer tools, agents should also be able to interact with a wide range of other agents, many of which have not been encountered previously. To meet these criteria, a common agent language needs to be developed. In order for agents to operate effectively in specific domains, ontologies (i.e., a taxonomy of concepts for a particular application area) need to be developed as well. The development of agent languages and ontologies is an active area of research.

Ability to Use "Tools"

Another common characteristic of agents is the ability to use software tools. Because agents act as surrogates for users, in many cases they have to access tools in the same manner as users. Many of the information resources available are independent of the agent and cannot (and should not) be integrated into the agent's core functionality (like one would integrate a new learning algorithm). These information resources are used "as is" by agents.

For example, the Alta Vista search engine indexes the majority of the sites accessible over the Internet and allows users to perform a keyword search over the content of each site. However, there is no special API that an agent can use to access the search engine directly. Any agent that wants to take advantage of Alta Vista's capabilities must do so through the HTML interface, just as a human user would. Accessing legacy systems is a common problem in many data management environments.

Mobility

Mobile agents are code-containing objects that may be transmitted between communicating participants in a distributed system. As opposed to only exchanging nonexecutable data, systems incorporating mobile agents exchange executable code fragments and state information as well as data.

Mobility is sometimes thought of as being synonymous with the concept of agents, but in reality that is not necessarily the case. Many mainframe batch processing systems move jobs between processors to improve performance, but those jobs are rarely considered to be agents.

Why should agents be mobile? In many cases, a task performed by a mobile agent can be performed by an agent resident on a single machine via a network connection to a server. However, mobile agents become valuable when:

- Communications costs are high. If it is necessary to examine many images on many different databases to select one, it is better to do the examination on the remote machine and transfer one image, rather than transferring all the images and doing the examination locally.
- Connections between machines are faulty or intermittent. With a mobile agent you can "fire and forget." For example, a submarine commander might want to locate some specific data, but the time available to issue the query and wait for the results may be unacceptable. The commander could send an agent to query the appropriate data sources and break the connections. The agent would do its job, then wait for the connection to be reestablished to download the results of the query.
- The task performed by the agent is best done on another machine because of limited local resources or enhancements (e.g., special software or hardware) on the remote machine.
- The task has a parallel component that can be exploited.

In many instances, it is more advantageous to the remote machine to receive agents rather than direct requests for services. The remote machine then has the luxury of scheduling when the agents would run rather than trying to satisfy remote requests for services immediately. By using mobile agents, a remote server has more flexibility in satisfying requests and can operate more efficiently.

AGENTS FOR HETEROGENEOUS DATA MANAGEMENT

The preceding sections described the characteristics of agents. This section examines how agents can be applied to data management problems. Some decisions-makers feel information technology has done them a disservice. A large amount of data that had been totally inaccessible, or only painfully accessible, is currently being made available to them in great volumes as the result of rapid advances in information access and integration technologies.

Yet, decision-makers often feel that huge quantities of possibly valuable data are raining down on their heads, without having the time or tools to make sense of it all. Even with this newly available data, important questions such as, "What actions should I take next?" may still be no closer to being answered than before. The rapid growth of the Internet and the concurrent popularity of the corporate intranet have meant that an immense body of potentially useful information has become readily accessible to anyone with a computer and an Internet connection.

The bad news is, of course, that it is difficult to find information useful to the task at hand. In addition to the sheer size of the search space, there are other factors that contribute to the difficulty of finding information. The information is distributed over a multitude of servers that are controlled by different people and organizations, even within a single corporation. The data are stored in many different (frequently unstructured) formats with many different access methods. The formats range from structured databases to semistructured or tagged text (e.g., E-mail messages or HTML), proprietary formats (e.g., Microsoft Word), or plain ASCII files. Access methods range from client/server database methods, HTTP, CGI scripts, FTP, and Telnet, each with its own domain-specific commands and responses. Indexing of the information sources is erratic at best, so there is no easy way to tell exactly what is in each information collection. Finally, the information space itself is very dynamic. Information sources rapidly appear, disappear, and change location.

Example Information Space: The MITRE Information Infrastructure

The MITRE Corporation Intranet (also known as the MITRE Information Infrastructure, or MII) is a good example of a collection of the types of information that proliferate. This intranet is accessible to all MITRE employees via any desktop computer and contains multiple sources of information on many different subjects. Information on employees, the projects they work on, and the amount of time they spend on each project is contained in an Oracle database. Many plain-text and semistructured documents are available on the MII as well. Newsletters, policy and procedure documents, and library holdings are available, and any staff member can publish up to 50 megabytes of documents. In addition, personal, project, and departmental homepages are available, along with internal and external newsgroups. All of these documents are indexed by a commercial text search engine on a regular basis.

All of this information (except for project financial information) can be retrieved via a browser (e.g., Netscape). Information can also be gathered through custom-developed scripts interfacing with APIs for the data sources as well. Staff-published documents are added via FTP and shared file systems. The documents themselves exist in multiple formats, including plain text, marked-up text, Microsoft Word, PowerPoint, and Excel documents. Specific documents are usually found via a text-retrieval tool that allows for keyword searches and performs relevance ranking on the results.

Systems such as the MII are good at finding large numbers of documents that meet simple criteria (e.g., finding documents that contain specific keywords). However, a major problem with searching wide area information systems is that it is difficult to specify a combination of keywords that will result in a reasonable number of hits. Anyone that has used an Internet search engine realizes that for most queries, recall (i.e., the percentage of relevant documents that were retrieved) is high, but precision (i.e., the percentage of retrieved documents that were relevant) is low.

Another problem is that the data are not always structured in the way that is needed for particular queries. An example of this is using the intranet to find people knowledgeable about specific subjects at MITRE. Queries to the search engine return documents; but because of the way the data are structured, finding the people associated with those documents requires several extra steps.

The many different types of data and their associated access methods pose a problem for users as well. Each data source differs in both syntax and semantics. Middleware tools provide a partial solution for structured databases, but there is no general solution for accessing and combining all the different types of available data.

The last major problem is that the data contained in intranets are constantly changing. This poses problems in both searching for and monitoring information. Information sources appear and disappear. This problem is addressed by regular indexing of the information space, but indexing becomes difficult as the information space grows. The number of information sources that change remains a constant percentage of the total, but grows in absolute terms. Since there is a fixed cost for indexing each data source, the ability of the indexing process to maintain current information decreases as the information space grows. This has implications for monitoring as well as searching for information. In large information spaces, the ability of a user to monitor multiple data sources is limited, not by connectivity, but by sheer volume.

How Agents Help with Data Management

As the previous examples indicate, it is easy to find information, but finding the right information is difficult. How can agents help a user find this information? There are certain classes of problems addressed by current agent research that are useful for data management tasks. These include searching, filtering, monitoring, and data source mediation.

It is important to note that agents are not a magic bullet that can solve all the problems associated with locating information in multiple, massive, distributed, heterogeneous data sources. However, agents can be developed that are targeted at solving a specific data management task. Then, by coordinating their efforts, groups of agents can be used to solve even more complex tasks.

Searching for Information. The amount of information available over a corporate intranet stretches the capability of most users to effectively retrieve useful information. Even a medium-size corporation such as MITRE can provide an enormous amount of information for its employees.

Search agents contain domain knowledge about various information sources. This knowledge includes the types of information available at each source, how to access that information, and other potentially useful knowledge, such as the reliability and accuracy of the information source. Search agents use this knowledge to accomplish specific search tasks.

One example of a search agent is the People Finder agent at MITRE (discussed in more detail later). People Finder is an agent that searches for MITRE employees who know about a specific subject area. It contains the knowledge about what information sources to look at and how the data in those sources is structured in order to locate people. This is an example of an agent that uses existing information for a new purpose. The information the agent searches is not structured properly for finding people. The People Finder agent makes this underlying structure immaterial to the user.

Another search agent example is Metacrawler. Metacrawler is an agent that knows how to use Internet search engines. A user enters the query once, Metacrawler employs all of the known search engines to search and then collates the results and removes duplicates. This is an example of adding another layer of abstraction between the user and the task. A user could perform all of the subtasks necessary to do the search on each separate engine, but Metacrawler encapsulates that knowledge in a single agent.

Information Filtering. Information filtering is another common task for agents. Information filtering agents attempt to deal with the problem of information overload by either limiting or sorting the information coming to a user. The basic idea is to develop an online surrogate for a user that has enough knowledge about the user's information needs so that it can select only those documents that would be of interest. These types of agents usually function as gatekeepers by preventing the user from being overwhelmed by a flood of incoming information. Filtering agents also work in conjunction with, or are sometimes incorporated into, search agents in order to keep the results from searches down to reasonable levels.

Typically, filtering agents incorporate machine learning mechanisms, which allow the agents to adapt to the needs of each user and to provide more precision than that typically provided by keyword filtering approaches.

Information Monitoring. Many tasks depend on the timely notification of changes in different data sources. A logistics planner may develop a plan for moving equipment from one location to another, but the execution of that plan could be disrupted by the onset of bad weather at a refueling stop. The logistics planner would like to know of any events that would be likely to affect his plan as soon as they happen. Agents are useful for monitoring distributed data sources for specific data. Being software constructs, they have the patience necessary to constantly monitor data sources for changes.

Alternatively, mobile agents can be dispatched to remote or otherwise inaccessible locations to monitor data that the user might not normally have access to.

Data Source Mediation. The data management landscape is populated with a multitude of different systems, most of which do not talk to each other. Agents can be used as mediators between these various data sources, providing the mechanisms that allow them to interoperate. The SIMS Project developed an information mediator that provides access to heterogeneous data and knowledge bases. This mediator can be used to create a network of information-gathering agents, each of which has access to one or more information sources. These agents use a higher-level language, a communications protocol, and domain-specific ontologies for describing the data contained in their information sources. This allows each agent to communicate with the others at a higher semantic level.

Interface Agents/Personal Assistants. An interface agent is a program that is able to operate within a user interface and actively assist the user in operating the interface and manipulating the underlying system. An interface agent is able to intercept the input from the user, examine it, and take appropriate action.

While interface agents are not directly related to data management, they have the potential to play a large role in assisting users of data management systems. This becomes increasingly important as data management systems become more distributed and group together to form large, complex systems of systems. Agents in the interface can function as a bridge between domain knowledge about the data management systems and the user. These agents could assist users in forming queries, finding the location of data, and explaining the semantics of the data, among other tasks. Examples of this include intelligent tutoring systems and Web-browsing assistants. In addition, Microsoft is now including interface agents in its desktop products to watch the actions of users and make appropriate suggestions.

AGENTS IN ACTION

Here, two agent examples are given that highlight some of the features of agents. The first agent exploits knowledge of the underlying information system to locate people who are knowledgeable about a particular subject. The second example describes a system for distributed situation monitoring. This system employs agents to determine what parts of a logistics plan are most vulnerable to disruption and dispatches agents to monitor a set of distributed data sources for any changes that may affect the ongoing plan.

It is important to note that these agents (as is the case with all other agents) are not doing the data management tasks. Those are left to the various data management systems with which they interact. Agents fill in the "niches" around the data management systems, making the user's life easier by performing tasks that the data management systems were not originally designed to do.

Example Agent 1: People Finder Agent

"Who knows about X?" is a common question in many organizations. This is the problem that the People Finder project addresses.

The MITRE People Finder agent was created to help users quickly find people who are knowledgeable about a particular subject area (such as "data mining" or "software agents") at the MITRE Corporation. This is accomplished using only existing corporate information sources (i.e., the MITRE Corporate Internet, or MII, described previously), thereby avoiding the creation of a separate, single-purpose "skills database." Experience has shown that these types of special-purpose databases are difficult to maintain and quickly become obsolete. By exploiting existing online documents, the results from the People Finder agent are always as current as the information in the system. As information about new technologies is added to the online information systems, the People Finder system can locate the people associated with those technologies with no additional effort.

People Finder uses the native intranet search engine to examine the many sources of information available for documents containing a keyword phrase (e.g., "software agents"). The list of documents returned is categorized into one of two types: documents published by employees and documents that mention employees in conjunction with projects and technologies.

Once the documents are found, the search for relevant people begins. Employee-published documents are indexed by employee number; it is a fairly trivial matter to find the employees associated with each document. Locating the MITRE employees in the "mentioning" documents is a more complicated matter. People Finder uses a commercial name extraction tool to locate the proper names within each document. People Finder then performs a statistical analysis of names and query terms, examining factors such as the proximity of the name to the relevant terms, the number of times the name and query term appear together, as well as many other factors.

The names retrieved from the mentioned documents are combined with the names gathered from the published documents, and each name is matched with names in the MITRE phone book. The final weighting of each name is determined by factors such as number of documents, distance between name and query term, and types of HTML tags that appear between name and term. The names are then presented to the user in ranked order, as shown in Exhibit 23-2.

People Finder is primarily an example of a search agent that uses available tools and does some learning. It uses three different tools (the MITRE intranet search engine and two different databases) that are available over the intranet. The results returned from those tools are further processed by the People Finder agent, which feeds the results into a Bayes Net for the final ranking. The Bayes Net also updates its probabilities in order to refine its rankings in the future.

The initial goal for the People Finder prototype was to create a system that could find people who were within a phone call of a person knowledgeable of a given subject (even if the person called did not know much about the subject, they would know someone who did). The prototype developed has met this goal in the majority of the test cases tried.

Example Agent 2: Software Agents for Situation Monitoring

Decision-makers in a wide variety of application areas are drowning in data. They often have great difficulty locating, in a timely way, the information needed to do their jobs. This situation is often called *information overload*, though it is more accurate to speak of *data overload* and *information starvation*.

The Software Agents for Situation Monitoring research project at the MITRE Corporation is investigating how software agents can be used to

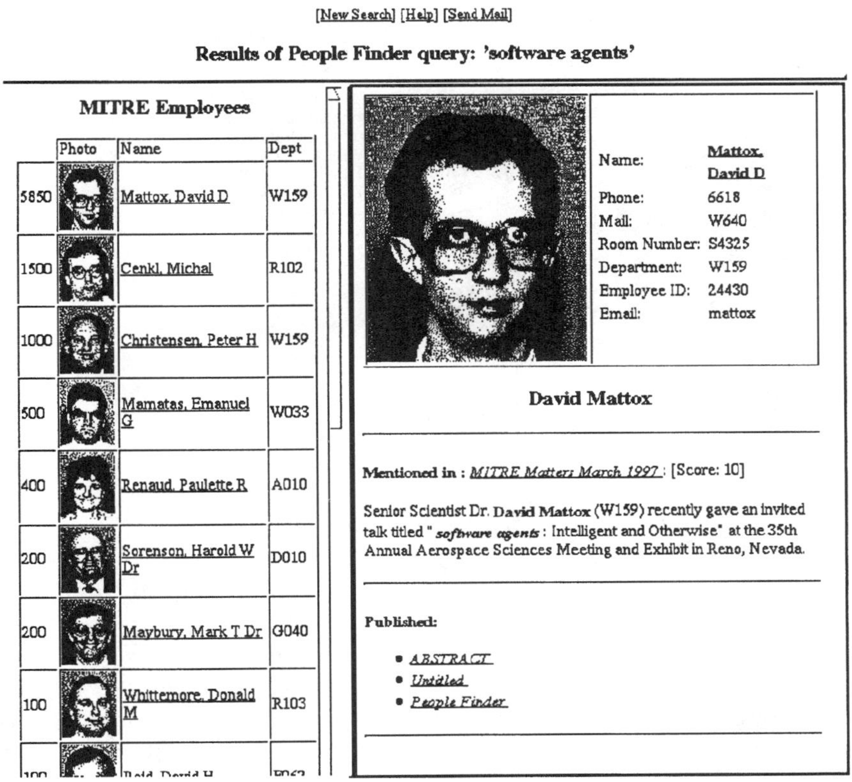

Exhibit 23-2. People Finder interface.

monitor distributed, heterogeneous data sources for the occurrence of specified situations, in order to ameliorate the data overload problem. In particular, the project is addressing the needs of users that must monitor the current state of a large-scale distributed situation and make decisions about managing its course. The situation may be a military logistics operation, an engineering design project, or any process represented piecewise in a set of dynamic, heterogeneous, and distributed data sources.

As an example, consider the problem of monitoring the execution of a logistics plan, which may require transporting troops and supplies to a targeted area by a certain date. A commander approves the plan and then wants to be informed if there is a high probability that the plan objectives cannot be achieved. Currently, the commander's staff must continually monitor information that resides in multiple, distributed data sources in order to detect possible problems.

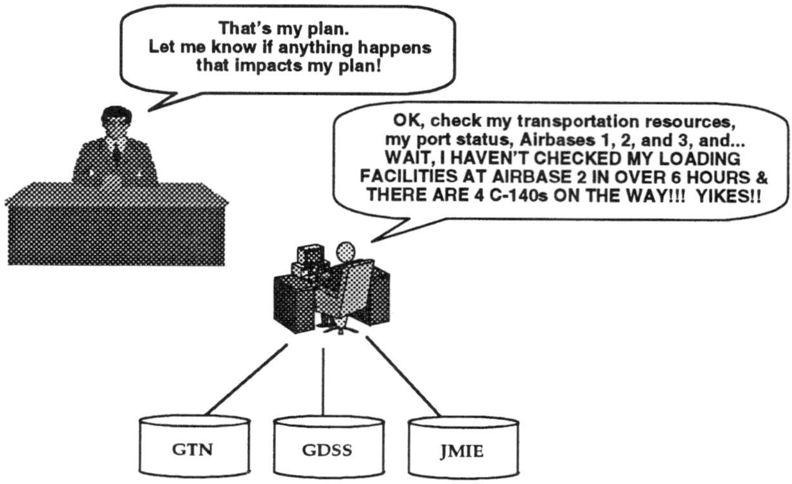

Exhibit 23-3. Manual situation monitoring.

While various efforts have made it easier to query multiple, heterogeneous data sources, they provide no facilities for monitoring those sources. The staff must determine which conditions to monitor, must continually query the data sources, and then must sift through the large amounts of data returned by those queries. In such an environment, it is easy to miss a critical indicator that could indicate a problem, as illustrated in Exhibit 23-3.

Given the complexity and error-prone nature of manual situation monitoring, there is a need for automated assistance with generating and monitoring standing requests for information (SRIs). An SRI is a set of conditions defined over a set of information sources. Our initial work has assumed that SRIs are equivalent to continuously monitored SQL queries (although MITRE is also investigating extensions of SQL).

An SRI, once issued, remains in place until the conditions that make up the SRI are satisfied by new or changed data in the information sources. Once the SRI is satisfied, an appropriate action can then take place.

Two major challenges must be addressed to support automatic generation of SRIs:

- Determining what conditions to monitor (i.e., those that are currently the highest-value indicators of plan failure).
- Monitoring those conditions efficiently, despite heterogeneity, autonomy, and distribution of data sources.

The Software Agents for Situation Monitoring project is developing and prototyping agent-based techniques for addressing both of these issues.

The determination of what conditions to monitor is based on analysis of a course-of-action plan. The goal is to generate monitoring agents (SRIs) for the highest-value information, where value is determined by the following factors:

- How good an indicator of plan failure is a particular condition?
- Timeliness (i.e., will the indicator event occur early enough in plan execution to permit corrective action to be taken?).
- Cost of acquiring the information (e.g., a database query is much less costly than tasking someone to gather information on the status of loading equipment).

A prototype agent has been developed for performing plan analysis and high-value condition identification that uses Bayesian belief networks.

Each of the high-value conditions identified by the plan analysis agent constitute the core of one SRI. Once these conditions have been identified, a set of SRIs can then be established. At this point, an agent is generated to perform the monitoring task needed for each SRI. Choosing an implementation strategy for these monitoring agents is a complex matter that must consider the following issues:

- *How do you monitor conditions that span multiple, heterogeneous distributed information sources?* Users (or software) must be able to specify SRIs in terms of an integrated view of the individual sources in order to insulate them from the details of how information is represented in each source or even which sources contain the information.
- *What data should be cached?* Caching is often required, both to meet response time requirements and to allow access to intermittently connected sources. On the other hand, cached data must be refreshed when the underlying sources change, possibly overloading low-bandwidth networks with refresh messages. These trade offs must be considered in deciding what to cache and how to refresh it.
- *How can sources be monitored nonintrusively, in a way that respects their autonomy?* For example, while triggers (i.e., database rules) provide a natural mechanism for testing intra-database conditions, many database administrators are unwilling to grant “create trigger” privileges to nonlocal users.
- *Graceful evolution.* In many domains, SRIs must be added and deleted frequently, as plan execution proceeds and the situation changes.

Given the complexity of monitoring SRI conditions, there is a need for automatic generation and installation of all required software and database objects to perform monitoring of the currently defined SRIs. Without this automatic generation, each time an SRI changed a major systems engineering project would ensue; this is clearly unacceptable in a dynamic environment in which the current set of SRIs is continually evolving to fit the current context.

This project has developed techniques for doing this automatic generation of monitoring agents. We call the software that performs this function a *monitor generator* because it automatically generates and installs monitoring agents that do the following: (1) selectively cache subsets of the component data sources, (2) refresh the cache, (3) monitor SRI conditions in the cache, and (4) alert decisions-makers when SRI conditions have been satisfied.

A prototype monitor generator has been implemented, and it is being used to support standing requests for information over a collection of databases that are used for military logistics planning. This architecture for monitoring SRIs is shown in Exhibit 23-4.

Either the plan analysis agent or a user defines SRIs that are fed to the monitor generator, which chooses an implementation strategy and generates one monitoring agent for each SRI (indicated by the dashed box in Exhibit 23-4). Whenever an SRI's condition becomes true, the monitoring agent associated with that SRI alerts the user (or software system) that requested the monitoring.

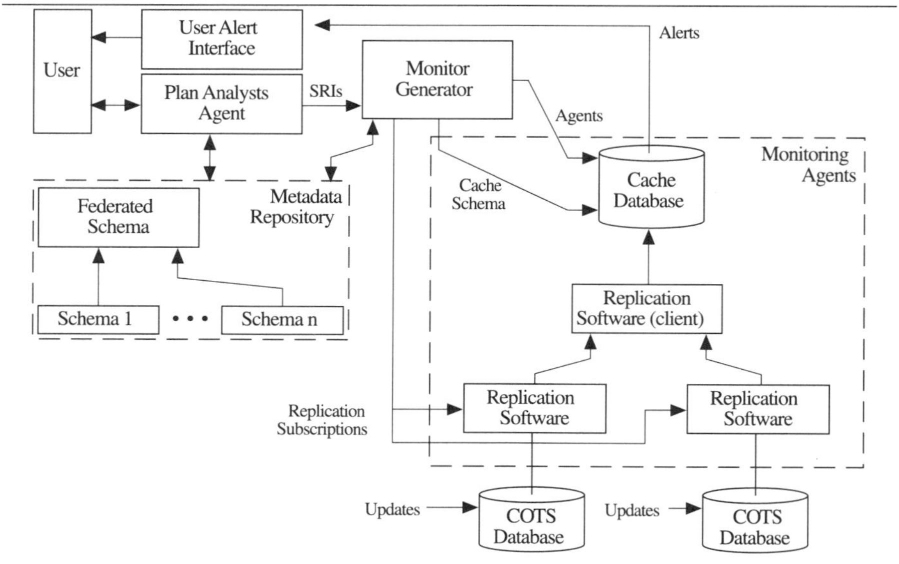

Exhibit 23-4. Architecture for distributed situation monitoring.

Two levels of information filtering automatically occur in the monitoring agent. These two levels act together to magnify the monitoring agent's power to filter data for the decision-maker, much as two lenses in a telescope can magnify its power to reach distant light sources for an observer.

The first level of filtering occurs at the data sources, leveraging commercial off-the-shelf (COTS) data replication software. A data replication product permits the user to specify a subscription: the subset of the data in a database to be replicated. A subscription can thus be used both to filter data at its source and to maintain a copy of the filtered data at the monitoring site. Each subscription filters out data, unless it is relevant to some of the monitoring agent's SRI.

The data at the monitoring site are called a *cache database* and always contain a synopsis of the current state of the situation being monitored. As relevant source data changes, those changes are automatically reflected in the cache database via replication. In addition, changes necessary due to source-receiver heterogeneity can be performed en route, "cleansing" the data to make it fit the cache database format.

Once in the cache database, this relevant data can be further filtered using active database technology. Triggers (i.e., active database rules) are placed in the cache database by the monitoring agent to represent the agents SRI. These triggers detect changes specific to the agents particular SRI. If these changes make the SRI true, an alert (notification) is issued and the user is made aware. Thus, users are insulated from many of the onerous tasks of sifting through massive amounts of data to perform their monitoring role; the most mundane, tedious, and voluminous tasks are done automatically, and the user simply responds to the issued alerts.

This project provides an example of how agents can be used in monitoring a distributed set of heterogeneous data sources. In doing so, they provide examples of some of the agent characteristics described earlier in this chapter.

The plan analysis agent and monitoring agents cooperate in providing the logistics planner with crucial information delivered in a timely manner. The agents in this system are goal-driven as well. The plan analysis agent passes down the information to be monitored and the monitor generator plans how the monitoring is to be accomplished, using domain knowledge about the available system to create a set of agents that can monitor the specific data sources. The monitoring agents exhibit some characteristics of mobility as well, by installing data subscriptions at each remote database site.

SUMMARY

Advances in data management technology have made large volumes of data available to any user with a desktop PC and network connection.

Unfortunately, these users have discovered that too much data is nearly as bad as no data.

Research in software agents shows promise in providing software capable of assisting users in managing data over a vast, poorly structured information environment. Agents are autonomous software entities that use existing data management systems in order to perform specific data management tasks on behalf of a user. This ability to autonomously manage tasks provides a level of abstraction between the high-level goals of the user and the low-level intricacies of data management systems. By employing an agent, a user no longer needs to be concerned with the petty details of a specific task and can be concerned with finding information rather than manipulating data.

Chapter 24 Selecting a Cryptographic System

Marie A. Wright

CRYPTOGRAPHY IS CONCERNED WITH THE DESIGN AND USE OF ENCRYPTION SYSTEMS, AND ITS PRIMARY OBJECTIVE IS TO ENSURE THE PRIVACY AND AUTHENTICITY OF DATA. Encryption provides privacy by transforming data into an unintelligible form through the use of a key, which is a symbol or group of symbols that controls the encryption or decryption processes.

Some cryptographic systems allow the same key to be used for both encryption and decryption. These private-key systems are so named because the disclosure of the key to anyone but the sender and the receiver will compromise the integrity of the transmitted data. Other cryptographic systems use different keys to control the encryption and decryption operations. These public-key systems typically use a public encryption key and a private decryption key. Although it is easy to calculate the public key from the private key, it is computationally infeasible to calculate the private key from the public key.

Public-key cryptographic systems readily provide authenticity by generating and verifying digital signatures. Of particular importance in financial and legal transactions, digital signatures are used to confirm the source of a message and to ensure that the message has not been inadvertently or deliberately modified.

Neither type of cryptographic system is inherently better than the other; each is used for different applications, and many practical implementations use both. Similarly, no single cryptographic system is suitable for all security needs. However, there are several key factors (i.e., the nature of the organization, the type of data maintained, the size and geographic distribution of the user population, and the system types and architectures) that render the use of some cryptographic systems more effective than others.

0-8493-0893-3/00/$0.00+$.50

This article offers guidelines for developing a comprehensive security plan that includes cryptographic measures. It then discusses the three most widely used cryptography alternatives: the Data Encryption Standard, the Rivest_Shamir-Adleman (RSA) algorithm, and the Digital Signature Standard.

SELECTING A CRYPTOGRAPHIC SYSTEM

Several steps should be followed in selecting a cryptographic system. Namely, the security manager should:

- Identify the data to be secured, as well as the length of time security must be provided.
- Determine the level of network security required.
- To the extent possible, estimate the value of the data to be protected and the cost to secure it.
- Evaluate the existing physical and logical security controls.
- Evaluate the existing administrative security controls.
- Determine how the cryptographic keys will be securely generated, distributed, stored, and used.

Identifying the Data to Be Secured

Before any thought is given to implementing a cryptographic system, the quantity, type, and sensitivity of the data to be secured must be clearly identified. The volume of data that must be securely transmitted or stored and the nature of the processing involved are fundamental criteria for a cryptographic system. So, too, are the nature and operations of certain organizations (e.g., financial institutions), the types of databases maintained, and the opportunities for economic gain for potential perpetrators. Although certain data (e.g., personnel records and Electronic Funds Transfer data) is clearly sensitive, the sensitivity of other data (e.g., inventory records) may not be as easily assessed.

Not all data requires encryption, and very little data needs to remain in encrypted form at all times. Certainly, any data that could cause competitive disadvantage, financial loss, breach of good faith, or personal injury or death if disclosed or modified in an unauthorized manner should be secured. In some cases, unencrypted sensitive data may be considered secure when stored within a large computer system with adequate access controls. However, the same data may be highly vulnerable and therefore should be encrypted when stored on a file server in a local area network or when transmitted through dial-up network connections, Wide Area Network, satellite communications, or facsimile machines.

Determining the Level of Network Security Required

There are two ways in which encryption may be applied to networks: link encryption and end-to-end encryption. These two approaches differ in the nature of security provided.

Link encryption performs the encryption of a message immediately before its physical transmission over an individual communications link between two network nodes. A message may be transmitted over many communications links before arriving at its final destination. Within each node, the incoming message is decrypted and the Routing Information extracted. The message is then re-encrypted using a different key and transmitted to the next node. Because the transmitted message is decrypted and encrypted at each node that it passes through, all data transmitted on the links, including the destination addresses, is encrypted. Because encryption is part of the transmission process, no special user intervention is required.

One disadvantage of link encryption is that it requires all nodes to be physically secured because the subversion of any network node will expose substantial amounts of information. In addition, key distribution and key management (discussed in a later section) are problematic in link encryption systems because each node must store the cryptographic key of every node to which it is connected.

End-to-end encryption provides a higher level of security in a network environment because the message is not decrypted until the final destination has been reached. Because the message is encrypted at the source and remains encrypted throughout its transmission, it will not be compromised if a node has been subverted. This level of encryption is more naturally suited to users' perceptions of their security requirements, because only the source and destination nodes must be secure. In addition, key management tends to be less problematic in this environment because end-to-end encryption does not require all of the network nodes to have special encryption capabilities.

However, this level of encryption does not permit destination addresses to be encrypted, because each node that the message passes through must have access to the address in order to correctly forward the message. Therefore, end-to-end encryption is more susceptible to attacks of traffic flow analysis because the origin-destination patterns are not masked. In addition, because individual users may elect to use this method of encryption, it is not as transparent to the users as link encryption.

Furthermore, end-to-end encryption requires each system to perform compatible encryption. As a result, the use of proprietary algorithms is less feasible in this environment. The options are effectively reduced to those cryptographic systems that are compatible with existing domestic or international standards (e.g., the Data Encryption Standard or RSA algorithms).

Estimating the Value of the Data to Be Protected

Because it is often difficult to assign financial values to the data to be secured, risk analysis methods typically prove to be beneficial. A risk analysis is a structured, methodical analysis of system assets and perceived threats. It realistically assesses the value of the resources to be protected, quantifies the probability of occurrence of identified system threats, calculates annual loss expectancies, and determines the cost of available security countermeasures. Undertaken by skilled professionals, a risk analysis can identify cost-effective security measures and enhance security awareness throughout the organization.

It is important to consider the impact of time on both the value of the data and the strength of the cryptographic system. Certain cryptographic algorithms are able to withstand cryptanalytic attack for longer periods of time than others. Because the value of data tends to decrease over time, variations in cryptographic strength should be carefully evaluated. A reasonable assessment of the time factors might show that a simpler and less costly cryptographic system could provide adequate security during the time that the value of the data remains at or above a critical threshold.

The use of cryptography can be an expensive means of providing data security. A realistic assessment should be made of the costs of acquiring and installing a cryptographic system; the processing costs of the encryption/decryption operations, and the costs associated with any adverse impact on data compression or data transmission rates. Cryptography should be used only when the value of the data exceeds the costs involved in securing the data.

Evaluating the Existing Physical and Logical Security Controls

Cryptography is only one component of total system security. Implemented alone, cryptography offers little protection in terms of avoiding the unauthorized disclosure of data, deterring inadvertent or deliberate modifications to data, preventing unauthorized data modifications, detecting the loss of data, or recovering after the occurrence of such events. Adequate physical and logical security controls must also be in place.

For example, access controls are of particular importance. These controls are designed to limit the number of individuals who can access the system and to constrain their activities once access is achieved. As a result, these controls should provide for the classification and isolation of data according to different levels of sensitivity, and they should allow only those individuals with authorized access rights to store, process, or retrieve data or to communicate with or make use of any system resource. Because cryptography operates as an adjunct to access controls, the security provided by a cryptographic system depends, at least in part, on the security provided by the operating system.

Evaluating the Existing Administrative Security Controls

Just as cryptography is only one facet of data security, data security is only one element of effective administrative control over system resources and operations. Safeguards—in the form of mandatory technological security mechanisms, operational and procedural controls, and accountability procedures—are required to support management control. Of particular importance to the implementation and use of cryptography are the following administrative practices:

Seeking expert advice before a cryptographic system is implemented. In-house experts and knowledgeable outside consultants should be used to analyze the strengths and weaknesses of a cryptographic system in light of the organization's current and future security needs.

Selecting the most inexpensive cryptographic system available that meets the organization's current and projected security needs.

Monitoring the technical operations of the cryptographic system after it has been implemented. Any changes in its operations should be made with extreme caution, because partial modifications often result in the degradation of cryptographic security.

Monitoring human interactions with the cryptographic system. Cryptographic keys are particularly vulnerable in the hands of inexperienced or inadequately trained personnel. For this reason, the handling of cryptographic keys should be transparent to system users and operators.

Determining How the Cryptographic Keys Will Be Managed

The security provided by a cryptographic system depends on the security of the keys. In fact, the importance of the keys suggests that they be given greater protection than the data to be secured. Key management focuses on the generation, distribution, storage, and use of the cryptographic keys, and its goal is to protect the integrity of the keys.

The issue of key distribution remains the most complex problem within key management. Private-key cryptographic systems require a cryptographic key to be secretly exchanged and therefore mandate rigorous key distribution procedures. When there are relatively few users, many methods could be used to distribute the limited number of keys. For example, the keys could be transported manually to the communicating sites or sent in a sealed envelope by overnight courier.

Most current systems are far more complex, however; there are a large number of users in widely dispersed communicating sites who request numerous keys and require frequent key changes. Manual key distribution is impractical for these systems. Instead, automated key distribution techniques are used.

In network environments in which terminal-host communication occurs, the host computer generates a session key for encryption purposes. The session key is generated on the request of a user at a terminal and is used only for that individual user's session at that terminal. After the session key has been generated, it is encrypted with the terminal key and transmitted from the host to the terminal. The session key is encrypted with the host's master key (or key-encrypting key) and stored at the host. Messages transmitted between the terminal and the host are encrypted and decrypted in secure modules at both sites.

In network environments with heavy data traffic and multiple communicating sites, a central key management system may be used. A standard describing this type of system has been established by the American National Standards Institute (ANSI). Published as ANSI X9.17, this key management standard is designed for use among wholesale financial institutions for electronic funds transfer systems.

The central key management system described in ANSI X9.17 calls for a key distribution architecture that uses either two or three layers of keys. In the two-layer architecture, the master key (or top-level key-encrypting key) is distributed manually, and the data keys (the cryptographic keys used to encrypt the data) are distributed automatically after they have been encrypted with the master key. The three-layer architecture also requires the master key at the top level to be distributed manually. A second layer of key-encrypting keys are then encrypted with the master key and distributed automatically. The data keys on the third layer are encrypted with the second-level key-encrypting keys and distributed automatically.

Automated key distribution may occur in point-to-point, key distribution center, or key translation center environments. In a point-to-point environment, at least one of the two communicating sites must be able to generate the top-level master key. Both sites share this master key so that the data keys (in the two-layer architecture) or the second-level key-encrypting keys (in the three-layer architecture) may be exchanged.

In a key distribution center environment, neither communicating site has the ability to generate the top-level master key. Instead, both communicating sites individually share a master key with the centralized key distribution facility. The site that wants to initiate communications requests the data keys from the centralized facility and provides the center with the identity of the receiving site. The center then generates two sets of data keys. The first set is encrypted with the master key shared between the center and the initiating site, and the second set is encrypted with the master key shared between the center and the receiving site. Both sets of encrypted data keys are transmitted from the center to the initiating site. This site in turn transmits the second set of keys to the receiving site.

In a key translation center environment, the initiating site has the ability to generate the data key and can encrypt it with the master key, which is shared with the centralized facility. The encrypted data key is then transmitted to the center along with the identity of the receiving site. The key translation center decrypts the encrypted data key and uses the master key shared between the center and the receiving site to re-encrypt the data key. The center then transmits the re-encrypted data key back to the initiating site, and from there the key is forwarded to the receiving site.

Public-key cryptographic systems (e.g., the RSA algorithm, discussed later) may be used to transmit the key-encrypting keys or data keys. Because public-key cryptography does not require the exchange of secret keys before the establishment of secure communications, these systems may be used to reduce the inherent complexities of key distribution.

Effective key management is one of the most crucial elements of the encryption process. Clearly, the number of individuals required to handle the keys and the manual operations involved should be kept to a minimum. Without exception, all cryptographic keys must be well protected and changed frequently to ensure the privacy and authenticity of the data.

CRYPTOGRAPHIC ALTERNATIVES

Different cryptographic systems provide varying degrees of strength. The three primary encryption algorithms currently in use are the Data Encryption Standard, the RSA algorithm, and the Data Signature Standard, which are discussed in the following sections.

The Data Encryption Standard

One of the oldest and most widely used cryptographic systems in the US is the DES (DES). An industry staple for more than 15 years, the DES is a private-key system designed to provide privacy.

Financial institutions use the DES extensively for the encryption of financial transactions. In fact, the DES is used to encrypt most of the transaction data (valued at approximately one trillion dollars) transmitted daily over such bank networks as the FedWire and CHIPS (Clearing House Interbank Payment System).

During the late 1960s and early 1970s, there were increasing concerns within the US that some information was being lost to foreign powers as a result of insecure communications media in the US. In response to the perceived need for the strong method of encryption to protect computer data, IBM Corp. developed a cryptographic system known as Lucifer.

In 1973, the National Bureau of Standards (now the National Institute of Standards and Technology) made a nationwide request for submissions for encryption algorithms that could be used to protect sensitive but unclassified data. Lucifer was submitted, and it was adopted as the national DES in 1977.

However, the DES was adopted amid controversy and bureaucratic compromise, much of which centered on the National Security Agency (NSA). As adviser on the DES project, the NSA convinced the National Bureau of Standards and IBM to weaken the key from its originally designed 128 bits to 64 bits. However, because eight of these bits are reserved for parity, the key was technically reduced to a relatively small 56 bits. In addition, the NSA advised IBM not to publish certain design criteria, leaving many to speculate that the algorithm may contain trapdoor mechanisms that could be used to circumvent or subvert its security features.

The only publicly known way to break the DES algorithm is by brute force: testing each of the cryptographic keys until the correct one is discovered. With an effective key length of 56 bits, the DES provides more than 72 quadrillion (256) unique cryptographic keys. Before computers with multiple parallel processors were introduced, testing all keys was believed to be computationally infeasible. This is no longer the case, because parallel processing significantly reduces the time needed to search through all of the keys, making it possible to identify the cryptographic key currently in use. With the growth of parallel processing, Data Encryption Standard security depends more than ever on random key selection and frequent key changes.

DES Cryptographic Process. The DES algorithm uses a 56-bit key to encipher a 64-bit block of plaintext into a 64-bit block of chiphertext. The 64 bits in the block of plaintext are initially transposed, then divided into two equal-sized blocks. These two blocks, referred to as L32 and R32, each contain 32 bits.

The bits in blocks L32 and R32 undergo 16 iterations of an intricate cryptographic process. Each iteration begins with a transposition of the 32 bits in R32, followed by an expansion of these bits into a 48-bit block. Next, an encryption key is computed that consists of 48 of the possible 56 bits. This 48-bit key is added to the expanded 48 bits in the R32 block, and the resulting 48 bits are split into eight 6-bit blocks. The eight 6-bit blocks are then input to eight different substitution functions. Each substitution function generates a 4-bit block as output.

These eight 4-bit blocks are consolidated into a 32-bit block. The 32 bits are transposed, added to the 32 bits in L32, and stored in a temporary location in memory. The 32 bits in R32 are then transferred to L32, and the bits temporarily stored in memory are transferred to R32. This process is repeated a total of 16 times, with a different 48-bit encryption key computed for each iteration. After 16iterations, the contents of L32 and R32 are interchanged. The bits in both blocks are transposed and then combined into a 64-bit output block of ciphertext.

The decryption process is accomplished by reversing this algorithm; the encryption process is effectively repeated with the order of the 16 keys reversed.

DES Variations. The conventional mode of the DES, previously described, is a basic block encryption method. It operates like an Electronic Code Book that contains 256 possible entries. The electronic code book (ECB) form of the DES provides privacy but not authentication, because there are inherent weaknesses in its operations.

For example, the encryption process is linear in nature; given a certain key and block of plaintext, the transformation process and the resulting ciphertext output will always be the same. Because most messages have some degree of redundancy, the plaintext could be constructed by examining several output blocks. Furthermore, because each block of plaintext is encrypted as an independent entity, a block could be modified without affecting any of the other blocks.

Other modes of DES operation eliminate the repetition of ciphertext blocks and provide both privacy and authentication. The cipher block-chaining mode encrypts 64-bit blocks of plaintext into 64-bit blocks of ciphertext. However, cipher block chaining overcomes the fundamental weakness of the electronic code book (ECB) mode by using the ciphertext for each block as feedback into the next plaintext block to be encrypted. As a result, repeated output patterns are hidden through the chaining process of repetitive encryption.

An alternative to cipher block chaining is the cipher feedback mode. Cipher feedback is used to encrypt individual bits or bytes of plaintext and is typically used when the plaintext cannot be framed into 64-bit blocks. Because each DES operation encrypts a much smaller unit of plaintext, cipher feedback is considered to be a stronger, but significantly slower, method of DES encryption.

The RSA Algorithm

The RSA algorithm, named for its inventors (Rivest, Shamir, and Adleman), was developed at MIT in 1978. It has proved its reliability through years of testing and public scrutiny and is now an internationally recognized encryption standard. The RSA algorithm provides both privacy and authentication.

Currently used by more than two-thirds of the US computer industry, the RSA algorithm is the de facto public-key encryption standard. The encryption key and the algorithm are made public, but the decryption key is kept private. Although the encryption and decryption keys are mathematically inverse pairs, it is computationally infeasible for an intruder to calculate the private decryption key from the known encryption key and algorithm.

RSA Cryptographic Process. The RSA algorithm is based on the fact that it is much easier to multiply two numbers than it is to factor the result. The algorithm used in the encryption process is referred to as a trapdoor one-way function. It calls for the product of two large prime numbers (integers with more than 100 decimal digits) to be computed and made public as part of the encryption key. To perform the decryption operations, however, the two prime factors must be known. Because the encryption key and algorithm are made public, the theoretical possibility exists that an intruder could determine the private decryption key through extensive mathematical analysis. In practice, however, the excessive number of calculations required to determine the decryption key renders this form of attack computationally infeasible.

The process of encryption begins with the random selection of two very large prime numbers (p and q). These numbers are multiplied, and the product (n) is made public. A calculation is then performed that computes the number of positive integers less than n that has neither p nor q as factors. The result of this calculation (x) is kept secret. Next, an enciphering integer (e) is randomly selected between the range of 2 and (x – 1). The resulting encryption key (e,n) is made public.

The plaintext to be encrypted is represented as a sequence of integers between 0 and (n-1). The public encryption key (e,n) is used to transform each plaintext integer into a corresponding ciphertext integer. Each plaintext integer is raised to the power of e, the result is divided by n, and the ciphertext is equal to the remainder.

A private decryption key (d,n) must be used to decipher the encrypted plaintext. The deciphering integer (d) is calculated from the values of e and x, such that the product of e and d differ from 1 by a multiple of x. Decryption is accomplished by raising each ciphertext integer to the power of d. The result is divided by n, and the plaintext is equal to the remainder.

RSA Applications. Although the encryption and decryption operations in the RSA scheme are computationally slower than those of the DES, use of the RSA algorithm is preferred for such applications as key management and digital signatures. The RSA algorithm is particularly effective in the area of key management. Key distribution is a significant problem with the DES, because the mechanics of the DES algorithm mandate that both the sender and the receiver share a secret cryptographic key.

The RSA algorithm overcomes many of the complexities involved in distributing the private cryptographic keys. Because the RSA scheme does not require the exchange of a private key before secure communications are established, it provides an effective method of securing the Data Encryption Standard keys.

The RSA algorithm is often used for certain financial and legal transactions, because the digital signatures produced are valid for legal contracts. A digital signature provides authentication by verifying the integrity and the source of a message as well as the identity of the sender.

The RSA algorithm provides an elegant method of producing digital signatures. The process begins with the encryption of a message with the sender's private key; this creates the digital signatures. The sender then encrypts this message with the recipient's public key, for additional privacy. When the message is received, the recipient's private key is used to decrypt the message and verify its integrity. The message is then decrypted using the sender's public key; this verifies the identity of the sender and validates the digital signature. The nature of the mathematics involved in the RSA algorithm allows the encryption and decryption operations to be reversed, thus allowing plaintext that was initially encrypted using the sender's private key to be decrypted and validated with the sender's public key.

The Digital Signature Standard

The Digital Signature Standard (DSS) was introduced by National Institute for Standards and Technology in 1991as the federal government's proposed standard for encrypting unclassified data. Developed by the NSA, the DSS was designed to compute and verify digital signatures, thus providing message authentication but not privacy. Despite this apparent weakness, the DSS was intended to become the nation's public-key encryption standard. If it is adopted, the DSS will be used in such business practices as Electronic Data Interchange, Electronic Funds Transfer, electronic mail, software distribution, and the software virus detection.

The need for a stronger, national cryptographic standard has been a matter of extensive debate since 1985, when the NSA announced that it would neither endorse DES-based products nor recommend re-certification of the DES algorithm after 1988. The NSA justified its decision by citing potential vulnerabilities of the DES resulting from its widespread use. There was considerable reaction to the NSA's announcement from the financial community, whose concern about the security provided by the Data Encryption Standard was overshadowed by the fact that a suitable cryptographic alternative had not been made available. The NSA rescinded its decision, and the DES was re-certified through 1992.

The need to develop a stronger domestic cryptographic system has been underscored by recent technological advances, which some believe have pushed the DES close to the end of its useful life. However, introduction of the DSS was a disturbing answer to the question of how best to provide data security.

Like the DES, the DSS owes its controversial beginnings to the NSA. The DSS was unilaterally developed by the NSA, a secretive government intelligence agency responsible for monitoring foreign communications. The absence of any involvement from business or academia on the algorithm's development stands in marked contrast to the origins of the DES and RSA algorithms. Unlike these algorithms, the DSS contains no method for encrypting data and will not be subject to government-imposed export restrictions. The potential imposition of this untested security standard has caused many to conclude that the NSA is more concerned with reducing the difficulty of crypt analyzing foreign communications than with increasing the security of corporate data communications.

NIST's role in proposing the DSS also has been the subject of intense scrutiny. The introduction of the DSS represents the government's overt rejection of the RSA algorithm. The impact of this is significant. It would be unduly expensive and complicated for businesses to use the DSS for domestic communications and the RSA scheme for international communications, yet multiple encryption technologies would have to be sustained to ensure compatible data communications. Furthermore, the DSS digital signature verification process is slower than that of the RSA algorithm. This creates the additional problem of noticeable performance delays for those applications requiring extensive use of signature verification (i.e., credit card or banking transactions).

Signature Generation and Verification. Because it was NIST's intent to offer a public-key cryptographic standard that was free of existing patents, the DSS uses a different algorithm than the RSA scheme. Although the RSA algorithm relies on the computational infeasibility of calculating the prime factors of large numbers, DSS security is based on the difficulty of calculating discrete logarithms.

The DSS uses two keys to control the digital signature generation and verification processes. The algorithm requires the sender the use a one-way hash function (i.e., a mathematical process) to generate a profile (or condensed version) of the message. The profile is encrypted with the sender's private key, creating the digital signature, which is attached to the message for transmission. When the message is received, the receiver uses the sender's public key to decrypt the profile. The receiver then uses the same hash function to create a profile of the message. If the receiver's profile matches that of the sender, the integrity of the message and the identity of the sender are authenticated.

The DSS requires all public keys to appear in a public directory, thus allowing any user to validate a sender's digital signature. To authenticate the public key registry, the DSS uses a mutually trusted arbiter (or certifying authority) to generate a certificate of credentials associating a given public key with the corresponding identity of the owner. However, details pertaining to the generation of such a certificate have not been fully specified by NIST.

CONCLUSION

Although cryptography is used as the primary means of protecting data in computer networks, it should be an integrated component of a comprehensive system security program. Selection of a cryptographic system should be undertaken after several factors have been carefully assessed including:

- The nature and operations of the organization.
- The quantity, type, sensitivity, and value of the data.
- The perceived threats to the data.
- The size and geographic distribution of the user population.
- The level of network security required.
- The effectiveness of existing physical, logical, and administrative security controls.

In addition, variations in the level of security provided by different cryptographic systems should be knowledgeably evaluated. Before a cryptographic system is chosen, consideration should be given to the level of privacy and authenticity provided; the reputed strength, speed, and efficiency of the algorithm; its recognized domestic and international use; and its associated acquisition, installation, and processing costs. The optimal choice is the most inexpensive cryptographic system available that meets the organization's current and projected security needs.

Chapter 25
Data Security for the Masses

Stewart S. Miller

CREDIT CARD NUMBERS ARE AN EXAMPLE OF INFORMATION THAT SHOULD BE PROTECTED WHILE USERS CONDUCT COMMERCIAL TRANSACTIONS OVER THE INTERNET. Because the Internet was originally designed to be an open system, implementing security has proven to be difficult for developers.

PASSIVE THREATS

Security threats can be passive or active (see Exhibit 25-1 and Exhibit 25-2). Passive threats include unauthorized:

- Monitoring or recording of data transmitted over a communications facility.
- Release of message contents.
- Analysis of traffic.
- Examination of packet headers to determine the location and identity of communicating hosts. From this information an intruder can also observe the length and frequency of messages.
- Reading of user data in messages.

ACTIVE THREATS

Active threats include:

- Unauthorized modification of transmitted data or control signals.
- Production of false data or control signals transmitted over a communications system.
- Modification, deletion, delay, or reordering of a genuine message to insert a false one (a technique known as message stream modification).

For example, an active threat might be a hacker who manipulates transmitted data and alters messages by gaining network access with stolen passwords. The attacker intercepts source information before it reaches its destination user. Hackers have password programs that try different

0-8493-0893-3/00/$0.00+$.50

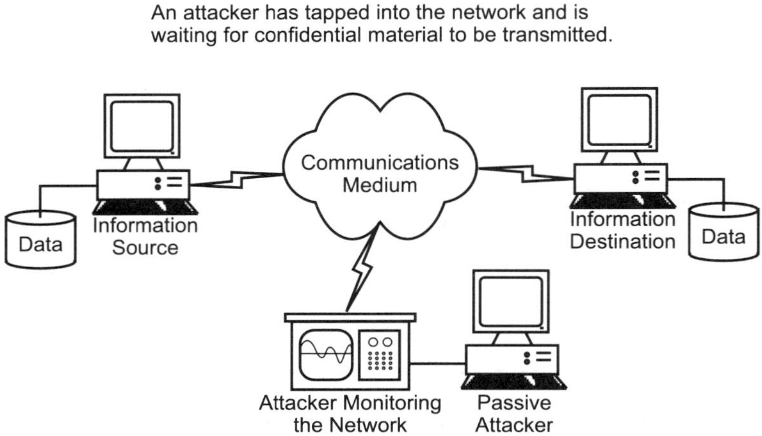

Exhibit 25-1. Passive security threats.

combinations of words until the hacker gains access. An attacker can also physically tap into to data or telephone lines to intercept, manipulate, or destroy confidential data.

PAYING SAFELY OVER THE INTERNET

CyberCash Inc. (Reston, VA), founded in 1994, works with financial institutions and goods and services providers to deliver secure Internet payment systems. CyberCash uses general security methods including the secure sockets layer (SSL) protocol and the Secure HyperText Transfer Protocol (S-HTTP). Users, however, may want to further protect themselves with an additional layer of software designed explicitly for secure financial payments.

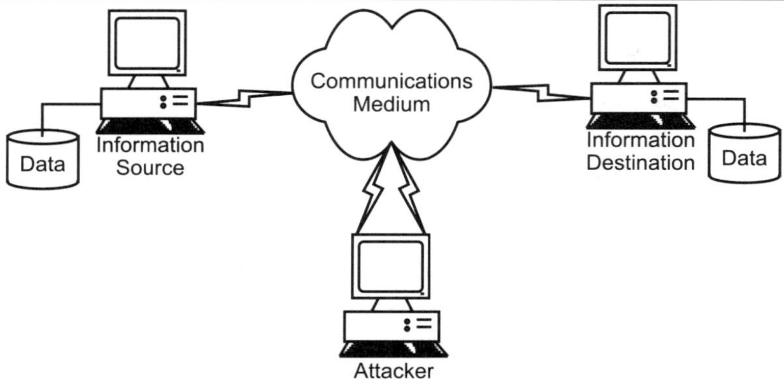

Exhibit 25-2. Active security threats.

The Rivest_Shamir-Adleman (RSA) Data Security (Redwood City, CA) industry standard is used by most security software developers. RSA's security features offer several levels of encryption. Generation of the encryption key should be hidden from the end user. However, users should know the frequency at which the software outputs a secure encryption key. If multiple encryption keys are used at once, and if a new key is generated each time users conduct a transaction, then the level of security and privacy will be greater.

Banks are testing Internet payment systems. Secure applications that are endorsed by a bank or financial institution are usually adequate safeguards for online transactions.

Firewalls

A firewall is one method of protecting a network from unauthorized access. The firewall is actually a pair of mechanisms: one that blocks traffic and one that allows traffic flow. Firewalls are employed to:

- Protect networks from vandals.
- Keep unwanted traffic out of the network to keep valuable resources free.
- Store data so users cannot access the system, yet allow the user to retrieve information stored in the firewall.
- Allow authorized users inside the network so they may communicate freely with the outside world.
- Provide a single cornerstone where security and audits can be imposed.
- Can be an effective tracing tool in the event of unauthorized network access.

Firewalls are usually inadequate protection against viruses, however, because there are too many ways of encoding binary files for transfer over networks. A firewall is designed to keep intruders out of sensitive corporate networks and maintain the security of confidential information. Firewalls, however, cannot replace user security. A firewall will not protect companies whose users threaten security by writing their passwords on monitors or keeping passwords exceedingly simple.

Netscape's Secure Courier

Netscape Communications Corp. (Mountain View, CA) uses Secure Courier, an open, cross-platform protocol that creates a secure digital envelope for financial data over the Internet. Intuit, Inc. and MasterCard International use this protocol to secure online credit card, debit card, and charge card transactions. Secure Courier uses the Secure Socket Layer protocol and the MasterCard/Visa security specification for bank card purchases on open networks.

Compatible with UNIX, Windows, and Macintosh, Secure Courier secures Internet business transactions by encrypting financial information between the PC and financial institutions. Secure Courier also authenticates consumer data for merchants. SSL encrypts data traveling between the client system and server; Secure Courier provides the additional security that keeps financial data encrypted (i.e., the secure digital envelope). The data remains protected at all sites along the path, which significantly reduces the risk of consumer and merchant fraud, allows global payment security, and consequently reduces merchant costs.

Netscape Security Updates. Netscape has completed security updates for its client and server software in response to the potential vulnerability in security discovered by two University of California at Berkeley students. In that case, encrypted data was decoded and users were able to break Netscape's SSL encryption code. Netscape has since corrected the problem.

Netscape is increasing the quantity of random information used to implement its random number generator. This security approach plugs a random number in a mathematical formula to create a session key used to encrypt information transmitted across the Internet. An increase in the amount of random information enhances security, preventing information thieves from identifying the encryption key.

ENCRYPTION AND DECRYPTION

Encryption transforms intelligible messages into unintelligible messages. Exhibit 25-3 shows the steps involved in encryption. Decryption uses a key to prevent unauthorized users from accessing message contents.

Data Encryption Standard

The Data Encryption Standard encrypts data in 64-byte blocks using a 56-byte key. Using this key, the 64-byte input is modified into the 64-byte output. Decryption follows these steps in reverse order. DES characteristics include:

- An input block of 64 bytes.
- A 64-byte key input where 8 bytes are parity bytes resolved by the other 56 bytes.
- Switch input that determines either encryption or decryption.
- A 64-byte block of output.

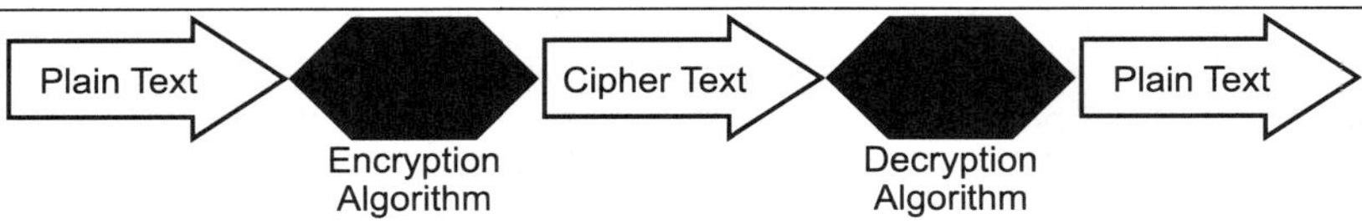

Exhibit 25-3. Standard encryption.

Single Key Encryption

Single key encryption uses a noncomplex algorithm to encrypt and decrypt. It permits large amounts of throughput, so data can be processed quickly. The key used to encrypt a message is the same key that decrypts the message. The drawback is that the sender and receiver must share the algorithm and key.

Public Key Encryption

Single key encryption requires users to distribute the keys securely. Public key encryption does not require the distribution of keys, but instead employs an algorithm that uses a key for encryption and a different companion key for decryption. Security is enhanced because private keys are produced locally by each user and never need to be distributed. In a public key encryption system:

- Each end system in a network produces a pair of keys used for encryption and decryption of received messages.
- Each system generates its encryption key and stores it in a public file (i.e., public key), with the companion key kept private.

Although public key encryption is a secure encryption method, public key throughput is less efficient than single key because the algorithm used by public key is much larger.

COMMERCIAL ENCRYPTION SOFTWARE

RSA Secure

RSA Data Security's software uses RC4 Symmetric Stream Cipher, which is an 80-byte encryption algorithm that provides significantly more security than Data Encryption Standard-based systems (i.e., the government encryption standard). RC4's 80-byte keys take more than 70 trillion million instructions-per-second (MIPS) years of computer time to decrypt. Emergency access and auto crypt features help larger enterprises handle emergency situations and permit all users to automatically or manually set encryption preferences.

Organizations using threshold-based emergency access can reach an individual user's encrypted files in urgent situations without degenerating systemwide security. Administrators are able to delegate emergency decryption authority through up to 256 different trustees. Commercial key escrow capability is possible through RSA's Public Key Cryptosystem, as well as advanced storage and confidential sharing technologies.

TimeStep Permit Security Gateway

TimeStep Corp. (Kanata, Ontario, Canada) provides a device that secures communications between remote users and local applications, eliminating the need for corporate information systems staffs to program security into each application because this device protects individual host computers.

TimeStep's Permit 1060 Security Gateway uses encryption, to authenticate users and ensure privacy, and Internet firewalls to keep invaders out of corporate networks. The Permit 1060 protects hosts behind a firewall from both internal and external trespassers.

Permit software uses public key cryptography (e.g., from RSA Data Security) to authenticate users. It uses the faster data encryption standard (DES) algorithm for line-speed encryption of file and message contents. Encryption designs are based on IP source and destination addresses, therefore systems administrators can choose which users can communicate with others.

DIGITAL SIGNATURE TECHNOLOGY

RSA Data Security, Inc. is one of the first companies to establish digital identification to authenticate a user's identity, which is an important element of electronic commerce. VeriSign, Inc. (Redwood City, CA) offers its digital signature technology for authenticating users as a component separate from encryption, which allows for export of stronger authentication.

VeriSign verifies digital identification for individuals, companies, World Wide Web (WWW) servers, Electronic Data Interchange servers, and Internet addresses. Its technology facilitates business transactions across the Internet using public key certificates for digital signatures and authentication.

Online Digital ID Issuing Service

VeriSign's digital ID issuing service allows users to instantly enroll and receive an individual digital ID. Both businesses and consumers can simply register for a unique digital ID online through the company's Web site at http://www.verisign.com. An auto responder processes noncommercial, class-one digital IDs at no cost to private users; commercial versions cost $6.

Public Identification Certificates

Multiple classes of digital IDs are available for a variety of products (i.e., Netscape Navigator 2.0). Public identification certificates are granted to individuals as well as merchant servers. The certificates are divided into four classes with increasing levels of identity assurance retrieved from either VeriSign or the online digital identification service.

Class One. Class-one certificates provide the unique name or E-mail addresses primarily used for casual Web browsing and secure E-mail, so users can safely communicate and identify themselves to merchants on the Internet.

Class Two. Class-two certificates offer a higher level of security for each user's identity. The registration process requires third-party proof of name, address, and other personal information. These IDs are primarily used for inter-company E-mail, online purchasing from electronic malls, and online subscriptions. Class-two IDs cost $12 annually.

Class Three. Class-three certificates offer an increased level of identity security by involving either personal presence or registered credentials. These IDs are used mainly for transactions that require more substantial assurance of an individual's identity. Uses for this ID level include electronic banking, large online purchases, and online membership services. Class-three IDs are available for an individual for $24 a year.

Class Four. Class-four certificates provide a maximum identity security assurance level for individuals and companies. Individuals or organizations are thoroughly investigated. In addition, personal presence is required to obtain the class-four ID. Uses of this ID include access to confidential information, authorization to trade financial securities, and access to corporate databases. Class-four digital ID pricing varies; users must contact VeriSign for details.

X. 509 Certificates

VeriSign is enhancing its certificate-issuing technology by offering the X.509 certificate (version 3 format), which will expand the use of digital IDs. Netscape Navigator 2.0 users will be the first to take advantage of version 3-compatible digital IDs. X.509 certificates allow corporate and individual users to customize IDs with respect to their needs by including authorization parameters in the digital ID. X.509 certificates may become an international standard identification on both public and private network.

SECURING E-MAIL WITH S/MIME

RSA Data Security enables encrypted messages to be exchanged between multiple vendors' E-mail applications through use of Secure/Multipurpose Internet Mail Extensions (S/MIME). In short, MIME has the ability to handle most content types and S/MIME secures them.

S/MIME is based on the inter-vendor Public Key Cryptography Standards (PKCS) established by RSA, Microsoft, Lotus Development Corp., Apple Computer, Novell, Digital Equipment Corp., Sun Microsystems, and the Massachusetts Institute of Technology in 1991.PKCS is the leader of commercial cryptographic standards in the US. PKCS specifications let developers develop secure applications independently that will work with other secured PKCS applications.

An S/MIME message composed and encrypted on one application can be decrypted and read on others. S/MIME yields a standard structure for

Internet mail content type. In addition, it allows extensions for new content type security applications. S/MIME provides customers with RSA encryption and digital signatures.

S/MIME secure E-mail plan vendors include Microsoft, ConnectSoft, QUALCOMM, SecureWare, and RSA. Frontier Technologies, an experienced developer of secure E-mail solutions, is one of the first vendors to support S/MIME in its networking software and will also make an initial implementation of the S/MIME protocol readily available as a reference to other vendors.

A LOOK AT THE FUTURE

Electronic commerce over the World Wide Web requires sophisticated encryption and authentication technologies. Secure communication over the Internet will allow the next generation of consumers to comfortably transact business online, performing daily purchases that today would be considered unsecured. These new advances will make the Internet the virtual marketplace of the 21st century.

Chapter 26 Firewall Management and Internet Attacks

Jeffery J. Lowder

NETWORK CONNECTIVITY CAN BE BOTH A BLESSING AND A CURSE. On the one hand, network connectivity can enable users to share files, exchange e-mail, and pool physical resources. Yet network connectivity can also be a risky endeavor if the connectivity grants access to would-be intruders. The Internet is a perfect case in point. Designed for a trusted environment, many contemporary exploits are based on vulnerabilities inherent to the protocol itself. According to a recent dissertation by John Howard on Internet unauthorized access incidents reported to the Computer Emergency Response Team (CERT), there were 4567 incidents between 1989 and 1996, with the number of incidents increasing each year at a rate of 41 to 62 percent. In light of this trend, many organizations are implementing firewalls to protect their internal network from the untrusted Internet.

LAYING THE GROUNDWORK FOR A FIREWALL

Obtaining management support for a firewall prior to implementation can be very useful after the firewall is implemented. When a firewall is implemented on a network for the first time, it will almost surely be the source of many complaints. For example:

- Organizations that have never before had firewalls almost always do not have the kind of documentation necessary to support user requirements.
- If the firewall hides information about the internal network from the outside network, this will break any network transactions in which the remote system uses an access control list and the address of the firewall is not included in that list.
- Certain types of message traffic useful in network troubleshooting (e.g., PING, TRACEROUTE) may no longer work.

0-8493-0893-?/00/$0.00+$.50

All of these problems can be solved, but the point is that coordination with senior management *prior to* installation can make life much easier for firewall administrators.

Benefits of Having a Firewall

So how does one obtain management support for implementation of a firewall? The security practitioner can point out the protection that a firewall provides: protection of the organization's network from intruders, protection of external networks from intruders within the organization, and protection from "due care" lawsuits. The security practitioner can also list the positive benefits a firewall can provide:

- *Increased ability to enforce network standards and policies.* Without a firewall or similar device, it is easy for users to implement systems that the Information Services (IS) department does not know about, that are in violation of organizational standards or policies, or both. In contrast, organizations find it very easy to enforce both standards and policies with a firewall that blocks all network connections by default. Indeed, it is not uncommon for organizations to discover undocumented systems when they implement such a firewall for the first time.
- *Centralized internetwork audit capability.* Because all or most traffic between the two networks must pass through the firewall (see below), the firewall is uniquely situated to provide audit trails of all connections between the two networks. These audit trails can be extremely useful for investigating suspicious network activity, troubleshooting connectivity problems, measuring network traffic flows, and even investigating employee fraud, waste, and abuse.

Limitations of a Firewall

Even with all of these benefits, firewalls still have their limitations. It is important that the security practitioner understand these limitations because if these limitations allow risks that are unacceptable to management, it is up to the security practitioner to present additional safeguards to minimize these risks. The security practitioner must not allow management to develop a false sense of security simply because a firewall has been installed.

- *Firewalls provide no data integrity.* It is simply not feasible to check all incoming traffic for viruses. There are too many file formats and often files are sent in compressed form. Any attempt to scan incoming files for viruses would severely degrade performance. Firewalls have plenty of processing requirements without taking on the additional responsibility of virus detection and eradication.
- *Firewalls do not protect traffic that is not sent through it.* Firewalls cannot protect against unsecured, dial-up modems attached to systems inside

the firewall; internal attacks; social engineering attacks; or data that is routed around them. It is not uncommon for an organization to install a firewall, then pass data from a legacy system around the firewall because its firewall did not support the existing system.

- *Firewalls may not protect anything if they have been compromised.* Although this statement should be obvious, many security practitioners fail to educate senior management on its implications. All too often, senior management approves — either directly or through silence — a security posture that positively lacks an internal security policy. Security practitioners cannot allow perimeter security via firewalls to become a substitute for internal security.
- *Firewalls cannot authenticate datagrams at the transport or network layers.* A major security problem with the TCP/IP is that any machine can forge a packet claiming to be from another machine. This means that the firewall has literally no control over how the packet was created. Any authentication must be supported in one of the higher layers.
- *Firewalls provide limited confidentiality.* Many firewalls have the ability to encrypt connections between two firewalls (using a so-called virtual private network, or VPN), but they typically require that the firewall be manufactured by the same vendor.

A firewall is no replacement for good host security practices and procedures. Individual system administrators still have the primary responsibility for preventing security incidents.

FIREWALLS AND THE LOCAL SECURITY POLICY

Cheswick and Bellovin (1994) define a firewall as a system with the following set of characteristics:

- All traffic between the two networks must pass through the firewall.
- Only traffic that is authorized by the local security policy will be allowed to pass.
- The firewall itself is immune to penetration.

Like any security tool, a firewall merely provides the capability to increase the security of the path between two networks. It is the responsibility of the firewall administrator to take advantage of this capability; and no firewall can guarantee absolute protection from outside attacks. The risk analysis should define the level of protection that can be expected from the firewall; the local security policy should provide general guidelines on how this protection will be achieved; and both the assessment and revised policy should be accepted by top management prior to firewall implementation.

Despite the fact that, according to Atkins et al.,[1] all traffic between the two networks must pass through the firewall, in practice this is not always technically feasible or convenient. Network administrators supporting legacy or proprietary systems may find that getting them to communicate through the firewall may not be as easy as firewall vendors claim, if even possible. And even if there are no technical obstacles to routing all traffic through the firewall, users may still complain that the firewall is inconvenient or slows their systems down. Thus, the local security policy should specify the process by which requests for exceptions[1] will be considered.

As Bellovin[2] states, the local security policy defines what the firewall is supposed to enforce. If a firewall is going to allow only authorized traffic between two networks, then the firewall has to know what traffic is authorized. The local security policy should define "authorized" traffic, and it should do so at a somewhat technical level. The policy should also state a default rule for evaluating requests: either all traffic is denied except that which is specifically authorized, or all traffic is allowed except that which is specifically denied.

Network devices that protect other network devices should themselves be protected against intruders. (If the protection device were not secure, intruders could compromise the device and then compromise the system[s] that the device was supposed to protect.)

FIREWALL EVALUATION CRITERIA

Choosing the right firewall for an organization can be a daunting task, given the complexity of the problem and the wide variety of products from which to choose. Yet the following criteria should help the security practitioner narrow the list of candidates considerably.

- *Performance.* Firewalls always impact the performance of the connection between the local and remote networks. Adding a firewall creates an additional hop for network packets to travel through; if the firewall must authenticate connections, that creates an additional delay. The firewall machine should be powerful enough to make these delays negligible.
- *Requirements support.* A firewall should support all of the applications that an organization wants to use across the two networks. Virtually all firewalls support fundamental protocols like SMTP, Telnet, FTP, and HTTP; strong firewalls should include some form of circuit proxy or generic packet relay. The security practitioner should decide what other applications are required (e.g., Real Audio, VDOLive, S-HTTP, etc.) and evaluate firewall products accordingly.
- *Access control.* Even the simplest firewalls support access control based on IP addresses; strong firewalls will support user-based access control and authentication. Large organizations should pay special attention to whether a given firewall product supports a large number of user profiles and ensure that the firewall can accomodate increased user traffic.

- *Authentication.* The firewall must support the authentication requirements of the local security policy. If implementation of the local security policy will entail authenticating large numbers of users, the firewall should provide convenient yet secure enterprisewide management of the user accounts. Some firewalls only allow the administrator to manage user accounts from a single console; this solution is not good enough for organizations with thousands of users who each need their own authentication account. Moreover, there are logistical issues that need to be thought out. For example, suppose the local security policy requires authentication of all inbound telnet connections. How will geographically separated users obtain the proper authentication credentials (e.g., passwords, hard tokens, etc.)?
- *Physical security.* The local security policy should stipulate the location of the firewall, and the hardware should be physically secured to prevent unauthorized access. The firewall must also be able to interface with surrounding hardware at this location.
- *Auditing.* The firewall must support the auditing requirements of the local security policy. Depending on network bandwidth and the level of event logging, firewall audit trails can become quite large. Superior firewalls will include a data reduction tool for parsing audit trails.
- *Logging and alarms.* What logging and alarms does the security policy require? If the security policy dictates that a potential intrusion event trigger an alarm and mail message to the administrator, the system must accommodate this requirement.
- *Customer support.* What level of customer support does the firewall vendor provide? If the organization requires 24-hour-a-day, 365-days-a-year technical support, is it available? Does the vendor provide training courses? Is self-help online assistance, such as a Web page or a mailing list, available?
- *Transparency.* How transparent is the firewall to the users? The more transparent the firewall is to the users, the more likely they will be to support it. On the other hand, the more confusing or cumbersome the firewall, the more likely the users are to resist it.

FIREWALL TECHNIQUES

There are three different techniques available to firewalls to enforce the local security policy: packet filtering, application-level gateways, and circuit-level gateways. These techniques are not mutually exclusive; in practice, firewalls tend to implement multiple techniques to varying extents. This section defines these firewall techniques.

Packet Filtering

Packet filters allow or drop packets according to the source or destination address or port. The administrator makes a list of acceptable and

Exhibit 26-1. Sample packet filter configuration.

Rule Number	Action	Local Host	Local Port	Remote Host	Remote Port
0	Allow	WWW server	80	*	*
1	Deny	*	*	*	*

unacceptable machines and services, and configures the packet filter accordingly. This makes it very easy for the administrator to filter access at the network or host level, but impossible to filter access at the user level (see Exhibit 26-1).

The packet filter applies the rules in order from top to bottom. Thus, in Exhibit 26-1, rule 0 blocks all network traffic by default; rule 1 creates an exception to allow unrestricted access on port 80 to the organization's Web server.

But what if the firewall administrator wanted to allow telnet access to the Web server by the Webmaster? The administrator could configure the packet filter as shown in Exhibit 26-2. The packet filter would thus allow telnet access (port 23) to the Web server from the address or addresses represented by <machine room>, but the packet filter has no concept of user authentication. Thus, unauthorized individuals originating from the <machine room> address(es) would be allowed telnet access to the WWW server, while authorized individuals originating from non-<machine room> address(es) would be denied access. In both cases, the lack of user authentication would prevent the packet filter from enforcing the local security policy.

Exhibit 26-2. Packet filter configuration to allow Telnet access from <machine room> to <www-server>.

Rule Number	Action	Local Host	Local Port	Remote Host	Remote Port
0	Allow	WWW server	80	*	*
1	Allow	WWW server	23	<machine room>	*
2	Deny	*	*	*	*

Application-Level Gateways

Unlike packet filters, application-level gateways do not enforce access control lists. Instead, application-level gateways attempt to enforce connection integrity by ensuring that all data passed on a given port is in accordance with the protocol for that port. This is very useful for preventing transmissions prohibited by the protocol, but not handled properly by the remote system. Consider, for example, the Hypertext Transmission Protocol (HTTP) used by WW servers to send and receive information, normally on port 80. Intruders have been able to compromise numerous servers by transmitting special packets outside the HTTP specification. Pure packet filters are ineffective against such attacks because they can only restrict access to a port based on source and destination address; but an application gateway could actually prevent such an attack by enforcing the protocol specification for all traffic on the related port.

The application gateway relays connections in a manner similar to that of the circuit-level gateway (see below), but it provides the additional service of checking individual packets for the particular application in use. It also has the additional ability to log all inbound and outbound connections.

Circuit-Level Gateways

A circuit-level gateway creates a virtual circuit between the local and remote networks by relaying connections. The originator opens a connection on a port to the gateway, and the gateway in turn opens a connection on that same port to the remote machine. The gateway machine relays data back and forth until the connection is terminated.

Because circuit-level gateways relay packets without inspecting them, they normally provide only minimal audit capabilities and no application-specific controls. Moreover, circuit-level gateways require new or modified client software that does not attempt to establish connections with the remote site directly; the client software must allow the circuit relay to do its job.

Still, circuit relays are transparent to the user. They are well-suited for outbound connections in which authentication is important but integrity is not.

See Exhibit 26-3 for a comparison of these firewall techniques.

DEVELOPING A FIREWALL POLICY AND STANDARDS

Reasons for Having Firewall Policy and Standards

There are a number of reasons for writing formal firewall policies and standards, including:

- Properly written firewall policies and standards will address important issues that may not be covered by other policies. Having a generic corporate policy on information systems security is not good enough. There are a number of specific issues that apply to firewalls but would not be addressed, or addressed in adequate detail, by generic security policies.
- A firewall policy can clarify how the organization's security objectives apply to the firewall. For example, a generic organizational policy on information protection might state that, "Access to information is granted on a need-to-know basis." A firewall policy would interpret

Exhibit 26-3. Advantages and disadvantages of firewall techniques.

Firewall Technique	Advantages	Disadvantages
Packet filtering	Completely transparent Easy to filter access at the host or network level Inexpensive: can use existing routers to implement	Reveals internal network topology Does not provide enough granularity for most security policies Difficult to configure Does not support certain traffic Susceptible to address spoofing Limited or no logging, alarms No user authentication
Application-level gateways	Application-level security Strong user access control Strong logging and auditing support Ability to conceal internal network	Requires specialized proxy for each service Slower to implement new services Inconvenient to end users No support for client software that does not support redirection
Circuit-level gateways	Transparent to user Excellent for relaying outbound connections	Inbound connections risky Must provide new client programs

this objective by stating that, "All traffic is denied except that which is explicitly authorized."

- An approved set of firewall standards makes configuration decisions much more objective. A firewall, especially one with a restrictive configuration, can become a hot political topic if the firewall administrator wants to block traffic that a user really wants. Specifying the decision-making process for resolving such issues in a formal set of standards will make the process much more consistent to all users. Everyone may not always get what he or she wants, but at least the issue will be decided through a process that was adopted in advance.

Policy and Standards Development Process

The following process is recommended as an efficient, comprehensive way to develop a firewall policy. If the steps of this process are followed in order, the security practitioner can avoid making time-wasting oversights and errors in the policy. (See also Exhibit 26-4.)

1. *Risk analysis.* An organization should perform a risk analysis prior to developing a policy or a set of standards. The risk analysis will not only help policy-makers identify specific issues to be addressed in the document itself, but also the relative weight policy-makers should assign to those issues.
2. *Identify list of topics to cover.* A partial listing of topics is suggested under Policy Structure later in this chapter; security policy-makers

should also identify any other relevant issues that may be relevant to the organization's firewall implementation.

3. *Assign responsibility.* An organization must define the roles and responsibilities of those accountable for administering the firewall. If necessary, modify job descriptions to reflect the additional responsibility for implementing, maintaining, and administering the firewall, as well as establishing, maintaining, and enforcing policy and standards.
4. *Define the audience.* Is the policy document intended to be read by IS personnel only? Or is the document intended to be read by the entire organization? The document's audience will determine its scope, as well as its degree of technical and legal detail.
5. *Write the policy.* Because anyone can read the document, write without regard to the reader's position within the organization. When it is necessary to refer to other organizational entities, use functional references whenever possible (e.g., Public Relations instead of Tom Smith, Public Relations). Be sure to list a contact person for readers who may have questions about the policy.
6. *Identify mechanisms to foster compliance.* A policy is ineffective if it does not encourage employees to comply with the policy. Therefore, the individual(s) responsible for developing or maintaining the policy must ensure that adequate mechanisms for enforcement exist. These enforcement mechanisms should not be confused with the clause(s) of a policy that specify the consequences for noncompliance. Rather, enforcement mechanisms should include such administrative procedures as awareness and training, obtaining employee signatures on an agreement that specifies the employee has read and understands the policy and will comply with the intent.
7. *Review.* New policies should be reviewed by representatives from all major departments of the organization — not just IS personnel. A special effort should be made to resolve any disagreements at this stage: the more low- and mid-level support that exists for a policy, the easier it will be to implement that policy.

Exhibit 26-4. Policy development process.

1. Risk analysis
2. Identify list of topics to cover
3. Assign responsibility for policy
4. Define the audience
5. Write the policy
6. Identify mechanisms to foster compliance
7. Review

After the policy has been coordinated with (and hopefully endorsed by) department representatives, the policy should be submitted to senior management for approval. It is extremely important that the most senior-level manager possible sign the policy. This will give the IS security staff the authority it needs to enforce the policy.

Once the policy is adopted, it should be reviewed on at least an annual basis. A review may have one of three results: no change, revisions to the policy, or abandoning the policy.

Policy Structure

A policy is normally understood as a high-level document that outlines management's general instructions on how things are to be run. Therefore, an organizational firewall policy should outline that management expects other departments to support the firewall, the importance of the firewall to the organization, etc. The structure of a firewall policy should look as follows:

- *Background.* How does the importance of the firewall relate to overall organizational objectives (e.g., the firewall secures information assets against the threat of unauthorized external intrusion)?
- *Scope.* To whom and what does this policy apply?
- *Definitions.* What is a firewall? What role does it play within the enterprise?
- *Responsibilities.* What resources and respective responsibilities need to be assigned to support the firewall? If the default configuration of the firewall will be to block everything that is not specifically allowed, who is responsible for requesting exceptions? Who is authorized to approve these requests? On what basis will those decisions be made?
- *Enforcement.* What are the consequences for failing to meet the administrative responsibilities? How is noncompliance addressed?
- *Frequency of review.* How often will this policy be reviewed? With which functions in the organization?
- *Policy coordinator.* Who is the point of contact for this policy?
- *Date of last revision.* When was this policy last revised?

Firewall Standards

Firewall standards can be defined minimally as a set of configuration options for a firewall. (Although firewall standards can and should address more than mere configuration issues, all firewall standards cover at least this much.) Exhibit 26-5 presents a sample outline for firewall standards. Because all firewalls come with default configurations, all firewalls have default standards. The job of the security practitioner is to draft a comprehensive set of standards governing all aspects of firewall implementation, usage, and maintenance, including but not limited to:

- protection of logs against unauthorized modification
- frequency of logs review
- how long logs will be retained
- when the logs will be backed up
- to whom the alarms will be sent

Legal Issues Concerning Firewalls

If firewall audit trails need to be capable of being presented as evidence in a court of law, it is worthwhile to provide a "warning banner" to warn users about what sort of privacy they can expect. Many firewalls can be configured to display a warning banner on telnet and FTP sessions. Exhibit 26-6 shows an example of such a warning.

FIREWALL CONTINGENCY PLANNING

Firewall Outage

What would be the impact on an organization if the firewall was unavailable? If the organization has routed all of its Internet traffic through a firewall (as it should), then a catastrophic hardware failure of the firewall machine would result in a lack of Internet connectivity until the firewall machine is repaired or replaced. How long can the organization tolerate an outage? If the outage were a catastrophic hardware failure, do you know how you would repair or replace the components? Do you know how long it would take to repair or replace the components?

If the organization has a firewall, the odds are that a firewall outage would have a significant impact on that organization. (If the connection between the two networks was not important to the organization, why would that organization have the connection and protect it with a firewall?) Therefore, the security practitioner must also develop contingency plans for responding to a firewall outage. These contingency plans must address three types of failures: hardware, software, and evolutionary (failure to keep pace with increasing usage requirements).

In the case of a hardware failure, the security practitioner has three options: repair, replacement, or removal. Firewall removal is a drastic measure that is not encouraged, it drastically reduces security while disrupting any user services that were specially configured around the firewall (e.g., Domain Name Service, proxies, etc.). Smaller organizations may choose to repair their hardware because it is cheaper, yet this may not always be an option and may not be quick enough to satisfy user requirements. Conversely, access can be restored quickly by swapping in a "hot spare," but the cost of purchasing and maintaining such redundancy can be prohibitive to smaller organizations.

Exhibit 26-5. Sample outline of firewall standards.

- I. Definition of terms
- II. Responsibilities of the firewall administrator
- III. Statement of firewall limitations
  - a. Inability to enforce data integrity
  - b. Inability to prevent internal attacks
- IV. Firewall configuration
  - a. Default policy (allow or deny) on network connections
  - b. Physical location of firewall
  - c. Logical location of firewall in relation to other network nodes
  - d. Firewall system access policy
    - 1. Authorized individuals
    - 2. Authentication methods
    - 3. Policy on remote configuration
  - e. Supported services
    - 1. Inbound
    - 2. Outbound
  - f. Blocked services
    - 1. Inbound
    - 2. Outbound
  - g. Firewall configuration change management policy
- V. Firewall audit trail policy
  - a. Level of granularity (e.g., we will have one entry for each FTP or HTTP download)
  - b. Frequency of review (e.g., we will check the logs once a day)
  - c. Access control (e.g., access to firewall audit trails will be limited to the following individuals)
- VI. Firewall intrusion detection policy
  - a. Alarms
    - 1. Alarm thresholds
    - 2. Alarm notifications (e.g., e-mail, pager, etc.)
  - b. Notification procedures
    - 1. Top management
    - 2. Public relations
    - 3. System administrators
    - 4. Incident response teams
    - 5. Law enforcement
    - 6. Other sites
  - c. Response priorities (e.g., human safety, containment, public relations)
  - d. Documentation procedures
- VII. Backups
  - a. Frequency of incremental backups
  - b. Frequency of system backups
  - c. Archive of backups (e.g., we will keep backups for one year)
  - d. Off-site backup requirements

Exhibit 26-5. Sample outline of firewall standards. *(continued)*

VIII. Firewall outage policy
   a. Planned outages
   b. Unplanned outages
      1. Reporting procedures
IX. Firewall standards review policy (e.g., this policy will be reviewed every six months)

Exhibit 26-6. Sample warning banner.

Per AFI 33-219 requirement:

Welcome to USAFAnet
United States Air Force Academy

This is an official Department of Defense (DoD) computer system for authorized use only. All data contained on DoD computer systems is owned by DoD and may be monitored, intercepted, recorded, read, copied, or captured in any manner and disclosed in any manner by authorized personnel. THERE IS NO RIGHT TO PRIVACY ON THIS SYSTEM. Authorized personnel may give any potential evidence of crime found on DoD computer systems to law enforcement officials. USE OF THIS SYSTEM BY ANY USER, AUTHORIZED OR UNAUTHORIZED, CONSTITUTES EXPRESS CONSENT TO THIS MONITORING, INTERCEPTION, RECORDING, READING, COPYING, OR CAPTURING, AND DISSEMINATION BY AUTHORIZED PERSONNEL. Do not discuss, enter, transfer, process, or transmit classified/sensitive national security information of greater sensitivity than this system is authorized. USAFAnet is not accredited to process classified information. Unauthorized use could result in criminal prosecution. If you do not consent to these conditions, do not log in!

Significant Attacks, Probes, and Vulnerabilities

To be effective, the firewall administrator must understand not only how attacks and probes work, but also must be able to recognize the appropriate alarms and audit trail entries.

There are three attacks in particular with which every Internet firewall administrator should be familiar.

Internet Protocol (IP) Source Address Spoofing. IP Source Address Spoofing is not an attack itself. It is a vulnerability that can be exploited to launch attacks (e.g., session hijacking). First described by Robert T. Morris in 1985 and explained in more detail by Steven Bellovin in 1989, the first known use of IP Source Address Spoofing was in 1994. Since then, hackers have made spoofing tools publicly available so that one need not be a TCP/IP expert in order to exploit this vulnerability.

IP Source Address Spoofing is used to defeat address-based authentication. Many services, including rlogin and rsh, rely on IP addresses for authentication. Yet, as this vulnerability illustrates, this form of authentication is extremely weak and should only be used in trusted environments. (IP addresses provide identification, not authentication.) By its very nature, IP allows anyone to send packets claiming to be from any IP address. Of course, when an attacker sends forged packets to a target machine, the target machine will send its replies to the legitimate client, not the attacker. In other words, the attacker can send commands but will not see any output. As described below, in some cases, this is enough to cause serious damage.

Although there is no way to totally eliminate IP Source Address Spoofing, there are ways to reduce such activity. For example, a packet filter can be configured to drop all outbound packets that do not have an "inside" source address. Likewise, a firewall can block all inbound packets that have an internal address as the source address. However, such a solution will only work at the network and subnet levels. There is no way to prevent IP Source Address Spoofing within a subnet.

TCP Hijacking. TCP Hijacking is used to defeat authenticated connections. It is only an attack option if the attacker has access to the packet flow. In a TCP Hijacking attack, (1) the attacker is located logically between the client and the server, (2) the attacker sends a "killer packet" to the client, terminating the client's connection to the server, and (3) the attacker then continues the connection.

Denial of Service. A strength of public networks like the Internet lies in the fact that anyone can create a public service (e.g., a Web server or anonymous File Transfer Protocol [FTP] server) and allow literally anyone else, anonymously, to access that service. But this unrestricted availability can also be exploited in a denial-of-service attack. A denial-of-service attack exploits this unrestricted availability by overwhelming the service with requests. Although it is relatively easy to block a denial-of-service attack if the attack is generated by a single address, it is much more difficult — if not impossible — to stop a denial-of-service attack originating from spoofed, random source IP addresses.

There are two forms of denial-of-service attacks that are worth mentioning: TCP SYN Attack and ICMP Echo Flood.

1. TCP SYN Attack. The attacker floods a machine with TCP "half-open" connections, preventing the machine from providing TCP-based services while under attack and for some time after the attack stops. What makes this attack so significant is that it exploits an inherent characteristic of TCP; there is not yet a complete defense to this attack.

Under TCP (used by Simple Mail Transfer Protocol [SMTP], Telnet, HTTP, FTP, Gopher, etc.), whenever a client attempts to establish a connection to a server, there is a standard "handshake" or sequence of messages they exchange before data can be exchanged between the client and the server. In a normal connection, this handshake looks similar to the example displayed in Exhibit 26-7.

Exhibit 26-7. Normal TCP handshake.

Client		Server
SYN	------------->	Server
<----------------		SYN-ACK
ACK	------------->	
Client and server may now exchange data		

The potential for attack arises at the point where the server has sent an acknowledgment (SYN-ACK) back to the client but has not yet received the ACK message. This is what is known as a half-open connection. The server maintains, in a memory, a list of all half-open connections. Unfortunately, servers allocate a finite amount of memory for storing this list, and an attacker can cause an overflow by deliberately creating too many partially open connections.

The SYN Flooding is easily accomplished with IP Source Address Spoofing. In this scenario, the attacker sends SYN messages to the target (victim) server masquerading a client system that is unable to respond to the SYN-ACK messages. Therefore, the final ACK message is never sent to the target server.

Whether or not the SYN attack is used in conjunction with IP Source Address Spoofing, the effect on the target is the same. The target system's list of half-open connections will eventually fill; then the system will be unable to accept any new TCP connections until the table is emptied. In some cases, the target may also run out of memory or crash.

Normally, half-open connections timeout after a certain amount of time; however, an attacker can generate new half-open connections faster than the target system's timeout.

2. Internet Control Message Protocol (ICMP) Echo (PING) Flood. The PING Flood Attack is where the attacker sends large amounts of ICMP ping requests from an intermediary or "bounce" site to a victim, which can cause network congestion or outages. The attack is also known as the "smurf" attack because of a hacker tool called "smurf," which enables the hacker to launch this attack with relatively little networking knowledge.

Like the SYN attack, the PING Flood Attack relies on IP Source Address Spoofing to add another level of indirection to the attack. In a SYN attack with IP Source Address Spoofing, the spoofed source address receives all of the replies to the PING requests. While this does not cause an overflow on the victim machine, the network path from the bounce site to the victim becomes congested and potentially unusable. The bounce site may suffer for the same reason.

There are automated tools that allow attackers to use multiple bounce sites simultaneously. Attackers can also use tools to look for network routers that do not filter broadcast traffic and networks where multiple hosts respond.

Solutions include:

- disabling IP-directed broadcasts at the router
- configuring the operating system to prevent the machine from responding to ICMP packets sent to IP broadcast addresses
- preventing IP source address spoofing by dropping packets that contain a source address for a different network

CONCLUSION

A firewall can only reduce the risk of a breach of security; the only guaranteed way to prevent a compromise is to disconnect the network and physically turn off all machines. Moreover, a firewall should always be viewed as a supplement to host security; the primary security emphasis should be on host security. Nonetheless, a firewall is an important security device that should be used whenever an organization needs to protect one network from another.

The views expressed in this chapter are those of the author and do not reflect the official policy or position of the United States Air Force, Department of Defense, or the U.S. government.

Notes

1. Atkins, Derek et al. *Internet Security Professional Reference,* 2nd edition, New Riders, Indianapolis, IN, 1997.
2. Bellovin, Steven M. *Security Problems in the TCP/IP Protocol Suite, Computer Communications Review,* 19:2, April 1989, pp. 32–48. Available on the World Wide Web at ftp://ftp.research.att.com/dist/-internet_security/ipext.ps.Z

References

Bernstein, Terry, Anish B. Bhimani, Eugene Schultz, and Carol Siegel. *Internet Security for Business,* John Wiley & Sons, New York, 1996.

Cheswick, W.R. and Bellovin, S.M. *Firewalls and Internet Security: Repelling the Wily Hacker,* Addison-Wesley, Reading, MA, 1994.

Garfinkel, Simson and Spafford, Gene. Practical Unix & Internet Security, Sebastopol, CA, 1995.

Huegen, Craig A. The Latest in Denial of Service Attacks: 'Smurfing', Oct. 18, 1998. Available on the World Wide Web at http://www.quadrunner.com/~chuegen/smurf.txt.

Howard, John D. An Analysis of Security Incidents on the Internet 1989–1995, Ph.D. dissertation, Carnegie Mellon University, Pittsburgh, PA, 1997.

Morris, Robert T. A Weakness in the 4.2BSD Unix TCP/IP Software, *Bell Labs Computer Science Technical Report #117,* Feb. 25, 1985. Available on the World Wide Web at ftp://ftp.research.att.com/-dist/internet_security/117.ps.Z.

Wood, Charles Cresson. Policies from the Ground Up, *Infosecurity News,* March/April 1997, pp. 24–29.

Chapter 27
Evaluating Anti-Virus Solutions Within Distributed Environments

Network Associates, Inc.

SINCE EFFECTIVE ANTI-VIRUS PRODUCTS ARE AVAILABLE, IT APPEARS THAT ORGANIZATIONS HAVE FOUND THE ESTABLISHMENT OF PROTECTIVE MEASURES TO BE CONFUSING, DISRUPTIVE, AND/OR POSSIBLY TOO EXPENSIVE. Indeed, the decision process is complex, especially in distributed multi-user, multiplatform environments (which typically undergo almost constant evolution). More important, it would seem that no two product comparison reviews offer similar assumptions, results, or conclusions.

As a leading provider of anti-virus software for networked enterprises, Network Associates proposes that the following evaluation process will enable decision makers to achieve cost-effective enterprise-wide protection and policies.

DISTRIBUTED SECURITY NEEDS

As in the evaluation and purchase of any other category of software, the difference in needs between individual PC users and networked users is great. In the case of virus infection, the very proliferation of networks and increasing mobile users is at once both a source of the problem and an obstacle to solving it.

Industry estimates for the introduction of new viruses/strains range from 100 to 300 per month, so anti-virus measures are important even for stand-alone PCs, which inevitably "contact" virus potential via modem use and/or sharing and borrowing data and programs from other users via disk or network.

0-8493-0893-3/00/$0.00+$.50

The creation of a new virus is a deliberate act (one often aided by multiple resources readily available to perpetrators). However, the introduction of viruses into corporate networks is most often innocent — employees take work to the home PC or exchange files via the Internet, etc., bring it back to the network, and have no idea their files, programs, and/or computers were infected.

In a networked enterprise, anti-virus strategies must take into account further complications as follows:

- Multiple system entry points for viruses
- Multiple platform constraints on compatibility
- Resource requirements for adequate protection
- Need for integrated support efforts
- Need to minimize "epidemic" potential
- Multilevel reporting of network/system activity
- Logistics of installation across enterprise
- Ongoing implementation and maintenance costs
- Need for company-wide policies, overlaying political considerations

The above factors may seem obvious, but it is important to review them, as their perceived difficulty has contributed to today's state of affairs — in which anti-virus products and strategies are seriously underutilized and network vulnerability increases daily. Currently, viruses already infect 40% of all networks.[1]

EVALUATION REASONING

The key evaluation criteria for choosing anti-virus solutions are detection, performance, features, and price. However, in choosing products to meet specific organizational needs, some typical assumptions about these factors need to be challenged in order to make the best decision.

Detection

Isn't the product that detects the greatest number of viruses always the best?

Not necessarily. The rate of virus proliferation is such that every vendor's current detection numbers are constantly changing. And although researchers have identified as many as 12,000 to 15,000 viruses, the same few hundred viruses continue to account for a vast majority of infections. Therefore, a sacrifice of other key criteria for the sake of a higher detection "count" may be a costly mistake.

Performance

Isn't the best product the one that works fastest and demands the least of system resources?

Maybe and maybe not. Performance statistics cited by vendors and reviewers, no matter how responsibly they were formulated, can only be taken at face value unless every aspect of the tested environment happened to be identical to that of the evaluating organization.

Therefore, experiments performed in one's own network environment are necessary, albeit time-consuming. Finally, virus detection rates, *measured at various performance configurations,* may add further meaning. What real difference will a few seconds (or milliseconds) make if damaging viruses were missed?

Feature Set

The product with the most features wins, right?

By now, most evaluators of technology products are aware of the features trap, but it is still important to analyze claimed features very closely. Some "features" are simply characteristics and may be beneficial to some environments while downright harmful to others. And it is not enough simply to decide whether or not a feature is needed by the enterprise. It should be attempted to assign *weighted importance* to each feature, and then weight test results accordingly (guidelines follow later in this chapter), before a given feature should be considered key to the decision.

Price

Wouldn't it be great if the lowest-cost product is also the best?

Definitely. But of course, there is far more to cost analysis than initial purchase price, especially with anti-virus software. Considerations that affect basic pricing are: license types, platform support, terms of purchase, and maintenance structure. Further, cost of ownership considerations include: internal and external cost of user support and training, cost of future changes, and ultimately, the perhaps incalculable cost of *inadequate* protection. (American businesses lost $2.7 billion due to viruses in 1994 alone.)[2]

When the evaluation team understands the basic pitfalls of relying too heavily on any one of the above factors, it is ready to move on. The next step is to establish the framework of tests and analyses in which all leading products will compete.

TODAY'S VIRUS PROFILE

Prior to recommendations for testing methodology, this overview of today's active virus types may be helpful.

Boot vs. File Viruses

IBM-compatible and Macintosh viruses (which constitute the majority of network infections) fall into two basic categories: "Boot" and "File." *Boot* viruses activate upon system start-up and are the most common type. They infect a system's floppy or hard disk and then spread (by replicating and attaching) to any logical disks available. *File* viruses are actually programs that must be executed in order to become active, and include executable files such as .com, .exe, and .dll. Once executed, file viruses replicate and attach to other executable files.

Four Special Challenges

Particularly troublesome virus classes today are known as *Stealth* (active and passive), *Encrypted, Polymorphic,* and *Macro.*

Stealth viruses are difficult to detect because, as their name implies, they actually disguise their actions. *Passive stealth* viruses can increase a file's size, yet present the *appearance* of the original file size, thus evading Integrity Checking — one of the most fundamental detection tactics. *Active stealth* viruses may be written so that they actually attack installed anti-virus software, rendering the product's detection tools useless.

The challenge of *encrypted* viruses is not primarily one of detection, *per se*. The encryption engine of this type of virus masks its viral code — making *identification,* as opposed to detection, more difficult. Therefore, detection and prevention of recurring infections is harder even with frequent anti-virus software updates.

The *polymorphic* category has grown considerably, presenting a particular detection challenge. Each polymorphic virus has a built-in mutation engine. This engine creates random changes to the virus's signature on given replications.

Recently, *macro* viruses have gained much notoriety and growth. A macro virus is a set of macro commands, specific to an application's macro language, which automatically executes in an unsolicited manner and spreads to that application's documents. Since macro virus creation and modification is easier than other viruses and since documents are more widely shared than applications, they pose the most significant new threat.

COUNTERACTION TECHNOLOGY OPTIONS

As the threat and number of viruses grew along with the conditions so conducive to their spread, so did the sophistication of the efforts to combat them. There are now five major virus detection methods:

- *Integrity Checking* — Based on determining whether virus-attached code modified a program's file characteristics.
- *Downside Examples* — Checksum database management, the possibility of registering infected files, inability to detect passive and active stealth viruses, no virus identification.

- *Interrupt Monitoring* — Looks for virus activity that may be flagged by certain sequences of program system calls, after virus execution.
- *Downside Examples* — May flag valid system calls, limited success facing the gamut of virus types and legal function calls, can be obtrusive.
- *Memory Detection* — Depends on recognition of a known virus' location and code while in memory.
- *Downside Examples* — Can impose impractical resource requirements and can interfere with legal operations.
- *Signature Scanning* — Recognizes a virus' unique "signature," a pre-identified set of hexadecimal code.
- *Downside Examples* — Totally dependent on currency of signature files (from vendor) and scanning engine refinements, also may make false positive detection in valid file.
- *Heuristics/Rules-based Scanning* — Recognizes virus-like characteristics within programs for identification.
- *Downside Examples* — Can be obtrusive and can cause false alarms, dependent on currency of rules set.

Usually, all five techniques can be used in real-time or on-demand, and on both network servers and workstations. The number of virus types and their many invasion and disguise methods, combined with the five counteraction methods' various strengths and weaknesses, has resulted in the fact that today all effective products leverage a combination of methods to combat viruses. This field is by no means limited to known methods, however. Constant involvement in virus counteraction steadily increases the knowledge base of anti-virus software vendors, enabling refinement of these methods and the development of entirely new ones for the future.

TESTING OBSTACLES

Detection Testing

The Test Parameter seems simple: Send a library of files and viruses through the client–server host and calculate the detection percentage of each competing product.

Obstacles to this process, and to a valid analysis of test results, are numerous. Evaluators should attempt to answer all of these questions before proceeding with detection testing:

- Where will we get the viruses? Should test files consist of only one library of viruses or multiple sources?
- Do the sample viruses replicate?
- What total number of viruses will we need for a valid test?
- What mix of virus types will reflect real-world best in testing (i.e., macro, boot vs. file viruses, polymorphics, encrypted, passive and/or active stealth, etc.)?

Performance Testing

For each product being evaluated, a library of files and viruses (the same used in Detection Testing) is sent through the client–server host, while both speed of operation and host degradation are calculated.

Obstacles to this test include:

- Determining the number, sizes, and types of control files to be scanned for viruses
- Determining all control conditions of the testing platform, i.e., what is "normal"? (Evaluators should average multiple test runs for both workstations and servers to produce a standard set of values.)
- How will we assure accurate timing metrics?
- The overriding concern in performance testing — that test conditions be as real-world as possible

Features Testing

A list of all product feature claims must be compiled. Decide which features the organization needs, tabulate the scores, and compare competing products.

Obstacles to features comparison are:

- Certain features will appear to be common to all products, but how comparable are their actual implementations?
- Not all implementations will be suited to all needs — what is really required to take advantage of a given feature, and is it really worth it?
- If a "standard" feature set (such as may be derived from Novell and NCSA certification) is the basis for comparison, in what ways does each product go beyond that standard set?
- Verifying the depth of analyses behind each claim (does the vendor provide empirical evidence?)

All features, common and unique, must be analyzed as to their true importance within a defined description of the evaluating organization's needs and desires. Inevitably, when evaluators adhere to a methodology of assigning a numerical weight of importance to each feature, certain features are revealed as far more critical than others, and those critical features may be very different from one company to another.

Additional Obstacles

The three key factors that can be tested (detection, performance, and features) share several *common* obstacles as well. In preparing to test each factor, evaluators should also assess:

- To what extent statistical inferences meet actual objectives
- Whether the latest releases of all products have been obtained for testing (remember that monthly signature file and regular engine updates are a *de facto* standard in the anti-virus software industry)
- To what extent the products can be *normalized* (for "apples to apples" comparison)
- In which tests should products also be *maximized* (letting the "oranges" stand out where they may, and finding a reliable way to quantify their value)

TESTING PREPARATION

Virus Sample Configuration

Evaluators should begin researching sources of testable viruses early in the process. Sources are critical to achieving reliable tests, and it may prove time consuming to obtain adequate numbers of the virus types determined necessary for testing.

Here are some considerations regarding virus sample size and type:

- How many viruses constitute a large enough sample? Is 1,000 out of a potential 7,000 (14%) enough? (Obtain samples in your environment)
- One standard deviation (66% of total universe) is potentially 5,600 viruses — possibly overkill and almost certainly too costly to fully test across competing products for both detection and performance analyses. (Again, most virus infections involve the same 200 viruses over and over.)
- Boot, file, and macro viruses should probably all be tested, and boot virus tests can demand significant time and resources. Because of that demand, the evaluation weight appropriate to such viruses should also be determined during sample design.
- Use pure viruses, which are those obtained from initial samples that have successfully replicated twice (avoid droppers). Example of pure virus model:

  virus 1, infected file 1, infected file 2 → validation

- Polymorphics, unto themselves, require a fair-size sample by their very nature. Example of preparation for polymorphic testing:

  Take polymorphic virus, replicate 100 times;
  take an infected file of that sample and replicate 100;
  take an infected file of that sample and replicate 100…
  Repeat until sample of at least 2,000 is achieved.

- From polymorphics, sample library should capture each of a given major type such as SMEG, MTE, etc.

- Tests must be set up so that file viruses can infect different file extension types, as appropriate (.com, .exe, .DLL...).
- Due to the fact that macros can be easily modified, it is suggested that one include only macro viruses deemed most likely to be found in your environment.

It should be clear from the above that collection of the virus test library alone is a fairly extensive project. Various on-line services and bulletin boards may be good resources, as are some independent testing bodies. Make sure to research how the sample library of viruses was obtained; is it possibly too vendor oriented?

Anti-Virus Product Configuration

Establish a cut-off date by which vendors must provide you with the latest releases appropriate to your platform(s), along with all appropriate documentation. Also make sure vendors provide virus signature files that are equally up to date. Take time for a general review of all competing products prior to testing (remember to build this time into the initial project schedule).

Testing Platform Configuration

In configuring a network or stand-alone platform for testing, and during actual detection and performance tests, it is critical to maintain a controlled environment. This environment should resemble actual workplace conditions as much as possible.

Today's anti-virus products must safeguard network servers, workstations, stored data, and remote users, so it is important that all tests must be run consistently across the same devices. Those devices must also be installed with the same "typical" software in all categories.

TESTING PRACTICES — DETECTION

Normalized vs. Maximized Protection

Normalization of the products being tested will tend to provide more dependable results, in terms of extending their meaning for real-world conditions. All products should be capable of performing as closely as possible on identical operations. Prior to testing, this required level of protection must be determined.

Maximization testing allows each product to perform to its full capability, with no set baseline or limit in the number of viruses that can be detected or the time allowed for detection. Evaluators may then calculate weighted averages for each product's maximized protection tests in order to compare them to each other and to normalized results.

TESTING PRACTICES — PERFORMANCE

Timed Tests

In timed tests, the biggest variable will be the server (and workstation) disk cache. Therefore, the first test should record performance without any anti-virus protection. Again, adequate timing mechanisms should already have been established. A timer program or even a stopwatch may be used. Below is a timer program example:

timer, map, timer off
timer, copy c:\test f:\sys\test, timer off

For statistical reliability, each test needs to be run at least five times; then the lowest and highest values are removed and the remainder averaged. Also, products being tested must share a common configuration for accurate results.

Throughout the testing process, one might double check that file and virus sample libraries are identical in each test. Evaluators must also down the server or workstation after tests of each product to clean the cache in preparation for the next product's test.

Resource Utilization Tests

Resource utilization testing actually began with the first Timed Test — in which the system's performance was measured without any virus protection installed. Now, with anti-virus products installed in turn, the effect of each on overall performance may be measured.

A fundamental test is how long it takes to launch programs from the file server. Windows (consisting of over 150 files) and Syscon are good samples to test.

Testing larger files will allow the server copy overhead delays, giving the virus scanner more time to meet outstanding file scans. Be sure to test files both read from and written to the file server.

Again, every aspect of the test environment must be controlled. To prevent interference, other users cannot be allowed to log on to the test environment. Product configurations must be similar, tested on identical computers, without cache or other bias.

Performance, in terms of speed, was measured with a timer program or stopwatch. Resource utilization of each anti-virus product is best judged using Novell's monitor. One can conduct resource utilization tests on workstations by implementing similar tests.

TESTING PRACTICES — FEATURE SET

Tabulation

For each product under consideration, list all the features claimed within the product package and any accompanying documentation. To make features comparison easier, use a common format and standard terminology on all product feature lists.

Feature Validation/Implementation

Validate all the apparently desirable feature claims by following documented procedures. If a feature does not seem to work as described, check the documentation again. Throughout the validation process, take detailed notes on each feature's implementation, particularly at any points which seem poorly documented or cumbersome.

Critical and/or highly desirable features, of course, should receive the closest analysis of their implementation and performance as promised.

Feature Rank and Weight

Each feature should be weighed as to its ability to meet requirements, and then ranked in relation to comparable features from competing products. After eliminating any products which have important implementation barriers (discovered during feature validation), determine the weighted average among remaining products.

Using Exhibit 27-1 as a guide, summarize each product's performance/delivery of desired features for both client and server platforms.

COST OF OWNERSHIP — PRICING

Throughout the software industry, product pricing is affected by four main issues that may differ greatly from one enterprise to another: type of license, platform support, maintenance agreement, and terms of purchase.

With anti-virus software for networks, one aspect is perhaps simpler than other applications — there should be little fact finding required to answer the "who needs and really uses this software?" question. The entire network requires protection, and every workstation, whether on-site or remote, must be viewed as a potential entry point and considered vulnerable to viruses that might originate from other entry points.

License Types

Several different licensing schemes are commonly available, and most vendors offer some degree of choice between concurrent use, per-node, per-user, home users, etc. Purchasers must assess the enterprise's overall

Exhibit 27-1. Feature set weighted average.

Server Platform Support Price (5 High...1 Low)	Client Platform Support Price (5 High...1 Low)
Detection	**Detection**
General	General
Polymorphic	Polymorphic
Macro	Macro
Scanning	**Scanning**
Performance	System Resources Requation
Options	Performance
Capabilities	Capabilities
Administration	**Ease of Use**
Manage/Security	Installation
Console/Interface	User Interface
Flexibility/Notification	Flexibility/Update Distr.
Client Support	Security Control
	Notification/Reporting
	Virus Encyclopedia
Client/Server Integration	**Support**
Auto Install/Update	Updates/Accessibility
Notify Log	Documentation/Package
Isolate/Enforce	Technical Support
Support	
Documentation/Package	
Technical Support	

network configuration, including authorized home users, to decide on the type of license that will provide adequate coverage at the lowest cost. Organizations should also consider their own growth potential and investigate vendor procedures for adding users and/or nodes as needed, with a minimum of disruption to network operations.

Platform Support

Another pricing factor that will vary from product to product is support of multiple platforms, which is often necessary in today's network environments. As prices might vary depending on the platforms required, buyers must confirm pricing specifics for all current platforms (preferably in native mode) as well as the cost associated with users migrating from one system to another. Availability and pricing variations, if any, for platforms the company may consider adding should also be checked.

Maintenance

Maintenance agreements usually fall into one of two basic plans:

- Base price plus stated cost per user per year (how much covers current users and how much for additional users in the future)
- Percentage of overall contract per year (platform by platform)

If a vendor can offer either type of maintenance plan, evaluators must compare any stated differences in degree of support, response time, etc., and then calculate actual cost estimates based on known platforms and user base over time. In evaluating maintenance plans, buyers should also consider each arrangement's potential impact on internal administrative resources.

Terms of Purchase

Because of its complexity of implementation, enterprise-wide network software, including anti-virus software, is most often purchased on a contract basis, intertwined with support and maintenance agreements.

A typical arrangement is an annual contract including maintenance, renewable each year. Longer-term contract periods, such as two to four years, should provide added value to the buying organization in terms of lower buy-in price, added support, simplified administration, etc.

TOTAL COST OF OWNERSHIP — SUPPORT

For a large distributed network, the initial price of new software is only the beginning of a careful cost-of-ownership exploration, especially with anti-virus solutions. Investment in an anti-virus system protects all other software investments and invaluable corporate information, yet it also necessarily adds complexity to the overall network operation. Without adequate support, this additional "layer" can disrupt network operations, resulting in hidden added costs.

Anti-virus software, least of any category, cannot just be installed and left alone, so evaluators must thoroughly analyze how competing products can satisfy the following support considerations.

Signature, Engine and Product Updates

To remain effective, even the best package must include frequent signature file and scanning engine updates in addition to product operational updates, because of the constant flow of new viruses/strains.

While most well-known anti-virus software vendors will certainly produce updated virus signature files, their methods, quality assurance, and timeliness of distributing the files to customers vary. Physical distribution, in the form of disks accompanied by documentation, is one method. Even if physical distribution is done via express courier, however, electronic distribution via file download is the faster (and if anything, lower-cost) method.

Training, Education and Consulting

In terms of logistics and cost (included or not in contract, on-site vs. vendor site, depth of staff included, etc.) training and education services will vary from vendor to vendor. Key network management and support staff should probably obtain direct training from the vendor.

Further training of the next personnel levels might be accomplished in-house, but organizations should weigh the cost and time required of their own internal resources against the cost of outside training (which may prove a relative bargain). The availability of the vendor to perform flexible consulting services may also improve implementation time and reduce costs.

General and Emergency Services

For ongoing maintenance services, proposals should detail what the vendor will provide as part of the contract, how often, how they may be accessed/ordered, and the availability of any special features.

Emergency services are a key aspect of anti-virus software maintenance. Customers need to know in advance the vendor's emergency-basis policies (and additional costs if any) for analysis of suspect files, cure returns, and cure guarantees. Often, if it sounds too good to be true, it is. What are the guarantees backed with?

VENDOR EVALUATION

Surrounding all the tests, analyses, and qualitative considerations about product features and performance are key questions about the vendor companies being evaluated. Decision-makers should thoroughly investigate the following aspects of each competing company.

Infrastructure

Assuming that vendors under strong consideration offer desirable technology, buyers should not neglect to research the *business* side of each vendor. A company's resources and the way it uses them are important issues for customers pondering a fairly long-term contract for critical anti-virus software and services. Simple and practical questions to be answered are: How many, and of what experience level are the support, development, quality assurance, and virus research people employed by the vendor? And what is the size and scope of its user base?

The vendor's economic health should also be assessed, as a struggling company will have difficulty servicing many large clients and supporting monthly ongoing product development.

Technologies

The company's product development track record, in the context of continued organizational strength, is an indicator of how well it will support future development. Have its new product releases been significant improvements and/or departures from standard technology of the time? Have updated releases been truly enhanced or mere "fixes"? Have those releases arrived on schedule, or is the company usually running behind?

Beyond its handling of individual products, the vendor's grasp of technological trends is important, too. Does it recognize issues about the future that concern its customers? In proposing anti-virus solutions, do its representatives ask knowledgeable questions that reflect this ability?

Relationships

Technological strength alone or excellent service without robust technology cannot provide the best anti-virus solution for a complex distributed environment. Gathering this information about a potential vendor's infrastructure *and* technological strength will give a clearer picture of its ability to fully support the relationship.

SUMMARIZED CRITERIA

In today's large network environments, the task of choosing an enterprise-wide anti-virus solution involves a multidisciplinary evaluation of many factors. Products and vendors that are strong in certain areas may have weak links in others that are of particular importance to a given organization. Ultimately, the best solution is the one that provides the best overall balance of these factors in relation to your needs:

- *Detection* — consistently high detection rates, tested repeatedly over time on appropriate virus samples.
- *Performance* — ability to provide security with minimal impact on network operations.
- *Administration* — practicality of central and distributed management, with convenient support.
- *Reporting* — mechanisms for communication and measurement of virus incidents.
- *Reliability* — stability of the product, vendor, and ongoing support.
- *Total Cost of Ownership* — as measured in real dollars and impact on other resources, initial and long-term.

- *Vendor Considerations* — ability to sustain key relationship based on technological expertise and healthy infrastructure.

REAL-WORLD EXPERIENCES

Research of products and vendors combined with analysis of data from customized tests provides a strong foundation for anti-virus software evaluation. However, decision makers should not neglect the highly valuable resource represented by peers from other, similar organizations.

Ask about their experiences in obtaining viruses to test, equipment utilized in tests, whether they normalized tests and their method of weighting results. The fight against viruses is a relatively popular area in which all involved can benefit from shared experiences.

The anti-virus software industry can provide more too, by formulating guidelines and supporting more in-depth education. Vendors should offer their own tests to supplement user-customized tests, and assist with virus libraries for sample configuration.

Anti-virus software certification by the National Computer Security Association (NCSA) serves both users and vendors by providing measurable industry standards. It is an ongoing process of independent "blind" testing of anti-virus product detection.

Over 30 participants from several different countries, including major software vendors and independent researchers, contribute to NCSA's effort to catalog all viruses, as they become known. Currently, NCSA is in the process of recertifying products against new, tougher standards for virus detection.[2]

CONCLUSION

To choose the anti-virus solution that best suits the needs of an organization, it is vital that the evaluation team have a thorough understanding of the following issues:

- The threat of virus exposure today
- Detection technologies currently available
- Trends in viruses and anti-virus countermeasures
- Functional requirements, present and future
- Environment constraints, present and future
- Pros and cons of various testing methodologies
- Evaluation methodologies and resources

It is hoped that this paper has enhanced potential evaluators' knowledge of these issues, in addition to providing a sound methodology for discovering solutions that satisfy their organizations' needs well into the future. We are prepared to provide further assistance to your evaluation effort.

References

1. Computer Security Association, *Virus Impact Study,* 1994.
2. National Computer Security Association, *NCSA Anti-Virus Certification Scheme,* November 1997 Edition, NCSA Worldwide Web Site.

Note: All company and product names, registered and unregistered, are the property of their respective owners.

Chapter 28
The Future of Computer Viruses

Richard Ford

COMPUTER VIRUSES ARE A FACT OF LIFE FOR THE INFORMATION SYSTEMS (IS) MANAGER. Since 1986, when the first virus was written for the IBM PC, the number of known viruses and variants has skyrocketed; the current total is over 8,000.This chapter describes the virus-related threats that users will face in future.

THE FIRST RECORDED VIRUSES

Although computer viruses are often associated with the burgeoning computing environment of the late 1980s and 1990s, self-replicating code has been around for far longer. In the mainframe environment, codes existed that could fork processes and, replicating wildly, undermine performance. These were the forerunners of today's computer viruses.

The Brain virus of 1986 is often identified erroneously as the first virus ever discovered. However, although Brain was the first PC virus, its discovery was preceded by that of a virus written for the Apple II in 1981 called Elk Cloner. Elk Cloner's payloads included inverting the screen and displaying a text message. In 1983, Dr. Fred Cohen developed self-replicating code in a series of VAX and UNIX experiments and, subsequently, Brain was discovered in 1986. Brain, like Elk Cloner, was a boot sector virus that spread from machine to machine through the boot sector of floppy disks. The Brain virus received a great deal of media attention, and the combination of growing public awareness and the 1988 publication of *Computer Viruses: A High Tech Disease* by R. Burger — the first published reference for virus source codes — fueled a sharp increase in virus development. Burger's book detailed the source code for the Vienna virus, which has many contemporary variants.

The Brain virus introduced the concept of stealth to the computing public. A stealth virus hides the changes that it makes to an infected system. For example, if a full-stealth virus infects the boot sector of a diskette, a reading of that boot sector on an infected system will return the original

0-8493-0893-3/00/$0.00+$.50

contents of the boot sector, not the virus code. Similarly, changes to the amount of free memory or to the length of infected files can be disguised. After the stealth virus, the next technical innovations in viruses were encryption and polymorphism.

The first encrypted virus, Cascade, was discovered by virus researchers in 1989. Decrypting an encrypted virus is simple. If a variable key has been used to encrypt the virus, a hex string can be used to identify the short decryption routine. Not long after the decryption of Cascade, the virus-writing fraternity realized that writing code that could produce many different decryption routines would render it impossible or, at best, impractical, to detect these viruses with a simple hex string. Thus, polymorphic viruses were born. Polymorphic viruses, plus add-on polymorphic modules that could be linked to ordinary, non-polymorphic virus code, were developed. The most famous of these was the Mutation Engine (MtE) written by the Dark Avenger.

Polymorphic viruses prompted the next level of virus scanner development, as vendors raced to catch the rapidly accelerating target that viruses had become. As recently as mid-1995, several products were still unable to detect MtE reliably. Over the last few years, virus designers have developed different methods of infecting files and have infected a wider range of targets.

VIRUSES TARGETED TO WINDOWS PLATFORMS

One of the most significant challenges that present and future virus designers face is the new generation of operating systems. Virus writers have not yet focused on Windows 95 and Windows NT. Although many of the existing DOS viruses can infect executables or boot sectors in these new operating systems, only one virus, Boza, has been discovered that explicitly targets these platforms. The Boza virus is unremarkable, however, and does not pose a serious threat to Windows 95 users.

The most significant threat to Windows 95 or Windows NT platforms currently are traditional boot sector viruses. If a Windows NT or Windows 95 system is booted from an infected diskette, the virus will infect the boot sector of the computer. Because neither of these operating systems accesses the fixed disk in the same manner as DOS, the virus will usually be unable to infect other diskettes and should spread no further. However, the virus may render the machine unbootable. Moreover, the virus can, in many cases, successfully execute its trigger routine. Thus, if the virus is configured to format the fixed disk at boot time on a particular date, that trigger routine will be executed. Windows operating systems' accommodation of ordinary MS-DOS executables also exposes the platforms to the existing crop of file-infecting DOS viruses.

It is expected that more virus writers will target Windows platforms soon, because many of the systems' inherent characteristics make them ideal hosts for malicious code. In a multitasking environment, it is much easier for programs to become resident. This fact may result in a variety of new strategies to subvert the systems. Furthermore, there will be more ways for a virus writer to hide a malicious code's presence in memory. Windows' functionality for sharing resources seamlessly around a company also places the system as risk, in that an application that a user accesses could be on the local fixed disk, on the fixed disk of a computer across the room, or on a machine linked across the Internet. This invisible networking could provide the perfect infection vector for a virus, allowing self-replicating code to spread across an organization rapidly.

Researchers estimate that these platforms have not been subjected to attack because youthful virus writers — the majority of virus writers are young enough never to have had a full-time job — do not yet have the resources to write viruses for high-end operating systems. The average home machine is still running Windows under MS-DOS. Additionally, programming tools are not readily available to general users. DOS contained a primitive assembler/disassembler (DEBUG) as a standard offering; however, the large software development kits required for Windows programming are comparatively expensive and difficult to use. Those programmers who do have the necessary skills and resources to write viable Windows NT and Windows 95 viruses tend to be experienced programmers who are not, statistically speaking, in the virus-designing business. For the time being, then, the platforms have been virtually virus-free. This will likely change when this new generation of operating system becomes the standard.

THE MACRO VIRUS

In the last quarter of 1995, the first macro virus was discovered in the wild. However, there was no virus in the wild that was capable of spreading by embedding itself in data files until the discovery of the WinWord.Concept virus. The idea behind macro viruses is simple. Many application programs allow for the inclusion of certain macros within data files. As application software has developed, macro languages have become increasingly powerful, allowing programmers to edit, delete, and copy files, and even on occasion to invoke the DOS shell. One application package allows for at least 150 macro commands in each template. These commands allow the programs to perform functions without user action.

Although several different packages are susceptible to macro viruses, Microsoft Word has been the most affected to date. There are also known macro viruses for Excel and AmiPro.

The WinWord.Concept Virus

When a user selects a Microsoft Word document and loads it, either from within Word or by double-clicking on the document icon, Word examines the document type. A standard Word document does not contain any embedded macros and is loaded into the program, ready for editing. However, if the loaded file is a document template file, Word automatically loads any macros that are contained within it. Should the document template file contain a macro named AutoOpen, the contents of this macro are automatically executed. The WinWord.Concept virus exploits this ability by adding macros to existing documents. These macros, once installed, add additional functionality to menu-bar operations and allow the virus to infect other documents on the system. Notably, AutoOpen is not the only auto executing macro in the Word environment; there are several others that Concept's creator could have taken advantage of. The Concept virus does not contain a trigger routine, but the words "That's enough to prove my point" are contained within the code.

Concept is now a widespread virus. The reason for this is twofold. First, although users rarely share executables or boot from diskettes, their jobs usually involve the exchange of data files. In many cases, users have been taught that viruses are only a risk when they are swapping binaries or diskettes, and thus do not suspect a macro virus. Moreover, many companies' policy and procedure manuals do not address the risk posed by macro viruses. The second reason for Concept's rapid spread is that it was accidentally distributed on CD-ROM and over the Internet.

The Future of Macro Viruses

In a straw poll taken at a recent firewalls conference, a speaker asked the audience members to raise their hands if they had heard of the dangers posed by embedded macros. Less than half of the attendees responded. This is not surprising. Time after time, systems administrators report that they have never heard about macro viruses. More disturbing is that many of them admit that, although they have heard of the viruses, they have not taken any protective measures and have no idea whether they may have an infected environment.

Macro viruses are intimately involved with data files. Although the Concept virus does not intentionally damage files on the system, the potential exists for macro viruses to cause data loss or corruption. Since the discovery of Concept, other viruses and Trojan horses designed for Word have been discovered, including one that modifies documents by adding the string "And finally I would like to say: STOP ALL FRENCH NUCLEAR TESTING IN THE PACIFIC."

The future of macro viruses will depend on how application vendors develop software products. Some applications are more resilient to the threat of macro viruses than others; however, resilience can often undermine functionality. For example, although creating macros that are portable across a suite of applications is a wise business decision for a Microsoft, it will allow a macro virus written for Microsoft Word to function and spread under Microsoft Access. Thus, added functionality increases the population of computers that can be infected.

ANTIVIRUS SOFTWARE

For years, security practitioners have predicted the death of the virus scanner. However, the scanner is still the most popular weapon in the fight against viruses. Predictions of the scanner's demise were based on the sheer number of new viruses that scanner vendors must process every month to keep their products current. Several of these viruses are polymorphic and require a great deal of analysis by the developer to ensure reliable detection. Thus, the work required maintaining a scanner continually increases.

Because scanning engines that are currently in use cannot keep up with the pace of virus development, most new products will be virus nonspecific in design. The latest crop of new products provide for the automatic detection and removal of viruses. In the last year, there has been a growing interest in studying existing viruses to create a definitive must-detect list for anti-virus products. Among the most important new developments are products that remove boot sector infections at boot time. Because boot sector viruses are the most common, this software could conceivably reduce the amount of time required to detect and repair damaged boot sectors. Although this software has certain limitations (i.e., it is vulnerable to those viruses that target it as well as to those that happen to meet its trigger conditions at boot time), it can provide a quick and easy method for catching boot viruses early.

Fully Automated Response for in the Wild Viruses

Some practitioners believe that new developments must be taken a step further. In a paper presented at the 1995 Virus Bulletin Conference, Mike Lambert proposed a concept called Fully Automated Response for in the Wild (FAR-ITW) viruses. Lambert's philosophy is that, where possible, virus incidents should be cleaned up automatically, with no user disruption. Furthermore, Lambert believes that anti-virus software should automatically and centrally report incidents, and gather samples of infected files for later analysis. Although several products can do part of this job, no product as yet is capable of fulfilling the role. FAR-ITW would allow vendors to concentrate repair and identification on those viruses that are known to be spreading. Additionally, the user does not necessarily need to be informed of a form-infected disk, although logging and reporting of the incident is vital in terms of evaluating the threat.

The level of automated response required by a company will depend on the type of business that the company is in and on the company's established policies and procedures. The principal advantage of automated removal is that it will not disrupt the workplace. Concerns about false positives must be addressed by identifying viruses before removal and by automatically removing only those viruses that are not likely to have caused data damage and that can be removed with certainty. Of course, the memory and performance impact of such a product would have to be thoroughly assessed before companies would opt to buy it. Although FAR-ITW is not yet available, several products seem to be addressing the automation goal.

VIRUSES TRANSMITTED OVER THE INTERNET

Corporate IS personnel exploring the new vistas offered by the Internet are finding themselves inundated with the amount of information that is presently available on Internet virus activity and security. The intentional distribution of viruses over the Internet is increasing as quickly as the new commercial opportunities it provides. Virus exchange has always been a standard practice of the computer virus subculture. Although some reports indicate that exchange is not a significant factor in increasing the number of viruses in the wild, the development of the Internet and the increased accessibility within corporate environments necessitate a reevaluation of the threat posed to users from this source.

Any service that is used to obtain binary files can be a source of virus infection. Several different Internet services, and the risks for users who access them, are discussed in the following sections.

File Transfer Protocol

Before the advent of the World Wide Web, the most common way for users to obtain information from remote systems was through the File transfer protocol (FTP). There are a large number of File Transfer Protocol sites around the world, many of which allow users to access anonymously certain files that are stored on them. FTP access is a useful facility for functions as diverse as locating the lyrics to an old pop song to obtaining the latest NetWare drivers for OS/2. However, users must be aware that the files they obtain may contain viruses.

Because of the volatile nature of the Internet, users should be taught to pay particular attention to where they obtain files. Although the well-known and popular archive sites have a good track record for containing clean files, lapses occur. The Computer Emergency Response Team (CERT) Coordination Center has received confirmation that some copies of the source code for wuarchive FTP daemon have been modified by an intruder and contain a Trojan horse. Any site running this archive should take immediate action by installing version 2.3 or disabling the File Transfer Protocol daemon. In this case, the software was "trojanised" to allow an intruder to access systems that were running the software. It would have been just as easy for a virus to have been planted.

Netnews

Usenet, or Netnews, is a widely circulated collection of newsgroups similar to a bulletin board system (BBS). Netnews membership is comprised of the entire online community. Netnews newsgroups range from the bizarre (e.g., alt.swedishchef.bork.bork.bork) to the useful (e.g., comp.virus, alt.security) and encompass a vast array of hobbies and pastimes. Although Netnews is a text-only environment, several newsgroups contain binaries that can be executed. These binaries are converted to text format with a UNIX utility known as uuencode and are posted to groups. A reader can then download the text, decode it, and recreate the original binary.

Aside from the usual problems of importing binaries onto a trusted machine, binaries obtained from a newsgroup are of highly questionable origin. There is little to prevent one user from masquerading as another. Further, several of the newsgroups contain files that have little or no work-related value. For example, the alt.binaries hierarchy contains a newsgroup called alt.binaries.pictures.erotica, and it is from this group that many users have contracted their first Internet-transmitted virus.

The virus that was spread in the newsgroup is the KAOS4 virus. An infected copy of a program named "Sexotica" was posted to the group. Several users downloaded it; some took the precaution of scanning it. Unfortunately, the KAOS4 virus was not familiar to the anti-virus community and therefore was passed by scanners as clean.

The KAOS4 virus is poorly written, and it was not long before infected users began to notice malfunctions on their systems. The virus was isolated shortly thereafter, and anti-virus software updated to detect it. One problem with tracking down the source of the infection within companies was that many users were reluctant to tell the staff how they had become infected — or that they were infected — because of the questionable source. Consequently, many systems were not cleaned up as effectively as they might have been.

This incident highlights the need to educate users about the dangers posed by text-encoded binary files that are available within the Usenet environment. Companies should restrict newsgroup access to those that are required for business functions. Virus code is not confined to accidental postings: there is a newsgroup dedicated solely to posting virus code.

The World Wide Web

In terms of viruses and the Internet, the most disturbing trend is the exposure of the World Wide Web (WWW) to infestation. Although viruses have been available through anonymous FTP for a long time, sites have been relatively hard to locate. With the advent of the WWW, it is possible to search out sites that provide large collections of viruses simply by using a Web search engine. Most of these virus collections are clearly labeled as such, so it is not likely that a user will unknowingly download an infected file. However, working with viruses is tricky, and it is easy for a user's experiment to get out of control.

Some users may feel that this availability of viruses will allow them to test anti-virus software easily and thus perform private evaluations. This is not the case, however, as the maintenance of a virus collection can be extremely difficult. Using this method to test anti-virus software is unwise for a variety of reasons. First, the majority of the virus threat comes from those viruses already known to be in the wild, rather than from so-called "zoo" viruses. Although there are over 8,000 different viruses written for the IBM PC, less than 200 have actually been encountered in the wild. Thus, the only way to test effectively the efficacy of a virus scanner is to create a collection of those viruses known to be in the wild. A collection obtained from a WWW site is unlikely to contain all of these viruses.

Another argument against testing antiviral software against virus collections is that the WWW collections contain many files that are not viruses, including text files renamed to COM extensions, damaged executables, and clean files. The only way to be sure that the files are real viruses is to replicate them onto clean files, known as goat files, and then to ensure that these files are also capable of replication. This is a very large job; if it is not carried out, the test results are meaningless at best and misleading at worst. Furthermore, many collections contain droppers or first generation samples of viruses. These are not suitable for testing scanners, because they are not the same as all further replications of that virus. Finally, the most common viruses are boot sector viruses; these are usually not found in such collections.

The correct way to test polymorphic viruses is to produce a large number of different samples. For a meaningful test of a product's polymorphic virus detection capability, thousands of samples must be replicated out, and samples that are missed must be confirmed as genuine replicants.

Although the ability of users to obtain viruses intentionally from the WWW is cause for concern, a far bigger problem is posed by the unintentional retrieval of viruses from the Web. Many corporate users are unaware of the risks to which they are exposed when browsing the Web. For example, one user searched for information on the Word macro virus, Concept. Finding a site, the user downloaded a document file that purported to contain more details. This document was infected with another Word macro virus. Consequently, when the browser passed control to the helper application, the virus code was executed and the local system became infected. The virus spread rapidly throughout the company.

In most cases, users are unaware of the risks to which they expose an organization's systems. There are several ways to address this problem. Two of the most effective strategies are comprised of technologically based solutions and denial-of-service solutions.

Technologically Based Solutions. The simplest way to provide virus protection for binaries received over the Internet is to install some form of continuous virus protection on the host machine. Terminate and Stay Resident programs (TSRs) or, for Windows 95, VxDs, can provide effective protection against these viruses in the wild. However, many memory-resident applications do not have the same detection capabilities as their nonresident counterparts. Furthermore, users should ensure that TSRs are capable of detecting macro-based viruses. A TSRs should detect macro viruses even if the host application is launched by another program, such as a WWW browser. A company's anti-virus software vendor will typically be able to supply this information. Publications such as *SECURE Computing* and *Virus Bulletin* are also reliable resources.

The threat posed by malicious electronic mail attachments can be limited at the mail gateway. Several vendors have developed products that attempt to scan incoming mail messages for binary file attachments before the messages are distributed to the eventual recipients. However, this is not a foolproof solution, because encrypted information that is transmitted across the Internet cannot be scanned by the gateway. Although it would be possible to supply the gateway with a copy of all of the encryption keys, this is an unacceptable solution.

Finally, there has been some discussion about the possibility of checking incoming files for viruses at a company's firewall. This is a relatively new idea, however, and technology has not as yet been developed to support it.

Denial-of-Service Solutions. A number of denial-of-service solutions have proven to be cost-effective security strategies. The idea of denying users access to particular services for security reasons has become unfashionable in recent years. Security as facilitator, not moderator, is the philosophy that has allowed security to become an accepted part of the IS manager's function. However, companies interested in accessing the Internet should, ideally, maintain a sensible balance between moderating and facilitating access to this powerful tool. In particular, the requirements for Internet access within a company should be closely examined. IS managers should evaluate how many users will need access over and above that required for E-mail. Most likely, the majority of the staff will not have a legitimate business need for unrestricted access. Further, for those users who require WWW access, the IS manager should consider providing isolated terminals that can connect to the Web. This approach has a number of benefits. With the use of limited terminals, anyone who wishes to use the WWW may do so, and the company will not be divided into those who have access and those who do not. Moreover, there will be a reduced opportunity for employees to waste time surfing the Internet. This approach does not preclude the installation of a wider net access if it is deemed necessary at a later date; it does, however, provide the benefits of the Internet within a controlled environment.

Firewalls can also be configured to limit the type of services that users are permitted to use. This is especially helpful if many users in a company require Internet access. For example, few Usenet groups will be used for business purposes. A full news feed is costly in terms of resources (e.g., disk space and bandwidth), lost time and productivity. Thus, companies should carefully prune the Newsnet hierarchy and, as a general rule, should set the default settings to deny particular newsgroups.

THE MODERN DAY VIRUS EXCHANGE AND ITS WRITERS

The ready availability of virus code on the WWW, both as precompiled binaries and as source code, has opened up the once-shadowy world of virus writers to the light of day.

Modern day virus exchange is a simple matter of point and click. In many ways, this has had the effect of legitimizing the activities of virus-writing groups. The moderated comp.virus Usenet discussion group has been, to a certain extent, supplanted by the anarchic but lively alt.comp.virus group, which is populated by a curious mix of virus writers, virus researchers, anti-virus product developers, and users. Whereas at one time virus writers shielded themselves from the public eye, they are now happy to be at the forefront of discussion. Further exacerbating the situation has been the publication of a CD-ROM filled with live viruses collected by Mark Ludwig, and the public position adopted by several experts who preach that viruses are useful and valid research.

Research has shown that the general profile of virus writers has been affected by the changing computing environment and high visibility of virus design and protection. Over the past two years, research conducted by Sarah Gordon has yielded some interesting results. Although, in 1994, virus writers generally fell within the ethical norms for their age groups, recent writers appear to be desensitized to the negative effects of the viruses that they write. When confronted with the facts, today's crop of writers seems not to care; in fact, they seem to thrive on the fame and attention that virus writers are receiving.

OBJECT ORIENTATION

As operating systems increase in complexity, users are moving away from programs that relate to particular data and towards an integrated approach in which the borderlines between programs and data files are no longer clearly defined. This trend will create problems for the anti-virus industry.

Already, the number of different objects that can be infected has grown immeasurably. Viruses currently exist that infect source code, bin files, SYS files, BAT files, OBJ files, and DOC files. Zhengxi, the latest virus that cannot be completely dissected and for which disinfection routines are difficult, is an example of these potent polymorphic viruses. Zhengxi infects EXE and OBJ files and attaches infected COM droppers to ZIP, ARJ, and RAR archives.

Windows Object Linking and Embedding provision, which allows users to plug executable code into many different objects, creates an environment in which a virus scanner must search through all Windows objects, regardless of their extensions, to find all of the OLE executables within a file and scan them. This results in slower scan times. Currently, no virus has been reported to target OLE. One company, however, was repeatedly reinfected by an infected executable OLE'd into a data file. Although the virus scanner was capable of detecting all of the subsequent replications of the virus, it could not detect the infected file within the document. One possible way to avoid this scenario is to use real-time virus protection in the form of Terminate and Stay Resident or VxDs.

CONCLUSION

It is difficult to make predictions concerning the future of viruses. The last decade of virus writing has demonstrated that virus writers are extremely resourceful. The list of objects that may contain virus code continues to increase, and the development of increasingly object-based operating systems and environments will fuel this trend. The only safe predictions are that the number and complexities of viruses will continue to increase, and that viruses will be designed that target Microsoft's new high-end operating systems.

Chapter 29
Strategies for an Archives Management Program

Michael J.D. Sutton

FEW PROFESSIONALS HAVE NAVIGATED THROUGH FEW ARCHIVES MANAGEMENT (AM) PROJECTS, TEAMS, SUCCESSES, AND FAILURES. Why? Because there have been few successes to point to, and because there has been no poignant business reason to proceed with such initiatives (at least until recently). Nonetheless, many corporations and public sector organizations are now experiencing significant pain and financial liability from the loss of their corporate memory. The lack of archives management strategies is holding back "well-intentioned" but untrained project directors and managers from coming to grips with the issues, concerns, problems, and obstacles associated with an archive repository (AR). The overall strategy outlined here could well be an important reference document for one's next initiative.

FOUNDATIONAL CONCEPTS

Why does one need a strategy? One needs a strategy because the AM initiative one has been asked to embark upon has no anchors to hold anyone to the *present*. Archives management is about time, and the effect time has on artifacts created in the *present*. Archives management is, paradoxically, about the *future* (which most people cannot see unless they profess to be prophets), but only when that *future* has become the *past*. AM does not incorporate in its conceptual model a classical linear timeline; it presents a reverse timeline where the *past* only becomes valuable again when it is many years old.

0-8493-0893-3/00/$0.00+$.50

Suppose one is asked to plan an archives repository in such a way that information objects created in the *present* can be "read" (or at least understood) in the *future*, within their original, rich context. However, someone (or some automated system) in the *future* must, at its *present* moment, contend with information objects from the *past*. The information objects at that point in the *future* never seem to have enough context or content to permit their proper understanding.

Archives management, especially as it is defined in digital terms, is a very young discipline. The key business drivers and benefits are not yet well-defined or clearly mapped. The project director has no means of testing whether information objects created as an output to an AM initiative will be usable in the future, other than through simulated testing. This testing cannot take into account software product or system evolution over a five- to ten-year period, or even worse, over a 25- to 100-year period. The best a project director can do is make an educated guess, and hope that when five or more years have passed, he may have been a prophet in his own land.

Although there is little to go on at this time to justify an AM initiative, there is anecdotal material that points to business drivers and benefits. There are **key business drivers** that can justify an AM initiative, including:

- an antiquated or traditional records management system that cannot cope with the emerging challenges and requirements of a digital workspace
- increasing online space requirements for current operational databases, data marts, and data warehouses
- short- and long-term technological obsolescence
- an enterprise's drive to harmonize all systems onto a heterogeneous environment
- an inability to find, locate, catalog, and use current or historical digital information objects
- new uses for "old" data from sales, human resources, marketing, facilities, engineering, and financial databases

There are numerous potential benefits in implementing an archives management program that may apply to an organization, including:

- decreased corporate exposure during audits or legal inquiries
- increased compliance with various levels of laws and regulation (international, federal, state/province, county/region, and city/municipal)
- improved records management and control
- appropriate retention and timely destruction of business records
- streamlined and rationalized processes where business owners do not have to be concerned with archiving information objects from their current systems

Take the Year 2000 issues and problems that most organizations are currently contending with, for example. These were a significant archives management problem. As automated systems grew in the 1960s and 1970s, no one could predict how memory costs would fall or how software would handle date-related information. In fact, most people who worked on such systems never expected COBOL, PL/I, RPG, or even Assembler compilers to last more than five years. Alas, one is now in the *future*, and trying to cope with the professional inability to plan for legacy applications that were just too poorly documented to re-write, and too integral to the business to throw away.

An AM initiative differs substantially from a contemporary information system project. The AM initiative can be described by a number of characteristics:

- generally five to seven years in length
- an average team size of five members for an enterprise of 1000 client users
- historical focus on record and file structures that are not currently in vogue
- primarily concerned with the disposition of the digital records of the enterprise after they are at least seven years old

Contrast this with the characteristics of a contemporary information system project:

- generally less than two years in duration (and preferably less than one year)
- an average team size of seven to ten members for an enterprise of 1000 client users
- *avant garde* focus on record and file structures that are just currently in use
- primarily concerned with the creation and use of digital records of the enterprise created in the *present*, less than two years from their date of creation

There is a significant difference in the business goals and objectives of the two projects. In addition, the owners and technology supporters of the current system projects have been allocated no time or budget to worry about or plan for the eventual retirement or disposition of the systems, data, or documents. These *present-focused* business and technology leaders have incentives, i.e., bonuses, dividends, or stock options, based on what they help the company accomplish *today* or *tomorrow* — not five to seven years from now.

The tools used within an AM project must contend with both old and new technologies, software, media devices, methods, file structures, record formats, etc. The tools of an AM initiative are Janus-like in their employment. (Janus was the classical Roman god who had two faces: one looked into the past while the second looked into the future. Janus was identified with doors, gates, and beginnings and endings). The AM project team must contend with having one foot in the *past* and one in the *future*, while the *present* passes them by.

Information management professionals — at the behest of private and public sector leaders — have worked for over 40 years to automate (digitize) less than 20 present of the enterprise information assets and intellectual capital. Regretfully, in doing so, they have forced most enterprises to be short-term in their vision of the value of information objects and systems, to rely too heavily on the digital nature of the information. Thus, many organizations almost ignore the digital as well as the hardcopy storage and long-term retrieval value of information. These enterprises may not have "lost their minds," but they have lost their corporate memory. When an audit or legal discovery process tries to contend with digital information that is five to ten years old (or even three years old), there are significant problems in reconstructing these information objects and their context. And for many enterprises today, this "corporate amnesia" results in hefty legal costs, fines, and lost revenue.

Archives Management Problem Statement

Most organizations that wish to survive in today's aggressive business climate must continually improve, evolve, and reposition their market, products, and services, and aggressively maintain their profitability. The enterprise must create and achieve short-term business goals, objectives, and strategies. Many businesses have invested heavily in automated legacy systems. These systems may be nearing or have already passed their retirement date. The valued corporate memories in these systems may be incorporated into new, emerging corporate systems; or, alternatively, the digital information objects may be stored offline to comply with legal and regulatory requirements. The worst case is that these out-of-date systems, data, and document objects are ignored until it is too late to determine how they could be migrated to physical media or logical format to be useful.

All enterprises are facing a challenge to preserve digital systems, data, and documents over short-, medium-, and long-term periods of time. Some companies have lost significant income from audits because substantiating data and documents (stored digitally) were lost years earlier; but not discovered until it was too late. The business owners of current operational information systems are generally preoccupied with operational challenges, issues, and concerns surrounding applications performance and availability. Managers are asked to contend with short-term business objectives and present problems, not with hypothetical problems that could emerge in the distant future.

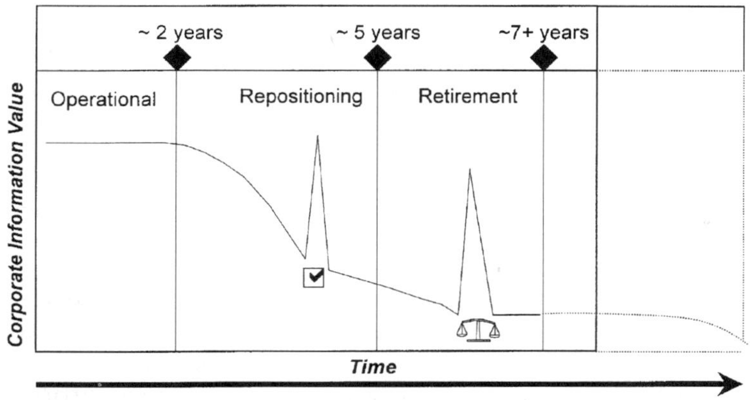

Exhibit 29-1. Information preservation stages.

The oversimplified diagram shown in Exhibit 29-1 might help to illustrate the preservation challenge that one faces. Current information systems create or acquire information objects that have immediate corporate value. This is the operational stage of a corporate information value life cycle. The operational stage may encompass one to two fiscal years. The requirement during this stage for instant retrieval dictates that the information objects are stored online. This stage might also encompass data marts and data warehouses that require relatively quick access and retrieval response times.

The corporate value of the information will decrease over time because it simply is no longer current; and current information is very important when generating profits or increased stock price value. The information objects migrate to the repositioning stage of the corporate information value life cycle. The repositioning stage may incorporate three to five fiscal years of information objects. The use of near-line or offline storage media (optical disks, CD-ROMs, QIC tapes, etc.) generally applies at this stage, and may continue for up to five or six years. Instantaneous retrieval is not as critical at this juncture in the life cycle. Nonetheless, during this period of time, external audits by regulatory or tax agencies may take place; this creates a peak in the perceived corporate value of the information where its value may be as much or more than its original corporate value.

Generally, information objects during this period of time exhibit certain characteristics of aging, which include:

- the loss of the original information and its context
- the original media may be unreadable or devices to read it are no longer manufactured

- the original file and record structure may be unknown, foreign, or undocumented
- any significant business rules stored in the software programs are unreadable, unusable, or unknowable
- any individuals who may have worked on the original system or database have moved on to other opportunities

In short, corporate amnesia exists.

Finally, the corporate information moves into the retirement stage of the corporate information value life cycle. Information objects can remain dormant here for six to 20 years, depending on legal, historical, and archival requirements. The information objects are loaded onto offline media such as magnetic tapes, DAT (digital archive tapes), or possibly CD-ROMs. Historians, social scientists, or lawyers are the expected users for these seldom-accessed information objects. Nonetheless, the information objects must retain enough content, logical structure, and context to be more useful than just a historical artifact.

A business framework or archival facility has rarely existed in present-day enterprises to accommodate the corporate information life cycle as described above. Thus, a digital archives repository rarely exists or is available in today's public and private sector institutions to use as a model. A digital archives repository is required to contextually preserve the database objects, document objects, business rules, system documentation, and other descriptive data (meta-data). Such a repository must accommodate information objects over a medium- to long-term period of time (i.e., from five to 20 years) in a software- and hardware platform-neutral format (e.g., that proposed in ISO Reference Model of the Consultative Committee for Space Data Systems White Paper, *Open Archival Information System (OAIS)*). The archives management strategy might help to position this commitment to a repository.

FOUNDATIONAL DEFINITIONS

Before describing an archives management strategy (AMS), some basic vocabulary intrinsic to archives management is required. An archives management program consists of specific information objects, facilities, processes, and preservation domains. One can start with the information objects.

At the fore of a good AMS is the *business record* — a by-product of a business transaction preserved for future use as evidence of transacting business. A business record must maintain a number of preservation characteristics. Charles Dollar, in *Ensuring Access over Time to Authentic Electronic Records: Strategy, Alternatives, and Best Practices,* proposes a number of preservation characteristics that help preserve the legal integrity of a business record while stored and archived; these characteristics include:

- *authentic:* the measure of the reliability of a record (i.e., its ability to remain unaltered, unchanged, and uncorrupted)
- *encapsulated:* the measure of the self-referential linkage of logical components in a record
- *identifiable:* the measure of the specification of unique identification boundaries in a record
- *intelligible:* the measure of the integrity of the bit stream represented in a record
- *readable:* the measure of the integrity of the bit stream device processing of a record
- *reconstructable:* the measure of the quality of rebuilding the same structure and intellectual content of a record
- *retrievable:* the measure of the capability to locate objects and parts of a record
- *understandable:* the measure of the quality of the context of creation of a record

Business records are aggregated into files. An *operational file* is an information object that contains information of immediate, instantaneous interest to a reader. Digital copies of operational files are normally created in the course of data management procedures, and are referred to as *backup files.* A *repositioned file* is a specially formatted copy of an original operational file that can be retrieved through near-line storage media instead of online storage media. For longer-term storage, repositioned files are migrated to retired files.

A *retired file* contains information objects that would be the foundation for reconstructing an authentic instance of a file in its original format and context. A retired file can encompass system, data, and document objects. The information content can be conveyed to the user or another computer as audio data, bit map data, data fragments and databases, spatial (geographical), spreadsheets, text, vector data, and video data.

The files are managed by different facilities (as illustrated in Exhibit 29-2). An *operational facility* is accountable for managing the current information assets of an enterprise. The information assets are digital and are stored online for immediate access. A *repositioning facility* manages the nearly current information assets (i.e., information that may be between two and five years old). The information objects are stored on near-line media for near-instant access. A *retirement facility* manages the dormant information assets (i.e., information that may be between six and 25 or more years old). The retirement facility can store the information objects in a hardware- and software-neutral format to diminish the problems of technological obsolescence. All the facilities execute specific processes upon the information objects under their control (see Exhibit 29-3).

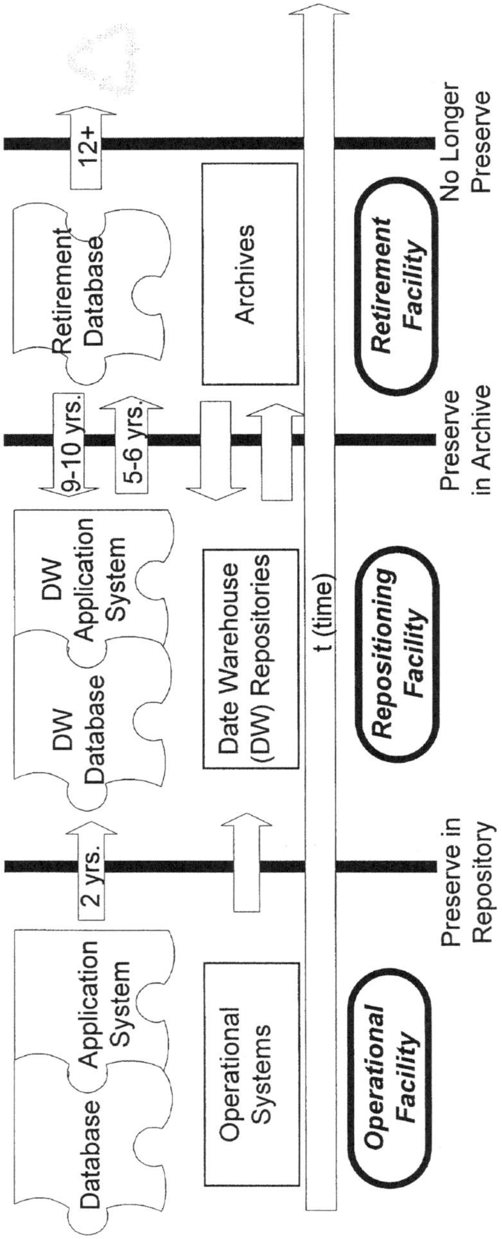

Exhibit 29-2. Time-based migration of information between current and successive stages.

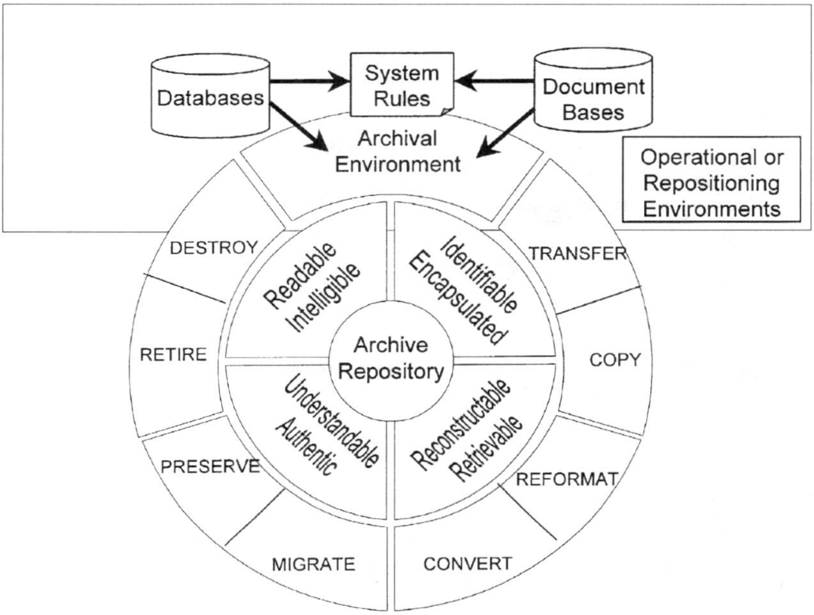

Exhibit 29-3. Archival management processes.

A number of specific processes can be executed on the operational and repositioning environments to move them into an archival environment, including:

1. *convert:* importing or exporting of records from one software-dependent environment to another while ensuring the preservation of structure, content, and context
2. *copy:* the creation of a digital binary twin of the original file
3. *destroy:* physically disposing of the media and information objects so as to make them totally unreadable (i.e., degaussing, crushing, melting, etc.)
4. *migrate:* moving authentic electronic records from legacy information systems in online systems to another storage media, such as near-line or offline storage, while preserving the logical view of the original records
5. *reformat:* transferring records from one medium to another without alteration of the bit stream of a record (e.g., with no change in appearance, content, or logical structure)
6. *retire:* moving information objects to very dormant offline storage to protect and preserve records from corruption and make them relatively inaccessible

7. *transfer:* repositioning electronic records from online or near-line storage to offline storage for infrequent retrieval

Finally, there is *metadata*. This is specific descriptive data about particular data objects which increases the precision in recalling information objects from a search of a repository of data, document, or systems. *Metadata* can describe an information object with fields such as author, business unit of the author, creation date, modification date, security classification, or subject. This overview of the emerging vocabulary of AM will serve as a foundation for subsequent discussion.

STRATEGIES FOR AN ARCHIVES MANAGEMENT INITIATIVE

The following set of strategies and guiding principles are proposed for constructing a framework to design and successfully engineer an archives management program.

Strategy 1: Develop a Repositioning Facility

The repositioning facility will depend on available budget as well as corporate technical resourcing, knowledge, and support. In addition, the enterprise will require skills in data mart and data warehouse design, and an informed and experienced digital records management group. The repositioning facility will ensure the availability of a corporate memory for between two and five years. The operational facility feeds the repositioning facility after two or three fiscal years have elapsed for the operational data.

Strategy 2: Develop a Retirement Facility

The retirement facility must construct a long-term program, which most enterprises are not willing to fund. This retirement facility will need long-term financing so that it is not cut from the budget during lean times. This is a corporate commitment to preserve the memory of the institution. This business unit will be responsible for the archival activities associated with appraisal, collection, migration, protection, reformation, retention, and, finally, the destruction of digital information assets. The retirement facility will warrant that valuable corporate memory is available and accessible. A corporate records management program may already handle many of these functions for hardcopy records. But beware, most records management staff are ill-equipped to cope with managing digital records, especially over such a long term; a new business unit may need to be defined in the organization.

Strategy 3: Employ Guiding Principles in Architecture and Design

The following guiding principles are proposed to jump-start the design and deployment of an AMS.

Principle 1: Manage long-term information assets in the same way one manages short-term information assets. Most organizations ignore the problems and challenges of storing information assets over the long term. This is metaphorically similar to the problems that industrial and manufacturing sectors are experiencing with pollution. If ignored in planning and design, it will cost 100 times as much to reconstruct information assets, or pay the fines and costs of mismanaged archival data.

Principle 2: Business owners of the information assets are concerned with the present — not the future. Business owners should not be made responsible for ensuring medium-term repositioning and long-term preservation of their information objects. They hardly have enough time to keep their current, operational systems performing within acceptable operational limits and backed up for disaster recovery. If the enterprise forces the operational facility to worry about repositioning and retiring, then these activities will never be done. (How many people have omitted backing up their hard disks when they first started on a PC? — my point exactly.) A separate set of facilities (with their own goals and incentives) must be brought into play to relieve the stress and pressure exhibited in the operational facility. This can even be outsourced to companies that are starting to sell services for digital records and archives management facilities.

Principle 3: Aggressively pursue the preservation of critical information assets. A digital retirement facility must be mandated to proactively collect and acquire the critical information objects that need to be preserved. Otherwise, corporate amnesia is guaranteed. Corporate amnesia is expected to increase as companies expend incredible budgets on the Y2K problem instead of on more significant areas such as enterprise document management systems. Neglect and incompetence invalidate any warranty for corporate survival.

Principle 4: Destroy archived information assets in a timely manner. Maintaining access and availability of all digital objects over a long-term period is both impractical and expensive. Assets must be categorized according to their records retention schedule to facilitate their timely destruction. Periodically evaluate the retention periods of archival information assets and destroy the records according to their legal requirements before they can be used against the institution in legal proceedings. The only thing worse than corporate amnesia is "photographic recall" — very risky in any court proceeding. Nonetheless, there may be corporate records of a historical nature that should be preserved longer than their normal destruction date. Make sure that only the historical records are preserved.

Principle 5: Assess compliance with all legal and statutory rules and regulations. Some business unit must be made responsible for maintaining a comprehensive checklist of relevant laws, statutes, and regulations. Often, the knowledge about retention is scattered among different business units; no one is really accountable for knowing or enforcing the legal and statutory requirements. This must change, and accountability must be assigned. There are too many financial liabilities that can cost an institution if these requirements are ignored.

These guiding principles should help in creating a firm foundation for AM activities.

RECAP

This chapter has presented a vocabulary, broad strategies, and guiding principles for embarking on an archives management program. The strategies revolve around the creation and staffing of a repositing facility and a retirement facility. The existence of these two facilities will relieve the operational facility of the stress and pressure to try and find a short-term solution for a long-term problem. The solution is not really within their mandate or skill set to achieve. Separate business units must be "anointed" with these tasks.

Beware of the lack of funding and commitment when starting an AM initiative. Because of the short-term thinking prevalent in most organizations, these would be the types of facilities that would be cut from the organization when times get tough. If the enterprise sees corporate value and the substantial benefits of an AM program, then it must be committed to keep that program intact. An archives repository with gaps is a corporate memory with missing fragments — it may take a great deal of effort to understand, and there will be gaps that could leave out important data, legally required data. Can the enterprise afford that?

Chapter 30
Managing EUC Support Vendors

Jennifer L. Costley
Edward F. Drohan

VENDOR RELATIONSHIPS OFTEN CONSTITUTE THE LION'S SHARE OF AN EUC ORGANIZATION'S BUDGET. Therefore, it is critical that EUC managers secure the best, most economical vendor support agreements that they can possibly arrange. This chapter presents the case study of a large financial institution that attained profitable, successful relationships with its EUC services vendors by:

- Benchmark test EUC vendor performance.
- Measuring EUC vendor profitability.
- Avoiding multiple markups in the distribution channel.
- Analyzing "Total Cost of Ownership" models.
- Correctly assessing an EUC vendor strategic fit.

BANKERS TRUST: A TALE OF SUCCESSFUL VENDOR MANAGEMENT

Bankers Trust Company is a large commercial bank based in New York with offices in major money centers worldwide. In the mid-1980s, Bankers Trust underwent a total realignment of IT goals and structures. Critical to this realignment was the creation of a centralized technology architecture and core IT functions supporting a distributed software development organization. Among the centralized groups was end-user technology procurement. At the same time, Bankers was aggressively seeking opportunities to transfer the risk and cost of non-banking activities to those companies who were best in class, which redefined the role of vendors and was essentially "outsourcing," before it had become a widespread practice.

Bankers' Service Distribution Model

The technology procurement organization participated in this redefinition. Because PCs were standalone and did not run mission-critical applications, they were considered outside the architecture. The goals in PC

0-8493-0893-3/00/$0.00+$.50

acquisition were simple: cost-effective purchasing, no on-site inventories, and minimal paperwork. Bankers also wanted to maintain standards for both hardware and software platforms and to make the vendor responsible for auditing adherence to these standards. This partnership survived several reorganizations on both the vendor and bank side and lasted for several years. The model has become an established service offering in a competitive marketplace.

The bank continued to evolve the distribution model, and with time was able to establish a true "cost plus" relationship with the vendor. This can only occur after both parties get past the jargon (i.e., marketing allowances, markups versus margins) and recognize that there are opportunities for mutual wins. This required direct negotiations with the manufacturers, with the idea of managing risk and cost. The bank committed to global purchase volumes for PC hardware and software and to simplified purchasing processes. They centralized support requirements by establishing internal escalation procedures. They agreed to future volume commitments, providing bookable cash flow. All of this led to reduced costs and better availability of the desktop and server products that were becoming more and more critical to business operations.

The bank began to apply the same strategy that had been successful in developing win/win relationships with distribution vendors to their end-user maintenance suppliers— most successfully in breaks and fixes, and moves, adds, and changes where the service parameters were clearly defined. The economies of scale inherent in a centralized environment were in their favor, as was finding a vendor who needed to establish a showcase account. They made sure to bound the risk on both sides and to establish performance targets that reflected the criticality of the various businesses.

Bankers Trust pursued other opportunities as well. As PC software became more critical to the enterprise, they were among the first to put in place global software licensing agreements for key desktop products. Structured as site licenses, these agreements allowed the bank to deploy software in a cohesive architecture without necessarily being concerned about how to manage this deployment at a granular level. More recently, the bank has successfully deployed a standard package for tracking and managing software across the enterprise. This has supplemented the site licenses and enabled better asset management.

Retaining Core IS Functions. Bankers currently retains "core" IS functions internally, including desktop engineering (which includes approval of all configurations and add-ons), network operations and engineering, data center engineering and operations, and software development and maintenance. The bank's business imperative is that the infrastructure be in place and working without issues on an around-the-clock basis, with support resources that are responsive and reliable.

THE NY TECHNOLOGY ROUNDTABLE: A CONSENSUS VIEW

The attitudes reflected in the discussion of Bankers Trust—aggressive vendor management and an aversion to having the service provider take over "core" IT activities—is consistent across the population that comprises the New York Technology Roundtable. The Roundtable is a loosely organized group of mostly financial service firms that was established in 1994 to compare best practices.

In 1993, Bankers' payments to its PC vendors were the largest single vendor expense category for its New York offices. Bankers felt valuable market information could be gained—information far beyond price benchmark test—and shared with a group of similarly concerned organizations. This would be accomplished by soliciting the potential members to participate in a carefully prepared study and to benefit from the resulting analysis.

Many hours were spent developing the PC procurement study. The final version of the survey covered 11 areas in depth, including distribution, pricing, administration, support, performance criteria, vendor performance, and manufacturer relationships. Respondents were also asked to describe the unique characteristics of their processes and distribution vendors and to identify their greatest challenges.

Using these surveys and its vision of the benefits of the resulting analysis, and pledging confidential handling of the participant's data, Bankers proceeded to sell its concept of a PC procurement study to its peers through letters and phone calls.

Twenty organizations, with contacts obtained mostly through Bankers' vendors, were invited to participate in the study. The 12 respondents represented an installed base of 109,000 PCs and an annual purchasing volume of $290 million. The surveys were collected, coded for anonymity, and analyzed.

The results showed a correlation between what the organizations were paying for PCs at that time (between 3-11% markup over manufacturer cost) and the number of value-added services that the PC supplier or distribution vendor was providing. These value-added services included hardware and software installation, freight, dedicated personnel, dedicated inventory, and special orders at no additional cost. The key to success with these customers was service, additional support after the sale, and knowledge of the products.

The PC Maintenance Follow-Up Study

Bankers followed up with a PC maintenance study that covered 16 areas in a more complex and analytically challenging survey. The areas covered included the users' PC support environment, software and hardware standards and support, vendor relationships, pricing methods, and performance criteria. Thirteen companies participated. Because responses were limited to the New York metropolitan area, the installed base was somewhat smaller at 60,000 PCs.

The results of the maintenance survey showed that the average respondent expected response times of 1-2 hours for workstations and one hour or less for servers. Times to repair or "fix," were somewhat longer in each case.

In summarizing the results of the study, Bankers had these observations regarding the end user organizations represented:

- Users strongly differentiate between PC workstation and server support requirements.
- Vendor reporting (i.e., performance and management) is a sore spot with most organizations.
- Breakages, fixes, and maintenance are generally outsourced.
- Software support, help desk, and LAN support are not generally outsourced.
- Organizations perceive a lack of vendor-supported asset management systems.
- There is a high level of dissatisfaction with vendors. (Less than 20% of the respondents were completely satisfied.)

The Roundtable meets irregularly to address common issues of technology management and recently met to discuss new directions in asset management.

ANALYZING EUC SERVICES VENDORS

This chapter presents a model for the EUC services industry to help organizations understand how to get better value and quality from the service vendors. The model takes into account the major drivers of cost and profitability for these providers, and relates those drivers to the profitability of the vendor for a particular client or customer. It is a valuable tool in negotiations and in obtaining successful vendor relationships.

As a simple example, consider the table provided by Information Week, as shown in Exhibit 30-1. The information as it stands is credible, but uninteresting. Adding one additional column, as shown in Exhibit 30-2, livens the data up quite a bit.

Service Revenue per Service Employee Ratios

The key ratio of service revenue per service employee (SR/SE) is one element of the model developed for end-user computing services vendors. There may be many explanations for the differences in this number—for example, how centralized the accounts are, how service employees are defined (i.e., direct versus indirect), or where corporate overheads show up. Organizations should make sure that they can clearly determine not

Exhibit 30-1. Information week table.

	Services Staff	1995 Revenue	Service as % of Total
Ameridata	700	$1.5 Billion	10%
Entex	2000	$1.5 Billion	10%
The Future Now	700	$795 Million	10%
Vanstar	2000	$1.4 Billion	14.3%
CompuCom	1080	$1.4 Billion	8%

Exhibit 30-2. Adding one column to information week's table.

	Services Staff	1995 Revenue	Service as % of Total	Revenue per Staff ($000)
Ameridata	700	$1.5 Billion	10%	$214
Entex	2000	$1.5 Billion	10%	$75
The Future Now	700	$795 Million	10%	$114
Vanstar	2000	$1.4 Billion	14.3%	$100
CompuCom	1080	$1.4 Billion	8%	$104

only the vendor's overall ratio, but also the ratio for their own accounts. Regardless of the vendor's overall ratio, an organization may be able to sustain a lower SR/SE ratio because service employees can be more productive if they are more centralized, have better desktop standards, or require less "high-end" support than the average account.

Managing Parts Inventories

Other key ratios in the model relate to parts inventories. From the EUC service vendor's perspective, there are two critical cost elements to every account—people and parts. Parts inventories are included in the model for several reasons. At the strategic level, inventory management is critical to the success of any vendor in this business. An organization should include detailed information on parts inventories in its request for proposal (RFP) and be concerned if the turnover ratio for a vendor is too low relative to their competitions. (A request for proposal is a document that invites a vendor to submit a bid for hardware, software, or services. It may contain a general or a very detailed specification of the system.)

At the account level, an organization should ask what parts are locally stocked and what accounts the vendor is dedicated to. A vendor's local or on-site inventories should be a significant proportion of their account revenue. Ratios of inventories should be examined for critical items (such as servers) and should be explicitly covered in the contract. If an organization is going to be a large customer, it should negotiate for on-site (i.e., dedicated) inventories.

Warranty Rebates, Non-Contract Labor Charges, and Software Support Ratios. There are several other aspects to the model, including warranty rebates, non-contract labor charges, and where appropriate, software support ratios. Bankers develops a specific model for the situation and challenges the vendor to agree or disagree with its analysis. The goal is not just cost reduction for the end user, but improvement in the vendor's ability to provide service.

For example, the end user may have a better manufacturer relationship for printer consumables than the vendor, and jointly agree that the end user will source them. Or both parties may agree to take equipment off maintenance if it is in neither party's interest to service it. These situations are often revealed by "red flags," that are set off when model parameters (such as parts cost/asset value) are exceeded.

Monitoring the Vendor's Financial Ratios. An organization should also keep a close eye on the vendor's financial ratios, both at the corporate level and at the account level. This is not as difficult as it may seem. The information at the corporate level is freely available, although not always as easy to interpret as this example from Ameridata's publicly-available filing, as displayed in Exhibit 30-3. The same kind of information can be generated from a company's internal accounting systems as a model of how its account appears to service provider. A corporate accounting system usually provides information on exactly how much the company has paid a vendor for what services or products.

An organization should know what staffing the vendor has allocated for its account so that it can accurately estimate employee costs and overheads. The company can get a record of the parts used for its account from the vendor, and estimates of the wholesale cost of those parts from third-party parts suppliers. The company can even estimate sales and marketing costs from the vendor's corporate financials.

Exhibit 30-3. Ameridata's publicly-available filing.

	($000)	
Net Product Revenues	389,040	
Cost of Product Revenues	345,993	
Gross Product Margin	43,047	11.1%
Net Services Revenue	37,235	
Cost of Services	22,041	
Gross Services Margin	15,194	40.8%

In summary, customers can become adept at figuring out where their vendor's profits and losses are and what their margins are on their accounts. This is critical information in managing both cost and risk effectively. It is no secret that the biggest vendor profits are in high-end services, not in distribution or the competitive and parts-intensive break/fix business.

THE "CONTINUUM OF SERVICES" PERSPECTIVE

Today's Fortune 500 company is rapidly transitioning toward networked PC workstation environments. Dispatch centers have evolved into sophisticated help desks. LAN support and PC software support now play a critical role in the IT infrastructure for most organizations. The end user recognizes the need for a "continuum of services" to support the PC workstation environment. This continuum, as shown in Exhibit 30-4, begins with product selection and includes management of:

- Configuration and installation of hardware and software.
- LAN design, implementation, and maintenance.
- Hardware breaks and fixes.
- Software support and training.
- Moves, adds, and changes.
- Help desk support.
- Technology refreshment.
- Technology assessment.
- Asset management.
- Product disposition.

The user looks to the marketplace for partial or total support in some or all of these areas.

Traditionally, because of the impracticality of controlling large parts inventories, the user has outsourced hardware breaks and fixes. This market is not only experiencing dynamic growth, it is redefining itself as it grows. It is now populated with "outsourcers" such as AT&T, Electronic Data Systems Corp., Digital Equipment Corp., Unisys Corp., and IBM Corp.; national third-party maintainers (TPMs); and value-added resellers (VARs).

Consider, for example, the perspective of an end user who is a technology executive with a Fortune 500 company with 5,000 PCs in a campus environment where 80% of the PCs are LAN-connected. As the user tracks the rampant acquisition and divestiture activity in the IT industry, he or she probably asks a few simple questions: "Will this newly emerging market benefit the organization?" "Will the economies of scale created by this oligopolistic market reduce the cost of support services?" "Does this provide a direct line of desktop support for the continuum of services?" These questions are logical. After all, product selection is larger and costs are lower in a chain supermarket compared with a local grocery store.

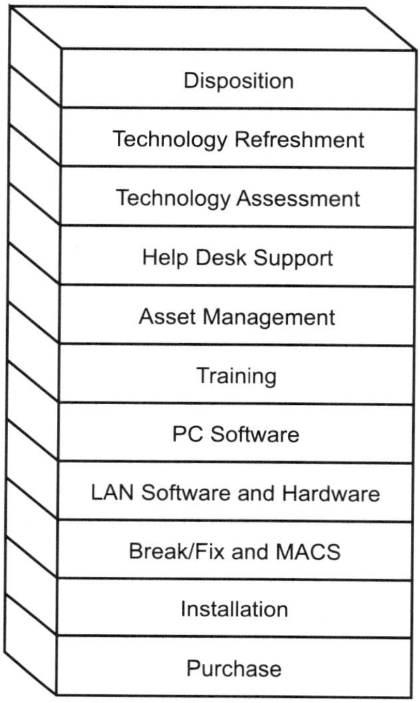

Exhibit 30-4. Continuum of services.

If users dig further into the marketplace, they may be disappointed. An RFP soliciting for the lower two-thirds of the "continuum of services"—PC procurement and distribution, hardware breaks and fixes through the help desk—would likely be sent to top-tier outsourcers, original equipment manufacturers (OEMs), national and local TPMs, and VARs. No one vendor is likely to satisfy the request for even this range of support services without subcontracting and alliances. No one vendor is likely to have strong references across the total range of requested services. Nor is any one vendor likely to have an existing relationship that they can clone to meet the user's request. The user would be forced to abandon the "total life cycle" concept for a one-piece-at-a-time solution.

COST OF OWNERSHIP AND THE END USER

The aggressive end user is constantly assessing the company's needs and studying the market for solutions. Users as well as vendors employ the services of large consulting organizations such as Dataquest or the Gartner Group for market assessment and strategic direction.

The most popular metric in the industry today is the Gartner Group's Total Cost of Ownership (TCO) PC Support Cost Model. In this model, "hard" costs include capital, administration, and support. End-user costs consist of peer support, supplies, data management, application development, and formal and casual learning. These end-user costs make up more than 50% of the total.

All major services vendors use the Gartner Group TCO concept in their sales efforts, ranging from sales support offerings to marketing claims. The differentiation is in how effectively they can implement services to support the TCO.

The most uncontrollable issue the end user sees in PC services is the inventory asset management problem. The vast majority of users are not satisfied with the inventory asset management systems they have in place. Unfortunately, asset management impacts all other support services and has a major impact on TCO. For example, leasing cannot be seriously considered without asset management, and technology refreshment and disposition needs inventory controls. Strategies cannot be developed if the users do not know where the equipment is and who is using it.

Gartner Group models and similar analyses can steer the user to tangible cost savings. However, vendors should not claim an ability to deliver service offerings that bring efficiency and affect savings in all areas of the PC life cycle, when more than 50% of the costs are intangible or immeasurable. And reliance on TCO from Gartner and others does not preclude the need to accurately measure the costs within the organization.

MOVING TOWARD CREDIBLE SERVICE OFFERINGS

The strategic consultants, industry watchers, and forecasters bring clarity to a complicated computer systems support industry. To the end users, however, it often seems as though vendors are using these resources not as helpful marketing input, but rather as the basis for marketing direction and strategy. VARs, OEMs, and TPMs all seem to be marching in lockstep with their commitment to the concept of "total life cycle support".

The vendors of this industry, instead of universally adopting the "total life cycle support" theme, should be using their own knowledge of their customers' needs and issues in developing an effective marketing strategy. Marketing departments should be developing service strategies that are strongly influenced by the company's sales strengths, resources, and hands-on experience. Expansion of service offerings should be planned and sold by the vendor in key accounts with pilot programs in such areas as asset management.

Despite the desire to retain control over all "core" technologies, the reality is that end users will be forced to cede to competent service vendors those areas where they can demonstrate a value added. It will be impossible for any user organization to focus effectively across the full spectrum of technologies. With the expanding scope of technology comes opportunity for the services provider who can clearly focus on adding value, particularly in those areas that are rapidly becoming standardized while retaining the promise of reasonable profit margins.

There is potential for vendors to provide help desk support and automation, asset management, LAN installation and support, and network management. Exhibit 30-5 shows how vendor support capabilities are expected to expand over the next few years. The ability to rely on standard protocols—such as TCP/IP—for internetworking and interoperability allows the end user to focus on vendor performance and cost rather than constantly working to resolve cross-vendor architecture and accountability issues.

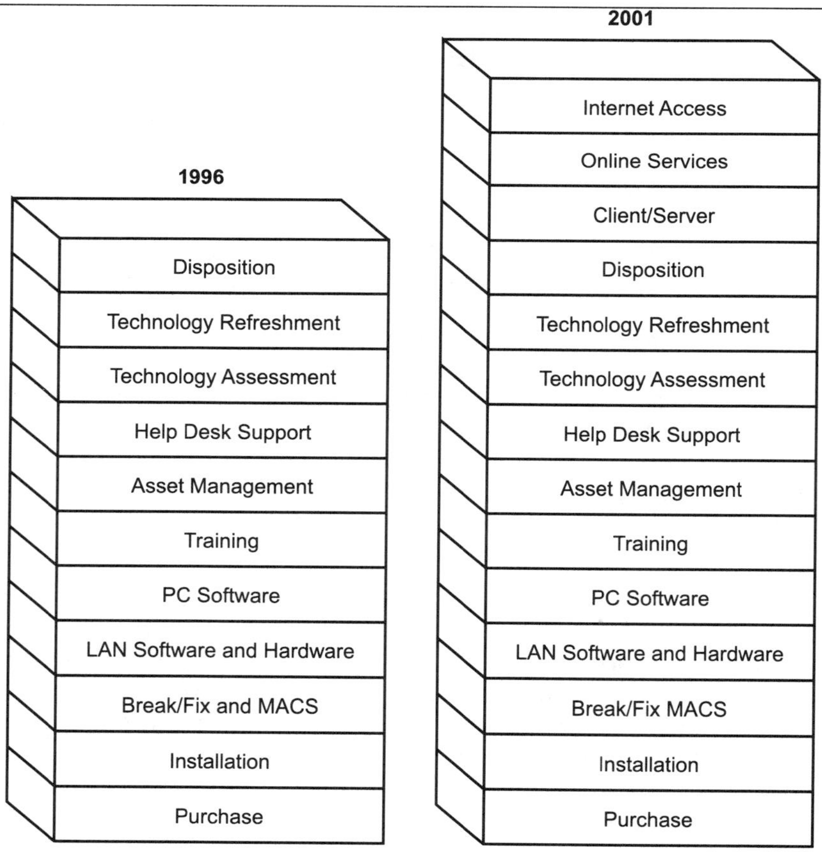

Exhibit 30-5. Continuum of services comparison.

RECOMMENDED COURSE OF ACTION

To effectively manage EUC support vendors, organizations should:

- Work toward a win/win relationship with the vendors.
- Commit to purchase volumes in exchange for a "cost plus" contract.
- If possible, negotiate directly with manufacturers and software publishers.
- Establish and track service performance metrics.
- Benchmark test with peers.
- Develop a model of profitability for the EUC services vendor.
- Avoid multiple markups by dealing directly with the service provider whenever possible.
- Monitor vendor financial performance and be alert to structural changes.
- Look for opportunities to outsource in cases where vendors can demonstrate value added.

Chapter 31 Organizing for Disaster Recovery

Leo A. Wrobel

LAN MANAGERS, COMMUNICATIONS MANAGERS, AND OTHER TECHNICAL SERVICE PROFESSIONALS ARE USUALLY CALLED ON TO WRITE DISASTER RECOVERY PLANS FOR THE SYSTEMS FOR WHICH THEY ARE RESPONSIBLE. Whether they realize it or not, these professionals already have a disaster recovery plan in place. These individuals are most familiar with the layout of the technical platform they are protecting, whether it is a LAN or PBX. They have probably been involved in the design, layout, and construction of the system since its inception. In short, they are the most knowledgeable and competent people to recover that system in the event of a disaster. They are a disaster recovery plan.

The problem is, this plan resides in their heads and is generally not committed to paper. Most key technologists are consumed by the daily operations of the network, leaving little or no time for long-term planning pursuits such as disaster recovery. Because these key technologists are highly skilled at their jobs, they may become offended when asked to put a disaster recovery plan to paper, viewing such a request as a test to prove that they know their jobs.

Nothing could be further from the truth. The plan is necessary for a simple reason: what does a business do if its key technical personnel are unavailable during a disaster? Or worse, what if these key personnel are injured or incapacitated during the event? A clearly written disaster recovery plan is essential to allow another reasonably competent technician to come in and recover the organization when key people cannot.

This chapter reviews several generic items that must be covered in any effective disaster recovery plan—some of which are easily overlooked in disaster planning. The purpose is not to document the recovery process so that the technologist can recover the network; it is to document the processes so that an outsider can come in and do the job in the event key personnel are unavailable.

0-8493-0893-3/00/$0.00+$.50

NOTIFICATION PROCEDURES

Scenario: A security guard is walking through the building and notices water coming from under the door of an equipment room. What is the notification procedure? The guard would probably call a supervisor at home to report the situation and request that someone from facilities come and open the door. Would the supervisor in the facilities department then know the right person to notify of the situation?

This is somewhat a simplistic example, but it is important to consider how information flows through an organization in an emergency to ensure that everyone who needs to know about a situation is notified. Many companies handle responses to broad-based disasters through an Executive Management Team.

The Executive Management Team

Whether a department is involved in providing the LAN, communications, or another technical function, it needs to be able to respond to two different types of disasters. The first type is confined solely to the technical platform (e.g., a LAN server, PBX, or a mainframe computer). The second type of disaster is a broad-based disaster affecting numerous company departments. In the event that the company declares a corporatewide disaster, many departments—facilities, security, human resources, technical services, telecommunications, corporate communications (i.e., the company spokespersons who deal with the media), and perhaps even legal departments — must pitch in.

Responsibility for coordination of broad-based disasters encompassing many departments clearly falls within the jurisdiction of a chief executive officer (CEO). The executive management team (EMT) should therefore include a small core group of individuals who provide timely information to the executive so that an intelligent coordination of resources geared toward recovery of the company can be accomplished. The makeup of the EMT does not have to be a constant; the right mix of people to participate on the EMT may depend on the event.

Typically, the EMT members would locate to another building outside the main headquarters of the company, possibly in a conference room or other facility equipped with a small complement of phones, fax machines, administrative supplies, and other items necessary to coordinating the recovery process. After being notified of a disaster, the managers from the departments affected by the event (e.g., telecommunications, data center, technical services, and others) would arrive on site and make a preliminary damage assessment. Each manager would, in turn, report directly to the EMT on the extent of the damage. These department managers must define the level of the disaster (e.g., physical destruction of facilities or technical problems, either hardware or software based), and then inform the EMT whether the damage is confined solely to one technical system or requires a more widespread disaster declaration. Provisions in the company's disaster recovery plan must be made to determine who can officially declare a disaster. Typically, it is the CEO, chief information officer, or other high-level person participating in the event's EMT.

Critical Events Log. Each reporting manager is expected to open a critical events log immediately on notification of the disaster. One of the reasons for requiring a critical events log is that many command decisions will have to be made in rapid succession, and the managers supporting the recovery process may literally forget what they have done. A second reason for the critical events log is that it could be useful later in assessing liability as to what went right and what went wrong and in fine-tuning the recovery plan.

To summarize, the written disaster recover plan should include an EMT or, at a minimum, identify the responsible management involved in declaring a companywide disaster. Second, adequate command and control should be in place in the form of telephones, two-way radios, and other devices as well as administrative supplies and personnel. Finally, reporting procedures must be in place so that the EMT can make an intelligent decision as to the extent of the disaster and the appropriate corrective measures to take.

COORDINATING OFF-SITE RESOURCES

Once initial command and control has been accomplished and responsible employees have arrived on site, the actual recovery process itself begins. Recovery is not limited to restoration of the equipment; recovery also means identifying and restoring the key business functions vital to the well-being of the company.

During the initial hours or days following a disaster, the business environment for the company may be quite different from what employees are accustomed to. First and foremost, it is important to provide business continuity. At the same time, the restoration process involves getting back to business as usual as soon as possible, in which case equipment restoration becomes important. These are two different phases of recovery, but they must commence concurrently as part of the recovery process.

Commonly Overlooked Procedures

One of the first steps in a recovery plan is to immediately contact all major equipment vendors and telecommunications carriers and requesting an on-site representative. If the company subscribes to a commercial recovery center, provisions for activation of this center should be made.

There are, however, some less apparent, sometimes overlooked areas where procedures are needed. A recovery plan should contain provisions for employee travel and for dispensing cash in order to facilitate the rapid movement of people to recovery facilities. For example, how many employees carry credit cards? Many times, the people actually involved in the recovery process are not management people and they may not be accustomed to making last-minute travel plans. They may also not have an adequate supply of money and may be unable to travel to the recovery facility, especially if it is in another state. The company should have in place procedures to:

- Retain a travel agent who, in the event of a disaster, can keep a preplanned travel itinerary for each critical person.
- Establish a line of credit to allow airline tickets to be dispensed promptly, without individuals needing to charge a credit card.
- Request services from its bank to solve the problem of dispensing cash. One recovery plan for a multimillion-dollar company called for its bank to have a mobile bank on-site within two hours of a disaster staffed by two people. The on-site bank handled all of the accounting for cash disbursements in order to move people around.

The establishment of an on-site bank to ensure employees' financial needs were met was an ingenious solution. Because the company demanded the services of a key vendor already familiar with and capable of the processes associated with dispensing cash, the work was accomplished in an afternoon. Had a technologist member of a recovery team been assigned the unfamiliar task of writing a procedure for dispensing cash, it might have taken weeks to coordinate all of the departments within the company. Further provisions should be made in the plan for calling companies that specialize in after-the-fact disaster restoration. These companies are familiar with dealing with many types of contaminants, resurrecting circuit boards and equipment, and even with saving magnetic media and paper documentation by various freeze-dry processes.

The importance of calling these companies promptly after a disaster cannot be overstated. Many times, 24 hours makes all the difference in the world as to whether equipment can be resurrected or has to be scrapped. For example, burning Permanent Virtual Circuit (polyvinyl chloride) on cable creates sulfides, which when mixed with water creates a diluted sulfuric acid. Once this hits the equipment directly or spreads through the building in the form of droplets through the air-conditioning system, the equipment becomes irreparably damaged within 24 hours. Salvage operations for equipment can commence immediately if telephone numbers for companies that specialize in clean-up operations are on hand. The 24-hour hotline for one such company, BMS Catastrophes, is (800) 433-2940.

EMPLOYEE REACTIONS TO THE RECOVERY PROCESS

Scenario: It is Sunday night and a gas explosion and fire have occurred at a principal place of business. The first thing that races through the technical services director's mind is to call in Pat, the department's top technologist. The director phones the employee's home to ask Pat to report to work immediately. Only the employee's spouse answers the phone and, with some alarm, says that Pat is supposed to be at work.

There are two important lessons here. The first is to be sensitive to the reactions of family members when calling employees in after a disaster. Many IS employees work at odd hours. In this case, the call to Pat's spouse caused some anguish.

The second point this example drives home is that it is not sound practice to rely too heavily on one key employee. LAN managers in particular are known for keeping critical information close to the vest. If information is not properly documented, what happens if they are unavailable, incapacitated, or unwilling to help with the recovery process?

Getting Employees Back to Work

To be workable, a recovery plan must make provisions for its employees' personal affairs and well-being or at least take into account the time it will take for employees to get their personal situations in order before reporting back to work. In the aftermath of major hurricanes, such as Hurricane Hugo, dozens of companies have had to activate disaster recovery plans. In most cases, the plans executed adequately, but only after employees attended to their personal business first. Once employees were satisfied that their families were safe, then and only then did they return to work.

On the West Coast of the US, with the earthquake potential, mobility is a problem after a disaster. Any recovery plan that directs employees to go to an off-site storage facility or a recovery center should be carefully thought out. How reasonably can employees travel to a remote location if, for example, traffic lights are not working or there is major damage to city streets? Both of these situations are possibilities after a major earthquake. Once again, employees will need to ensure that their personal situations are in order before reporting back to work and it is difficult to set a time limit on them. What if, for example, there is the threat of looting in an employee's neighborhood, such as has occurred after some hurricanes of the past years? There are no easy answers to handling employees' personal commitments prior to a disaster. Some West Coast companies have gone as far as instructing employees to bring their families to the office with them. The reasoning is that a business facility would be a safe place for families after a major earthquake. From a liability standpoint, however, this arrangement could prove to be a nightmare.

Dealing with Disasters in Stages

Once employees are back at work and actively engaged in the recovery process, the problems are not over. Exhibit 31-1 graphs the typical level of employee motivation and drive at various stages after the disaster declaration.

The vertical axis in Exhibit 31-1 is a measurement for employee motivation, productivity, and drive; the horizontal axis represents time. Initially, the graph charts slope downward. At first everyone is confused or thinking about either the difficulty of the situation or about their need to find another job. At some point, however, the organization begins to realize that it can pull out of the situation. Everyone rallies and productivity skyrockets. Employees work 16-hour shifts, sleep on the job, and extend superhuman efforts to save the company and their jobs.

In Exhibit 31-1, point A corresponds roughly with the two- or three-day point in the recovery process. Even though people have begun to rally, productivity and drive drop. Productivity drops essentially because this is the point where employees drop. Most people can get four hours sleep, come in, and work the following day without any problem at all. If they get four hours'

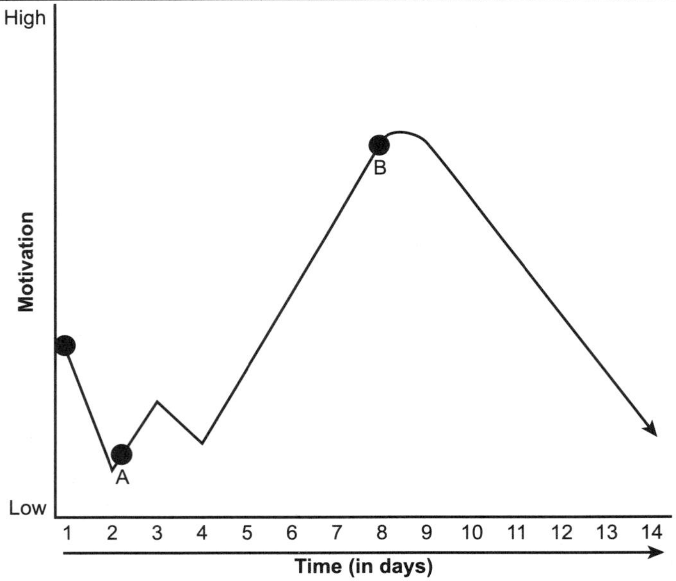

Note:
The slight sag on the rising line between points A and B is attributed to employees who simply work themselves to exhaustion in the first 72 hours of a disaster. Make provisions to force employees to cut back to 12-hour shifts at perhaps the 48-hour point.

Exhibit 31-1. Stages of employee motivation during a disaster.

sleep the second night, the third day when they come in, they are not working at the peak of their mental capacity, and they are tired. If a third night passes with only four hours sleep, most people are on the verge of not being able to work at all. This is what happens in the recovery process. After two or three days of 16-hour shifts and little sleep, the staff literally begins to burn out.

A business can make provisions to address this problem in the recovery plan by establishing a policy that on the second day, some employees will be sent home and the organization will begin alternate 12-hour shifts. This is not to say that 12-hour shifts are pleasant, but they are at least sustainable over time and will alleviate the employee burnout problem. Without this type of provision, employees sometimes literally work themselves sick, which does not benefit anyone in the long run.

At a later stage in the recovery process, point B in Exhibit 31-1, something equally predictable happens. Just as the organization realizes it is going to make it, the chart drops significantly. By this time, employees have had several weeks of working double shifts. They may be situated in a dark basement, working on a temporary configuration. They begin to miss their old offices and social relationships within the office. In essence, they become burned out once more. Recruiters may start calling employees. Some of them will leave. Others will simply crack under the pressure and have to go on disability. What if one of these people is a key technologist?

To summarize, management must consider the human element in the recovery plan and how employees will react to stressful personal and work situations. Human factors should be reflected in the company's notification procedures, in procedures that eschew an overreliance on a handful of key individuals, and in provisions that can help alleviate employee burnout at a time when they are needed most.

RECOMMENDED COURSE OF ACTION

Disaster recovery planning is a complicated process, but it need not be an overwhelming one. Technical service managers must write a plan in concert with the normal flow of information within an organization and with the involvement of other departments that contribute different areas of specialty. Managers can use the checklist that follows, which includes several emergency procedures that are not always readily apparent or included in many recovery plans:

- Pay attention to coordination between departments, such as between security and facilities and the technical service staff, to ensure that the people who should be notified in a disaster are notified promptly.
- Explore or suggest the concept of using an Executive Management Team to facilitate command and control in a disaster and to coordinate a companywide response if required.

- Keep accurate listings of vendors and carriers, as well as an escalation list, and request that a vendor representative is present on site immediately after a disaster to aid in the recovery process.
- Keep telephone numbers of restoration companies on hand and document provisions for initiating the restoration process, especially during the first critical 24 hours, when equipment can still be salvaged.
- If the company subscribes to a commercial recovery company, work in concert with its representatives to codify the recovery plan and make sure it meshes seamlessly with what the commercial recovery company can provide.
- Pay close attention to the well-being of employees, from the initial notification procedures throughout the duration of the disaster. Employees may rally under a stressful situation and even appear to give superhuman effort, but they will reach a point where they will burn out unless the company pays close attention and creates a work schedule to alleviate some of the pressure.
- Consider providing outside resources well-versed in recovery planning methodologies to assist the current technical service staff, which are undoubtedly consumed in operations and may not have the time to pursue recovery planning. Especially in a time of downsizing or rightsizing, outside support can be merited and justified. Even with this support, recovery plans can take months or years to completely underwrite. Without adequate support, a formal disaster recovery plan is generally not underwritten, and the company remains vulnerable indefinitely.

Section V
The Future Today

CIO PROFESSIONALS REALIZE THAT THE FUTURE HAS ARRIVED. The changes emerging in data management incorporate technology that was only under development in the mid-1990s. The capabilities for data warehousing and data mining offer a wealth of opportunity to an enterprise. Distribution of information and the tools for ready access are available for optimization of the Web.

Change is observed in how data management staff can use data link switching to transport SNA traffic over an IP network and offers new advantages for an alternative in enterprise extender. Comparisons and contrasts between the two technologies within this section provide data management staff assistance in determining the most appropriate techniques for a given enterprise.

In addition, Web-to-host connectivity tools offer an entire range of tools for end-user to data source access. Implementing these state-of-the-art tools is easier with the framework provided.

Looking into the future of technology involves lessons learned from effective technology still in use today. Manufacturing concerns are using refined ERP systems to streamline their planning and resource allocation as well as integrate their business processes across the enterprise. Along with these systems is a look at the changing manufacturer distribution model. This changing model is refined for Internet and short product lifecycle considerations. Full details of the change are captured in the business-to-business and business-to-customer model. Chapter 36 reveals the flexibility required by current CIO professionals.

Finally, a full discussion of the tools available to help gain and maintain customer loyalty is offered in the discussion on customer relationship management tools. As discussed, these tools provide a method of integration in stages throughout an enterprise to optimize resources as well as measure effectiveness.

This section will assist the CIO in planning the direction of the enterprise, using as many of the components currently available within the data management environment. It also strives to help the CIO plan for the chaotic change environment that is prevalent across industries in today's marketplace. The chapters listed below permit the CIO to focus on the vision necessary for the needs of the specific enterprise to position for data management for the future.

- Web-enabled Data Warehousing
- Enterprise Extender: A Better Way to Use IP Networks
- Web-to-Host Connectivity Tools in Information Systems
- Business-to-Business Integration Using E-commerce
- Customer Relationship Management

Chapter 32
Web-enabled Data Warehousing

Nathan J. Muller

A DATA WAREHOUSE IS AN EXTENSION OF THE DATABASE MANAGEMENT SYSTEM (DBMS), WHICH CONSOLIDATES INFORMATION FROM VARIOUS SOURCES INTO A HIGH-LEVEL, INTEGRATED FORM USED TO IDENTIFY TRENDS AND MAKE BUSINESS DECISIONS. For a large company, the amount of information in a data warehouse could be up to several trillion bytes, or terabytes (TB). The technologies that are used to build data warehouses include relational databases; powerful, scalable processors; and sophisticated tools to manipulate and analyze large volumes of data and identify previously undetectable patterns and relationships.

The benefits of data warehousing include increased revenue and decreased costs due to the more effective handling and use of massive amounts of data. Data warehousing applications are driven by such economic needs as cost reduction or containment, revenue enhancement, and response to market conditions. In being able to manage data more effectively, companies can improve customer satisfaction and cement customer loyalty. This can be done by sifting through the data to identify patterns of repeat purchases, determine the frequency and manner with which customers use various products, and assess their propensity to switch vendors when they are offered better prices or more targeted features. This kind of information is important because a change of only a few percentage points of customer retention can equate to hundreds of millions of dollars to a large company.

The benefits of data warehousing now can be extended beyond the corporate headquarters to remote branch offices, telecommuters and mobile professionals. Virtually anyone with a Web browser and an Internet connection can access corporate data stores using the same query, reporting and analysis tools previously reserved for technically elite number crunchers using expensive, feature-rich client/server tools. The Web-enabled data warehouse makes it possible for companies to leverage their investments

0-8493-0893-3/00/$0.00+$.50

in information by making it available to everyone who needs it to make critical business decisions.

SYSTEM COMPONENTS

The data warehousing framework typically encompasses several components:

- An information store of historical events (the data warehouse).
- Warehouse administration tools.
- Data manipulation tools.
- A decision support system (DSS) that enables strategic analysis of the information.

A key capability of the DSS is data mining, which uses sophisticated tools to detect trends, patterns, and correlations hidden in vast amounts of data. Information discoveries are presented to the user and provide the basis for strategic decisions and action plans that can improve corporate operational and financial performance.

Among the many useful features of a DSS are an automatic monitoring capability to control runaway queries; transparent access to requested data on central, local, or desktop databases; data-staging capabilities for temporary data stores for simplification, performance, or conversational access; a drill-down capability to access exception data at lower levels; import capabilities to translators, filters, and other desktop tools; a scrubber to merge redundant data, resolve conflicting data, and integrate data from incompatible systems; and usage statistics, including response times.

The latest trend in data warehouses is to integrate them with the corporate intranet for access by remote users with browser-enabled client software. The primary purpose of Web-enabling a data warehouse is to give remote offices and mobile professionals the information they need to make tactical business decisions.

A variety of toolkits are available that allow developers to create canned reports that can be hosted on the corporate Web site. In some cases, users can drill down into these reports to uncover new information or trends. With more sophisticated Web-based online analytical processing (OLAP) tools, users can access directly the corporate data warehouse to do simple queries and run reports. With the resulting information, reports can be culled to provide information that remote users need for their everyday decisions.

At a retail operation, for example, a store manager might tap into a canned sales report to figure out when a specific item will run out of stock, whereas a business analyst at the corporate headquarters might use client/server OLAP tools to analyze sales trends at all the stores so strategic purchasing decisions can be made.

For users who need more than static HTML documents, but like the convenience of Web browsers, there are plug-ins that dynamically query the back-end database. With such tools, employees can do things like drill down into the reports to find specific information. At an insurance company, for example, users might have the ability to drill down to a particular estimate line within a claim. This granularity might let a user determine how many claims relate to airbags and how long and at what cost it takes to repair them. Such information can be used to determine the discount drivers qualify for if their vehicle is equipped with airbags.

Making a data warehouse accessible to Web users solves a dilemma faced by many companies. On one hand, they do not want to limit users by only providing predefined HTML reports that cannot be manipulated. On the other, they do not want to overwhelm users with an OLAP tool they are not trained to understand. A Web-based OLAP tool that allows some interactivity with the data warehouse offers a viable alternative for users who are capable of handling simple queries. In turn, this makes corporate information more accessible to a broader range of users, including business analysts, product planners, and salespeople.

Because not everybody has the same information requirements, some companies have implemented multiple reporting options:

- Canned reports: these are predefined, executive-level reports that can only be viewed through the Web browser. Users need little to no technical expertise, knowledge of the data, or training because they can only view the reports, not interact with them.
- Ready-to-run reports: for those with some technical expertise and knowledge of the data, report templates are provided that users fill in with their query requirements. Although dynamic, these reports are limited to IS-specified field values, fill-in boxes, and queries.
- Ad-hoc reports: for the technically astute who are familiar with the data to run freeform queries, unlimited access to the data warehouse is provided. They can fill in all field values, choose among multiple fill-in boxes, and run complex queries.

WEB WAREHOUSE ARCHITECTURE

Many vendors offer Web tools that support a tiered intranet architecture comprising Web browsers, Web servers, application servers, and databases (Exhibit 32-1). The Web servers submit user requests to an application server via a gateway such as the common gateway interface (CGI) or server API. The application server translates HTML requests into calls or SQL statements it can submit to the database. The application packages the result and returns it to the Web server in the proper format. The Web server forwards the result to the client.

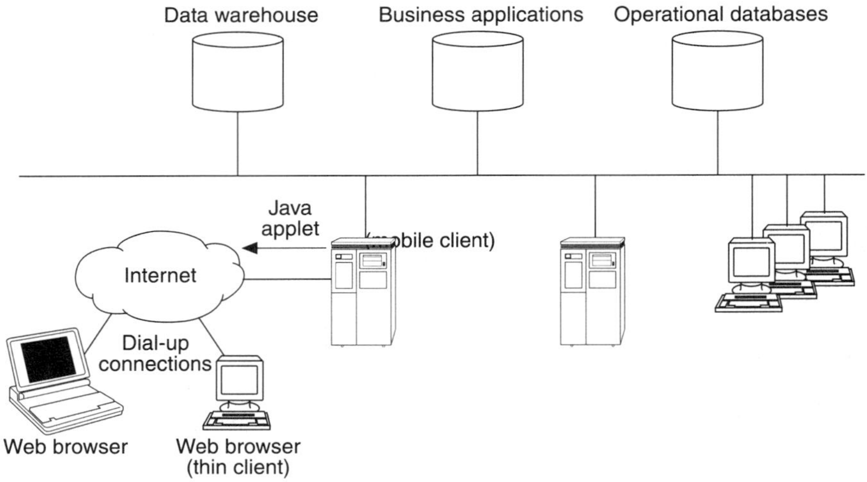

Exhibit 32-1. Tiered architecture for web-enabled warehouses.

This model can be enhanced with Java applets or other client-side programs. For example, the query form can be presented as a Java applet, rather than the usual CGI. Among the advantages of a Java-based query form is that error-checking can be performed locally rather than at the server. If certain fields are not filled in properly, for example, an appropriate error message can be displayed before the query is allowed to reach the server. This helps control the load on the server.

An all-Java approach provides even more advantages because connecting clients and servers at the network and transport layers is much more efficient than doing so at the application level using CGI scripts. This means users can design and execute queries and reports much more quickly than they can with other types of tools.

SECURITY

Obviously, a data warehouse contains highly sensitive information, so security is a key concern for any company contemplating a Web-enabled data warehouse. Not only must the data warehouse be protected against external sources, many times it must be protected against unauthorized access from internal sources as well. For example, branch offices might be prevented from accessing each other's information, or the engineering department might be prevented from accessing the marketing department's information, and all departments might be prevented from accessing the personnel department's records. Security can be enforced through a variety of mechanisms from user names and passwords to firewalls and encrypted data transmissions.

The use of Java offers additional levels of security. Applets that adhere to the Java cryptography extensions (JCE) can be signed, encrypted and transmitted digitally via secure streams to prevent hackers from attacking applets during transmission. Specifically, JCE-based applets make use of Diffie-Hellmann authentication, a technology that enables two parties to share keys, and data encryption standard (DES) for scrambling the data for transmission.

Some Web-enabled OLAP and DSS tools are designed to take advantage of the secure sockets layer (SSL) protocol, which protects data transferred over the network through the use of advanced security techniques. The SSL protocol provides security that has three basic properties:

- Connection privacy: encryption is used after an initial handshake to define a secret key.
- Data protection: cryptography algorithms such as DES or RC4 are used for data encryption. The peer's identity can be authenticated using a public key.
- Connection reliability: message transport includes an integrity check based on a keyed message authentication code (MAC).

SSL is being considered by the Internet Engineering Task Force (IETF) as the official Internet standard for transport layer security (TLS).

OPTIMIZATION TECHNIQUES

Some Web-based development tools optimize database interactivity by giving users the ability to access back-end databases in real time. Users can submit queries against the entire database or refresh existing reports to obtain the most up-to-date data. In addition to providing for more flexible report generation, this dynamic report creation environment minimizes the need to manage and store physical reports online, which streamlines storage requirements. However, some servers also can deliver copies of pre-executed reports to users who do not need to filter existing reports and want to optimize data delivery.

Other Web tools optimize functionality by giving users the ability to manipulate returned data in real time. Users can drill up, down or across data, apply calculations, toggle between charts and tables, and reorganize the local data. Through the use of Java and ActiveX, a high degree of interactivity between the user and data is now possible over the Web.

VENDOR OFFERINGS

Many vendors of DSS and OLAP tools now offer Web versions of their products, each differing in terms of features and ease of use. Exhibit 32-2 summarizes the offering of the five vendors discussed here. All of them strive to extend data warehouse query and reporting capabilities to a

Exhibit 32-2. Select vendors of web-enabled DSS and OLAP tools.

Company	Product	Platform	Databases
Brio Technology, Inc. 3950 Fabian Way Suite 200 Palo Alto, CA 94303 USA Tel. +1 650 856 8000 Fax. +1 650 856 8020	brio.web.warehouse	Windows NT, Macintosh, Unix	Oracle Express
Business Objects, SA 2870 Zanker Road San Jose, CA 95134 USA Tel. +1 408 953-6000 Fax. +1 408 953 6001	WebIntelligence	Windows NT	Arbor Essbase, Oracle Express
Information Advantage, Inc. 7905 Golden Triangle Drive Eden Prairie, MN 55344 USA Tel. +1 612 833 3700 Fax. +1 612 833 3701	DecisionSuite Server, WebOLAP	Unix	IBM DB2, Informix, Oracle, Red Brick, Sybase, Tandem, Teradata
Infospace, Inc. 181 2nd Avenue Suite 218 San Mateo, CA 94401 Tel. +1 650 685 3000 Fax. +1 650 685 3001	SpaceOLAP, SpaceSQL	Unix, Windows NT or IBM mainframe	Arbor Essbase, IBM DB2, Oracle Express
MicroStrategy, Inc. 8000 Towers Crescent Drive Vienna, VA 22182 Tel. +1 703 848 8600 Fax. +1 703 848 8610	DSS Web	Windows NT	IBM DB2, Informix, Oracle, Red Brick, Sybase, SQL Server, Tandem, Teradata

greater number of users who otherwise may not be able to access corporate information stores and database systems, because conventional tools are either too complex for the average person to use, or too expensive for general distribution and maintenance by IS staff.

Brio Technology

Brio Technology, Inc. (Palo Alto, CA) offers a scalable server suite called brio.web.warehouse that provides a full-featured Web-based query, reporting and analysis solution for the extended enterprise. Through the use of push and pull technologies, organizations efficiently and economically can distribute business-critical information to a broad range of users, across mixed computing environments.

Brio offers a choice of servers. One provides information on-demand through the use of client pull technology and the other distributes information on a scheduled basis through the use of server push technology. The choice depends on how the organization wants to make information available to users. Both servers are available in Windows NT and UNIX versions.

The company's Broadcast Server runs scheduled queries and pushes precomputed reports and documents to Internet, client/server and mobile users via FTP, E-mail, Web, and file servers. Reports also can be sent directly to any network printer from the Broadcast Server. With push technology, the user subscribes to predefined reports and documents, which are delivered automatically when ready — without having specifically to request them. The canned reports are viewed with Web client software called Brio.Quickview.

The company's OnDemand Server is a Web application server that delivers full-featured ad-hoc query, reporting, and analysis functionality over the Web using client pull technology. Pull technology simply means that the user specifically must request information from the server using a query form.

The OnDemand Server provides users with the capability to conduct queries across the Web. Query execution is performed on the server, which then builds reports and transmits them in compressed form back to Brio.Insight Web clients. Recipients then can engage in personal reporting and analysis using the exact same functionality and user interface offered in the company's client/server based BrioQuery Navigator product.

However, analysis often leads to new questions, which require ad-hoc querying. Brio.Insight can adapt its functionality based on the contents of the report and the user's security profile. This means that users can do a certain amount of ad-hoc querying, but without having free-form control over information they only should be allowed to view.

The reporting backlog of busy IS departments can be reduced by granting analysis and ad-hoc querying capabilities to specific users or groups of users on a report-by-report basis. Five different functional modes dynamically can be enabled from view-only to full query-and-analysis. A built-in Wizard creates a Web page where decision makers can find a list of available reports — each with its own set of analysis and formatting functionality privileges. This frees IS staff to focus on publishing or giving access to data anywhere in the extended enterprise.

The OnDemand Server also supports zero-administration of clients. The server automatically installs and updates Brio.Quickview and Brio.Insight on client machines. Upon opening a report on the Web, users are notified to download the appropriate Web extension, new patch, or latest upgrade. This capability lowers the total cost of ownership for IS organizations because the need to install and maintain complex middleware and client/server software across diverse platforms is eliminated.

Business Objects

Business Objects, SA (San Jose, CA) offers IS organizations the means to deploy broadly DSS capabilities and extend DSS beyond the enterprise to reach suppliers, partners, and customers over the Web. The company's multitier, thin-client WebIntelligence solution provides nontechnical end users with ad-hoc query, reporting, and analysis of information stored in corporate data warehouses, data marts, and packaged business applications.

Via a Java query applet, users autonomously can request data using familiar business terms, analyze the data by viewing it from different perspectives and in different levels of detail, and share the information with other users in the form of formatted reports.

The WebIntelligence report catalog and search engine enable users to find and access specific documents quickly. Like Brio Technology's product, WebIntelligence takes advantage of both the push and pull models of document distribution. With a few drag-and-drop actions, users can pull fresh data in new or existing documents and, after applying simple formatting options, push the reports to wide populations.

Users also can reach beyond the corporate data mart or data warehouse and tap into the resources of the Web to enrich their reports with other useful information. WebIntelligence includes a feature called hyperdrill, which allows the report cells themselves to be hyperlinks that can drill out of a report and into any Internet-based data source. Using hyperdrill, for example, an accounts receivable report can include a hyperlink for each customer that, when pressed, activates a credit service to produce a current credit report for that customer.

WebIntelligence can run on a single machine or be distributed across multiple servers. With multiple servers, WebIntelligence automatically performs load balancing to make the best use of system resources and ensure optimal response times. A multiserver configuration allows a backup server to be designated for automatic cutover in case another server becomes unavailable. It also allows components to be added easily to the system to meet increased user demand.

Together, the distributed architecture and Java query applet eliminate the need for client-side installation and maintenance of both application software and database middleware. As a Java-based solution, users require only a standard Web browser on their desktop to access to the information they need. Because the Java query applet does not take up permanent residence on the client machine, the most current copy of the applet is called by the Web browser when the user wants to perform a database query. This zero-administration client eliminates one of the key obstacles to wide-scale deployment of decision support technology — deployment cost.

User administration can be streamlined by assigning new users to groups. For each user or group, the resources they are allowed to access can be specified by the system administrator. In addition, WebIntelligence is designed to work with Web security standards such as the secure socket layer (SSL), which protects data transferred over the network through the use of advanced encryption algorithms.

With the WebIntelligence administration utility, distributed components can be started, stopped, configured and tuned over the Internet. At any time, the administrator can check which users are connected to the WebIntelligence system and monitor their activity. This information can be stored in a system log file for auditing purposes.

WebIntelligence can share the same metadata (e.g., the same business representation of the database) and the same security information as BusinessObjects, the company's client/server tool for decision support systems. The business representation of the database (also called a semantic layer), which is created to insulate users from the complexity of the data source, is available to both WebIntelligence and BusinessObjects users. Similarly, the security privileges defined to control each user's access to database information apply to both tools. Thus, only one DSS environment needs to be set up and maintained to support both Web and client/server users.

Information Advantage

Information Advantage, Inc. (Eden Prairie, MN) offers WebOLAP, a browser-based reporting and interactive analysis tool that extends the delivery of warehoused data over a corporate intranet, to business partners over an extranet, or to remote users over the Internet.

WebOLAP is supported by the company's DecisionSuite Server, a system that maximizes throughput in high-volume reporting environments by dynamically adding, managing and deleting concurrent processes initiated by requests from multiple users. This multi-user, network-centric design eliminates bottlenecks by maintaining persistence and state between the server and database, providing the means to create as many concurrent server processes as required to fulfill incoming requests.

Unlike Brio Technology and Business Objects, Information Advantage's WebOLAP does not provide a Java-based query applet. Instead, a CGI script is used to provide a link between the Web and its application server, which is still the most prevalent integration method. The DecisionSuite Server outputs OLAP report files in XLS, WK5, ASCII, or HTML formats.

WebOLAP indexes the data warehouse to corporate intranet or extranet metadata. Live, interactive OLAP views can be accessed directly from search engines, bookmarks, directories, hyperlinks and E-mail attachments for seamless integration of data warehouse analysis into corporate intranet sites.

Users can create, pivot, drill, and save reports and convert and download data to popular desktop productivity tools, such as spreadsheets and word processors. The WebOLAP system retains each new report so users have a clear audit trail of their journey through the data warehouse. WebOLAP saves and shares reports as live objects that contain the data and instructions used to create the reports. More than one user can interact and explore a single report. Each user receives a temporary instance of the object, so that he or she is free to take the analysis in any direction without affecting other users or the original report.

Users also can benefit from the monitoring and filtering capabilities of intelligent agents that work on their behalf to find information stored in the data warehouse. Agents filter out low-priority information and proactively deliver personalized OLAP information back to the user. Agents can deliver results to directory listings and/or notify the user directly through alerts or E-mail with interactive report attachments. A number of agents can be launched by the user and be active at the same time within the data store. Agent requests run in the background, keeping desktops free for other tasks. Agents save the user from having to personally surf and filter through gigabytes and terabytes of warehoused and derived data.

WebOLAP develops reports using a personalized library of private and published filter, calculation, and report template objects. Information objects can be recombined to create new and different analyses of the data warehouse. Reports can be delivered in multiple file formats, allowing users to integrate information within their current business workflow and personal productivity tools.

WebOLAP gives users the ability to cross-analyze data simultaneously from multiple data marts or data warehouses, regardless of data location or vendor RDBMS. A report subscription feature provides access to previously built report templates that can be personalized quickly with a user's parameters to save time and prevent the reinvention of popular reports. A groupware application provides seamless sharing of interactive reports and their assumptions to eliminate duplication of effort, ensure consistent analysis, and encourage collaboration.

Infospace

Infospace, Inc. (San Mateo, CA) offers two scalable, server-based data access and analysis solutions that work over the Web: SpaceOLAP and SpaceSQL. Both applications are written in Java. With the familiar Web browser, users are provided with data access to any relational or multi-dimensional database, data mart, or data warehouse, and even to other legacy data sources and objects via an open API.

Persistence and state are maintained between client and server and server and database, allowing data to pass freely and efficiently. To improve efficiency and performance, the server caches data and only delivers small packets of information to the user as needed. As the number of users increases, a load-balancing option also allows additional machines to start up automatically to meet demand.

Operating in UNIX, Windows NT, or mainframe environments, SpaceOLAP delivers most of the same functions as traditional client/server-based data analysis tools. It provides native access to Oracle Express Server 6.0, Arbor Essbase, and IBM DB2 OLAP Server.

SpaceOLAP consists of three client modules and one server module. Each client module is a different application that is accessed through a browser. The server module, called the Infospace Java Server, resides on the Web server. This module pulls data from data sources as requested by modules running on the client. SpaceOLAP Administrator is where administrators set up the users, user groups, and data sources of the system. SpaceOLAP Designer lets users and administrators create reports and graphs for the system. OLAP queries can be built from scratch, or the user can simply use predefined queries. SpaceOLAP Runtime lets users view the reports and graphs that have been created for them in their browsers.

SpaceOLAP enables the user to interact fully with the data in real time. In addition to drill-down, drill-up, pivoting, and selection capabilities, interactive presentations can include Java-based charts (SpaceCharts) and Java-based pivot tables (SpaceTable). With SpaceCharts, users can sort and select data dynamically, and resize and rotate charts. With SpaceTable, users can present the information with a Java-based pivot-table, which allows the user to slice and dice via pivoting and drill-down in a spreadsheet-like environment.

The company's other product, SpaceSQL, is a Java-based query, reporting, and charting tool that provides Web access to relational databases. It integrates graphical reporting with the Web-based point-and-click interface for direct access to Oracle, Informix, Sybase, and other relational databases over a corporate intranet.

The architecture comprises a client that runs within a Web browser and a server that resides alongside the Web server. SpaceSQL includes a Java-based design version for query, report, and chart definition and a runtime version for end-user viewing. It installs itself automatically on the client system when called.

The SpaceSQL designer allows users to define queries through a point-and-click interface. Advanced users can also use the SQL editor to directly import or enter SQL queries. Query results can be presented and analyzed by designing customized reports and interactive three-dimensional charts using the browser's intuitive interface. A Java-enabled Web client, like Netscape Navigator, is the only requirement on the client system; no additional hardware or software is required.

SpaceSQL produces output in a variety of formats including HTML, Java charts, .GIF, VRML, CSV (for Microsoft Excel compatibility), and Java tables. This allows users to gain insights into data, then communicate their ideas through standard E-mail by attaching one of the chart formats suited for the recipient's system.

Existing chart technologies provide static images only and offer less flexibility in presenting and viewing the chart according to each user's preferences. However, SpaceSQL enables users to interact with data and manipulate the displayed data. The interaction takes two forms — drill-down reports and three-dimensional charts.

Native RDBMS drivers and the multithreaded server provide database interaction. The persistent database connection is an improvement over typical HTML-based solutions, which constantly need to reconnect to the database. The charting is done completely on the client side, freeing up the server and facilitating scaling to a large number of users.

Reports can be scheduled to run when the system load is low. SpaceSQL also allows for periodic scheduling of reports — daily, weekly, or monthly. This is especially useful for running large reports without tying up network and processor resources. Depending on the sophistication of the user, he or she can design, run, and view reports and charts and immediately communicate the insights gained from this analysis over the corporate intranet.

MicroStrategy

MicroStrategy, Inc. (Vienna, VA) offers DSS Web, an OLAP tool that provides all types of end users with dynamic, interactive access to decision-support information. Starting with version 5.0, users can take advantage of webcasting for decision support. DSS Web 5.0 incorporates Internet push technology to automate the delivery of information to end users. Users can decide which reports they wish to subscribe to and have those reports automatically pushed to their desktops. DSS Web's Alerts & Exception Reporting feature enhances the automation of report delivery by allowing users to run reports that provide text alerts to exception conditions, such as record weekly sales or low item in stock. This feature allows users to focus on immediate business action instead of report creation.

Via a Web browser, remote users can share a central, corporate information repository to access data and conduct sophisticated analysis. For example, the DSS Web Report Wizard provides step-by-step instructions that allow users to define and save new reports. DSS Web AutoPrompts provide runtime customization of reports. And with features such as On-the-fly-Sorting and Outline Mode, users can view and modify their data in a variety of different ways. Reports in grid and graph modes can be sliced and diced with drill everywhere functionality. Interactive reporting features are achieved with Java and ActiveX technologies.

System administrators have the ability to manage the system from remote locations. Administrative changes can be made once through DSS Web and distributed to all Web browsers, eliminating complicated and expensive upgrades. In addition, decision support systems deployed with DSS Web can have up to four tiers of security at the browser, firewall, DSS Web and RDBMS levels.

Among other enhancements scheduled for later this year by MicroStrategy, DSS Web will support newspaper-like overviews of canned reports and other enhancements aimed at less technology-savvy users.

SELECTING A TOOL

In selecting a Web-enabled DSS or OLAP tool, attention must be given to the critical areas of security, data management, ease of use, and scalability.

Security

A data warehouse solution must include authentication so that the organization can be certain that each party requesting access to its information is indeed who they say they are. Authentication will prove the identity of a remote user, whether on the public Internet, an intranet, or an extranet that is shared by several business partners.

End-to-end encryption is vital to the protection of data during transmission, preventing eavesdropping. Public key technology is an effective solution. It uses a secret and a public key — the public key is sent with the query. The system encrypts the return data using that key. The user's secret key is then used to decrypt the coded information. If the DSS or OLAP vendor does not provide encryption, it can be added with a third-party solution.

The data warehouse solution should also provide the administrator with tools that control the access level each user should have. These tools can be used not only to stop departments from stepping on each other's toes, but to minimize the chances that databases will be corrupted by user error or mischief. Being able to set access levels is an important enforcement mechanism that imposes order on the otherwise chaotic flow of data to and from the company.

Data Management

Virtually everyone within an organization has the ability to create the documents that go into databases. What organizations lack most are the skills to manage all this data. Therefore, the warehouse product must include tools that facilitate the management and ongoing maintenance of vast stores of information.

At a minimum, the product should provide authors with the means to prioritize, label, and set expiration dates on the documents they create and, ideally, allow them to set access levels based on a corporate policy. If the documents are to have embedded hypertext links, there has to be some automated way of checking periodically the integrity of the links, which can become broken over time as new data is added and expired data is deleted.

Regardless of the warehouse product under consideration, it must be remembered that none is going to substitute for experienced staff who have a thorough understanding of the business and who can establish appropriate data definition parameters.

Ease of Use

Ease of use is perhaps the most difficult criterion to apply to the selection of a Web-enabled data warehouse solution, especially within an environment of diversely skilled users. The reason is that the same product must appeal to both low- and high-skilled users if the organization expects to leverage its investment in information systems.

Ideally, the product should not overwhelm less-experienced users by requiring technical mastery before a basic query can be launched. A warehouse product that supports push technology to serve predefined reports and documents automatically may be adequate for most users and does not require any training. Power users, however, must be provided with the features they need to dig deep into the information store and perform sophisticated trend analysis.

Picking the right tool requires an understanding of how various users intend to use the information. Do they just need to look at and refresh reports, for example, or do they need the capability of inputting new values and building queries from scratch? Can a range of user needs be accommodated in the same product, without imposing feature and performance tradeoffs on everyone?

Scalability

Scalability refers to the ability of the data warehouse solution to grow and adapt incrementally as organizational needs change. The data warehouse application must be scalable in several ways: the amount of data to be managed, the amount of users to be accommodated, and types of functions to be supported.

Because data tends to accumulate rather than diminish over time, the data warehouse solution must be able to maintain an acceptable level of performance to ensure optimal response, regardless of how much data there is to plow through. There are a number of ways to enhance server performance, such as implementing caching and balancing the load across several connected machines. In addition, the database server should be designed to accommodate easily such components as processors, memory, disk drives, and I/O ports to meet increased user demand.

In terms of functionality, the data warehouse solution should not only support the broadest range of users, but allow new functionality to be added with minimal disruption to business operations. Furthermore, it should be easy for users to migrate to higher level functions as they become more experienced or as their information needs change over time.

CONCLUSION

The Web enables organizations of all types and sizes to provide applications that deliver content to the end user without the traditional, costly barriers of installation, training and maintenance. Web-based decision support tools and data warehouses provide scalable solutions that can handle diverse requirements in dimensional analyss, support a large variety of financial calculations and enable secure collaborative analysis across all levels of the company.

In the mainframe-centric environment of the past, employees had to submit their information requirements in writing to IS staff and then wait two or three weeks for a report. Today, with a Web-enabled data warehouse, users can have immediate access to the information they need. The Web offers unparalleled opportunity to deliver business reports to huge numbers of users without the information bottlenecks of the past and without the headaches typically associated with rolling out and configuring new software.

In addition, the Web is easy to access on a global basis, supports a high degree of interactivity, and provides platform interoperability — capabilities that are difficult and expensive to achieve over non-TCP/IP networks. All the end user needs is a Web browser. The two most popular Java-enabled

Web browsers — Microsoft's Internet Explorer and Netscape Navigator — are free. End users get the most updated versions of Java applets automatically whenever they log onto the data warehouse, which virtually eliminates the need for IS staff to extend software support to every client machine.

Although the rich functionality and high performance of client/server tools cannot be duplicated yet on Web-based data warehouse offerings, this is not necessarily a handicap because the overwhelming majority of users only need to access predefined reports or execute limited queries. For this class of users, basic Web OLAP and DSS tools are appropriate. The relatively small number of technically elite users, who require the ability to interact with large data sets or create decision-support applications for others in the corporation, will continue to use the more powerful client/server tools to which they have become accustomed.

Chapter 33 Enterprise Extender: A Better Way to Use IP Networks

Richard J. Tobacco

MOST BUSINESSES RELY ON LEGACY APPLICATIONS RESIDING ON MAINFRAMES. Access to these applications and databases were through networks based on Systems Network Architecture (SNA). Newer application development is often aimed at E-business, and these applications are generally based on TCP/IP networks. Initially, business created and supported these SNA and TCP/IP networks separately. Today's cost-conscious network managers are seeking ways to consolidate their SNA traffic onto the TCP/IP network. Rewrite of the estimated $3 billion dollar investment in legacy SNA-based applications is clearly not justified.

Many businesses use TN3270e as their method of accessing those SNA applications. The TN3270e client communicates over a TCP/IP network to a TN3270e server that transforms the IP data-gram into an SNA data flow. The TN3270e server can be located within the application server, on a device channel attached to the application server, or on a branch office router. Unless the TN3270e server resides within the application server, there is a SNA data flow between the TN3270e and application servers. This SNA data flow can be transported across an IP network.

In 1992, IBM introduced Data Link Switching (DLSw) as a means for transporting Systems Network Architecture (SNA) data across a TCP/IP network. As the only nonproprietary TCP/IP encapsulation scheme, DLSw gained widespread acceptance by all routing vendors, and many customers use this as their method for accessing SNA applications across a TCP/IP network. Five years later, IBM created Enterprise Extender as an open alternative way to integrate SNA applications onto an IP network. Recently, Cisco Systems, Inc., announced that its routers will also provide the enterprise extender function — called SNA Switching Services (SNASw).

0-8493-0893-3/00/$0.00+$.50

Enterprise Extender is a network integration technology that provides the flexibility to build the networks that cost-conscious network managers demand. It is a technology that extends the reach of SNA applications and data across IP networks to IP-attached clients, while providing users with the levels of reliability, scalability, and control they have come to expect from mission-critical SNA-based applications. Enterprise Extender provides this integration using standard IP technology and requires no new hardware or software in the IP backbone network. The following is a quick look at the nomenclature of protocol transport and some of the differences between DLSw and Enterprise Extender.

TALKING TRANSPORT

A few transport analogies may aid network managers trying to describe the transport differences to fellow workers.

By Air, Land, or Sea: Link Selection

Companies have long had the option of selecting the mode of product shipment. Perishable goods might go by air, "normal" deliveries by truck, and bulky products via barge or container ship. SNA provides a similar selection; part of class-of-service, where different types of data can be transported across different links, for example, satellite, modems, or fiber. The capability to select network links based on application-specified class-of-service is only provided by SNA networking. Recent Internet Engineering Task Force (IETF) work on Differential Services has improved the ability to affect the link selection; however, Enterprise Extender allows the link to be selected.

Taking Familiar Routes: Connection Oriented

One drives to a favorite vacation spot along familiar roads, not altering one's route unless an unexpected detour is encountered. One knows the travel time and progress toward the final destination is readily apparent. If delayed, concerned friends might be able to ascertain one's progress by checking at one's favorite "stopping spots." In networking terms, one is *connection oriented.* Had one been out joyriding and decided the route at each intersection, one would (in networking terms) be *connection-less.*

Data path consistency, provided by a connection-oriented network, provides similar benefits to network managers. They can view data progress, check for congestion roadblocks, and monitor and plan for increases in traffic. High performance routing (HPR), a lower-overhead less-complex SNA, creates connection-oriented networks by providing the data path information to the routers and virtually eliminating router overhead for the SNA sessions. With Enterprise Extender, HPR-capable endpoints provide connection-oriented routes for the UDP/IP datagrams forwarded by the intermediate network routers (see Exhibit 33-1).

Exhibit 33-1. SNA and TCP/IP transport.

- First versions of SNA, designed to support networks with unreliable links, were very tightly coupled with data integrity checked at each path step. Improved link quality enabled SNA to be restructured with data verification only at the endpoints. This advanced SNA — High Performance Routing (HPR) — separates transport functions from data integrity functions.
- The similarity of HPR — an improved Advanced Peer-to-Peer Networking (APPN) SNA routing protocol — with TCP/IP may be apparent; end stations ensure data integrity and intermediate devices forward traffic. The intermediate — Automatic Network Routing (ANR) — nodes forward packets, have no session awareness, and rely on the endpoints for error recovery. The endpoint — Rapid Transport Protocol (RTP) — nodes provide end-to-end error recovery, nondisruptive rerouting, and selective retransmission of lost packets. People familiar with TCP/IP networks will relate RTP to the TCP portion and ANR to IP part of the TCP/IP stack. Both transports are valid and leading networking products will continue to support TCP/IP and SNA.
- A key difference between SNA and TCP/IP transport is that HPR sessions use the same path as long as it is available, whereas TCP/IP sessions may often change paths. Because the HPR endpoints establish a path and maintain it until a failure occurs, the intermediate routing devices use routing information contained within the transmitted packets. This eliminates the need for the routing devices to make routing decisions. If there is a path change, the packet labels are changed by the RTP endpoints.
- Separating transport and integrity functions also means that SNA messaging characteristics can be applied to SNA applications crossing an IP network. Enterprise Extender code provides priority queuing for SNA sessions, making IP transport appropriate for business-critical applications.

First Class or Coach: Priority Queuing

We have become accustomed to priorities in business. CEO air-travel arrangements are made first; they travel first class and avoid having to wait in long lines boarding or exiting the aircraft. Likewise, some data transmissions are more important to a business than others. Being able to assign priority based on the data type (e.g., interactive or batch) can mean business-critical data gets transmitted first. Access devices such as routers often create queues for data placed on the network. And IP networks can provide Type of Service (TOS) or port prioritization such that both SNA networks and the new application transport, Enterprise Extender, can provide priority transmission throughout the entire network.

Registered Shipments: Reliable Transport

Many have sent or received registered mail. At transfer points, the mail (or contents of a shipment) is accounted for prior to being forwarded. This additional effort of accounting for shipment integrity often results in slower and more costly delivery. If one generally finds that "normal" shipments reach their destination, one will rely on the final recipient to verify shipment integrity, thus reducing the cost of shipment. In TCP/IP networks, registered shipments are analogous to *reliable transport* and "normal" shipments are comparable to *unreliable transport.*

Network links have become more reliable and transmission error rates have declined significantly. Although it was more efficient, if not necessary, for SNA to verify message integrity at each transfer node in the 1960s, it is now possible to avoid the cost of additional processing overhead. Enterprise Extender uses unreliable UDP transport for forwarding SNA application data across a TCP/IP network. Message integrity is guaranteed by the session endpoints instead of each intermediate router within the network.

Packaging: Encapsulation

In networking parlance, placing a letter in an envelope is encapsulation. The envelope has an external address that is used by a carrier to route the letter to its destination. Once received, the envelope is discarded and the contents distributed as appropriate. DLSw is the encapsulation of SNA protocols within a TCP/IP "package." The package is a usable TCP/IP address that has been discovered by the DLSw-capable routers. Likewise, Enterprise Extender is the transport of SNA protocols within a "lighter" UDP package.

WHAT IS ENTERPRISE EXTENDER?

Enterprise Extender is an extension to HPR technology that provides efficient encapsulation of SNA application traffic within UDP frames by HPR-capable devices at the edges of an IP network. To the IP network, the SNA traffic is UDP datagrams that get routed without hardware or software changes to the IP backbone.

The Enterprise Extender session is "normal SNA" with predictable performance and high availability. Unlike gateways, there is no protocol transformation and, unlike most common tunneling mechanisms, the encapsulation is performed at the routing layers without the overhead of additional transport functions. Enterprise Extender enables efficient use of the IP infrastructure for support of IP-based clients accessing SNA-based data.

Enterprise Extender is currently supported on all IBM Communication Servers and routers, on IBM Personal Communications products (TN3270e client), on Cisco routers (as SNASw), and within the operating system of System/390 servers.[6] Enterprise Extender can be implemented in traffic consolidating communications servers or remote routers or within a single end user's Personal Communications product. Terminating this traffic within a System/390 enables pure IP transport by existing routers and eliminates many shortcomings of DLSw TCP encapsulation.

Larger Number of SNA Users

At both the sending and receiving locations, DLSw-capable routers terminate the SNA connection and locally acknowledge transmissions. Connection setup and maintenance is process intensive, involving link-level acknowledgment, TCP retransmit, congestion control, protocol translation, and data store-and-forward. This is a significant router burden even to the more powerful routers. Very often, the expensive data center DLSw router is incapable of supporting more than a few hundred SNA users. Enterprise Extender eliminates the termination and acknowledgment workload, thereby enabling the routers to handle a much larger number of users.

Because Enterprise Extender uses end-system to end-system congestion control and connectionless UDP, there are no TCP retransmit buffers, no timers, and no congestion control logic in the router. Because of these savings, the edge routers can concentrate on the job they do best — forwarding packets — rather than providing protocol translation and maintaining many TCP connections. Enterprise Extender allows the existing data center routing platforms to handle larger networks and larger volumes of network traffic. In similar network configurations, the same router has been measured to be up to ten times faster when using Enterprise Extender rather than DLSw.

No Single Point of Failure

Enterprise Extender leverages the inherent availability features of IP to provide failure-resistant SNA application access. With DLSw, the data center router, where termination and acknowledgment occurs, is a single point of failure. Should this router fail, although an alternate path may exist, all SNA connections would be disrupted and would have to be reestablished. Because Enterprise Extender does not terminate the session flow, it can support the IP reroute capability, maintain the connection, and switch to an alternate path without session disruption.

When Enterprise Extender is operating within S/390 Parallel Enterprise Servers (Parallel Sysplex), the UDP/IP flow extends into the sysplex. The HPR-controlled session — over an IP network — is from the end user all the way to the application on the server. This provides applications full parallel sysplex support — in the event the original application processor fails, it can move to another processor without terminating the original session. This results in "five nines" availability of the legacy SNA application (99.999 percent availability) running on OS/390 — with no changes to the SNA applications.

Enterprise Extender eliminates a TCP/IP network connection into the server with a "stub" SNA session between the gateway routing device and the server. Extending the UDP/IP flow into the S/390 server also eliminates the complexity of multiple gateways each supporting several hundred TN3270 sessions. The data center router or switch can be ESCON channel attached or use the recently available gigabit Ethernet adapter for high-speed IP attachment to the S/390 server. And, recent S/390 operating system enhancements have eliminated the single access and further improved TCP/IP stack availability.

Traffic Priority

Most routers provide some form of prioritized queuing; however, the difficulty has been to properly identify the priority at which an SNA packet should be sent. With DLSw, for example, where traffic prioritization is handled on a link basis, multiple links must be defined to the same SNA device. Other traffic prioritization techniques either have no capability to provide SNA priority, require guesswork, or adherence to addressing conventions. Enterprise Extender ends this guesswork and configuration overhead and provides real priority by mapping the priority of SNA packets to UDP port numbers that routers within the IP network can easily use to properly handle the traffic.

Efficient Message Sequencing

DLSw uses TCP/IP reliable transport to avoid messages arriving at their destination scrambled or out of sequence. This is because although higher layers of SNA could correct scrambled messages, correction can require significant retransmission that would severely impact response times. Enterprise Extender employs congestion avoidance (*Adaptive Rate-Based*) and selective retransmission of lost packets. When only an occasionally missing message part has to be selectively retransmitted, instead of the missing segment and all segments following it, the HPR-capable endpoints manage the retransmission with little effect on response times.

Choosing Between Enterprise Extender or DLSw

Today there are no ubiquitous network solutions. Thousands of native SNA transport networks have provided unsurpassed reliability and predictability. Emerging E-business opportunities rely on the Internet, intranets, and internal TCP/IP networks. Companies deciding how to merge these SNA and TCP/IP networks should consider both Data Link Switching and Enterprise Extender.

Consider the total cost of ownership. Are the routers currently in the network capable of supporting DLSw? Do existing routers have the capacity to handle the increased DLSw workload? Are the current network devices capable of providing HPR support to Enterprise Extender? What is the skill set of the people within the organization? Will education offset any savings in initial purchase prices? How much will it cost to maintain the solution?

Consider implementation implications. Are skills currently available or will they have to be recruited? How long will it take to redesign and upgrade the current network? Does one want to maintain the current IP network without change? Does one want gigabit Ethernet attachment into the S/390 server? Does one want to use TN3270 servers to transform from IP-based to SNA-based data flows? Where will one locate and how will one maintain any TN3270e servers? How will current decisions affect future network plans?

How one consolidates the networking will affect future growth and acquisition plans. External E-business customers, business partners, as well as internal executives may see one's network performance. Therefore, choose wisely — network consolidation decisions will impact business.

Chapter 34

Web-to-Host Connectivity Tools in Information Systems

Nijaz Bajgoric

IN INFORMATION TECHNOLOGY (IT) HISTORY, THE INVENTION OF THE GRAPHICAL USER INTERFACE (GUI) WAS A REVOLUTIONARY STEP IN IMPROVING BOTH THE EFFICIENCY AND EFFECTIVENESS OF IT END USERS. The GUI has become dominant not only in operating systems, but also in application software. After introducing Web technology in 1994, it turned out that a Web browser is the most convenient way of using computers for end users because it is completely based on a mouse-click operation. Of course, this became possible thanks to HTTP, HTML, and other Internet/Web-related facilities

The job of IT people, both IT vendors and IS staff, in organizations is to make information technology seamless and easy, so that end users can do their jobs as easily and efficiently as possible. From the perspective of ease of use, it is the Web technology that can help in that sense. Web-to-host connectivity tools are software products that ease the process of connecting to several types of host data (also known as legacy data), both from end users and state-of-the-art client/server (c/s) applications.

FRAMEWORK FOR IMPLEMENTATION OF WEB-TO-HOST ACCESS TOOLS

Today, Web technology can be used in contemporary information systems (IS) in three modes:

1. for Internet presence, intranet and extranet infrastructures
2. for improving access to corporate data, both legacy and c/s applications
3. for rapid application development

0-8493-0893-3/00/$0.00+$.50

Also, Web technology can significantly cut the costs of accessing systems and reduce the time required to connect users to corporate data. The role of Web technology in improving data access can be considered from the following perspectives:

- End-users' perspective: with the main objective defined as: how to provide end users with efficient access to corporate data
- Application developers' perspective: how to improve applications' efficiency using:
  - —Web technology in creating middleware and gateway applications that provide more efficient access to the existing applications (legacy data and c/s apps)
  - —Web technology in development of Web-enabled c/s applications with the primary aim to provide a "thinner" client side (based only on Web browser)
  - —Web technology in creating dynamic Web pages for corporate intranet and extranet infrastructures (dynamic HTML, ASP, etc).

Exhibit 34-1 represents a framework for implementation of Web-to-host connectivity tools in an information system (IS).

The IS subsystems that can be accessed via Web technology are:

- transaction processing system, which usually consists of legacy data and c/s data
- messaging system
- document management and workflow system
- business intelligence system
- ERP system (if IS infrastructure is based on an integrated ERP solution)

The remainder of this chapter provides some examples of Web-to-host tools that connect to these systems.

WEB-TO-LEGACY DATA

According to a recent study (http://www.simware.com/products/salvo/articles_reviews/linking.html), about 80 percent of all enterprise data is in legacy data structures, and rules for access are within legacy applications. The Gartner Group (www.gartner.com) also estimates that 74 percent of all corporate data still resides on legacy mainframes.

Legacy systems (legacy data or legacy applications) refer to older or mature applications that were developed from the late 1950s to the early 1990s. Such systems are primarily mainframe systems, or distributed systems where the mainframe plays the major processing role and the terminals or PCs are used for application running and data uploading-downloading.

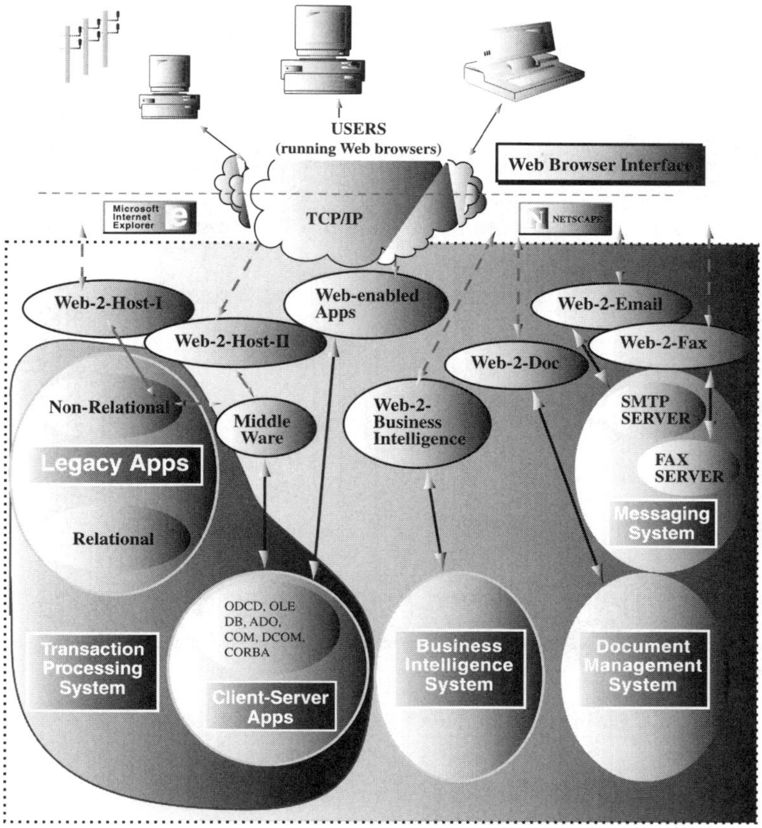

Exhibit 34-1. Framework for implementation of Web-to-host connectivity tools.

Access to legacy data through user-friendly applications (standard c/s applications and Web-based applications for intranets and the Internet) requires a processing layer between the applications and the data. Web-to-host technology makes it possible for users to access the data stored on legacy hosts just by clicking a Web link. Moreover, it cuts the costs of software ownership through centralized management.

Example: WRQ Reflection EnterView (www.wrq.com). Reflection EnterView is a Java-based legacy host access program from WRQ. As can be seen from

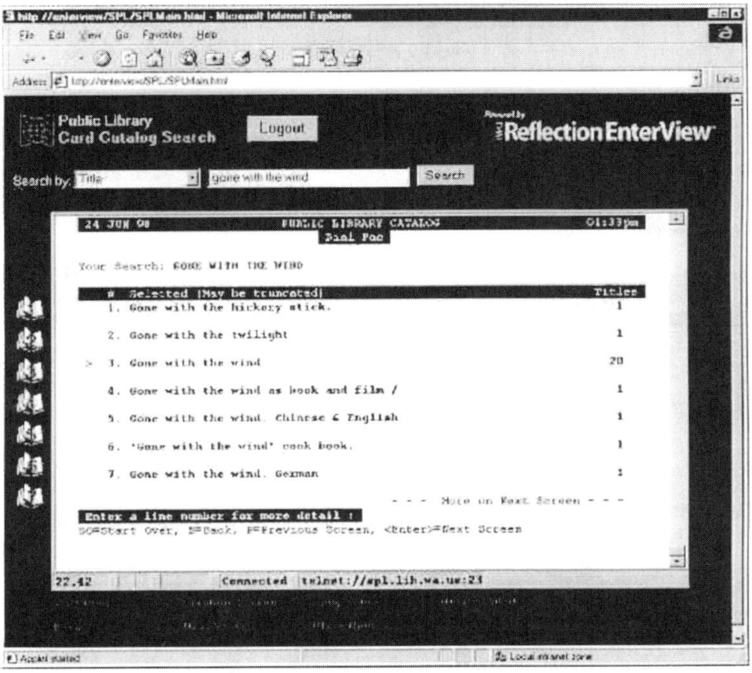

Exhibit 34-2. WRQ Reflection EnterView.

Exhibit 34-2, it gives users easy access to IBM, UNIX, and Digital hosts — right from their desktop browsers.

Example: Network Software Associates' Report.Web (www.nsainc.com). Report.Web is another Web-to-legacy program and intranet report distribution tool from Network Software Associates, Inc. At the heart of Report.Web is the enterprise server, a powerful and robust engine that automates the entire process of delivering host-generated reports to the Web — from almost any host, including IBM mainframes, AS/400s, DEC VAXs, and PC LAN servers, to the corporate intranet/extranet.

Report.Web provides a variety of Web-accessible outputs, including:

- spreadsheet output
- WRF (Web reporting format) output
- HTML output

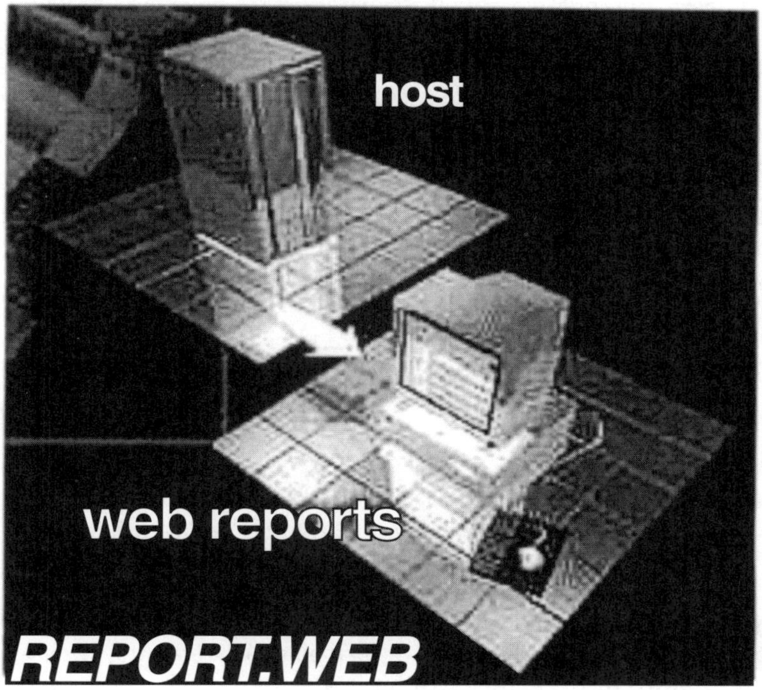

Exhibit 34-3. Network Software Associates ReportWeb.

- PDF output
- thin client (all reports published by the enterprise server are readable by standard Web browsers)

See Exhibit 34-3.

Report.Web supports also distributing ERP-generated reports across the corporate intranet, without deploying ERP clients at every desktop.

WEB-TO-MESSAGING SYSTEMS

Example: Web-to-Mail (www.mail2web.com). The Web2Mail or Mail2Web program is a service that lets users to use their POP3 e-mail accounts through an easy Web interface. If this program is installed on the server side (SMTP server), then the only program users need on the client side is a Web browser. They do not need any e-mail program like Eudora, Pegasus, MS Exchange Client, MS Outlook, or character-based telnet-pine program. From the end-users' perspective, this is very important because the Web browsers' GUI is based on a very simple "point-and-click" interface. Hence, this approach is more user friendly. As an example, mail2web's URL address is a public site that allows people to use a Web-based interface to their e-mail accounts (for those SMTP servers without the web2mail program). See Exhibit 34-4.

Example: Web-to-Fax (http://www-usa.tpc.int). The Web2Fax program, which is very similar to Web2mail, gives an opportunity of sending and receiving fax documents from Web browsers with no additional software (see Exhibit 34-5).

WEB-TO-DOCUMENT MANAGEMENT AND WORKFLOW SYSTEMS

Web-Based Index-Search Tools

Example: Microsoft's Index Server (www.microsoft.com). Microsoft Index Server is the Microsoft content-indexing and searching solution for Microsoft Internet Information Server (IIS) and Peer Web Services (PWS). Index Server can index documents for both corporate intranets and for any drive accessible through a uniform naming convention (UNC) path on the Internet. Users can formulate queries using the Web browser. Index Server can index the text and properties of formatted documents, such as those created by Word or Excel (see Exhibit 34-6).

Even the Office97 package includes Web-searching facilities. Its Web Find Fast is a search utility that allows a Web server to search HTML files and summary properties of Office97 documents (Author, Title, Subject, etc.) (see Exhibit 34-7).

Example: Compaq's AltaVista Search Intranet (http://altavista.software.digital.com/). AltaVista Search Intranet is search and retrieval software that provides search and retrieval for information in several formats, including HTML, Microsoft Word, Adobe PDF, and many other formats (over 150) of files located on Internet and intranet Web servers, Lotus Domino Servers, and Windows LANs. AltaVista Search also includes multi-national support (see Exhibit 34-8).

Web-Enabled Document Management and Workflow Software

Example: Keyfile from Keyfile Corporation (www.keyfile.com). Keyfile document management application provides Web-based access to user documents. It also supports integration with Microsoft Exchange/Outlook messaging system. The client side does not need any extra software installed beyond a Web browser (see Exhibit 34-9).

Exhibit 34-4. Web2Mail interface.

Exhibit 34-5. Web2Fax interface.

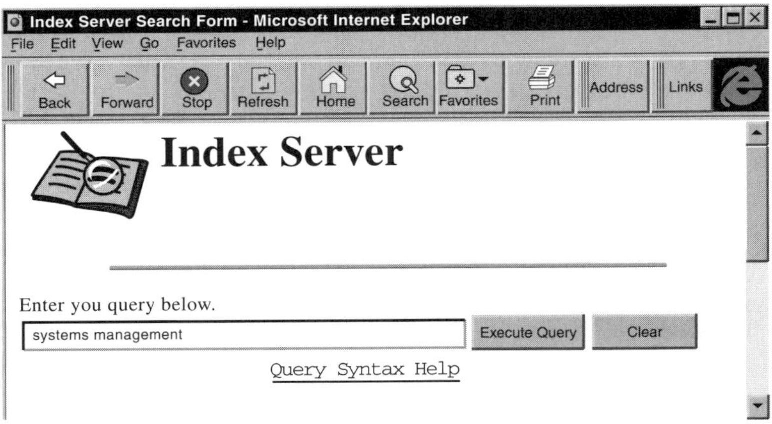

Exhibit 34-6. Microsoft index server.

Example: FileNET Panagon and Waterflow (http://www.filenet.com). FileNET Panagon is enterprisewide integrated document management software that represents a solution for capturing, accessing, managing, utilizing, and securing business information. Information is also available via Web interface (see Exhibit 34-10).

Example: SAP Internet-Based Workflow (www.sap.com/internet/index.htm). SAP Business Workflow module is another example of a Web-enabled workflow management system. With SAP Business Workflow, a user can initiate a workflow (via Internet/intranet application components, BAPIs, forms), track his or her work via the Internet application component "Integrated Inbox," respond to requests for other users, or review the workflow history via the Internet application component "Workflow Status Reports."

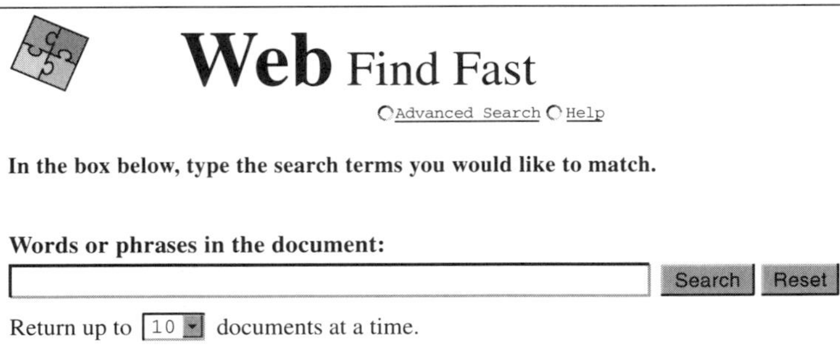

Exhibit 34-7. Microsoft Office97 Web Find Fast.

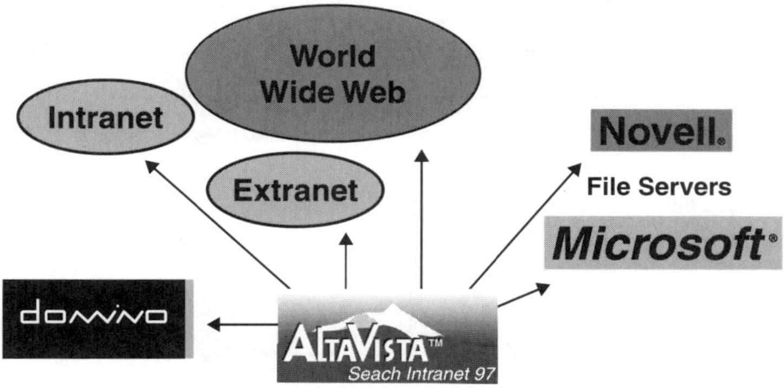

Exhibit 34-8. Compaq AltaVista search intranet.

WEB-TO-BUSINESS INTELLIGENCE SYSTEMS

Browser-based access to so-called business intelligence systems (decision support systems, executive information systems, data warehousing systems, etc.) is very important for decision makers because of its ease of use.

Web-Enabled Desktop DSS Tools

Decision modeling is now available via the Web browser. The decision maker can use a model that is already created and stored on a server from his or her computer through the Web browser.

Example: Vanguard DecisionPro Web Edition (www.vanguardsw.com). The Web version of DecisionPro, a powerful desktop DSS tool, allows decision-makers to run DecisionPro models remotely. They do not need special software on their computers other than a standard Web browser. For example, a model developed to assist salespeople in determining prices dealing with customers can be installed on a server and run remotely on a salesman's notebook computer.

What follows is an example of "loan qualification model," a model developed with DecisionPro and accessed through the Web browser. Users explore information with a browser so there is no client software to deploy (see Exhibit 34-11).

Web-Enabled EIS (Reporting)

Executive information systems (EIS) or reporting applications provide user-friendly access to corporate data. These applications are usually DBMS-based and can contain both direct data from c/s applications or

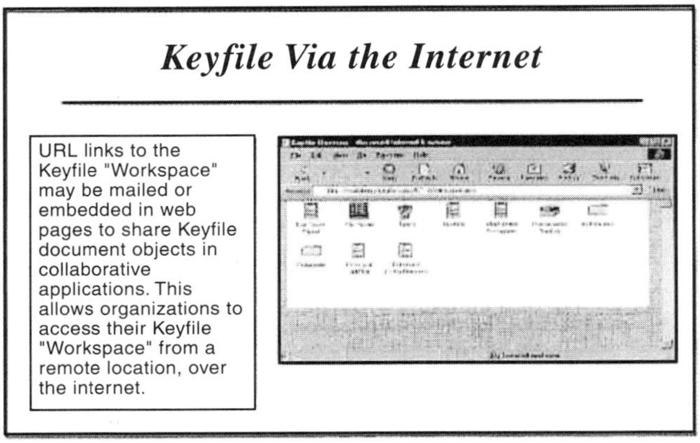

Exhibit 34-9. Keyfile Web-based interface.

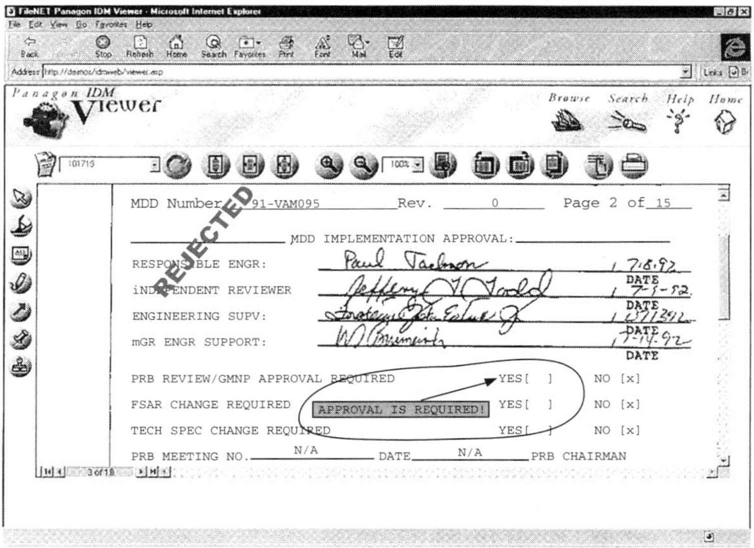

Exhibit 34-10. FileNET Panagon.

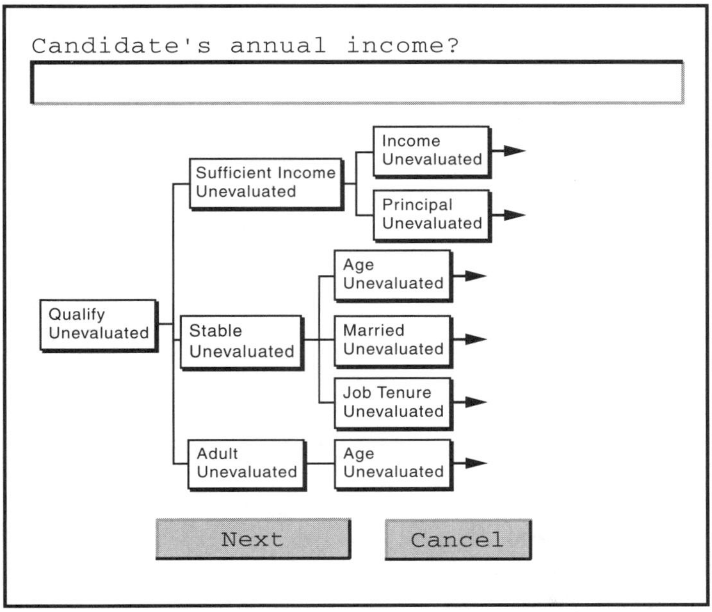

Exhibit 34-11. Web-based modeling feature of decision pro.

extracted and converted data from legacy systems. This conversion can be done manually or automatically through middleware or gateway programs (e.g., ISG Navigator, http://www.isg.co.il/home.asp).

Example: Cognos Impromptu Web Reports (www.cognos.com). Cognos Impromptu Web Reports delivers reporting facilities over the Web, providing end users with quick and easy access to the latest company reports — directly from their browser (see Exhibit 34-12).

Web-to-Enterprisewide DSS

In addition to Web access to desktop DSS tools, such GUI interfaces are supported by enterprisewide decision support systems as well.

Example: Business Objects' WebIntelligence (www.businessobjects.com). Business Objects' WebIntelligence is a multi-tier, thin-client decision support system (DSS) that provides end users with ad hoc query, reporting, and analysis of information stored in corporate data warehouses (see Exhibit 34-13).

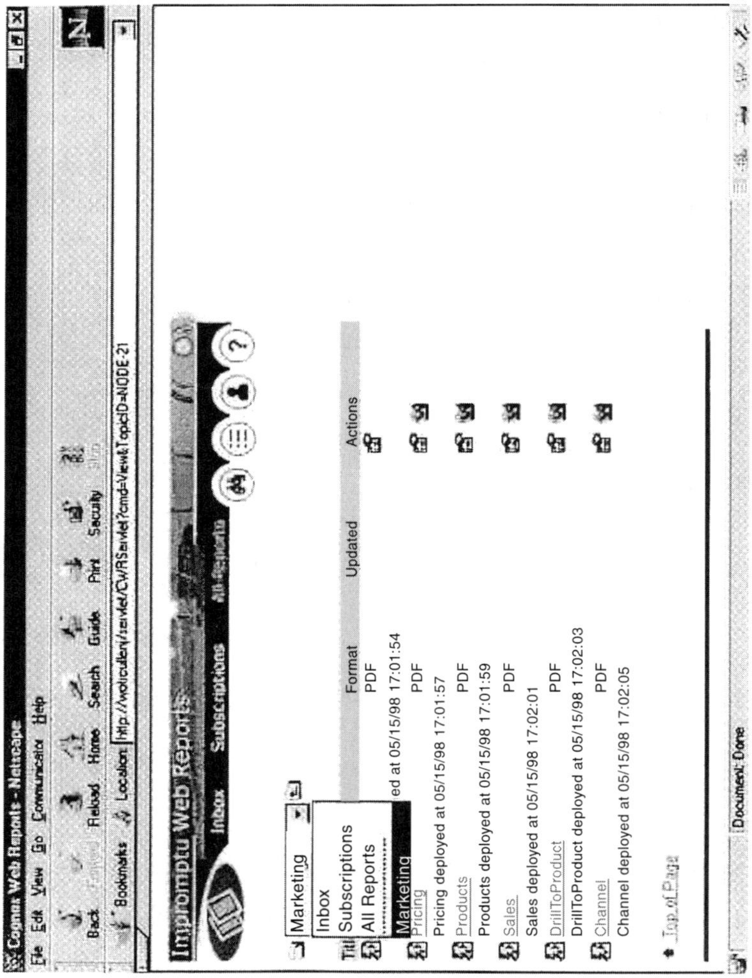

Exhibit 34-12, Cognos impromptu web reports.

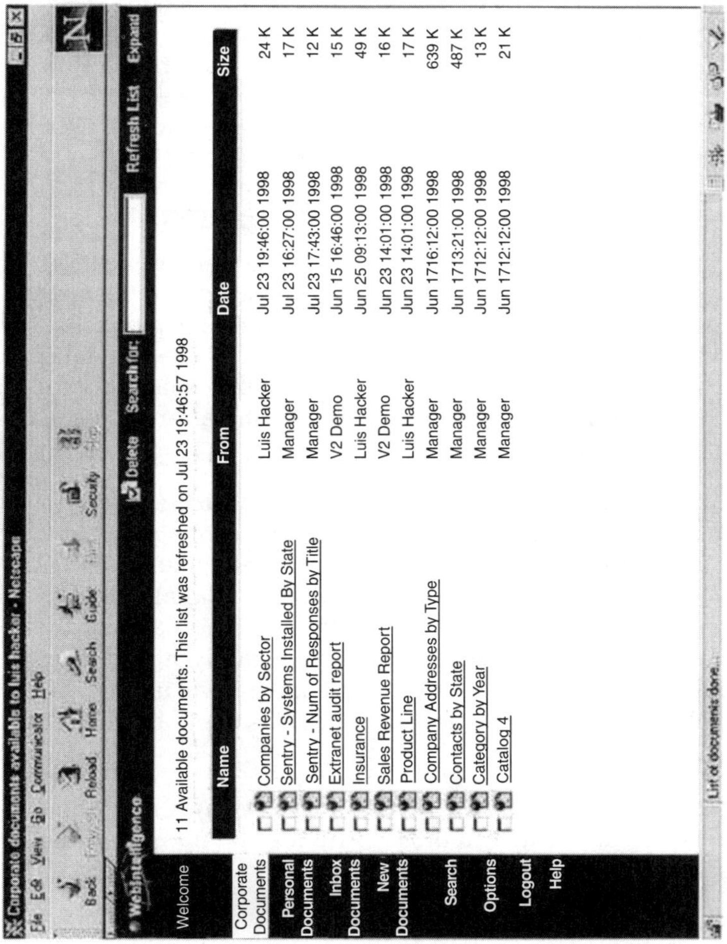

Exhibit 34-13. BusinessObjects WebIntelligence.

Example: MicroStrategy's DSS Web (www.strategy.com). MicroStrategy DSS Web is a user-friendly interface that connects corporate data warehouse across the World Wide Web (see Exhibit 34-14).

WEB TO ERP

Example: SAP R/3 System (www.sap.com). The SAP R/3 application suite includes Internet application components that enable linking the R/3 System to the Internet. These components enable SAP users to use the R/3 System business functions via a Web browser. SAP R/3 Internet applications can be used as they are, or as a basis for creating new ones. SAP R/3 architecture is based on a three-tier client/server structure, with distinct layers for presentation, application, and database (see Exhibit 34-15).

WEB-TO-HOST MIDDLEWARE AND RAD DEVELOPMENT TOOLS

Efficient access to legacy data is important from an application developer's perspective as well. The development of new c/s applications that will exchange data with existing legacy systems requires a type of middleware that overcomes the differences in data formats. Different data access middleware products exist and they are specific to a single platform; for example, RMS files on OpenVMS machines, IBM mainframes, or different UNIX machines. Two examples are given.

Example: ISG Navigator (www.isg.co.il). ISG Navigator is a data access middleware tool that provides an efficient data exchange between Windows platform and several host platforms such as OpenVMS for Digital Alpha and VAX, Digital UNIX, HP-UX. Sun Solaris and IBM AIX. ISG Navigator (Exhibit 34-16) enables access to non-relational data in almost the same way that relational data is accessed. More importantly, application developers can build new Internet-based applications that will use data from legacy systems by using data integration standards such as OLE DB, ADO, COM, DCOM, RDMS, CORBA, etc.

Example: ClientBuilder Enterprise (www.clientsoft.com). ClientSoft ClientBuilder Enterprise and other solutions provide the following important capabilities in the development of Web-enabled c/s applications and their integration with legacy data:

- data integration between desktop Windows applications and legacy data from IBM S/390 and AS/400 machines
- developing GUI interface to existing host-based legacy applications
- provides ODBC support to relational databases
- provides access to applications residing on IBM systems through the use of wireless communications technologies
- provides access to IBM host machines through the use of Web technologies within the electronic commerce systems (see Exhibit 34-17).

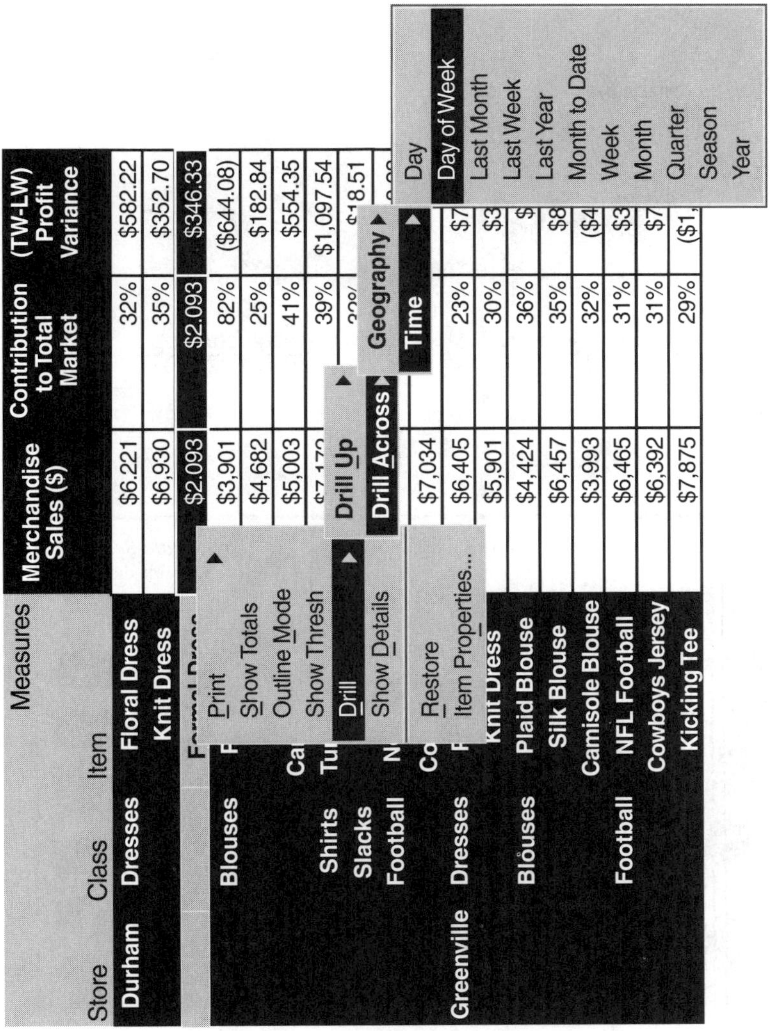

Exhibit 34-14. MicroStrategy DSS Web.

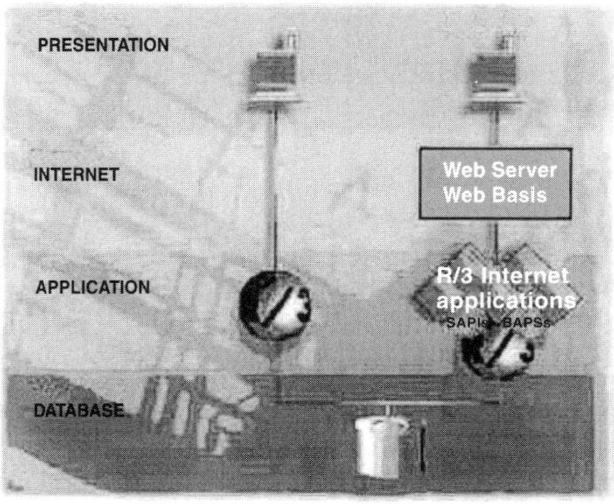

Exhibit 34-15. SAP Web-based infrastructure.

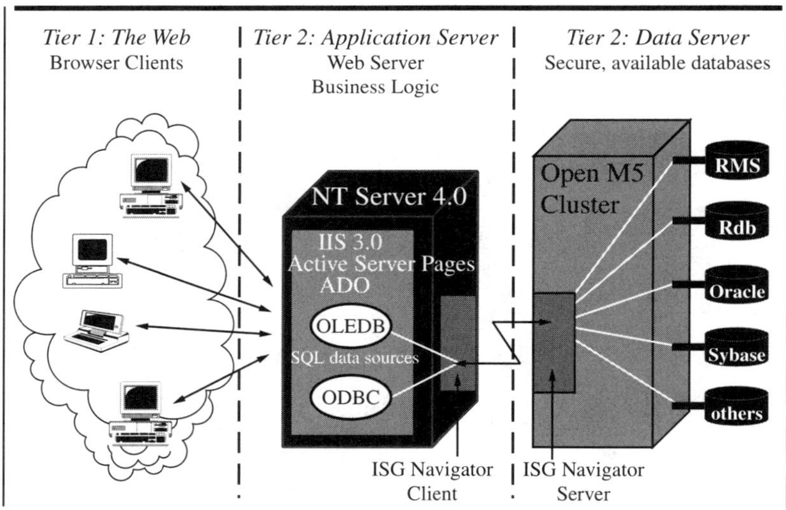

Exhibit 34-16. ISG Navigator.

Exhibit 34-17. ClientSoft.

While middleware products serve as a data gateway between legacy systems and Windows-based c/s and desktop applications, Web-based application development products support building Web-enabled c/s applications.

Microsoft Visual InterDev (www.microsoft.com) is a rapid application development tool for building dynamic Internet and intranet applications based on ASP feature of Microsoft Internet Information Server. It is available as a stand-alone product or as a part of Microsoft's Visual Studio integrated application development suite. Visual InterDev provides Web-based access to databases supporting ODBC standard (see Exhibit 34-18).

In addition to specific Web development tools, most contemporary standard rapid application development tools provide features for developing Web-enabled applications. Exhibit 34-19 illustrates such features supported by Borland C++ Builder (www.inprise.com).

CONCLUSIONS

This chapter presents a framework for an effective integration of Web-to-host connectivity and development tools in information systems. This issue was considered from both end user and developer perspectives. This means that an emphasis is put on how to improve data access and data exchange, no matter where that data comes from: standard legacy data, e-mail or fax message, document, business model, report, ERP module, etc. The IS subsystems in which these tools can be used were identified, and some examples of software packages that can be found on the market were presented.

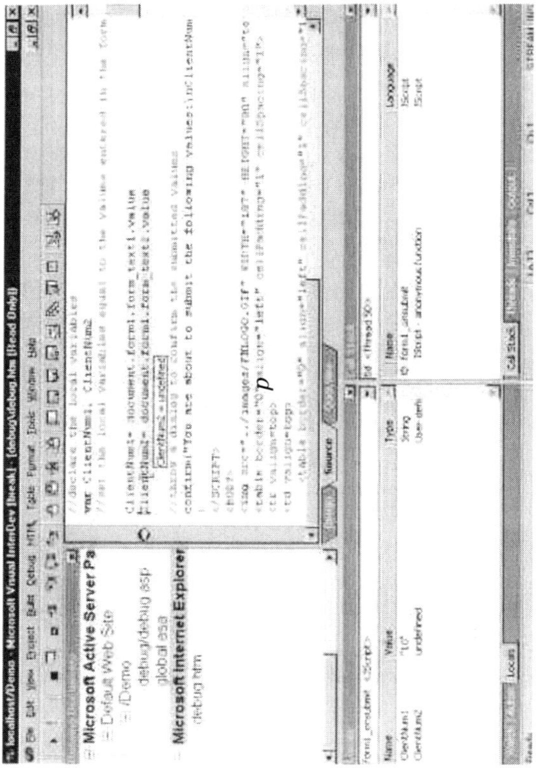

Exhibit 34.18. Microsoft Visualf InterDev.

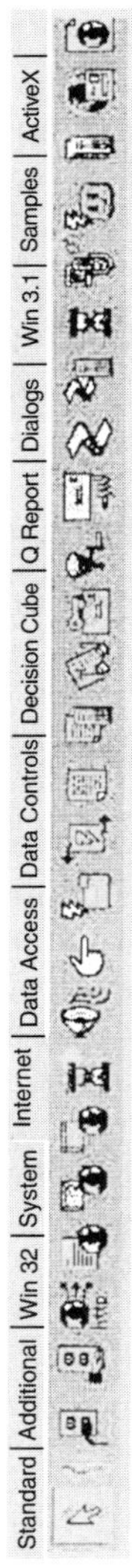

Exhibit 34-19. Borland C++ Builder: Internet Component Bar.

References

- www.simware.com
- www.gartner.com
- www.wrq.com
- www.nsainc.com
- www.mail2web.com
- www.tpc.int
- www.microsoft.com
- www.altavista.software.digital.com
- www.keyfile.com
- www.filenet.com
- www.sap.com
- www.vanguardsw.com
- www.isg.co.il
- www.cognos.com
- www.businessobjects.com
- www.strategy.com
- www.clientsoft.com
- www.microsoft.com

Chapter 35
Business-to-Business Integration Using E-commerce

Ido Gileadi

NOW THAT MANY OF THE FORTUNE 1000 MANUFACTURING COMPANIES have implemented ERP systems to streamline their planning and resource allocation as well as integrate their business processes across the enterprise, there is still a need to be integrated with the supply chain.

To reduce inventory levels and lead times, companies must optimize the process of procurement of raw materials and finished goods. Optimization of business processes across multiple organizations includes redefining the way business is conducted, as well as putting in place the systems that will support communication between multiple organizations that have their own separate systems, infrastructure, and requirements.

This type of business-to-business electronic integration has been around for some time, in the form of EDI (Electronic Document Interchange). EDI allows organizations to exchange documents (e.g. purchase orders, sales orders, etc.) using standards such as X.12 or EDIFACT, and VANs (Value Added Networks), for communication. The standards are used to achieve a universal agreement on the content and format of documents and messages being exchanged. EDI standards allow software vendors to include functionality in their software that will support EDI and communicate with other applications. The VAN is used as a medium for transferring messages from one organization to the other; it is a global proprietary network that is designed to carry and monitor EDI messages.

The EDI solution has caught on in several market segments, but has never presented a complete solution for the following reasons:

- High cost for setup and transactions meant that smaller organizations could not afford the cost associated with setup and maintenance of an EDI solution using a VAN.

0-8493-0893-3/00/$0.00+$.50

- EDI messages are a subset of all the types of data that organizations may want to exchange.
- EDI does not facilitate online access to information, which may be required for applications such as self-service.

With the advance of the Internet, both in reliability and security, and the proliferation of Internet-based e-commerce applications, e-commerce has become an obvious place to look for solutions to a better and more flexible way of integrating business-to-business processes.

The remainder of this article will discuss a real life example of how internet and e-commerce technologies were implemented to address the business-to-business integration challenge.

BUSINESS REQUIREMENTS

The business requirements presented to the e-commerce development team can be divided into three general functional area categories:

- General requirements
- Communicating demand to the supply chain
- Providing self-service application to suppliers

General requirements included:

- 100 percent participation by suppliers—The current EDI system was adapted by only 10 percent of suppliers
- Minimized cost of operation to suppliers and self
- Maintainance of high security level both for enterprise systems and for data communicated to external organizations
- Utilization of industry standards and off the shelf applications wherever possible. Minimized custom development
- Supplier access to all systems through a browser interface

Demand requirements included:

- The sending of EDI standard messages to suppliers
  - —830 — Purchase Schedule
  - —850 — Purchase Order
  - —860 — Purchase Order Change
- Advance notice of exceptions to demand through exception reports.

Exhibit 35-1 describes the flow of demand messages (830,850,860, exceptions) between the manufacturer and supplier organization. The demand is generated from the manufacturer ERP system (Baan, SAP, etc.); it is then delivered to the supplier through one of several methods we will discuss later. The supplier can load the demand directly into their system or use the supplied software to view and print the demand on a PC. The supplier can then produce a report indicating any exception to the expected delivery of

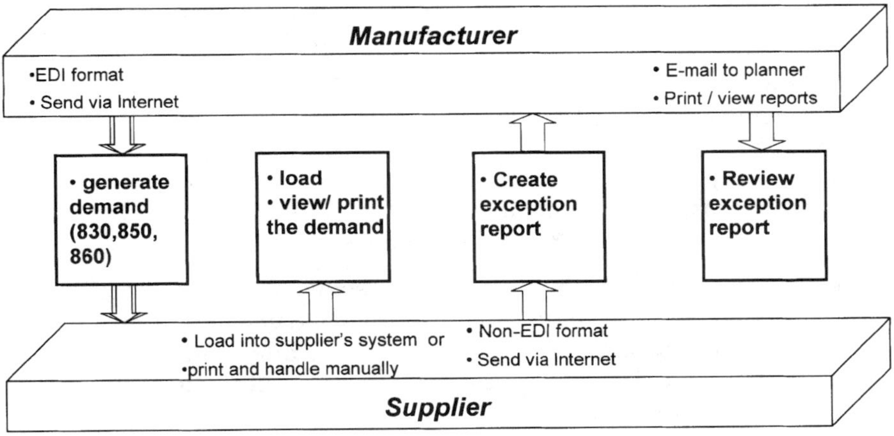

Exhibit 35-1

goods. The exception report is sent back to the manufacturer and routed to the appropriate planner, who can view the report and make the necessary adjustments later. The supplier can load the demand directly into their system or use the supplied software to view and print the demand on a PC. The supplier can then produce a report indicating any exception to the expected delivery of goods. The exception report is sent back to the manufacturer and routed to the appropriate planner, who can view the report and make the necessary adjustments. Self-service application requirements included:

- The means for suppliers to update product pricing electronically thereby ensuring price consistency between manufacturer and supplier
- The provision of online access with drill-down capabilities for suppliers to view the following information:
  - —Payment details
  - —Registered invoices
  - —Receipt of goods details
  - —Product quality information

TECHNICAL REQUIREMENTS

The technical solution had to address the following:

- Transportation of EDI messages to suppliers of various levels of computerization
- Complete solutions for suppliers that have no scheduling application
- Seamless support for small and large supplier organizations
- Batch message processing and online access to data
- Security for enterprise systems as well as data transmission.
- Utilization of industry standards and off the shelf products

Once again we can divide the technical requirements into three categories:

- General requirements
  - Low cost
  - Low maintenance
  - High level of security
  - Industry standards
- Batch message management
- online access to enterprise information

A review of the three main categories of technical requirements reveals the need for a product to support message management (EDI and non-EDI); and for the same or a different product to provide online access. The selected products will have to possess all the characteristics listed under general requirements.

E-COMMERCE PRODUCT SELECTION

Selection of e-commerce products for the purpose of developing a complete solution should take the following into consideration:

- What type of functionality does the product cover (online, batch, etc.)?
- Is the product based on industry standards or is it proprietary?
- Does the product provide a stable and flexible platform for the development of future applications?
- How does the product integrate with other product selections?
- What security is available as part of the product?
- What are the skills required to develop use of the product, and are these skills readily available?
- Product cost (Server, user licenses, maintenance)
- Product innovation and further development
- Product base of installation
- Product architecture

The E-Commerce team selected the following products:

- WebSuite and Gentran Server from Sterling Commerce—This product was selected for handling EDI messages, communication EDI, and non-EDI messages through various communication mediums. This product provides the following features:
  - Secure and encrypted file transfer mechanism
  - Support for EDI through VANs, Internet and FTP
  - Browser operation platform using ActiveX technology
  - Simple integration and extendibility through ActiveX forms integration
  - Simple and open architecture
  - Easy integration with other products
  - EDI translation engine

Baan Data Navigator Plus (BDNP) from TopTier was selected for online access to the ERP and other enterprise applications. The product has the following main features:

- — Direct online access to the Baan ERP database through the application layer
- — Direct online access to other enterprise applications
- — Integration of data from various applications into one integrated view.
- — Hyper Relational data technology, allowing the user to drag and relate each item data onto a component, thereby creating a new, more detailed query that provides drill-down capabilitie.
- — Access to applications through a browser interface
- — Easy to use development environment

Both products had been recently released at the time we started using them (Summer of 1998). This is typically not a desirable situation as it can cause the extension of a project due to unexpected bugs and gaps in functionality. We have chosen to select the products above for their features, the reputation of the companies that developed them, and the level of integration the products provided with the ERP system we had in place.

E-COMMERCE SOLUTION

Taking business and technical requirements into account, we put together a systems architecture that provided appropiate solutions.

On the left side of Exhibit 35-2 are the client PCs located at the supplier's environment. These are standard Win NT/95/98, with a browser capable of running ActiveX components. Both the applications (WebSuite and TopTier) are accessed through a browser using HTML and ActiveX technologies. As can be seen in the diagram, some suppliers (typically the larger organizations) have integrated the messages sent by the application into their scheduling system. Their system loads the data and presents it within their integrated environment. Other suppliers (typically smaller organizations) are using the browser-based interface to view and print the data, as well as manipulate and create exception reports to be sent back to the server.

Communication is achieved using the following protocols on the Internet:

- http, https—for delivery of online data
- Sockets (SL), Secure Sockets (SSL)—for message transfer

On the Enterprise side, the client applications first access a web server. The Web Server handles the http/https communication and invokes the server-side controls through an ASP page.

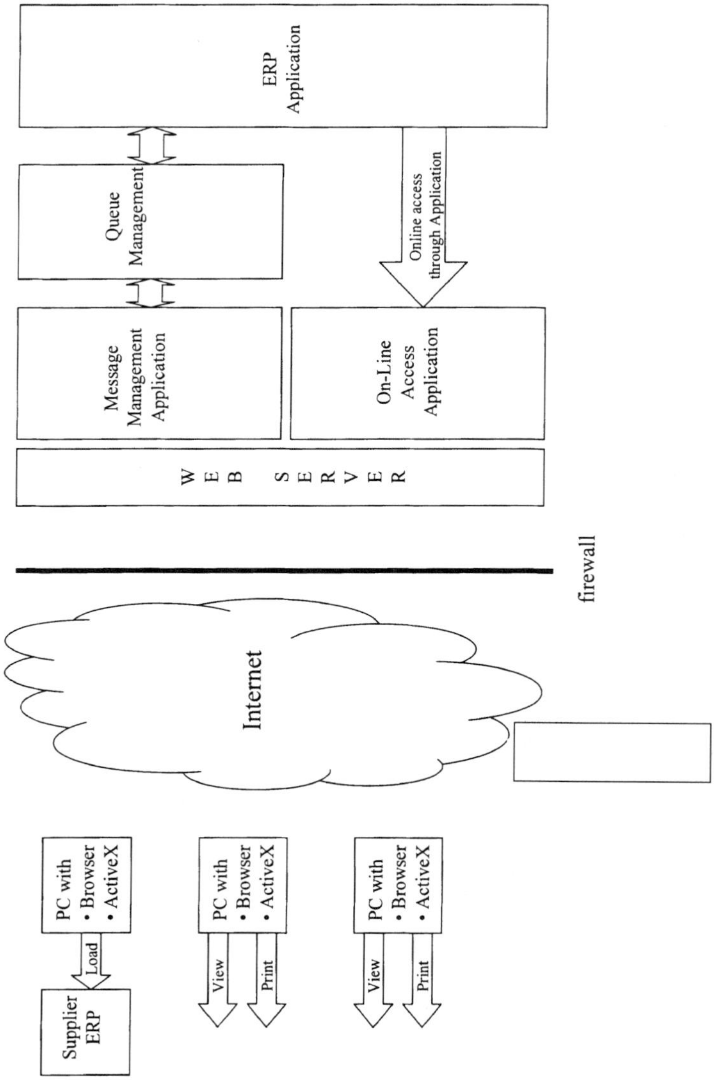
ERP
Application
Queue
Management
Online access
through Application
Message
Management
Application
On-Line
Access
Application
WEB SERVER
firewall
Internet
PC with
• Browser
• ActiveX
Load
Supplier
ERP
PC with
• Browser
• ActiveX
View
Print
PC with
• Browser
• ActiveX
View
Print

Exhibit 35-2

The online application (TopTier) intercepts the http/https communication address to it and interprets the query. It then provides a result set, which it integrates through an HTML template, to be sent back to the client PC as an HTML page. The online access application communicates with the ERP application through the application API, or through ODBC.

The message management application, WebSuite, communicates to the message queue using server-side ActiveX controls and ftp to send and receive files between systems. The message management application communicates with the ERP and other enterprise applications, using a set of processes that can read and write messages, to a shared mounted disk area.

This system architecture supports a mechanism for transferring messages in a secure and reliable fashion, as well as providing online access to data residing in the enterprise systems; this is accomplished through a browser interface with minimal requirements from the supplier and minimal support requirements.

SECURITY

The are two categories of security that must be handled:

- Enterprise systems security from outside intrusion
- Data security for data communicated over the web

Security for the enterprise is intended to prevent unauthorized users from accessing data, and thus potentially damaging enterprise systems and data. This is handled by various methods that are far too many to have a meaningful discussion in this article. The following is a review of the steps taken to secure the system on this project; these are by no means the only, or the complete set of, measures that can be taken. In addition, each organization may have different security requirements. On this project we have

- implemented a firewall that provided the following:
  - limited IP and PORT addresses
  - limited protocols allowed (http, https, IP)
  - required User Authentication at the firewall level
  - abstracted Server IP address
- provided for authentication at
  - front office application layer
  - back office application layer
  - operating system layer
  - firewall layer
- provided domain settings
  - the web server machine is not part of the enterprise domain
  - the web server machine has IP access to other servers

Data security is required to protect the information that is transferred between supplier and manufacturer over the public domain of the Internet. The intent is to secure the data from unauthorized eavesdroppers. There are many methods to protect data; these methods can be grouped into two main categories:

- Transferring data through a secure communication channel (SSL, https), a method that utilizes
  - authentication
  - certificates
  - encryption
- Encryption of data. This method is typically used in conjunction with the previous method, but can be used on its own. There are various encryption algorithms available. The encryption strength, or cipher strength, defined as how difficult it would be to decrypt data without the keys, can vary and is designated in terms of number of bits (i.e. 40bit, 128bit, etc.). For our project, we have selected Microsoft Crypto API, which is supported both by the web Server (IIS 4) and by the client browser (IE 4). The cipher strength selected was 40bits, to allow access to the application from outside theU.S. and Canada, where 128bit cipher strength for browsers is not available.

CONCLUSION

Manufacturing organizations striving to reduce inventory levels and lead times must integrate business processes and systems with their supply chain organization. E-commerce applications utilizing the Internet can be used to achieve integration across the supply chain with minimal cost and standard interfaces.

When implementing e-commerce applications, it is recommended to select those that can be used as infrastructures in the development of future business solutions that address new requirements. Selecting applications that provide technology solutions with a development platform, rather than those that provide an integrated business solution, will provide a platform for the development of future business applications, as the use of e-commerce proliferates through organizations.

Chapter 36

The Effect of Emerging Technology on the Traditional Business-to-Business Distribution Model

Doric Earle

Hey! We are almost halfway through the year 2000! Aren't your customers supposed to be sizing, configuring, modeling, identifying, pricing, and buying your products by the containership, over the Web by now? You got rid of that pesky, whiny, channel partner already; downsized the sales department; and hired that new Web portal wizard. So how come sales haven't shot through roof like those other Internet direct sales sites? Were we not all supposed to blow up our dealers, dismantle our channels, disenfranchise our distributors — because the PC revolution and the Internet were going to allow us to get rid of the middlemen in the business-to-business transaction model?

TECHNOLOGY, SPECIFICALLY AS IT IS APPLIED ON THIS PLANET TO CREATE AND PERPETUATE THE INTERNET, WAS SUPPOSED TO PERMANENTLY EVISCERATE THE TRADITIONAL COMMERCIAL INTERMEDIARIES, by bringing buyer and seller together to complete the commercial transaction, without needing the assistance of the traditional intermediary or distributor. That has obviously not happened. What has happened, is what this author calls the paradox of technology: the ability of technology, to both enhance and make obsolete one or more aspects of business, work and play. In the case of the traditional commercial distribution channel, this paradox holds

0-8493-0893-3/00/$0.00+$.50

true. The Internet has both enhanced and destroyed commercial channel selling. This chapter examines several ways technology (i.e. the Internet) affects this paradox.

The Internet and the application of its technology by consumers, both commercial and private, have altered forever how our venerable institutions of channel-based economics function in the world of E-business. In the case of business-to-consumer transactions, the likelihood of the consumer continuing to support the old notion of intermediation and the typical price mark-up by retail channels, is moving toward a zero, zippo — the cat is out of the bag. Consumers are not paying the middleman for zero value add in their commodity product purchases. In commodity industries, in industries where scarce information controlled the transaction (financial transactions), in markets where the distribution channel does not add much perceived value (consumer electronics), the Internet is replacing many distributors and retailers. This is called disintermediation.

On the business-to-business (B2B) side, however, this disintermediation is not as widespread as early Internet sages would have us believe. Some industries are more prone than others. While the PC, automobile, travel, and insurance industries are particularly vulnerable, one sees firms like IBM, Nortel Networks, Cisco, and Compaq Computer enhancing their channel partners through the deliberate and thoughtful use of technology and the Web. IDC's opinion sees the role of the middleman as changing over time. The following discussion highlights some of the negative and positive effects technology is having on the channel model of commerce. As Walid Mougayar notes in his article, "Don't Automatically Cannibalize Your Channels", many companies may have a dual strategy: one to enhance and grow the current, traditional channel, and the other to create what Mougayar calls "MySecondCompany.com" — a spin-off that keeps selling over the Internet with the core channel partners. Typically, these companies will be small and start slow, feeling their way along, while the parent continues in a traditional fashion, until the new disintermediated approach can be evaluated for its viability.

DISTRIBUTION MODEL BUSINESS BASICS

Modern business-to-business transactions (i.e., commerce, at least in the last 200 hundred years) have often flowed through a simple, but efficient model. This model included the manufacturer of the goods; a middleman or broker who distributed the goods; and the ultimate buyer who took delivery of the goods from the distributor. The value proposition of this tried-and-true model is centered on the distributor's ability to find and create markets for the manufacturer and to find and deliver goods to the buyer. The distributor was valuable to the manufacturer in that the distributor theoretically represented access to markets that the manufacturer needed into which to sell its goods — many distributors or channels, selling the manufacturer's goods, again theoretically, could sell more than the manufacturer could alone.

In addition, the distributor also provided the sales and marketing resources that the producer/manufacturer either did not have or did not want to employ for a variety of economic reasons. The distributor traditionally added value to the buyer of the goods by having product knowledge, pricing flexibility, and delivery resources to deliver the goods at a price that was attractive to the buyer and with the expertise to put the goods into service. This model is used to deliver every kind of product imaginable from Fruit Loops™ to brain surgery (hospitals distribute surgeons services to patients), and from jet fuel to copiers. The distributor's value continues to be its product and positioning knowledge. Knowledge of the manufacturer's goods — knowledge of which customers need and want these goods — is the value-add factor. The channel found buyers, found manufacturers, helped sell, service and represent both the buyer and seller because of its specialized knowledge of the complete transaction and all of the various components.

HISTORICALLY, TECHNOLOGY WAS EMBRACED BY THE CHANNEL

Up until very recently, technology was used primarily to enhance the efficiency and effectiveness of this distributor-centric model. The telephone and the personal computer are two examples of technology that have greatly enhanced the traditional channel model. The telephone greatly increased the speed of response the distributor could affect to the business wants and needs of their customers and it enabled the channel to keep abreast of the manufacturer's product information. The telephone also greatly increased the range that a single distributor could create and fulfill the transaction. The personal computer again increased the efficiency of the channel by allowing vast amounts of information (i.e., transactions) to be processed quickly and the history of each transaction retained for future use — by sales, marketing, and service agencies of the channel. But neither actually changed the producer-distributor-business consumer model radically, technology just made the model more efficient, and in many cases drove prices down, opened new markets, expanded territories, etc.

ENTER THE INTERNET

Technology is now in a position, through the complete and utter shift toward "E-commerce" and all that the term implies, to simultaneously destroy and empower the traditional vendor/channel, distribution model. This E-channel technological paradox may exist for several business cycles, perhaps forever. It depends how the three parties to the model —

the manufacturer, the distributor, and the buyer — choose to employ the Internet.

The Internet has opened the direct lines of communication between manufacturer and buyer, but it has also provided new opportunities for the distributor, the smart ones, to find other ways to add value back into the E-commerce transaction. First examine what is meant by the technology of the Internet.

CORE INTERNET TECHNOLOGY

Once the domain of government and science, primarily a text editor-driven, UNIX-based system, the Internet has evolved and grown by providing new technologies based on IBM-compatible PCs, Microsoft Windows based operating systems, and HTML-based browsers.

The concept of multimedia applications and hyper-linking Web pages greatly increased the range of content and the volume of information that could be retrieved over the original UNIX-based Internet. These technologies also moved the user from text-based content viewing to a graphics oriented, user interface, which improved the experience for the Web user. Users find today that the Internet is:

- Networks providing dramatically higher bandwidth with range and throughput.
- Communications devices offering faster communications at lower costs (hub, bridges and routers).
- All manner of devices, PDAs, cell phones, laptops, personal computers all possessing substantially improved processing, storage, and media-handling capabilities.
- Client/Server software with vastly increased software functionality.

There are several founding or early applications and companies that played a major role in creating the Internet. Some of the more significant products and companies include:

- *Netscape.* Netscape completed one of the most successful initial public offerings in history during 1995. It spurred Microsoft to create its now-infamous Internet Explorer browser; the two browsers account for 90 percent of all Web sessions.
- *Mosaic.* An early browser like CompuServe and AOL.
- *Java.* Developed by Sun Microsystems, the ubiquitous development language that allows for applets to be written that work across most operating systems and desktop PCs.
- *RealAudio and RealVideo.* Developed by RealNetworks, RealAudio and RealVideo provide real-time streaming of audio and video on-demand.

- *Internet phone.* Developed by VocalTec, Internet Phone allows full duplex voice conversations anywhere in the world for the cost of an Internet connection.
- *MP3.* An audio capturing technology that allows downloading and playing back of large audio streams.

HOW THE INTERNET IS NEGATIVELY AFFECTING THE TRADITIONAL CHANNEL VALUE PROPOSITION

Information Availability

The availability of information to the buyer was once the key factor in sustaining the distribution chain value proposition. The channel had the information that allowed it to leverage the knowledge it had of the producer's products, prices, and target markets. In addition, the channel also had direct knowledge of the market, the business customer; internal wants, internal requirements, pricing tolerances, and other preferences. The channel typically knew substantially more than the manufacturer or the business consumer in any given transaction. Both parties were dependent on the channel to make the transaction as profitable, economical, and timely as possible. The distributor could make everyone happy or not.

The channel can and would assist the buyer in comparison-shopping for better prices among manufacturers, and pit producers against one another to lower prices or to obtain other concessions from the producers. The distribution channel can recommend products based on its relationship with a particular producer (which could include special deals in which the distributor would make significantly higher margins) rather the most appropriate products for the business customer. The customer may never know that there might have been better products and services from a different producer because the channel was the only party to competitive or pricing information. Both ends of the transaction, the producer and buyer, were dependent on the distributor for information. The distribution channel often filtered the information in both directions to its advantage and not necessarily to the producers or buyers. The Internet and its vast universe of information, its affinity for allowing E-commerce to thrive, fertilized by the true currency of the Internet — knowledge — broke the monopoly the distribution chain had on the knowledge necessary to conduct B2B commerce. The value of the information once held only by the distribution chain is eroding (see Exhibit 36-1). The same proprietary, hard-to-find, scarce, and rare information about producer's products and buyer's preferences and identity that once was the leverage point of the value of the distributor is now available to hundreds of millions of Internet E-commerce participants. Producers like Dell Corporation, Charles Schwab, Ford Motors, Boeing Corp., and thousands more, provide all the information

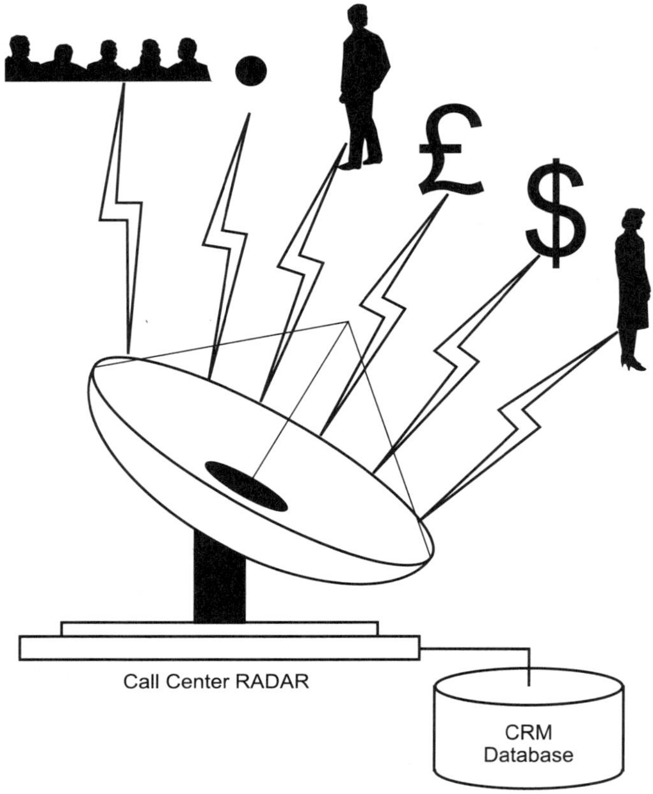

Exhibit 36-1. The hybrid effect of the Internet on the channel sales model.

their customers need to make a purchase decision — all without the channel or middleman.

Depending on the industry, the Web may have no effect on the product lifecycle at all — airline tickets, hotel rooms, Christmas toys. Rather, the Net affects the relationship between the manufacturer, channel, and the "consumer" through the information now available to the ultimate consumer. The Internet provides the information to the end consumer (business or retail) that was once only available through the middleman — because of the middleman's relationship with the manufacturer. Proprietary tools (EDI) and scarce information about product availability, pricing, where to buy it, and how to use it, keep the channel value high; the Web has not changed how the manufacturers build their products, but it has changed how they communicate with their customers. The channel can no longer charge what it wants in markups because end users now enjoy the same advantage in information that the distributor does — a critical value point. The Web has empowered consumers with all the same information, tools, and technology once enjoyed only by the distribution chain in their relationship with the manufacturer.

The Web–time factor betrays the distributor due to shortened product cycles and the distributor choice on where to place training for sales and engineering to insure ROI. The ROI on training and sales dollars may not be realized before products change. Higher technical industries are facing shorter product life cycles.

Self-service Takes Hold in B2B Transactions

After the shock and indignation wore off over the disappearance of the full-service gas station (at no extra charge), the bank teller, the receptionist, the telephone operator, the secretary, and the neighborhood hardware and grocery stores, a strange phenomenon occurred: people started to get used to having control over when they did things, who they talked to, what they bought, when they received their purchases, and how much less things cost by dealing directly with manufacturer or purveyor of goods or services in which they were interested. Cost-cutting on the manufacturer side led to technological conveniences that led to the introduction of the self-service model. ATMs, voice mail, dial-up banking, IVR (interactive voice response), and local area networks (LANs) have prepared us for the Internet and self-service. The Internet has ushered in the age of self-service in B2B transactions. Commercial buyers have become so accustomed to the availability of information about the products they wish to buy, and to the mechanisms allowing them to buy commercial products online, that it is difficult to imagine doing business any other way.

Standardization of Systems

Those business professionals around long enough to remember when EDI was still a novel concept, when Arcnet was the standard networking protocol, and local area networks where really, really local, also remember being totally dependent on proprietary technology, controlled by suppliers and intermediaries to complete most B2B transactions. Large fulfillment houses, distribution chains, and re-marketers grew up in the B2B space because most businesses did not have the time, capital, or resources to invest in the many different systems required to make a simple transaction like buying a replacement part for a PBX (telephone switching system for small to medium-sized business). Only one's local telephone company had the knowledge and the EDI systems to contact the manufacturer directly to order and take delivery of the part, let alone even identify the part number and order code. Typically, the manufacturer granted dial-up access only to authorized distributors, who had the correct modem, access software, terminal type, and access codes. No ordinary B2B customers could dial in and order the part for themselves.

It is the ubiquitous technology and access that make the Internet an EDI killer. EDI had examples of one to many. Johnson & Johnson, at its height, connected several thousand channels and customers to its EDI system, but one had to use their hardware and software and one had to invest in a proprietary solution. This investment had no application elsewhere, unlike the typical hardware and software investment in Internet access. Again, the ubiquitous nature of the Internet, and the personal computer revolution that preceded the Internet - making the Internet possible - has leveled the technological playing field. All manner of computing devices and systems have access and use the 'Net'. Manufacturers are building the portals, hubs, pages, exchanges, auctions and catalogs to serve them.

Brick and Mortar Being Replaced by Hubs, Portals, Aggregation, Auctions, and the Like

Drugs.com. Enough said, right? If one owns a retail outlet or is a commercial wholesaler of highly interchangeable goods that can be shipped easily and are very price elastic, then the dot.com portal and aggregation of sellers and buyers in one's space must be terrifying. There are hubs and portals to handle a wide range of consumer- and commercial-oriented goods. PaperExchange (paper), Cattle Offerings Worldwide (beef and dairy), Brand-x (telecommunications), Drugs.com (online drug store), pcOrder.com (build your own PC online), Travelocity (online travel arrangements), and flowers.com (flowers) are all examples as of this writing of disintermediation at work. These are examples of various new methods of commercial enterprise and transaction models that are replacing traditional retail and wholesale channels in favor of direct interaction between manufacturers or producers of goods and services and private and commercial consumers.

Ease of the Transaction

Why is the Internet invading every nook and cranny of our commercial consciousness? Simple, it is easy to use. The global deployment, especially in North America, of the infrastructure, the cabling, hubs, routers, bridges, servers, and personal computers to support the Internet, the World Wide Web, combined with new and exceptional transaction processing and user interfacing application software, make the Web a relatively easy, predictable, and today (save for random attacks of hacking) relatively secure place to do business. Having the power to look up the exact lawn mower model, part number, price, and availability of a part one desperately needs for one's Weed Whacker, in a matter of minutes, is a compelling argument against putting on one's clothes, shaving, and trotting down to Joe's Lawn Mower Parts on Saturday morning. One is pretty much in control.

WAYS THE INTERNET IS ENHANCING THE B2B DISTRIBUTION MODEL (FOR THOSE SAVVY ENOUGH TO RECOGNIZE IT)

Lowering Transaction Costs

Through the use of better, faster, and easier-to-use and maintain technology, the Internet has given the channels new tools to wrest the value proposition back in their favor, or at least to equal footing, with direct sales models. Channels can employ this technology to make the cost of completing a transaction very low, perhaps even lower than the consumer going to the manufacturer. It requires continued vigilance and investment in new technologies and strategies by the distributor. However, direct sales models between the manufacturer and the consumer become vulnerable when the transaction costs are equivalent to the original value proposition of the channel for the value-add of marketing and sales expertise.

Quality of Information Available Makes Better Educated Buyer

Again, if the channel grabs the attention of the B2B consumer, through either its old position in the economic equation or through a new position as a portal, hub, vertical or horizontal hub, as an aggregator or exchange host, it may maintain its position by providing the consumer with better information on a class or group of products than the manufacturer could in the direct model. The channel has access to multiple manufacturers' products and service information. If channels can provide more timely and accurate information and can allow the B2B consumer to act on the choices, channels can maintain and enhance their market presence.

Larger and New Markets

Who would have thought with all the push for direct sales, availability of all products, everywhere, that the supply channel would still have a play in the new economy? They do and here is why.

According to the Internet business and technology magazine *Business 2.0* (www.business2.com), one of the top ten driving principles of the new economy is markets (concept of managing and delivering to one's markets). Channels who genuinely offer unique services or lower costs will flourish, benefiting from a rush of new opportunities and customers. Those who have relied on physical barriers to lower competition are doomed.

Combine the explosion of market-making strategies by channels with the simple principle of unique services at a lower cost, the once supposedly *doomed* channels now have a new lease on life—using strategies such as commerce service providers, application service providers, enterprise service providers, information and internet service providers. Simultaneously, the portal notion, usually associated with consumer markets, is being applied to business markets as well.

American automobile dealers in the late 1970s and 1980s sold primarily a worst-in-class product as compared to the European and Asian manufacturers and their dealers. What changed the industry was that competition from other channels began to educate the market on alternative offerings (autos) that met the consumer's needs in quality, fuel efficiency, and price. This new information, just like what the Net is providing, wiped out several manufacturers and their dealers (AMC, for example). Distributors are market makers but vary widely, often based on the competition in the market, on performance, and on product offerings.

Walmart is another example of a huge distributor (and in some cases, manufacturer) of consumer products. They do not necessarily sell best-in-class products; they sell based on price and volume. Quality is very secondary. The Internet could impact them if consumers began finding similar pricing for similar products on the Web—provided the method and cost of delivering the goods to the customer are not unacceptable.

Vertical and Horizontal Opportunities

Market researcher Net Market Makers defines horizontal marketplaces as those that are hosted by trusted third parties to provide online selling and buying services to a set of identified customers. With that definition in mind, the opportunities for the traditional distribution company to reinvent itself into an E-supplier and E-market maker are many. The Gartner Group has estimated that the potential of business-to-business E-commerce transactions will reach U.S.$7.29 trillion by 2004, up from U.S.$145 billion in 1999. That is a lot of E-widgets.

So, the savvy channel that has grasped the fundamentals of E-selling (aggregation of valuable, timely and accurate information, provide reliable services, react and change quickly based on market and customer demands, to name a few principles), has a vast opportunity to create a new market, an E-commerce portal through which they can attract and retain sellers and buyers because of their unique value. Vertical and horizontal market makers are redirecting traditional and E-commerce transactions back to their sites. The extent to which the channels are working the B2B markets is evident in this recent sampling from a B2B "market maker" Web site chosen at random. In Exhibit 36-2, notice the range of markets they are supporting, as taken from the *biz2bizGuide2000* (http://biz2biz.eguide2000.com/) site.

Although the categories are not particularly revolutionary, the 27 categories represent real opportunities for the channels to regain control of their markets and buyers.

Exhibit 36-2. Business-to-business markets.

Advertising	Employment and staffing	Media
Aircraft	Food and restaurants	Moving and storage
Automobiles and boats	Furnishings	Office supplies
Chemicals and waste	Gardening and agriculture	Packaging and delivery
Clothing and cleaning	Health, sports, and recreation	Printing
Computers and data processing	Home repair, upkeep, and materials	Real estate
Construction, contractors, and materials	Insurance	Sales and marketing
Electronics (general)	Legal and accounting	Telecommunications

Renewed Support for Channel Partners by Manufacturers

As IDC reports in one study conducted—including interviews with Compaq Computer Corporation, Cisco System, Nortel Networks, and IBM—there is still a tremendous effort being made in many industries by the manufactures and service providers to maintain and enhance their channel partners. IDC contends that the Internet will be used to strengthen and enhance the channel relation and will not be viewed as a "nemesis." IDC also predicts that the "middleman" role will evolve away from a product focus, toward a more ancillary role. This role will push the channel to deliver service and support around the sale of the goods or service, rather than be responsible for the original product sale as they once were. Keep in mind this was done to maximize on economies of scale that kept the overall unit cost of handling and distributing the product to the consumer, via the channel, low.

Techniques being used and activities undertaken by manufacturers to support their channel partners include:

- online account status information
- Net-to-phone contextual support
- pricing and quoting with added features
- collaboration forums for partners
- matchmaking partners with aftermarket customers

After all, a strong E-channel partner can still yield huge benefits in terms of customer satisfaction, maintaining relationships, service, support, and buyer education—value that the manufacturer has built into its channel over a long period of time. Many producers realize this value in their channel and are finding that the Internet can help them retain their investments in their channel, while still creating their own relationships with their buyers when they do go direct.

CONCLUSION

Without a doubt, the new technology of the Internet is a double-edged sword for the traditional "middleman," the distributor, the channel, and the dealer. It cuts you and it slays your competitors, in the sense that certain industries are more prone to disintermediation than others. The travel and PC industries are classic examples of how the private consumer feels better served by shopping and buying direct.

On its face, the theory of disintermediation has been viewed as the death-knell for the traditional business-to-business distribution channel. The key values a traditional channel brought to both the manufacturer and the buyer—such as customer service and support; aggregation of information for pricing, availability, configuration of products; supply and delivery logistics; market making etc.—were thought to have been supplanted by the Internet. The Internet, in the way it empowers manufacturers to directly manage and inform its customers, was seen as the main threat to the traditional channel. The channel was theoretically no longer needed to provide pricing, availability, delivery, and customer service because the manufacturer could extend its touch points and deliver these values. The consumer, after all, is now accustomed to self-service and the way the Internet does business.

However, what really has happened is twofold: the first being the best news for the traditional distributor. The Internet has in fact enhanced the position and value of the best traditional channels in many markets. These distributors have strengthened their position with their manufacturers. They have realized the need to focus on the areas that still see their unique value proposition, that being primarily customer service and support. Technology has allowed the channel to minimize their investment in custom systems, sales engineers, and other selling infrastructure, but has also allowed channels to enhance the information provided to the B2B consumer, and leave the channel in the role as the provider of that value-add not available online—that is, custom interaction, usually with a human element, between the channel and customer.

The second effect is quite the opposite. Several markets have shed or are shedding their middlemen—travel, electronics, various commodities, etc.—in favor of direct selling and delivery between manufacturer and business consumer. Markets that can be operated in a complete automated fashion. Markets using hubs, portals, and other aggregation sites are shedding the traditional channel partner. Sometimes, a new distribution player evolves. Some examples of this are shown in Exhibit 36-3.

The key for the traditional channel that feels as if has been disintermediated is to completely reevaluate the old and new value proposition for its market to determine if reinventing itself, or realigning with new suppliers

Exhibit 36-3. Markets operated in an automated fashion.

Catalog	Auction	Exchange
Chemdex	AdAuction	e-Steel
PlasticsNet.com	IMark.com	PaperExchange
SciQuest.com		Ultraprise

and providing different value, will work. An industry where this is occurring today is insurance. The traditional distributors (i.e., agents) are finding ways to mix the speed and information-carrying capacity of the Internet with judgment, experience, and customer service of the personal interaction approach. It may mean the agent does not interact in the same way for the small issues, but may choose to interact with the customer on nontraditional insurance issues (e.g., financial security, health, etc.) to become a full-service personal insurance agent.

Tips for the distributor to remember when reviewing strategy to deal with E-business:

1. Technology is an enabler, not an end in itself. Do not accept technology only for technology's sake. Cool toys are great, but do they serve the customer and business decisions?
2. Customer service is key in business-to-business commerce. Speed and quality of service are huge drivers in business-to-business transactions.
3. Multimedia communication is driving enhanced customer service by allowing companies to interact with their customers in a fashion dictated by the customer.
4. How can one measure whether one will be successful? Plan the evaluation first. It is easier to design measurement systems up-front than add them as an afterthought to the Web site.

Look at the big picture. Lift your head up from the grindstone and listen to world around you. What are your manufacturers doing in your market? What are your customers saying? Communication is flowing throughout the transaction. Listen, learn, adapt, and prosper.

Other, more complex industries and markets, usually characterized as business-to-business (B2B), as opposed to consumer focused, have seen different models and reactions by the channel to the Internet technology. In many cases, companies are embracing a two-channel strategy: one direct sales and one through spinoffs of "secondcompany.com." Results are mixed.

Companies are finding ways to make their channels more efficient, responsive, and cost-effective through the application of Internet technology. In addition, channels are reacting by reinventing the approach to their roles through re-intermediating as hubs, portals, and E-market makers. The sword cuts both ways.

Chapter 37 Customer Relationship Management

Roxanne E. Burkey
Charles V. Breakfield

TRADITIONALLY, CUSTOMER RELATIONSHIP MANAGEMENT (CRM) IS A BUSINESS-TO-BUSINESS OR BUSINESS-TO-CUSTOMER RELATIONSHIP BASED ON KNOWLEDGE OF THE PURCHASER'S BUYING HABITS. These buying habits until recently were typically based on knowledge of the marketplace, trends, demographics, prices, and product availability. Responding to shifts in buying habits has the added burden of product availability from a wider selection of sellers and shortened product lifecycles, forcing enterprises to optimize technology tools to retain competitive leadership. CRM technology has expanded to a point where it contains the tools, if correctly applied, to impact business profitability.

A small enterprise may hold details about a few customers that were catered to because of the knowledge of preferences and historical buying patterns. For example, a local dress shop may have detailed records of specific customers sizes, colors, and styles, thereby allowing clerks to reserve merchandise and proactively call customers upon arrival of new merchandise. Luxury automobile dealers are tracking the buying patterns of high-end cars to cater to the historical patterns of their customers and ensure a proactive approach. Catering to a customer's desires and preferences has kept many a customer returning for subsequent purchases.

A large enterprise may hold many details about many customers but as enterprises grow, that information becomes more difficult to manage and associate with given customers to optimize revenue generation. Maintenance of customer trends in some cases is elusive or not cost-effective. Some enterprises have maintained automated CRM functionality for a number of years using trouble or ticket tracking systems and automated tickler files for service, scheduling, or maintenance issues.

0-8493-0893-3/00/$0.00+$.50

Recent shifts in business trends and insight to adaptation of technology to other business applications have turned CRM into a method to retain customers and optimize revenues through tracking customer interactions and using that information to develop long-term relationships. When an enterprise, either large or small, begins to compile and maintain the information needed for effective analysis of customers buying trends, the costs for CRM systems become a factor. First, a look at how business arrived at its present state, followed by a review of how businesses might apply the new CRM tools as well as the prevailing costs seems appropriate.

HIGH-LEVEL ECONOMICAL SHIFTS REVIEWED

Following World War II, consumers in the United States began an expansion explosion for consumable products. In general, businesses were providing products and services to consumers to keep up with buying demands. The overall marketplace was a dominant sellers' market. If Customer A did not want to buy something, Customer B was just minutes away. The population was moving toward the suburbs and a new set of requirements for keeping up with the Jones. The advent of credit purchases, coupled with the addition of increased advertising sophistication, has orchestrated buying trends to continue to rise for the last 50 years.

As countries put their economies back together after World War II, businesses went into either supplying governments or consumers with desired goods. This is the classic bullets-or-butter model from which companies had to choose. Incredible amounts of intellectual, monetary, and raw materials went into supplying governments the armaments desired from the 1950s through the 1980s. Those resources were not available to the private sector to service the end user. By the early 1990s, the environment was changing to invert the two roles.

Companies heavily dependent on government defense contracts were fighting for smaller contracts and began to consolidate to stay alive. By the late 1980s, General Dynamics employees, seeing their industry shrink before their eyes, placed a sign outside the Fort Worth plant facing the street that said, "Will trade stealth for food."

Countries that did not have this particular problem, like Japan and West Germany, were almost exclusively investing in consumer goods manufacturing. Post-war economics allowed these countries to not only rebuild their shattered economies, but to also export to other countries. The investments in consumer goods sales began to accelerate as the Soviet Union and other eastern European countries began rethinking their resource allocation. As countries collapse and are reborn, the economies are retooled to produce consumer goods—not military goods. All loans from the World Bank and IMF are extended to countries based on their ability to demonstrate good economics, not military strength.

With countries channeling their intellectual, human, and raw materials toward consumers rather than aggression, the business environment now has more resources invested and new competitors showing up daily. Global competition is now the rule, not the exception. In this global marketplace, the fight is not just for the American consumer (as in the 1960s, 1970s, and 1980s), but every consumer on the planet.

This is a trend that will potentially remain intact with the sheer number of choices a consumer has on where and how to shop. With that shift comes the realization by businesses that customers have no need to remain loyal to a business that does not provide service. If Enterprise X cannot meet one's requirements as a customer, then Enterprise Y may fill those needs. In a predatory buyers' market, Enterprise Y will often take a loss to gain a customer. The Internet has only exacerbated that effect, creating choices at the touch of a keyboard.

E-COMMERCE

Internet business has opened up entrance to the marketplace through a lower cost of doing business globally. Web customers cruise the Web and face buying opportunities during every session. Internet economy is a sales vehicle that few companies can ignore for long. Here, customer relationship management is even more tightly knit to the sales acquisition process. With so many competitors, it is critical for the E-commerce enterprise to use every tool to preserve customer relationships. Electronic responses are often faster than real-time discussions of traditional call centers, but people still buy from people. The difference then is the knowledge of the people facing customers for high customer satisfaction and promotion of business-to-business or business-to-customer loyalty.

At first glance it might seem that there are two types of E-commerce competitors: the lowest cost Web advertiser and the value-add Web retailer. The lowest cost Web advertiser is looking at the Internet as the "holy-grail of profitable sales." The belief here is that a virtual address can replace standard retail infrastructure. It cannot. Even Amazon.com created a huge call center and warehouse to support its virtual storefront. The proper approach is much like what the value-add Web retailer is doing by providing yet another "portal" into its retail environment. Offering, but not being able to fulfill goods or services, will not keep customers or help get new ones.

Customers have greater freedom to shop and browse before making buying decisions with a wider selections of businesses offering comparable products. The choice of when and where to buy is much more flexible through this consumer media. Customer relationship management on the Internet can track customer preferences and objections, evaluate Web site effectiveness, and provide a method to understand customer desires before manufacturing. Trends for colors and styles of products done electronically can minimize manufacturing costs of potentially unfavorable products. Weaving this information into an effective return on CRM investment is a complex project not taken on lightly by an enterprise.

Historically, enterprises would contract with an independent marketing firm to find out what consumers were willing to buy. Once the data was obtained, certain assumptions were made about a subset of that data and manufacturing decisions were made on what to build next. This model ignored two important issues: the first was that a company's competitors were also doing the same thing, which led to multiple corporations conducting "business assaults" on the same target group. The second issue was that companies targeting the group in this market research often ignored their installed customer base.

CRM begins with the premise that an enterprise's installed customer base is the proper place to start one's marketing research. An existing customer represents the successful acquisition of a revenue source based on the product offering. This existing customer has valuable marketing information for the enterprise and should be managed at two levels.

1. The first level is because they are an existing customer and have a high probability of being a repeat customer.
2. The second level is that because they are a current purchaser they can tell the enterprise about their next purchase and, as a consequence, the company's next offering.

If leveraged correctly, CRM can help capture existing customer information that can be used to design the company's next product offering.

While the rules of engagement on the Internet are written differently from those of a pure brick-and-mortar business, there is still a strong need for real-time contact points in the marketing, sales, and customer support cycle. Tailored services to meet customer needs are clearly needed to manage the relationship to preserve customers. The bar for competing for customers has merely been raised higher because the balance of power between enterprises has shifted. The convergence of traditional customer relationship management methods with E-commerce is placed squarely in the midst of the convergence of telephony and data within the enterprise infrastructure. Few enterprises will remain competitive if business is only conducted from a brick-and-mortar standpoint.

CALL CENTER IMPACT

Traditional customer support call centers service a variety of customer needs, often into a central location. Mergers, acquisitions, and the general realization that more call center specialization was needed have found call centers restructuring functions to meet customer demands. Special call routing and techniques have taken advantage of the newest technologies to improve call routing. This, coupled with other business changes, has expanded call center support to include some of the following:

- special lines for calls on marketing promotions
- caller selections to direct calls to a specific group
- internal help desk support
- collections staff
- self-help for inquires on balances in accounts or latest transactions
- emergency routing to alert customers that calls cannot be handled
- Web response/multimedia transactions

Different industries have naturally gravitated to one or more of these technology choices to service customers. Banking and credit cards certainly offer self-help, while expanding technology within the workplace requires an internal help desk to field information system questions readily for the internal user community, and enterprises deal with an expanding number of Web transactions as E-commerce is further explored and redefined.

Call centers are changing to meet the enterprise and customer responsiveness expected. Call center staffs that have adopted CRM tools to respond to callers more personally are more productive and customers are more satisfied. Efforts to bring this technology to the average call center is not only an investment in hardware, software, and often networking infrastructure, but also an investment in the review and assimilation of years of customer information into a repository that knowledge workers can readily access.

Competition with expansion of an E-commerce presence has merely required that staffs be cyber-enabled. Different skill sets and knowledge bases are required to understand the enterprise Web page offerings as well as the need to personalize an electronic response. While tools are used to evaluate the value of a given Web page and changes employed to attract more customers, it is important to remember that in most cases, the humanizing factor still closes the sale. Many buyers still want to talk to a real person and gain that sense of immediacy that the telephone has always provided real-time before they actually purchase. Market leadership will go to enterprises willing to develop mutually beneficial customer relationships to retain customer loyalty with E-commerce as one facet of the marketplace.

CUSTOMER SERVICES: CALL CENTERS

With the assumption that managing a customer relationship is as important as acquiring new customers, a different business approach is required. Simply dumping the responsibility of customer management on a company's call center and saying handle it is a poor approach. Shifting the business model to a relationship model means investing resources, time, and hard dollars into determining and implementing a CRM that maximizes existing infrastructures of call centers. This concept dovetails nicely into the business direction to integrate support and management overhead into the cost of sales based on expectations that call centers are capable of increasing revenues per transactions, per customer, providing the right tools are in place. As with many sales opportunities, customers often buy because they are pleased with the company representative and impressed by the personal knowledge that representatives may have about the customer history with the enterprise.

Example 1

When a caller hears the following after dialing the sales line of a company, how might the enterprise respond? "Hello Michael, how are you? We haven't spoken with you since you received those new speakers. How are they sounding these days? How may I be of assistance to you today?" Even if Michael wanted to register a complaint about those speakers, the representative has taken part of the wind out of the complaint with the knowledge clear that speakers were purchased. Customers feel better when they place a call and are immediately recognized for their last transaction. If there is only a positive response from the original query, the representative could go on to ask if a new DVD player is on the horizon, or some other companion product to a prior purchase.

Example 2

When a caller hears the following after dialing the product complaint or returns line of a company, how might the enterprise respond? "Hello Michael; glad you called. Have you had any issues with your new speakers? I received a notice that there have been several issues with the woofers and have you on my list to follow up with. Our company will not permit even one dissatisfied customer." If Michael had a problem or was angry, he now knows that the representative is familiar with product issues and knows the company stands behind its products. It might even be an opportunity to trade the item and offer an up-sell for an add-on product offered as a deal to account for the inconvenience being experienced. Customers like feeling that they are being taken care of with special deals or just good product service.

Example 3

When a caller dials a sales line, but the system learns that the caller is extremely past due on accounts, how might the enterprise handle the caller. Rather than interrupt the sales representative for a customer that has payment issues, the call might route straight to collections. Here, the interaction might take on a different note. "Hello, Ralph, it is good to hear from you. We were going to contact you to see if we can help rearrange your payment schedule. Right now, it appears that you might be having some problems and we want to make sure your line of credit remains up to your expectations. We are here to help." Ralph may have a problem with payments that he is unaware of, and this alert may keep him out of trouble. Ralph might also be embarrassed, as most folks are when they get behind, and welcome the kind offer to help. Ralph now also knows that he probably will not get to the purchasing group until this problem is resolved. Most of all, Ralph was treated as an individual with special needs and the right staff handled the interaction.

Example 4

The enterprise recently began using a Web page featuring comments, information, or products. Handling or managing this information, including knowing where the Internet shopper made the request or to gauge the effectiveness of the Web page, might be useful for Web page expansion or appropriate response to the query. At the very least, it is a different point of customer contact. As more businesses enter the marketplace, their main customer presentation could likely be the Internet. Without a process to manage, analyze, or review the effectiveness of a Web page to generate business, it may not return the cost of producing and maintaining the Web page. Seeking response from various types of pages or tracking frequency of returned entry is possible with some CRM tools. Integrating this with other CRM tools inside the enterprise may be warranted based on the industry. At the very least, gauging the level of satisfaction or interaction may be important to the external perception of the enterprise.

These examples are merely broad samplings of a shift from pure marketing return on transaction counts, to CRM long-term returns to the enterprise bottom line. Therefore, it is safe to assume that effective CRM contains elements of major importance to an enterprise bottom line. Determination of which tools should be employed and to what degrees is based on product mix, types of services, returned goods, past due accounts, customer base, enterprise reputation, and Web presence. Rating the priorities of the enterprise and then implementing the CRM technology tools to intelligently use data information to route calls and interact person to person with each customer. Radar O'Riley was always invaluable to Colonel Henry Blake, the commanding officer of M.A.S.H., because he anticipated and planned for the request in advance. Technology can make all the customer interactions a RADAR model.

The evolving RADAR (Recurring Avarice Demands Additional Revenue) model (see Exhibit 37-1) suggests that a company's revenue growth needs are better achieved by trying to leverage existing customers for additional

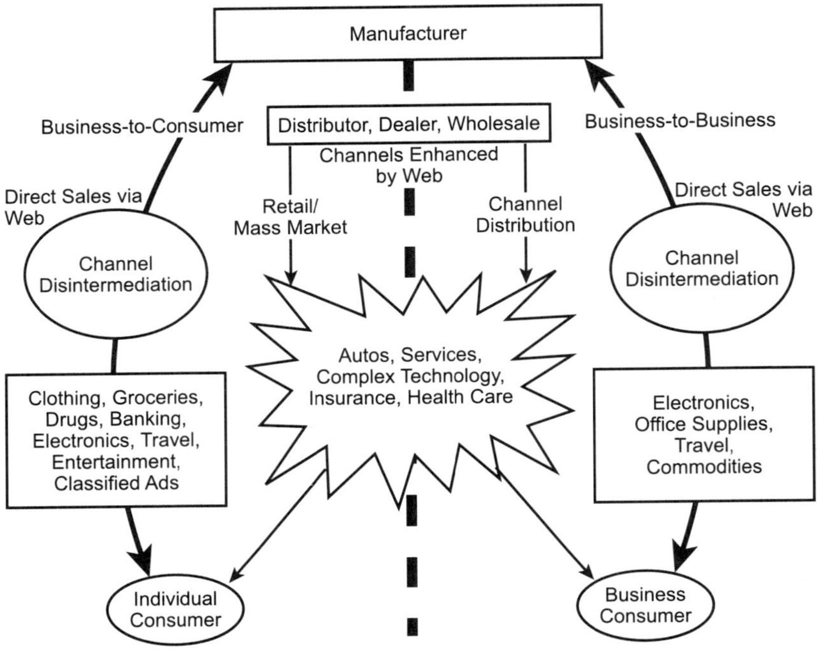

Exhibit 37-1. CRM RADAR model.

purchases, or continued loyalty, first and then add new, but qualified buyers to the installed base. The old business model of just selling, moving on to the next buyer, and ignoring the installed base is not a good long-term approach in today's marketplace.

The tactical value of CRM is to provide an automated view of a customer to the media center agent so that the agent can help maintain the relationship on behalf of the enterprise. In minutes or even seconds, the call center media agent must not only help, but also reinforce the customer relationship with the caller to retain that client. The collective effort to maintain a positive effect on the calling (Web) client is at the very heart of a CRM initiative.

AUTOMATED CRM STRUCTURE

Technology tools that promise customer relationship management begin with a detailed, structured database. The elements of that database are typically stored in a relational database structure as a point to gather and analyze customer information. Data collected from a caller on a marketing campaign needs to join with the accounting and historical purchases data. Weaved into this are the visits to the Web site and all other customer interactions. Gathering the information into a usable structure is necessary for any of the CRM tools to work effectively. The old data adage of garbage in, garbage out has not changed, even with the advances in technology. Therefore, it is necessary to rate the priorities of the enterprise so that correct information is maintained to support those priorities.

This structure is so critical for the tools of the trade to work, that many vendors require the conversion of enterprise data into a predetermined structured database. Even converted data has an element of accuracy that must be reviewed and then maintained by the enterprise workers. This requires a set of rules and processes for adding information into either a centralized or decentralized database. The database structure is typically classified into groups of information. Groups that are frequently found include:

- primary customer information
- order entry
- invoicing
- accounts Receivable
- customer complaints
- customer requests or inquires
- product promotions
- follow-up services
- inventory
- scheduling
- Web transactions

The level of analysis and relationship review required by the enterprise determines the fields of information contained in each of the groups. In general, the more detailed the data stored, the more cost associated with maintaining the data. The thread that binds them altogether for a customer history would be the customer identification number.

Each staff member who has an interaction with the customer will update the information or add information to the existing data structure, based on the rules. Data screen design would ensure that the fields of information needed for a given interaction were available, whether contact points are telephone, in person, or Internet. This design structure and development would present the most challenge for not only content, but also the usage expected over time. The structure would require the flexibility to grow and change. A simple example would have order entry tie to the inventory information to help ensure product availability and stock reduction as purchases are made. This relational data interaction is a fairly refined technology that database development is capable of addressing. It is the planning for the needs short- and long-term that is essential.

There are many vendors that have the CRM tools to both assist with development of the data structure and provide the needed data structure to store information in the format necessary to add the use and analysis layer. Such companies as Clarify, Remedy, Seibel, Alteon, etc. have the experience in not only the use of relational databases, but also the tools to interactively use the information as a tool to respond to customers. Each has tools that contain various strengths and weaknesses. The evaluation of the needs of the enterprise is critical prior to review of vendor capabilities.

When selecting a system, three areas of key evaluation might be included in the vendor selection decision process:

1. customizable system functionality without a dedicated programmer
2. real-time database interaction
3. vendor infrastructure to meet changing needs

Customizable system functionality would include the capability to modify screen presentation, following the initial installation design, to meet rapid business changes. Changes to screen presentation would be intuitive enough to have a trained staff member initiate such changes as needed. Therefore, training for enterprise staff members should be a part of the package offering and planned for in staffing commitments.

Immediate database updates are expected to replace older batch modes. This requires providing staff with the standards for completing data requirements, and along with notifications of required entry fields would ensure a smooth maintenance process. The real-time update capability guarantees that the very next customer interaction would include visibility to the last transaction completed. This permits staff who interact with the customer on any level to know the customer's current interactions. This sends a positive professional message to customers that their exchanges with this enterprise are important.

Vendor infrastructure must include a professional staff familiar with the general business needs of the industry at hand, as well as integration expertise, and a consulting staff with experience in current technology trends along with the right application of the technology to a given enterprise environment. The latest and greatest technology is not necessarily the best technology for an enterprise. Current enterprise infrastructure, business dynamics, and customer requirements must all interact effectively with any technology application. A commitment, however, on the part of the vendor to stay abreast with trends to offer the product enhancements that make sense in the highly competitive business marketplace and escalation processes to ensure effective customer service should be required.

From these basic requirements then, enterprises can have the data information available and updateable in order to build a strategy for customer retention. This retention is based on anticipating customer needs, responding to customer concerns, and making sure that all in the organization who provide customer contact points can readily access the information. Development of the tools can streamline services and consequently associated costs, evaluate responsiveness of individuals within the enterprise, and target the key customer base from the various automated analyses of the database information. As with any automated process, certain human review is still necessary to make sure the analysis criterion was properly requested. Database information is still only as good as the human interaction.

CRM MIGRATION/EVALUATION

Migrations of any type have little chance of success without adequate planning that includes development, cost analysis, implementation, and post-implementation reviews. The most critical phase is the planning and development. This would include a high-level review of the needs and details of what can realistically be accomplished based on the costs, resources available, hardware and software requirements, and infrastructure changes required to optimize the change. Determining the type of data available within the enterprise and the usefulness of the data are important in estimating the cost of storage components and time required to initiate/maintain the information.

Utilization of a hybrid CRM technology tool requires an enterprise to assess the following prior to deployment of the technology:

- points of customer interaction
- customer expectations
- responsiveness standards
- revenue expectation per customer
- service levels based on revenue points
- new product development drivers

Customers potentially have access to an enterprise from several ports: telephone, e-mail, Web page, fax, etc. Any of these might become the initial focus for CRM tools, depending on what the customer expectations are for the enterprise. Telephone or call center interactions are enhanced when customer information is presented with the call. If calls routing into the enterprise are distributed by various departments (e.g., customer service, scheduling, order desk, problems, etc.), then CRM tools can be utilized to pull customer information related to the department based on the database information along with screen representative of the activities expected in that area. When a response from a Web page is received, it too could be matched with the appropriate information related to it in the database.

Each of the entry points into the enterprise requires evaluation and determination for inclusion in the CRM. When the bulk of the data stored from a specific entry point to the enterprise is not used to retain or gain customers, then the capture of the information must be eliminated. It is pointless to track each visit to the Web site for the casual visitor. If the visitor is interacting and supplying feedback, then at some level it should be captured for evaluation and or inclusion into long-term marketing or product development plans. If callers frequently call the call center for information that is suitable for an automated process that will satisfy the customer and free up resources, then the shift to an automated IVR is recommended. These points should be reviewed on a routine basis to make sure changes to the customer's methods of reaching the enterprise are incorporated into the processes.

RELATIONSHIP COSTS

Costs for reaching new customers are even more than costs for maintaining customers. It is merely a matter of satisfying the customer needs, embracing shared loyalty with innovative products and responsiveness to meet the changing tastes of a broader customer base. Enterprises are turning to CRMs to optimize relationships with customers and turn them into long-term profits.

The costs include the initial investment in hardware and software required to run the CRM product selected. These costs are estimated based on requirements models provided by the vendor of choice. A good baseline for a single, focused tool begins at $40K. Hidden costs include the staff time and effort to standardize the database information and relocate it as needed for CRM functionality, as well as the respective staff training based on responsibilities to the system.

The most difficult hurdle to overcome is changing the way people think. Costs here are nebulous. Changing systems requires that people perform duties in a different manner, including customer interaction methods, data capturing standards, learning new software programs, responsiveness, desktop screen changes, and initially tracking what does or does not work and why. Even the most well-planned system requires evaluation to make sure it fits into the working environment effectively. Many people are resistant to change. The buy-in for the success of the transition by the staff is critical, or the costs become lost or staff becomes unhappy. Incentive structures integrated into and readily tracked by most CRMs can overcome this hurdle by rewarding customer relationship development. The tools assist in this effort and provide analysis results for review.

Some results are readily apparent shortly after system implementation. There are tools to help staff interactions respond to the callers with information pertinent to the caller particular requests. Reports for management evaluation are available in a variety of forms to analyze at any level of the business that the CRM is interacting with. If the call center agents were the focus of screens at the desktop to provide not only customer information when receiving call presentation, but also to show the historical purchases along with potential up-sell or cross-sell options, this in turn provides reporting at each level to evaluate the tools and tool usage by the staff: the number of calls received and the number of those calls completed with additional sales to determine the value of the investment.

As each point of contact is integrated with the CRM, the return value is measured with converted sales responses and a high percentage of repeat business. Finite routing of calls to specific groups or agents to fulfill the caller sense of immediacy is often employed for valued customers based on a standard criterion. The tools are available to automate those processes and automate the tools to evaluate each step. CRM users should expect and gain more sales per advertising dollar, better profitability through improved staff productivity, and lower overhead costs with word of mouth and repeat business. Customer loyalty levels will increase when customers know they can count on an enterprise to provide the same level of services, regardless of request origin, consistent product value, and selection based on the customer requests.

CASE STUDIES

A retail store had used traditional methods to increase sales, primarily with increased advertising and price discounts. The profitability then relied mainly on volume sales and aggressive cost controls. Any downturn in discretionary spending by the public severely affected profitability. To minimize the impact of spending shifts, the store implemented a CRM to track customer relationships and trends. In addition, it implemented a Web page and invited customers to visit and share with their friends. The Web page contained wish lists of what customers would want if available for various styles and colors, inviting them to mix and match. Analysis of the information by the CRM tool armed buyers with the customer wants prior to attending markets and resulted in inventory that turned over more rapidly. The store gained the reputation with customers of meeting the requests without being invasive (value proposition) and the advertising dollars spent were focused on altering customers who wanted merchandise that was available. Even a modest-sized store can benefit from a computerized system that helps focus on enterprise goals.

The travel industry is making increased efforts to apply CRM tools. A case in point is the travel agency that adopted automated processes to access traveler preferences while booking travel arrangements. Traveler preferences for airlines, flight seating, hotel chains, room types, and ground transportation were available at call initiation to streamline the process time. In addition, travelers felt their preferences were adhered to during the process. The automation technology integration to the airlines, hotels, and ground transportation providers also permits transference of identification numbers that relate to the value of the customer to each of the providers. Airlines have mileage programs that are available to agencies to ensure traveler credit via that identification code for each trip transaction. Failure of a travel agency to meet those business or personal traveler expectations would limit enterprise life expectancy. Adoption of the integrated system resulted in a growth of 25 percent by an agency during the first six months of use, with over 75 percent of the customers repeat business.

A manufacturing concern that uses partners for the majority of its sales and fulfillment of products began providing consolidated information on a given partner's customers via a Web site. They also took it a step further when their CRM was integrated with their call center for new product information. They found that customer contacts requesting new product information could easily route to the partner either in the geographical territory or previously used to ensure customer follow-up. This resulted in quicker follow-up to customer inquires and more leads in the hands of partners. A natural by-product of the effort was a better tracking of a partner's representation of the manufacturer's product, resulting in focused product training by the manufacturer where needed or discontinuation of partners that fell short of the manufacturer's requirements for product representation.

A financial banking institution that had undergone several mergers over the last ten years made a business decision to determine the high-end customers and extend greater services to those customers. In addition, they determined that the customers who were not doing a certain level of business should be charged for services above a specified level. Integration of a CRM here permitted intelligent call and Web response distribution based on information extracted from the database. Business accounts considered profitable were routed to a group of agents not only familiar with these customer banking needs, but also armed with the tools to know what the institution could offer in the way of services in line with customer needs. High-end personal accounts were routed in a similar fashion to a separate group knowledgeable in personal banking needs. Low-end customers who consistently overdrew their accounts and created additional load on the systems were routed to the lowest service levels in an effort to minimize services and human interactions. Plans are to integrate changes permitting routing for seniors that having different banking requirements and require additional time for each transaction. The reporting capabilities of the CRM of choice permitted transaction times and productivity standards of the operations to focus on the type of customers to optimize human interaction. They also discovered that many customers were very satisfied with self-service banking through voice systems and Web pages that permitted access at times convenient to the customer.

The key to effective integration is consistent use, accurate database information, and analysis and review. Expansion should only be considered when it aligns with the business goals. Effective customer relationship management can account for growth and expansion for an enterprise. Demographic information can also provide for insight into the future products and services needed for any customer-based enterprise, regardless of the industry.

CONCLUSION

Treating customers as respected partners in the business is part of building loyalty factors. Details about customers must be relevant, without being invasive. Response vehicles offered to a customer must permit the same level of immediacy as a telephone call and let them know their business is important to the enterprise. Asking for suggestions on merchandise and services needed as they change and grow is taken from demographic information to help shift product trends as the shape of the buying community changes. These kinds of touch points are easy with the right tools.

Information on customers is typically spread throughout an organization. Marketing knows the last products presented, accounting knows the customer payment patterns, order processing knows the order and shipment details, and customer service holds another link in the chain of satisfaction. The role of each of these inter-departments with the customer is also greatly dependent on the type of business. With the explosion of Web interaction, there is yet another element of customer preferences that is available to gain valuable insight into a customer's buying habits. Pulling all of the information spread throughout an organization becomes the challenge of effective customer relationship management and the basis for a strong foundation for enterprise growth.

Enterprises approach this in many ways, especially in recent years, as the need to hold onto customers is as much a business requirement as generating new customers. Both electronic and paper customer information and high turnover rates, coupled with the often-lacking standard procedures, find this information difficult to consolidate to then access companywide. Possible methods for how to gather and use this information will help gain true profitability with long-term business retention. Technology, coupled with solid processes, is the key to making promises to customers a reality by use of CRMs.

Index

A

B

C

F

G

H

I

J

K

L

N

O

P

Q

R

S

X

Y